Reprint Publishing

For People Who Go For Originals.

www.reprintpublishing.com

DETERMINISM: FALSE AND TRUE

DETERMINISM:
FALSE AND TRUE

A Contribution to Modern
Philosophy and Ethics

BY

FRANK BALLARD,
D.D., M.A., B.Sc. (Lond.), F.R.M.S., &c.

AUTHOR OF

'Haeckel's Monism False,' 'Theomonism True,' 'The True God,'
'Christian Essentials,' 'Does it Matter What a Man Believes?'
'New Theology,' 'Guilty: A Reply to "Not Guilty,"' 'The
People's Religious Difficulties,' 'Eddyism: A
Delusion and a Snare,' &c.

London

CHARLES H. KELLY

25-35 CITY ROAD, AND 26 PATERNOSTER ROW, E.C.

DEDICATED TO MY ELDEST SON

MAXWELL BALLARD,

AS A VALID AND WORTHY INSTANCE

OF THE

PRINCIPLES HERE ADVOCATED.

CONTENTS

INTRODUCTION

(1) Principles involved - - - - - - - 1
(2) Determinism in the past - - - - - - 9
(3) Present-day recrudescence - - - - - - 12

I—FALSE DETERMINISM

(1) *In name:*
(2) *In fact:*
    (i) The individual conscience - - - - 35
    (ii) The moral consciousness of mankind - - 38
    (iii) Human speech - - - - - - 39
    (iv) Literature of all nations - - - - 44
    (v) Practical life - - - - - - 46
(3) *In principle:*
    (i) As to religion - - - - - - 54
    (ii) As to moral philosophy - - - - 57
        (1) Self-respect - - - - - 60
        (2) Personal responsibility - - - 62
        (3) Morality in general - - - 63
        (4) Human character - - - - 67
        (5) Communal ethics - - - - 71
    (iii) 'Soft' Determinism and its pleas - - 75
    (iv) As to Psychology - - - - - 145
    (v) As to Metaphysics - - - - - 165

II—TRUE DETERMINISM

(1) *Philosophical:*
    (i) The reality of the self - - - - 186
    (ii) The creative activity of the self - - 201
    (iii) The free self - - - - - - 210
    (iv) The sufficient cause - - - - 225
    (v) The relation to heredity and environment - 242
    (vi) The true explanation of experience - - 263
    (vii) The sufficient estimate of the future - 270

CONTENTS

II—True Determinism—(*continued*)

(2) *Practical:*
- (i) The only valid foundation of morals - - 281
- (ii) The only possibility of character - - - 303
- (iii) The only way of upward evolution - - - 345
- (iv) The only basis of religion - - - - 373

III—Epilogue - - - - - - - - - 417

PREFACE

ELSEWHERE[1] I have definitely endorsed the avowal of Canon Henson that 'before the gospel can be reasonably considered, there must be at least agreement in the postulate of Theism, and as following from that, in the moral responsibility of man.'[2] That Christian churches on all occasions assume the former, and ordinary members of human society the latter, is too manifest to call for proof. Speaking generally, such a proceeding is in each case equally necessary and wise. But in days when literally everything is called in question, it becomes also wise and necessary not only to justify assumptions, but to repeat such justification even to the point of weariness; for it is only by means of repetition that even fundamental truths obtain permanent hold of the average human mind. Certainly, so far as the Christian faith is concerned, the refusal to do this, in modern light, will increasingly be ascribed either to cowardice in fearing to defend a cause which is held to be true, or hypocrisy in refusing to face the exposure of what is known to be false.

Leaving others to their own convictions, I have endeavoured in preceding volumes[3] to set forth the claims of Theomonism, or Christian Theism, as against the recent assertions of Naturalistic or

---

[1] *Theomonism True*, p. ix.
[2] *Notes on Popular Rationalism*, by Canon Henson, p. 221.
[3] *Haeckel's Monism False: Theomonism True: The True God* (C. H. Kelly).

Materialistic Monism. The promise made in the preface to the second of these (p. viii) to deal with the other two great postulates of Christian faith, i.e. Freedom and Immortality, has been hitherto unfulfilled through the demands of ceaseless public work in all parts of the country, together with the publication of popular replies to the plausible and so far effective issues of Mr. R. Blatchford, on behalf of his alleged Determinism.[1] These replies having to some real extent achieved their purpose, it remains to consider more fully, and on more definite lines of psychology and metaphysics, the larger theme of scientific 'Determinism,' as it is maintained, not by popular journalists, but by other writers on science and philosophy, some of whom at least have brought to such advocacy both acknowledged reputation and philosophical ability.

How vast, intricate, and difficult, is the task of facing yet again the problem which has not only occupied but baffled some of the acutest human minds for ages, cannot but be apparent to every sensible reader. Only the student knows how much is really involved in any endeavour to track what is termed 'free will' to its ultimate significance and source, especially under the rigid conditions of modern science. When, indeed, the popular writer just mentioned jauntily asserts that the 'free will delusion is not very difficult,' that it only requires attention 'because it has been tied and twisted into a tangle of Gordian knots by twenty centuries of wordy but unsuccessful philosophers,' and that 'the cause of all the confusion on this subject may

---

[1] See *Not Guilty: A Defence of the Bottom Dog*, by R. Blatchford (Clarion Press); and *Guilty: A Tribute to the Bottom Man*, by the present writer (C. H. Kelly).

be shown in a few words,'¹ the twenty pages which follow serve to show that it is but a display of ruthless superficiality, repeating Alexander's treatment of the genuine Gordian knot and virtually endorsing the later burning of the Alexandrian library. But when we come to the stronger words of one who has been described by a competent authority as 'the most daringly destructive and at the same time the most elaborately constructive of all living philosophers'²—to the effect that

'the doctrine which is vulgarly termed "free will" may in philosophy be considered obsolete, though it will continue to flourish in popular ethics. As soon as its meaning is comprehended it loses all plausibility; but the popular moralist will always exist by not knowing what he means'³—

one cannot but feel a touch of indignation at the contemptuousness, not to say insolence, with which so vast and complex a theme is thus dogmatically dismissed. The scorn here flung upon 'popular ethics' may be fine, but it is not philosophy. It is on a par with the further assertion of the same writer that 'most of those who insist on what they call the personality of God, are intellectually dishonest.'⁴ For apart from the falsity of the above statement, if it were not for the moral responsibility upon which 'popular ethics' confessedly insist, where is there any point in such a remark? What indeed would it matter whether men were honest or 'dishonest'?

In contra-distinction from the dogmatism thus displayed, alike on popular and philosophical lines, the following pages hold out no hope of a perfectly

---

[1] *Not Guilty*, pp. 169, 170.
[2] *Idealism and Theology*, C. F. D'Arcy, B.D., p. 141.
[3] F. H. Bradley, *Appearance and Reality*, p. 393.
[4] ibid., p. 532.

lucid and logical solution of this greatest human problem. We may none the less comfort ourselves with the discovery that we are in good company, seeing that the 'daring and elaborately constructive philosopher' just mentioned, himself assures us that the conclusion of his own whole performance 'has explained and has confirmed the irresistible impression that all is beyond us.'[1] Whilst the popular echo in the pages of 'Deterministic' Journalism is—'What we want is mystery, and more mystery, and still more mystery. What we strive for is mystery. Mystery is the object of life.'[2] If, then, for journalist and philosopher alike, *omnia exeunt in mysterium*, one may suggest that a little more modesty on their part would be in place, whether Theism or Agnosticism is the truth concerning God, and Realism or Idealism the final finding of philosophy.

Under existing circumstances the best result at which we can hope to attain is philosophical justification for a pragmatism which shall save us alike from intellectual confusion, moral wreckage, and social chaos. The notion that a few picked words will put an end to all our ignorance and difficulty in any department of human thought, most of all in this, is as childish as the suggestion to navigate the Atlantic in a toy yacht. There is no one single event, however commonplace, that Science can completely explain, no phase of reality that philosophical analysis can exhaust. In the present case we may venture to affirm, as modestly as earnestly, with Prof. Lloyd Morgan, that 'there is Determinism all along the line, but it is the self which determines.'

---

[1] F. H. Bradley, *Appearance and Reality*, p. 549. To insist—as on p. 552—that 'reality is spiritual' contributes nothing towards the logical explicability of the real.

[2] Issue of *Clarion*, February 12, 1909.

Or, with Dr. C. F. D'Arcy, that 'when it is shown that Will, to be Will, must be conscious, the battle against Determinism has been won.' We cannot, however, but add, in all honesty, as does this latter writer, that 'at the same time every one feels that this answer to the question, conclusive though it ought to be, is not quite satisfactory.' As rational beings we are bound to endeavour to get as near to what is satisfactory as we can. This only, but this certainly, is attempted in the pages that follow. How surprisingly difficult it is at once to do justice to the far-reaching subtlety and all-embracing comprehensiveness of true philosophy, and then translate its most valid conclusions into thought and speech of ordinary men and women, only those who have attempted it will know. These, however, at is hoped, will feel sympathy for faults and omissions which they alone will perceive.[1] To give always exact quotation for every reference to those modern writers who, as influencing the authority of to-day, are more especially contemplated, would make this volume too bulky. As much of this as seemed necessary has been done, and the utmost endeavour made, in every case, towards fair representation. The bibliography at the end may be taken as a general and grateful acknowledgement of indebtedness. I desire also specially to thank three able friends, Revs. S. E. Keeble, now of Southport, Dr. J. Warschauer, of Bradford, and R. Christie, M.A., of Gorebridge, N.B., for their valued assistance in reading the proof-sheets.

FRANK BALLARD.

HARROGATE, *July*, 1911.

---

[1] Perhaps the more so seeing that this attempt to deal with so complex a theme has had to be undertaken amidst the pressing demands of public work and the distractions of ceaseless journeyings.

INTRODUCTION

(1) Main Principles Involved

SANITY demands that in all intercourse between human minds there should be some common ground of certainty as an acknowledged basis. Whether in speech or in print, this is found to-day, for all men worthy of regard, in the universal assumption of moral responsibility. For the moment it matters not whence or how that ever-present human conviction arises. The fact that with one single pitiful exception, i.e. the intercourse between lunatics, or the necessary attendance upon them, all men hold each other responsible, alike for speech and action, remains as unshaken amid all the welter of disputes about 'free will,' as a granite rock swept by sea or blast. When popular fatalism, masquerading under the name of 'Determinism,' openly asserts that 'no man is answerable for his own acts,'[1] no one heeds it, no one attempts to act upon it, least of all the writer himself. There is no one place or phase of human society where it is acted on. Its only practicable sphere is the lunatic asylum. If humanity is developing upwards towards a time when the only war shall be that of words, then it is because already every speaker from a platform, every writer of a book—to say nothing of pulpits—takes always for granted that readers or hearers will appreciate truth, and so far as they can comprehend it, will

---

[1] *Not Guilty*, by R. Blatchford, p. 10.

reject untruth. It is indeed assumed on all hands, that whatever is shown to be true, *ought* to be received, and every statement shown to be untrue *ought* to be rejected. This principle applies, utterly regardless of age or circumstance, wealth or poverty, to every member of human society. Were it not for such an assumption and its universal acknowledgement, all moral effort would be as utterly wasted as rhetorical eloquence upon sheep.

Upon this assumption, moreover, all literature is based. Whether in the form of poetry or history, fiction or philosophy, that which each writer desires to convey is the truth. If it were made manifest, on the contrary, that he had no regard for truth, his words would remain unread or be read only to be scorned. In every realm of thought the truth is not only every man's birthright, but that which he can appreciate, and therefore ought to prefer above all else. The man to whom truth is nothing, dehumanizes himself. As a man he is morally responsible for thinking, speaking, acting the truth, to the very utmost of his conscious ability. This is certainty. It is the axiom without which not another word would here be written, or if written would be worth reading. It is simple fact, which does not admit of denial.

But it is no less certain that only a moral being can be morally responsible for anything. How man became a moral being, is at this point irrelevant. Whether, or how, he be naturally evolved from non-moral beings, no more affects the fact, than the actuality of any man's lofty intelligence or noble character is lessened by the record of his gradual growth through indefinable gradations from helpless babyhood to adult life. The evolution of morals or

INTRODUCTION

moral capacity, is matter of history. Human moral responsibility, with the connoted moral capacity, is matter of fact and of philosophy. It is the hallmark of the human, as distinct from the animal. All other animal life known to us is non-moral. It is only in leaving that stage behind that the *genus homo* becomes human. It is only through the development of that super-animal excess, that human society becomes possible. This is the crown of glory and honour which, whether he wear it with dignity or trample it beneath his feet, is man's distinctive characteristic and noblest possession. Well, therefore, does modern science, by one of its most eminent exponents, acknowledge this his high estate.

'What is the distinctive character of man?

'The distinctive character of man is that he has a sense of responsibility for his acts, having acquired the power of choosing between good and evil with freedom to obey one motive rather than another. Creatures far below the human level are irresponsible; they feel no shame and suffer no remorse; they are said to have no conscience.'[1]

Yet it is this, all this, nothing else, nothing less, which is now at stake. Not now, indeed, for the first time, but now more than ever before, by reason of the vast increase in modern populations and the hitherto unparalleled facilities for popular discussion through an ever-cheapening press. There are, happily, few who put the case with the ruthless bluntness of Prof. Hamon, in his open declaration that—

'To-day it must suffice us to have shown that there is no such thing as moral responsibility, and that all men are irresponsible.'[2]

Or of Mr. Cotter Morison, who avows that—

'The sooner the idea of moral responsibility is got rid of, the better it will be for society and for moral education.'[3]

---

[1] *The Substance of Faith allied with Science*, Sir Oliver Lodge, p. 24.
[2] *The Illusion of Free Will*, p. 138.
[3] *The Service of Man*, cheap edition, p. 111.

Or of Mr. R. Blatchford, who reiterates the statement—

'I do seriously mean that no man can, under any circumstances, be justly blamed for anything he may say or do.'[1]

But that these wild assertions are largely supported by some who claim to be modern teachers of science and philosophy — even as flimsy though flaring posters may be pasted upon a solid wall—will presently appear only too plainly.

Others there are who loudly proclaim themselves 'Determinists,' but make strenuous endeavour to save the notions of duty and responsibility from the wreck so luridly exhibited in the above. Whether that can logically be done, remains to be seen. Such a position certainly demands the closest scrutiny, not merely in the interests of academical philosophy, but even more on behalf of ordinary human society. In the whole matter of the relation of alleged 'Determinism' to morals, the philosophical and practical interests are always at least equal. There is abroad to-day a keener desire than ever for the truth, along with a larger capacity to appreciate it, thanks to the spread of modern education. There is also greater need than ever for wise and worthy principles of life and conduct in human society, both because of the greater numbers concerned, and the deteriorating influences of the high pressure under which present-day civilization compels so many to live.

On all the greatest themes that can occupy human thought, much has yet to be unlearned and more to be learned. No volume, however carefully prepared, even by expert intelligence, will put an end to the age-long controversy associated with our present

---

[1] *God and My Neighbour*, p. 137.

INTRODUCTION

theme. Yet it may be possible so to summarize the results thus far attained, as to mark a stage in the progress of the truth which shall not need in future to be retraversed. It may also be both possible and useful to set forth the actual mental facts in language which may be 'understood of the people,' instead of in a jargon of verbal complexities and monstrosities through which philosophy has too often been synonymous with profitless mystification. The scorn poured upon 'metaphysics' has been sometimes only too truly deserved, by reason of the extent to which counsel has been darkened by words that ought rather to have been illuminating.[1]

---

[1] Since the above was written Mr. Jacks' interesting volume on *The Alchemy of Thought* has appeared, in the first chapter of which the author strongly represents 'The bitter cry of the plain man.' The protest is certainly called for, and might be abundantly illustrated. When a person of ordinary intelligence is told that 'The positive relation of every appearance as an adjective to Reality and the presence of Reality among its appearances in different degrees and with diverse values—this double truth we have found to be the centre of philosophy' (*Appearance and Reality*, p. 561)—he may be forgiven for thinking that philosophy is beyond his comprehension. Or when he is assured in the name of metaphysics that—'The causality of phenomena, that is their being conditioned, is comprehensible, but not that which, occasioned by cause, appears as effect; and one can follow, step by step, how the comprehensibility of natural phenomena decreases in proportion as in the scale of mechanical, physical, chemical and organic phenomena, the effect gradually overwhelms the cause in becoming, in comparison to it, more dissimilar, mighty and independent; which is due to a gradually increasing susceptibility or so to say sensibility of organic and inorganic beings' (Deussen's *Elements of Metaphysics*, p. 99)—it is small wonder that he should heave a sigh of despair. If the object of philosophy be to mystify men, they do not want it. If it be to clarify their thoughts, then at least its terms and statements should be intelligible, and—if we may for once copy its phraseology—should not repulse inquirers with epistemological differentiations whose tortuous convolutions in labyrinthine sentences leave the average intellect only dazed amidst confusion confounded.

It cannot be too plainly pointed out that if that theory of the working of the human mind in volition which calls itself 'Determinism' be warranted, very much in all our intellectual, moral, social, and religious affairs is altogether wrong, and must be for ever abandoned. The deliberate avowal of the late Prof. W. James is assuredly as serious as any philosophical result can ever be—

'Calling the thing bad means, if it mean anything at all, that the thing ought not to be, that something else ought to be in its stead. Determinism, in denying that anything else can be in its stead, virtually defines the universe as a place in which what ought to be is impossible.'[1]

If that be so, then the dilemma is unmistakable; either 'Determinism' is false, or duty is a delusion. But if the conviction of duty is inseparable from manhood, then no effort can be too costly, no pains too great, no language too emphatic, to show where this much-proclaimed philosophy is as false in principle as ruinous in practice.

The term 'free will,' which is always popularly, and not seldom philosophically, employed as including the whole question at issue, is doubly misleading. It is both redundant and ambiguous. The former, because 'will' that is not, in some real measure, 'free,' is a contradiction in terms. A will, 'completely determined,' no matter by what, is no 'will' at all, but a mere mental nexus between some antecedent and some consequent.[2] The latter, because

---

[1] *The Will to Believe*, p. 161.

[2] The favourite simile with some writers is, in Mr. Blatchford's words, 'Will is like the action of balance in a pair of scales. It is the weight in the scales that decides the balance.' Is there then to be found any sane person who will credit the grocer's scales with possessing a will? Until there be, such talk is mere nonsense. The dilemma is absolutely inevitable. Either the grocer's scales are human or the man is a mere machine. Perhaps

INTRODUCTION

the suggestion conveyed to some minds is that there are no limitations to the function of the will. Whereas the most convinced Indeterminist, or the most ardent Libertarian, will acknowledge that the freedom which the very conception of 'will' necessarily involves, is as unmistakably limited as it is real. What these limitations are, will appear in due course. Here, we simply register a protest and pass on. On the whole, the nearest help that words can give to express an inexpressible reality, is probably to be found in the phrase 'self-determination,' which is as Dr. Illingworth says—

'only another name for free will. But it is a more accurate name, for it implies the necessity of motives as against mere indeterminism or liberty of indifference; whilst it reminds us that these motives are not mere desires, but objects of thought to a self-conscious subject, who, as such can distinguish himself from them and freely decide or decline to make them his own.'[1]

It is the reality and significance of this true Determinism by the self, as against the false Determinism by the not-self, which we here desire to elucidate, both for the sake of truth in philosophy and moral progress in human society.

One would think that to all ordinary mental vision it was clear enough, without verbal elaboration, that the repudiation of moral responsibility which is by some 'Determinists' openly, and by all logically, demanded, would very unfavourably affect if not altogether subvert moral progress in human

---

the popular journalist may be forgiven such superficiality as not being able to see—what I have plainly shown in 'Clarion' Fallacies, p. 69—that such a will is no will at all. But what to say to an avowed religious teacher who in *The Clarion* (for June 11, 1909—report of sermon by Rev. G. T. Sadler) avows that 'a will is a pair of scales,' I do not know. It is beyond respectful characterization.

[1] *Divine Immanence*, cheap edition, p. 109.

society. But when one of the latest and most erudite advocates of this theory vehemently asserts that 'it is free will, not Determinism, which has subversive consequences for the moral life of humanity,'[1] the need of further and thorough statement of the case becomes too manifest to call for apology. In this respect no line of distinction need be drawn between ethics and morals; the questions which emerge from their relationship to 'Determinism' are large and clear. Is man an automaton or not? Does 'Determinism' involve human automatism or something else? Is morality possible on 'Deterministic' lines? Does 'Determinism,' or its opposite, offer us most valid hope of progress in individual character? Is 'Determinism' the panacea, or the nemesis, of social reform? These queries all press for unequivocal answer, and must be met on the plain lines of experience and observation. The appeal cannot be made to Christian principles, because the Christian faith is so unmistakably and wholly arrayed on one side of the discussion. Without the moral freedom which is the inalienable essence of moral responsibility, Christianity would be but a colossal delusion. Such a sweeping affirmation, however, need here neither be made nor denied. Experience, rightly interpreted, will be our safe guide so far as we can follow it. When truth refuses to end there, the scrutiny which seeks to go beyond, must at least conform to what has preceded. The self may defy analysis, and refuse to be photographed, but it cannot be rationally contradicted. Not one whit too strongly has Prof. J. A. Thomson said that 'If a man is to deny the accuracy, or even the

---

[1] *Philosophical Essays*, by Bertrand Russell, M.A., F.R.S., first essay.

reality, of his mental consciousness, then there is nothing for it but to sit down and whittle a stick until death passes our way.'

(2) Determinism in the Past History of Philosophy

It must be clearly recognized that many of the great minds of past ages have not only seriously concerned themselves with the problems here suggested, but have with profound deliberation and profuse argumentation allied themselves to the views which are now known as 'Deterministic.' The variation in names is of little consequence. Whether we speak of fatalism, or predestination, or necessitarianism, the results for personality and moral responsibility are the same. If all a man's actions are irresistibly fated; if he is predestined, or foreordained before birth, to a certain course of life; if all that he is and does is but the expression of a necessity which he can no more gainsay than the earth can resist the force which drives it round its orbit[1]; then there is an end of personality, and with it of moral freedom, as also necessarily of moral responsibility. This plain issue has not always been frankly faced or definitely acknowledged. Theologians have joined with philosophers in putting velvet on the mailed fist which crushes manhood out of man. It cannot be denied that their attitude has been marked by strong speech, no less than by subtle acumen. Their views have been, however, so fully absorbed and reproduced in the vast area of

---

[1] 'The actions of a man's will are as mathematically fixed at his birth as are the motions of a planet in its orbit.'—*God and My Neighbour*, p. 144.

modern thought, that the merest reminder of their positions is all we here require, to bring us into clear apprehension of the present position. It will suffice, therefore, to mention but one or two of the more prominent representatives.

What is known now so well as the 'Free Will controversy,' as distinguished from the positive attitude of Aristotle,[1] may be said to have originated with the Stoics, though their own ultimate attitude towards it was ambiguous. Actually they asserted the freedom of the will, but their doctrine of a universal necessity or fate was so applied to the question of human volition, as to pave the way for the theological development of the question which received such impetus at the hands of Augustine. His uncompromising doctrine of predestination, which represented moral freedom as having been literally lost in Adam, and therefore lost to all men except those who were unconditionally elected by divine grace, dominated Christian philosophy for centuries, finding stricter formulation afterwards at the hands of Calvin, and, through his influence, amongst the Protestant churches of the Reformation. The vigorous polemic of Jonathan Edwards in the eighteenth century, expressed, in his famous treatise on *The Freedom of the Will* (1754), the utmost that philosophical theology has ever said, or probably ever will say, with equal intellectual force or metaphysical subtlety, to the same effect. Spinoza, in the seventeenth century, inaugurated a Pantheism which excluded all possibility of human free will.

---

[1] 'Morality supposes freedom. This exists whenever the will of the agent meets no obstacles and he is able to deliberate intelligently. It is destroyed by ignorance or constraint (Eth. Nic. III inst.).'—Uberweg's *History of Philosophy*, Vol. I, p. 172.

INTRODUCTION

For his system there was no such thing as contingency, in man or in nature. Belief in free will was simply the result of ignorance. Men thought themselves free because they were conscious of their actions, but not conscious of the causes of those actions. Thomas Hobbes about the same time was mainly devoted to political philosophy, but it is also recorded that 'his ethical theory, based on pure selfishness on the one hand and the arbitrary prescription of a sovereign power on the other, determined negatively the whole course of ethical speculation in England for a hundred years.' The influence of his trenchant style was cast undoubtedly into the Deterministic scale. So we come to Hume, of whose life and words Prof. Huxley has given so lucid an account in his little monograph.[1] In the chapter upon 'Liberty and Necessity,' the anti-free-will views of Hume are not only vividly summarized, but supported to the uttermost by every kind of comment on the part of his acute biographer. Not satisfied with pointing out how

'The last asylum of the hard-pressed advocate of the doctrine of uncaused volition is usually that, argue as you like, he has a profound and ineradicable consciousness of what he calls the freedom of his will. But Hume follows him even here'[2]—

he quotes Hume to the effect that 'By liberty we can only mean a power of acting or not acting according to the determinations of the will,' and then adds—'Half the controversies about the freedom of the will would have had no existence, if this pithy paragraph had been well pondered by those who oppose the doctrine of necessity.' He goes on to emphasize Hume's contention that so far from the

---

[1] Published by Macmillan, pp. 183-208.
[2] p. 189.

doctrine of necessity destroying responsibility, 'the very idea of responsibility implies the belief in the necessary connexion of certain actions with certain states of the mind.'[1]

How thoroughly the necessitarian view of the question, as against any doctrine of free will, was advocated by James Mill, and his more famous son John Stuart Mill, is too well known to call for comment, though it may be necessary to quote the latter as we proceed. It is not perhaps so well known that Schopenhauer, whilst especially distinguished as the philosopher who virtually founded his system upon will, was none the less as really a 'Determinist' as a pessimist. In his prize essay in 1839 on the 'Freedom of the Will,' he defends the phenomenal necessity or determinism of the will, no less than its 'supra-sensible' freedom. How far the utilitarian school, of which the Mills were the best-known representatives, adopted the same notion of necessity or Determinism, together with its manifest consequences, may be sufficiently illustrated by the avowal of Bentham, in his *Deontology*, that 'if the use of the word "ought" is admissible at all, then it ought to be banished from the vocabulary of morals.' As for Prof. A. Bain, whose ability is unquestioned, his attitude hereon may be summed up in a sentence. The will, according to his philosophy, is but a collective term for all the impulses to motion or to action. To ask whether such a complexity is free, is absurd.

(3) PRESENT-DAY RECRUDESCENCE

In face of all these deliberate and elaborate discussions, and together with a host of others

---

[1] p. 192.

INTRODUCTION

which do not here call for detailed notice, it is no wonder that the late Prof. James should remark, at the commencement of a contribution of his own, that—'A common opinion prevails that the juice has ages ago been pressed out of the free will controversy, and that no new champion can do more than warm up stale arguments which every one has heard.' He adds, however, also that 'this is a radical mistake. I know of no subject less worn out.' That this estimate is true, is abundantly confirmed by facts of recent date. The recrudescence of necessitarianism and fatalism, under the guise of 'Determinism,' in many publications, both erudite and popular, is manifest enough. There is considerable truth in the reference by Haeckel's best-known representative in this country, to 'the enormous spread of deterministic principles in our time.'[1]

Not all modern advocates of 'Determinism,' it must be confessed, identify it so uncompromisingly with fatalism, as do some of the books which have done most during recent years to popularize it. Says the author of *God and My Neighbour*—

'We are all creatures of heredity and environment. But this, you may say, is sheer fatalism. Well! it seems to me to be truth and philosophy and sweet charity.'[2]

But the careful consideration of a few plain extracts from recent publications, will show that the writer of such sentiments is far from being alone. His position is truly the only logical conclusion from the premisses. Whilst, however, in some cases, tortuous efforts are made to save the notions of responsibility and duty from the logical wreck, in others they are wholly jettisoned. Moreover, under the plea of

---

[1] Mr. J. McCabe, *R.P.A. Annual*, 1911, p. 75.
[2] pp. 140, 141.

natural causality, as rigid and mechanical sequence is urged for events in the mental as in the physical realm. Thus the reality of personality is ignored, and its unmistakable assertions treated as illusion. Whence also moral freedom becomes nothing more than mental action *in vacuo*, or causeless and therefore unscientific volition. So we see that Prof. James was well warranted in affirming that the question has become more full of interest than ever. The religious notion that because a powerful wave of sentiment in popular journalism during the last half dozen years may be truly said to have spent itself, therefore the whole suggestion of 'Determinism' may be pronounced obsolete, is as fatuous as the irreligious conceit which declares all that is connoted by 'free will' to be but an ecclesiastical delusion, at last and for ever exploded. The confidence with which the latter is asserted would indeed be amusing, were it not for the moral tragedy involved. But the ignorance—wilful or otherwise—displayed in regard to the present psychological or philosophical situation, is amazing and inexcusable. Thus the famous Professor of Jena says, without a tremor of hesitation—

'The freedom of the will is not an object for critical scientific inquiry at all, for it is a pure dogma, based on an illusion, and has no real existence.'[1]

The echoing popular journalist declares that—

'The deterministic case for the bottom dog is as simple as it is complete. It is not a mere theory of opinion, it is a demonstrated truth. It is not a matter for argument. There is nothing to argue about. There is no possible refutation. To argue against my case is as absurd as to argue against the statement that three times four are twelve. You may not like the

---

[1] *The Riddle of the Universe*, Ernst Haeckel, cheap edition, p. 6.

result. But you cannot answer me. It is a mere waste of words to argue. In fact, I am not arguing with you, I am telling you.'[1] With those who deny that there is any moral tragedy involved in the substratum of this blatant dogmatism, we will reckon presently. For the moment it seems most necessary that the modern attitude adopted by so many in our midst should be fully stated, irrespective of any minor differences in their avowed standpoints. It will be for the jury composed of the readers of these pages to decide whether, in face of such avowals, there is left any room for those moral actualities by which, as a social fact, all worthy living in civilization is ruled. Assuredly if humanity is in any real sense to move upward, somehow or other the great sacred cardinal realities of personality, duty, responsibility, character, must be not only rescued alike from the vandalism of popular ignorance and the subtleties of fatalistic or absolute-idealistic philosophy, but must become more than ever hitherto the watchwords of individual life and conduct.

The following statements, then, speak for themselves, and are typical of others. They are taken with scrupulous exactness from works of which they express, in condensed form, the total and unmistakable attitude. Turning first to the Continent, we learn from Prof. Haeckel that—

'The great struggle between the Determinist and the Indeterminist, between the opponent and the sustainer of the freedom of the will, has ended to-day after more than 2,000 years completely in favour of the Determinist. We now know that each act of the will is as fatally determined by the organization of the individual, and as dependent upon the momentary condition of his environment, as every other psychic activity. The character inclination was determined long ago by heredity from

[1] *Clarion*, March 9, 1906.

parents and ancestors; the determination to each particular act is an instance of adaptation to the circumstances of the moment, where the strongest motive prevails, according to the laws which govern the statics of emotion.'[1]

Again; Prof. Günther, in his *Darwinism and the Problems of Life*, informs us that—

'In reality the world has no place for duty from the scientific point of view. The cosmic process goes on inexorably. How ridiculous and aimless it must be in view of this conception of things, to direct a man how he shall act! As if he could make the slightest change in the inexorable march of cause and effect! There is no teleological occurrence in the world; even human actions are determined by causes that lie *behind*, not *before* them. The utmost that science can say is that an ethic, a setting-up of things to be attained, has no meaning. It can only direct a man to let himself be borne in peace on the stream of cause and effect, without doing anything, because his action could have no aim and no result. The only possible scientific ethic is resignation.'[2]

With equal perspicuity speaks Prof. Hamon, of the new University of Brussels, in his *Universal Illusion of Free Will*.

'Man is determined. His volitions are the result of the multifarious environments in which he moves. Historically and theoretically responsibility is based upon free will. As the latter does not exist, responsibility vanishes. Scientifically, man is the inevitable product of the surroundings in which he lives, and in which his ancestors lived. Logically, he is not responsible for his actions, for he could not help wishing them, the conditions once given. It is only by a collection of fictions that moral responsibility subsists in our codes and our customs. Universal Determinism being the scientific truth, it follows that moral responsibility does not exist. It cannot be conceived. It is, in fact, contrary to human reason to consider automatons responsible, being unavoidably obliged to be as they are. The rock which in breaking away crushes whoever is on its path, is not considered responsible. Nor is the tiger responsible who

---

[1] *The Riddle of the Universe*, cheap edition, p. 47.
[2] p 423

kills a man. We ought no more to consider the man who acts responsible, for he is as much an automaton as the tiger or the rock. General irresponsibility, such is scientific truth.'"[1]

In seeking a definition of freedom, Prof. Delboeuf of Liége says—

'The fundamental proposition of Determinism is the following. The present state of the universe, and consequently the movement of the least of its atoms, is the necessary and the only possible consequence of its immediately preceding state, and the sufficient cause of its immediately following state, so that a sufficient powerful intelligence would be able, from a single glance at the present state of the universe, to infer its entire past and its entire future.'[2]

Returning from the Continent, we find that writers on these themes in our own country express themselves with equal lucidity and emphasis. Concerning the attitude of Prof. Huxley, there can be no doubt. Thus in his essay on 'Science and Morals' he says—

'If physical science in strengthening our belief in the universality of causation and abolishing chance as an absurdity, leads to the conclusions of Determinism, it does no more than follow the track of consistent and logical thinkers in philosophy and theology before it existed or was thought of. Physical science did not invent Determinism, and the Deterministic doctrine would stand on just as firm a foundation as it does, if there were no physical science.'[3]

Again, in his little monograph upon Hume, we learn that—

'The passionate assertion of the consciousness of their freedom which is the favourite refuge of the opponents of the doctrine of necessity, is mere futility, for nobody denies it. What they really have to do if they would upset the necessitarian argument is to prove that they are free to associate any emotion whatever with any idea whatever: to like pain as much as pleasure;

---

[1] pp. 115, 134.
[2] *Bulletin de l'Académie Royale de Belgique*, 3me serie, No. 2.
[3] *Essays on Controverted Questions*, pp. 231, 233

vice as much as virtue; in short, to prove that whatever may be the fixity of order of the universe of things, that of thought is given over to chance."¹

Nor was Prof. Tyndall wanting in the expression of similar convictions—

'My physical and intellectual textures were woven for me, not by me; processes in the conduct or regulation of which I had no share have made me what I am. If, then, our organisms, with all their tendencies and capacities, are given to us without our being consulted; and if, while capable of acting within certain limits in accordance with our wishes, we are not masters of the circumstances in which motives and wishes originate; if, finally, our motives and wishes determine our actions, in what sense can these actions be said to be the result of free will?'²

Still more confident in his automatism, we know, was Prof. W. K. Clifford—

'We are to regard the body as a physical machine which goes by itself according to a physical law. If anybody says that the soul influences matter, the statement is not untrue, it is nonsense.'³

And even more outspoken, if possible, was always Dr. H. Maudsley, who in his *Life, in Mind and Conduct*, thus delivers himself—

'Good and evil, right and wrong, and their intermediates, have their natural causes, functions, and consequences, which are not outside the scope of scientific inquiry and ought, therefore, to be studied, not as abstractions but as concrete processes. The criminal is not inscrutable nor inexplicable, any more than a chemical compound, though the inquiry be more difficult; the sinner equally with the saint is a product of cause and effect in a fixed order of things; the fall of an individual or a kingdom is as natural a consequence as the fall of a leaf or a thunderbolt.'⁴

Mr. Herbert Spencer, as a philosophical necessitarian,

---

[1] p. 191.
[2] *Fragments of Science*, Vol. II, pp. 362, 364.
[3] *Lectures*, Vol. II, p. 33.
[4] p. 162.

INTRODUCTION

of course leaves us in no doubt concerning his attitude.

'That every one is at liberty to do what he desires to do, supposing there are no external hindrances, all admit, though people of confused ideas commonly suppose this to be the thing denied. But that every one is at liberty to desire or not to desire, which is the real proposition involved in the dogma of free will, is negatived as much by the analysis of consciousness as by the contents of preceding chapters. Psychological changes either conform to law or they do not. If they do not, no science of psychology is possible. If they do conform to law, there cannot be any such thing as free will.'[1]

During more recent years, if we follow a general chronological order, the following are also explicit statements on the part of writers who have contributed to the above-mentioned 'enormous spread of Determinism.'

Mr. Cotter Morison, in his *Service of Man*, writes that—

'Nothing is more certain than that no one makes his own character. That is done for him by his parents and ancestors. It will, perhaps, be said that this view does away with moral responsibility; that those who hold it cannot consistently blame any crime or resent any injury; that we should not on this hypothesis reproach a garrotter who half murders us: he is a machine, not a man with free will, capable of doing and forbearing according to the moral law. It is no more rational to blame him than it would be to blame a runaway locomotive which knocks you down and mangles or kills you. To which the answer is, that the sooner the idea of moral responsibility is got rid of, the better it will be for society and moral education.'[2]

Mr. Mallock, in his desperate attempts to establish Pyrrhonism with a view to Pragmatism, puts the modern case for 'Determinism' thus—

'Here then we arrive, by yet another and a final route, at one demonstration more, that free will is impossible. The gap in

---

[1] *Principles of Psychology*, Vol. I, pp. 500, 503. Cheap edition, p. 111.

the argument of psychology, physiology has filled up by its exposition of the facts and its establishment of the principle of heredity. It has thus stopped the last earth in which the phantom of freedom could hide itself. It has thus supplied the last link in the chain by which man is bound to the mechanism of universal nature; has shown him to be part and parcel of one single and inexorable process, no more responsible for any one of his thoughts or actions than he is for those of his grandfather, for the colour of his eyes, or for the history and temperature of the earth which have rendered his life possible. We have seen, as to his will, that he is nothing but a mere machine, who, whatever he does, deserves neither praise nor blame, since whatever he does, he could not have done otherwise.'[1]

Writing in *The Hibbert Journal*, Mr. Bertrand Russell expresses himself thus, in an attempt to show that 'Determinism does not in any way interfere with morals '—

'The principle of causality, that every event is determined by previous events, appears to apply just as much to human actions as to other events. When several alternative actions present themselves, it is certain that we can both do which we choose, and choose which we will. What Determinism maintains is that our will to choose this or that alternative is the effect of antecedents. There is no reason to regret that the grounds in favour of Determinism are overwhelmingly strong.'[2]

Mr. N. Pearson, in his volume on *Some Problems of Existence*, seeking to establish what he terms 'religious Determinism,' writes that—

'Every act of a man is the latest link in an immense chain of causation, in which the slightest element of uncertainty would be impossible. At a given moment, there may be several courses apparently open to a man, but in reality there is only

---

[1] *Religion as a Credible Doctrine*, pp. 148, 149.

[2] October, 1908, pp. 115, 118, 121. In a footnote the writer explains that he uses the term 'free will' simply to mean 'the doctrine that not all volitions are determined by causes.' This, it need hardly be said, is not the meaning it conveys to those who most earnestly oppose the ordinary statements of 'Determinism,' as illustrated in the instances given here.

INTRODUCTION

that course open to him which his character and environment make the only course possible. This, put quite shortly, is the doctrine of Determinism. It seems, then, that the doctrine of free will breaks down at every point where it comes into contact with the realities of existence. Those who insist upon the freedom of man's will must abandon any intelligible belief in the divine government of the world. The belief in free will is at present propped up rather by groundless fears of the dangers of discarding it, than by any solid evidence in its favour.'[1]

In an elaborate work entitled *Some Dogmas of Religion*, Prof. J. E. McTaggart, the Hegelian specialist and lecturer of Trinity College, Cambridge, seeks to get rid of all valid grounds for belief in God, freedom, and immortality—as this last is generally interpreted—and points to Spinoza as the 'great religious teacher in whom philosophical honesty and religious devotion were blended as in no other man before or since.' Some forty-five pages of his subtle dialectic are directed against 'free will,' with the avowed intention of showing that Indeterminism, not 'Determinism,' would injure or destroy morality.

'The main argument against it is that which proceeds by establishing the universal validity of the law of causality, and so showing that volitions like all other events must be completely determined. The law of causality asserts that every event is determined by previous events in such a way that if the previous events are as they are, it is impossible that the subsequent event should not be as it is. Determinists maintain that our volitions are as completely determined as all other events. From this it is generally, and I think correctly, held to follow that it would be ideally possible to deduce the whole of the future course of events from the present state of reality, though of course a mind enormously more powerful than ours would be required to do it.'[2]

Strangely enough, Mr. J. McCabe, to whose cultured and energetic advocacy Haeckel's works owe their

---

[1] pp. 92, 109, 115. [2] pp. 177, 143, 145.

vogue in this country, though himself a 'Determinist,' is distinctly removed from the blind dogmatism of the continental professors, and shows remarkable sensitiveness to psychological fact. We shall have occasion to appreciate his candid and scientific acknowledgements later on. For the moment his general summary is worth recording.

'The question is settled in the minds of an enormous proportion of the more thoughtful people of any modern community. Two more or less separate influences have been at work for more than half a century in the education of the people on this point. The teaching of science, eagerly caught up by a Rationalism that sought to discredit the unique claims that were made for the human mind, seemed to reduce man to an orderly and regulated atom in a vast system of inexorable, inevitable forces. The most recent theories of heredity add incalculable strength to the Determinist position. On the other hand, a large portion of our social moralists were driven to adopt the same position—to recognize heredity and environment as the predominant and tangible influences that mould character. Socialism, apart from a few leaders who linger lazily on the fringe of orthodoxy, is wholly Determinist, and has imbued millions of followers with the heresy. Every great leader of Socialism in Europe to-day is a Determinist. When we add the leading anti-Socialist moralists, Mill, Huxley, Spencer, Stephen, with their wide following; when we remember that dramatists and novelists like Ibsen and Zola set the same fashion in their worlds; when we find essayists like Mr. Mallock confessing that they would sign the creed gladly, but for the dogma of free will, we understand why Determinism pervades our literature and is so generally accepted.'[1]

Dr. C. Callaway, in an earlier issue of the same *Annual*, lays himself out to show that 'scientific Determinism' will rather help than hinder the sense of moral responsibility. Against 'the arrogant pretension of free will' he strongly protests.

'Man's assertion of free will betrays itself as a hindrance to the progress of the race. Whence comes the force in us which

---

[1] *R.P.A. Annual* for 1910, p. 59.

INTRODUCTION

is to overcome both heredity and environment? By the free will hypothesis such a force would be uncaused. A phenomenon without a cause! To such loose thinking does vanity condemn mankind! It is hardly too much to say that the moral improvement of the race has proceeded *pari passu* with a decline in men's belief in free will.'[1]

Popular writers against Christianity such as 'Philip Vivian,' of course join in such denunciation.

'No metaphysical argument can reconcile this inflexible causality with true freedom of will. How can the will be at one and the same time fettered and free? There is, I grant, every appearance of free will, but it belongs to the category of appearances which deceive. Is it not that there are two forces and two forces only, heredity and environment, acting upon our brain, and our choice is the resultant of them? Undoubtedly man, as a self-conscious and reflecting animal, has what may be called the power of choice, but the way this power will be used would be a foregone conclusion did we know the sum total of the effect of heredity and environment up to the moment of its use. Determinism is completely subversive of Christian teaching.'[2]

In direct contravention of the last sentence quoted, sometimes 'Determinism' is defended by avowedly Christian advocates. Thus the Rev. G. T. Sadler declares, from the pulpit of a Congregational church, that—

'Our actions are caused by laws which we did not make, but which make us live as we do. We choose, but our choice is governed by all our past and by present circumstances. A will is a pair of scales, and the motives are the weights, the stronger sending the scale down. All is law. All is inevitable by the laws of life. Our moral acts are caused by our characters, and our characters are built up from tendencies and ideas which have come from heredity and environment.'[3]

As a further specimen of the way in which the matter appears to many minds, take the following, contributed to *The Hibbert Journal*, in the course

---

[1] *R.P.A. Annual* for 1905, pp. 17, 26.
[2] *The Churches and Modern Thought*, pp. 248, 249.
[3] Reported in *Clarion*, June 11, 1909.

of a review of the philosophy of Prof. Bergson, by Mr. H. W. Carr—

'It is no longer the relation of man to his Creator which troubles and weighs upon the human conscience It is the sense of the insignificance of man, of the negligible part he plays in the vast and limitless activities that make up the universe, the rigid necessity characterizing the interdependence of its parts There seems to be no freedom, no real creation, possible in the universe as science represents it. Everything seems to be mutually fixed and determined. It is true that science cannot solve the problem of the prime mover, nor the beginning of time; but so far as thought can go, everything seems conditioned. Real origination, real creation, is for science inconceivable. All reality is mathematically measurable; the future is completely determined by the present state of the universe as the present has been conditioned by the past.'[1]

Amongst the artisan population of this country the most effective recent pleading on behalf of 'Determinism' has undoubtedly been that of Mr. R. Blatchford, whose two books and ceaseless editorials in his journal, have reached and influenced thousands of men and women otherwise unaffected by modern thought. His 'Determinism' differs altogether from the cautious scientific attitude of Mr. McCabe, and in its thoroughgoing assertions not only antagonizes Christianity but endorses the moral irresponsibility of man as alleged by Prof. Hamon and others above. His typical and characteristic statements, in addition to those already quoted, are such as these—

'If God is responsible for man's existence, God is responsible for man's acts. Man is what he is by the act of God, or the results of heredity and environment; in either case he is not to blame. You have power to choose, but you can only choose as your heredity and environment compel you to choose.'[2]

---

[1] July, 1910, p. 876.
[2] *God and My Neighbour*, pp. 131, 144, 146.

INTRODUCTION 25

'The conclusion is that everything a man does, is at the instant when he does it, the only thing he can do: the only thing he can do then. I base this claim upon the self-evident and undeniable fact that man has no part in the creation of his own nature. I shall be told that this means that no man is answerable for his own acts. That is exactly what it does mean.'[1]

The latest popular avowal to the same effect is a work by Mark Twain, dated February, 1905, but only recently published in this country by the Rationalist Press Association. The author claims to have written it many years ago, and to have continually revised it, until confident that all its assertions are 'unassailable truth.' The conclusions are not so avowedly anti-Christian, but quite as dogmatically uncompromising, as those just quoted—

'The human being is merely a machine. Man and a machine are about the same thing, and there is no personal merit in the performance of either. Man is the impersonal intelligence. Whatsoever the man is, is due to his make and to the influences brought to bear upon it by his heredity, his habitat, his associations. He is moved, directed, commanded, by exterior influences, solely. He originates nothing, not even a thought. A man is never anything but what his outside influences have made him A man's temperament and training will decide what he shall do, and he will do it. He cannot help himself, he has no authority over the matter. To me, man is a machine made up of many mechanisms, the mental and moral ones acting automatically in accordance with the impulses of an interior master who is built out of brain, temperament, and an accumulation of multitudinous outside influences and trainings.'[2]

It is not here necessary to criticize the psychology or the philosophy of this curious production. A humorist who is made an Oxford Doctor of Laws, *honoris causâ*, may perhaps be permitted to substitute the imaginary for the scientific and the mechanical for the philosophical. But his words,

---
[1] *Not Guilty*, pp. 202, 10.
[2] *What is Man?* pp. 1, 6, 8, 69, 140, 149.

the last popularly issued at the moment on this vast theme, may be taken as a fitting close to the statements and influences of 'Determinism' exhibited above. The inane young man who is made the cat's paw in the Socratic dialogue form of Mark Twain's book, ventures timidly to ask for pardon in regard to the suggestion that the publication of such doctrine might do harm. 'Pardon you!' is the reply; 'you have done nothing; you are an instrument; a speaking trumpet.' Upon which the following summary is stated and endorsed. Says the young man—

'Well, to begin with it is a desolating doctrine; it is not inspiring, enthusing, uplifting. It takes the glory out of man, it takes the pride out of him; it takes all the heroism out of him, it denies him all personal credit, all applause; it degrades him to a machine, it allows him no control over the machine—makes a mere coffee mill of him, and neither permits him to supply the coffee nor turn the crank; his sole and piteously humble function being to grind coarse or fine, according to his make, outside influences doing all the rest.'

And the oracular old man replies—

'It is correctly stated.'[1]

Such a conception of humanity, one cannot but think, is a poor legacy for any man to bequeath to his fellows as the result of a long life's literary toil. When Mr. McCabe in his review of this work[2] affirms that 'the enormous spread of Deterministic principles in our time has led to no demoralization,' the answer, as we shall presently more fully see, is simple enough, viz. that no one goes upon them. How utterly, for instance, our pseudo-scientific humorist, whose last words insist that man is but a machine, contradicts himself, may be judged from these other words of his.

'Man is the only animal that blushes—or needs to. As for me, all that I think about in this sad pilgrimage, this pathetic drift

---

[1] *What is Man?* p. 155.
[2] In *The R.P.A. Annual for* 1911, p. 75.

between eternities, is to look out and humbly live a pure and high and blameless life and save that one microscopic atom in me that is truly me; the rest may land in Sheol and welcome for all I care.'

A remarkable soliloquy, truly, from a machine! And a blushing machine!

Out of the total of the preceding statements manifestly two Determinisms emerge: the one denying moral responsibility and dismissing it as a mischievous fiction, the other acknowledging it, and claiming to intensify it. This difference is surely enough to make the problem overwhelming as to how out of any one scheme of thought such contradictories can be extracted. But we are driven to affirm, with reasons to follow, that the former is as logical and demoralizing as the latter is inviting but impossible. For the moment it is sufficient to have shown, by these unmistakable utterances from modern sources, that 'Determinism' is in the air and must be reckoned with; and that any notion of ruling it out of court by philosophical hauteur, or of ending it by pious disregard, is sheer fatuity. It is not enough to say with the late Prof. James, that 'the theme is as juicy as ever.' It is fraught with more importance than ever before in the world's history, by reason of the greater populations and pressing, not to say threatening, problems of civilization. The truth of philosophy, the good or evil influence of science, the possibility and worth of morality, the very existence of the Christian religion, all turn upon the inquiry—What is man?—and no equivocal answer can be sufficient. Nor will any reliance upon the authority of great names, or the venerableness of tradition, avail. There is, certainly, on the non-'Determinist' side a host of thinkers[1]

---

[1] For Bibliography, see end of this volume.

whose names and numbers should carry weight. But the final appeal is and must be to individual minds, whether they may be more or less capable of the required clear and patient thought. Mr. Bradley's scorn for the 'popular moralist' is as futile as unworthy. The suggestion that only professional philosophers can think, is in itself an absurd conceit. Both the need and the capacity for sustained thought on the part of the 'common people,' are increasing year by year. Whether Mr. Kidd's estimate of the ethical character of the new democracy be optimistic or not, it is certain that even the problems of the hour are being solved by the many rather than by the few. Moreover, it is the mind of the people, much rather than the mind of university Dons, which will decide and carry out the pragmatism of the future. No better summary of the present situation can be framed than a sentence from Mr. McCabe— 'There will be no human evolution save by the exercise of human power, and the re-assertion of that power is urgently needed.' In face of present-day facts, it is impossible to say which merits greater emphasis, the need for upward evolution, or the impossibility of obtaining it without all that is connoted by 'human power.' The purpose of these pages is to show that the whole hope of the future rests on the true, as against the false, 'Determinism.'

I
FALSE DETERMINISM

I

FALSE DETERMINISM

THE distinction in the preceding collection of avowals between what the late Prof. James expressively termed 'hard' and 'soft Determinism,' has been freely acknowledged, and the further confession may be made that from the non-'Determinist' standpoint the softer form is the harder to deal with. It will have to be fairly faced when we come to consider the ultimate nature of morality. Here it is imperative to point out that whether it be confessed that this 'Deterministic' attitude makes morality impossible, or stoutly contended that morality is thereby made more real and applicable, in some respects these varying forms and degrees of 'Determinism' are all alike. They all insist that the realm of human consciousness is as rigidly subject to law as the physical realm in which his body moves; that the principle of causation is the absolute *sine quâ non* of all science and philosophy; that human volition is, therefore, nothing more than the inevitable effect of which the strongest motive is the cause; that the forces whereby some particular motive is rendered the strongest, are external and beyond the man's own control. These unmistakable items in the theory bring us, whether by rougher or smoother paths matters nothing, to the conclusion that man is 'determined' in the sense so vividly defined by Prof. Hamon, Mr. Blatchford, and Mark

Twain. It is this 'Determinism' that we now take in hand to show that it is trebly false ; (1) in name ; (2) in fact ; (3) in principle.

(1) 'Determinism' False in Name

It is perhaps too late, in this as in some other cases, to protest against a name which has become a technical term. From the genuine Christian standpoint, for instance, the names 'Rationalist,' 'Free Thinker,' 'Agnostic,' 'Spiritualist,' 'Socialist,' 'Catholic,' are all actually fraudulent and touched with more or less of impertinence. But they have become, in the course of only a few years, such technical appellations that it is probably beyond the power of any modern writer or speaker to bring them back to their true signification. The same apparently applies to the name 'Determinism.' It is as convenient as it is unwarranted a title for the suggestion that heredity and environment are everything and human personality nothing. But there are other names, much more accurate and honest, which are not yet wholly repudiated. 'Fatalism' has been applied ever since the time of the Stoics, to views which involved the same conclusion, so far as human nature was concerned. From the time of Augustine, 'predestination' has been accepted as true, and, from powerful minds such as John Calvin and Jonathan Edwards, has received such emphasis that in spite of its essential immorality,[1] it still holds in its grip numbers of 'religious Determinists.' The

---

[1] 'Calvinism is not accidentally, but essentially immoral, since it makes the distinction between right and wrong a matter of positive enactment, and thereby makes it possible to assert that what is immoral for man is moral for God.'—Aubrey L. Moore, *Science and the Faith*, p. 119.

school of Mill and Spencer strongly avowed the doctrine of philosophical necessity. And in spite of Mill's attempt to distinguish between necessitarianism and fatalism, it is plain that the necessitarian doctrine reduces human nature to the same mere negation as fatalism. The latest, most expressive, and in some respects most true name for the theory we are considering, is 'Automatism.' Man in its view becomes really and merely a 'conscious automaton.' Prof. Huxley was not ashamed of the term, although he did not commit himself to such blunt dogmatism as the Belgian Professor who declares that a man 'is as much an automaton as a tiger or a rock.'

Thus we have had four names for virtually the same thing, 'Fatalism,' 'Predestination,' 'Necessitarianism,' 'Automatism.' These were all alike in this, that they endorsed what the old Persian pessimist has so vividly expressed—

> With Earth's first Clay They did the last Man's knead,
> And then of the Last Harvest sowed the Seed:
> Yea, the first Morning of Creation wrote
> What the Last Dawn of reckoning shall Read.[1]

Now, however, it appears that these four names, illustrating the varying fashions of philosophical speech, are to become obsolete, giving place to a fifth which, with exacter science and more precise philosophy, is to include them all, i.e. 'Determinism.' Concerning which we do not shrink from affirming that whatever else is right, this is wrong. Whether the others be true or not, this is false. For what is intended? A name for that scientific conception of human nature which regards man as a helpless no less than infinitesimal part of the cosmic process. Now the only phrases that can possibly do justice

---
[1] *Omar Khayyám*, LIII.

to such a conception are those above quoted ; viz. that 'man is determined'; 'man cannot help himself'; man is but a 'necessary result of forces external to himself'; 'he and his fellows are a mere procession of marionettes,' &c. In which case, the only place for the -ism which betokens a theory, is at the end of the term which expresses the conviction. If to such an extent as this, man is 'Determined,' then assuredly 'Determined-ism,' and not 'Determinism,' is the proper term to apply to such an emphatic assertion of pure passivity on his part. It is altogether misleading to claim that 'Determinism,' as an active term, stands here for the natural forces of heredity and environment. For 'active' these forces certainly are not ; seeing that by the very theory they are themselves determined, being nothing more than effects of preceding causes, which are again effects, and so on *ad infinitum.* The principle of causality which they are assumed to represent is, ultimately, as Prof. James said, nothing more than ' an empty name.'

'An empty name covering simply a demand that the sequence of events shall some day manifest a deeper kind of belonging of one thing with another, than the mere arbitrary juxtaposition which now phenomenally appears. It is as much an altar to an unknown God as the one that St. Paul found at Athens.'[1]

But since 'Determinism' unmistakably connotes purposeful activity, whatever else is right, to describe absolute open passivity as 'Determinism' is wrong. Strictly speaking, the 'forces of nature,' or 'heredity and environment,' no more determine anything than man does, on these naturalistic lines. From beginning to end the spontaneity which is the true essence of activity is absent. No one would say that a truck

[1] *The Will to Believe*, p. 147.

in the midst of a goods train is active, because it moves. In point of fact it does not move. It is moved. And the only determining force in the whole concern is the will of the engine-driver. If, therefore, in any form, this insistence upon absolute, unbroken, unbreakable, mechanical, causation, is to be maintained, and a new name has to be coined for its application to human nature, the least untrue name for it is ' Determinedism ' ; though any of the former appellations might be not unsuitably employed—except ' Determinism.'

(2) False in Fact

Dr. Rudolf Otto well says that the ' Theories opposed to freedom of the will cannot be refuted in any way except by simply saying that they are false. They do not describe what really takes place within us.'[1] But no theory can afford to dash itself opposingly on fact. The result will be as sure as that of a collision between an aeroplane in swift descent and a granite rock. Prof. Haeckel's cheap sneers at Kant's ' kategorical imperative ' do not in the least diminish the fact that the hall-mark which distinguishes true human nature from everything else on earth, is found in the threefold and ineradicable conviction of the normal man—'I ought; I can; I will.' However much the relations between these may vary in individuals, their total truth to fact yields a fivefold direct and unequivocal contradiction to the Determinedism which is now in some quarters alleged to be scientific truth concerning human nature.

(i) Such a theory is flatly contradicted by the fact of conscience in the individual. The voice of conscience says within the normal man, ' I ought.'

[1] *Naturalism and Religion*, p. 319.

But for the man who is 'determined' before he is born, such a word is utterly meaningless. Bentham was well warranted, from his standpoint, in the self-contradictory avowal above mentioned, that the word 'ought'—'ought to be banished from the vocabulary of morals.' But human nature cannot be banished from humanity. Fact remains, false theory dissolves into oblivion. Three notes of caution only are required in order to appreciate the force of this fact of conscience. (1) It must not be confused with moral judgement. A common but careless misrepresentation is to speak of conscience as 'a kind of heavenly voice whispering to us what things are right and wrong,'[1] and then out of that false definition to conjure up a vision of conflicting consciences by means of historical, geographical, personal, differences. But all such acknowledged differences in moral judgement between savage and saint, Nonconformist and Romanist, Aristocrat and Socialist, only serve to emphasize the reality and authority of conscience. For all these are absolutely one in the conviction which alone forms the inalienable principle of conscience, viz. 'I ought to do right.' And the felt intensity of such obligation is the very reason of the severity of the conflict which ensues when judgements differ. (2) The evolution of conscience from lowly beginnings, is utterly irrelevant. An acquired conscience is no less real for being acquired, than a man's intelligence is less real for having slowly developed from babyhood. There was a time when Newton could not count ten, but his *Principia* remains no less a monument of mathematical genius. (3) Variations in the degree of intensity with which conscience is acknowledged

---

[1] *Not Guilty*, p. 149.

as authoritative, do not diminish, let alone destroy, its reality. A grey dawn, or a morn of fog, is as real evidence of day as a summer noon. Sir Oliver Lodge's definition of human nature above quoted—according to science and consciousness in one—holds good on the firm ground of fact, whatever becomes of Palaeontology.

'The distinctive character of man is that he has a sense of responsibility for his acts, having acquired the power of choosing between good and evil, with freedom to obey one motive rather than another.'

Postponing for the moment all stress upon the latter half of such a definition, the former finds its true and sufficient expression in conscience. Wherever this obtains, Determinedism is unthinkable. The extent to which the Determinedism which so desires to be known as 'Naturalism' and 'Determinism,' herein contradicts itself, is worthy of exhibition in a museum Take but a couple of instances. A Professor writes a book in order to demonstrate that free will is an 'illusion,' and that therefore 'moral responsibility does not exist.' Suppose, then, that the demonstration is complete, and the conclusion apparently true ; the very question which cannot but arise concerning it, immediately contradicts it. For if sanity and honesty appreciate it, they are bound to go on and ask *ought* it to be received and acted on ? If not, what is the use of writing it ? But if so, if a man *ought* to act upon the truth, what becomes of irresponsibility ?[1]

Again; we have seen above that the latest effort of Mark Twain is to demonstrate that 'Man is a mere

---

[1] Rightly does Dr. Rudolf Otto also point out that the vaunted search of Naturalism for the truth ' is worthy of honour, but implies a curious self-deception. For if Naturalism be in the right, thought is not free, and if thought be not free, there can be no such thing as truth, for there can be no establishing of what truth is.'—*Naturalism and Religion*, p. 321.

machine'; that his 'brain works automatically, not by will-power'; that 'his temperament and training decide what he shall do, he cannot help himself.' And yet he assures us that 'conscience is a colourless force seated in man's moral constitution.'[1] The perfect representation of human nature, then, being a steam-engine[2] or a nugget of gold,[3] we have the remarkable suggestion of a moral steam-engine and a moral lump of metal. Such suggestions come well from a humorist. But the humour here surely becomes intense, when we once more recall the fact that it is Mark Twain himself who reminds us that 'Man is the only animal that blushes, or needs to.' So on the shelves of our museum we must find room for a blushing steam-engine, and, animals being prohibited, for a blushing bar of metal! Meanwhile, as long as reason remains and consciousness is worth regarding, the man who feels that he *ought* to do right, because he believes it to be *duty*, is not, never was, never can be, 'determined' by any force whatever, or under any conceivable circumstances.

(ii) Such a contradiction is sufficient, as regards a single individual, to put an end to Determinedism. But this is a case in which quantity may well add to quality. That which is true of an individual man, becomes emphatic when found to be also true of mankind. If conscience be defined as the human inborn sense of responsibility, so that the creature without a conscience ceases to be a man and becomes a mere biped, then the possession of conscience becomes the hall-mark of humanity. Man is distinguished from other creatures by the possession

---

[1] p. 151. How, under any circumstances, 'force' could be other than 'colourless,' we are not told.
[2] *What is Man?* p. 1.   [3] p. 90.

of an unmistakable moral consciousness. There is no need here to discuss the question whether any races of man have been found devoid of conscience or religious feeling. Prof. Tiele's view is well substantiated—

'The statement that there are nations or tribes which possess no religion rests either on inaccurate observation or on a confusion of ideas. No tribe or nation has yet been met with destitute of belief in any higher beings; and travellers who asserted their existence have been afterwards refuted by the facts.'[1]

So, too, says Prof. Tylor in his *Primitive Culture*—

'The assertion that non-religious tribes have been known in actual existence, though in theory possible, and perhaps in fact true, does not rest on that sufficient proof which for an exceptional state of things we are entitled to demand. The evidence given is often mistaken and never conclusive.'

But the truth concerning human capacity is to be learnt from its highest, not its lowest point. Kant's verdict, indeed, remains undeniable that 'the truth of these ideas of God, freedom, and immortality, no sophistry will ever wrest from the conviction of even the commonest man.' Moreover, the common sense of mankind has ever estimated the height of human nature from the degree of sensitiveness to moral obligation; whilst the denial or ignoring of that obligation has been, and is, regarded as the mark of the brute.

(iii) About one thing there neither is nor can be controversy, viz. that the faculty of speech is distinctively human. The intercommunications of animals are interesting and wonderful, but there is no approach, even in the highest of them, to the use of language as in the intercourse between man and man. Whatever be the history of the development

---

[1] *Outlines of History of Religion*, p. 6.

of this faculty,[1] it not only exists, but marks the degree to which man has evolved beyond all other animals. It is that fact, and the contents of the fact, which concern us here.

Now speech, as a fact, may be truly termed the incarnation of thought. We need not deny that animals think, after their fashion, even as children do. But it is all decidedly too elementary to be seriously deemed intellectual, in that there is no sign whatever of any capacity for abstract thought. Nor is there any such perception of right and wrong, or sense of the oughtness of right, as can permit them to be called moral.[2] But in man the acquisition of mental and moral capacity demands expression, and the expression reacts upon the development to its further stimulus. Hence all languages contain words intended to convey moral reality. Speech thus clothes thought, as suitable dress covers the body. It may be coarse or refined, rough or polished, scanty or plentiful, narrow or comprehensive, beautiful or ugly; but it is the outer embodiment of an inner conviction. As such, all languages, in the degree

---

[1] As a matter of psychological study, it may be conceded to Mr. McCabe that a 'careful comparison of a severe analysis of the primitive minds of the lowest known races of man, with the mental equipment of a higher ape, ought to be the indispensable starting-point of any speculation on the differences between the human and the infra-human intelligence' (*The Evolution of Mind*, p. 266). We are, however, here concerned not with the history of the evolution of speech and reason, but with their significance.

[2] 'No race of animals has ever yet developed, apart from man, mental powers beyond the range of its physical necessities; and no race has ever yet developed a moral sense so as to recognize quality and responsibility in its actions. By no process of evolution, either in the natural or in the domestic state, has any animal ever yet passed up into the plane of moral being: and there are no facts which may lead us to the expectation that any animal ever will, or ever could.'—*Fiat Lux*, by 'Inquisitor,' p. 98.

to which those who use them rise above savagery, abound in terms which unmistakably give the lie to Determinedism. Thus the ultramontane 'Determinist' above quoted says, in one issue of his paper—

'Can any one who knows what women and children should be, look upon the wrecks and *shames* of our contemptible and mean civilization without *remorse* and *shame*? It is all so ugly, so painful, such a *wicked* waste, and we are *angry* and hurt.'[1]

Yet every one of the words we have italicized here flatly contradicts both his principle of 'Determinism,' and the strong statements already quoted both from this writer himself and from others, in which it is set forth. If men are, as is affirmed, no more capable of moral action than a 'steam-engine' or a 'machine,' 'no more responsible than a tiger or a rock,' no more spontaneous than an electric current, assuredly there is no room for 'remorse,' or 'shame,' or 'wickedness,' or 'anger.' Many such words as these, we know, flash like jewels on a royal robe, in the human garb with which speech enwraps thought. But they are utterly destroyed by Determinedism. They become but meaningless babble on 'Deterministic principles.' Some desperate advocates openly accept this conclusion. Others, more wary, seek to refill the emptiness with subtle suggestions. Meanwhile, all continue to use such terms, and expect the old meanings to attach to them. Can any refutation of a theory be more complete? Science knows nothing of theories that will not work. If 'Determinism,' as above stated, be true, then Bentham must be heeded, and such words as 'ought,' 'duty,' 'repentance,' 'shame,' 'remorse,' 'justice,' 'right' and 'wrong,' must be for ever dismissed from human speech as ruthlessly as Mr. Cotter

---

[1] *Clarion*, 1906.

Morison and Prof. Hamon would fling away 'moral responsibility.' Not only then is Prof. James right in his estimate, above quoted, that 'Determinism virtually defines the universe as a place in which what ought to be is impossible,' but the case is worse than that, for what ought to be becomes both unutterable and unthinkable. The richest jewels of earth's languages are thus reduced to paste, their most precious coins are turned into worthless counters, and the dignity of thoughtful utterance becomes nothing more than such soulless sounds as issue from a gramophone. If it be absurd in ordinary parlance to say that my watch 'ought' to keep correct time, or that it is the 'duty' of a bicycle tyre not to get punctured; then it is equal mockery to apply these terms to men, if whatever they do 'is the only thing they can do,' because 'the action of their will is mathematically fixed at their birth.' On such principles, Nelson's famous signal at Trafalgar might as well have been addressed to the guns of the fleet as to the men who handled them.

Moreover, language is as full of recognitions of contingency as of words indicating the consciousness of power, and of power to choose. All these also become null and void on 'Deterministic' principles. The fate of a nation may turn upon an 'if.' To Determinedism there can be no 'if,' and there is no 'may.' The old wives' formula—'it was to be'—becomes the only philosophy of history. For the 'Determinist' there is no 'should be' but only 'shall be'; no 'perhaps,' no 'might have been.' All such terms, though they unmistakably indicate the very throbs and thrills of actual human life, become nothing more than the fantasies with which purblind bipeds mock themselves and hoodwink each other. So

FALSE DETERMINISM

undeniable, so manifest, so resistless, is this result of what is called 'Determinism,' that the theory can only live by abjuring its natural consequence in downright self-contradiction. One or two specimens will suffice—out of a host—by way of illustration.

We have noted how Dr. Günther, in his work upon *Darwinism and the Problems of Life* writes—

'The utmost that science can say is that an ethic, a setting-up of things to be attained, has no meaning. It can only direct a man to let himself be borne in peace on a stream of cause and effect, without doing anything, because his action could have no aim and no result. The only possible scientific ethic is resignation.'[1]

But if we turn over four pages, we are forthwith told that—

'Thus all science presupposes a will to attain the truth, a will to reach the goal of knowledge—we are justified in believing in a sense of life, and that there must be duties, since the idea of duty precedes all knowledge.'

Again, the well-known popularizer of 'Determinism' tells his fellows with an emphasis which cannot be exceeded that—

'No man can under any circumstances be justly blamed for anything he may say or do. All praise and all blame are undeserved. The tramp who murders a child on the highway could not help doing it. The actions of a man's will are as mathematically fixed as the motions of a planet in its orbit. There are no good or bad men but only weak and strong.'

Whilst on other pages we learn from him that the people in London are a 'blood-guilty' mob[2]; that he joins in a chorus of 'indignation' against Christians[3]; that his new religion teaches men 'to love each other'[4]; that there can be no true religion without 'sincerity'[5]; that 'the lifeboat man is a hero'[6]; that 'good' people have been very kind to him.[7]

---

[1] p. 423. [2] *God and My Neighbour*, by R. Blatchford, p. ix.
[3] ibid., p. 163. [4] *The New Religion*, p. 4. [5] ibid, p. 9.
[6] p. 13. [7] p. 15.

Again; Dr. Callaway, after insisting that 'by the free will hypothesis the force within us which is to overcome both heredity and environment would be uncaused,' which would be 'loose thinking' and 'vanity,' closes his elaborate denial that Determinedism destroys responsibility, with the assertion that 'it teaches that our wills are not forced by an external power, but are regulated by our own consciences.' Nothing would be easier than to multiply such specimens. But any theory which can only be perpetuated by the self-contradiction of its advocates, is surely sufficiently discredited. On the whole, it is not only true, as Prof. Tyndall wrote, that 'practically, as Bishop Butler predicated, we act as the world acted when it supposed the evil deeds of its criminals to be the products of free will'; but we talk, and must talk, if society is to hold together, as if men were both free and responsible beings. No one will accuse Mr. H. G. Wells of being a slave to conventional philosophy. Hereupon, however, he writes—

'I take the theory of free will therefore for my every-day purposes, and as a matter of fact so does everybody else. I regard myself as a free responsible person among free responsible persons.'[1]

(iv) In the course of ages, the use of language between human individuals has developed into an ever-growing literature. Thoughts which first struggled for expression on human lips, soon also incarnated themselves in writing. First by graphic representation in picture form, then through alphabets, utilized by means of rocks and parchments, rolls and books, the records of the past have come into

---

[1] *First and Last Things*, p. 52.

the possession of the men of to-day, and history, philosophy, religion, poetry, the drama, and the limitless products of the imagination, all find place in the multiplied libraries of every civilized nation. It is all so stupendous a testimony to the wondrous workings of the human mind, that it would be truly overwhelming, if we had not become accustomed to it from our very childhood. None the less, when appreciated, it testifies to the marvellous capacity and dignity of human nature. In the matter before us its witness is unmistakable and unequivocal. If consulted as to whether man should be regarded as a machine; whether the terms which in human language imply moral freedom should be discarded; whether it should be assumed that man can no more do moral right or wrong than a steam-engine,—the reply of all literature is a unanimous and overwhelming negative. Even if we here omit altogether the estimate of theology, as being pledged to human freedom and responsibility, the testimony of all other realms of literature is far more than sufficient.

As we are concerned for the moment more especially with the modern situation, we need not ransack antiquity for specimens. Does history, in the hands of Gibbon, Macaulay, Hallam, J. R. Green, Gardiner, and Lord Acton, represent man as an irresponsible automaton? Do the best-known poets such as Milton, Wordsworth, Browning, Tennyson, to say nothing of lesser bards, regard man as a mere creature of heredity and environment? Did our greatest dramatist in his *Macbeth*, or *Hamlet*, or *Richard III*, or indeed in any of his matchless creations, intimate that man was a 'mere machine,' the mechanical result of antecedents and surroundings? Have our most appreciated writers of fiction given us to understand that men are never to be praised or blamed, never to be held responsible for their words or actions, say in the pages of Sir Walter Scott, Hawthorne, Dickens, Charles Reade, George Eliot, Thackeray, Kingsley, Meredith, Mrs. Humphry Ward, and all the rest? Nay, even on the level of to-day's ordinary stage-play and sixpenny novel, is anything approaching such an estimate of human nature represented? We know that it is not. It would neither be believed nor tolerated. The theory, therefore, which can only establish itself by giving the lie direct to all literature worthy of the name, may be relegated to another planet. In this world it can find no place.

(v) Even if we were content to disregard the witness of literature, the philosophy which styles itself 'Deterministic' would be hopelessly wrecked on the rock of facts. For nothing is plainer than that the principles indicated in the specimens given above, are both practically intolerable and actually disregarded, in the daily life of the whole community, including unmistakably the behaviour of those who advocate them. This applies with the most manifest emphasis to 'hard Determinism.' But if we employ the terms 'hard' and 'soft' with a rather wider connotation than that intended by the eminent psychologist who coined them, and understand by 'soft Determinism' the system of thought which professes to maintain and sometimes even to increase personal responsibility, the special consideration of this latter may well be postponed for a moment, in order to deal plainly and conclusively with the former. Understanding, then, by 'Determinism' what Profs. Haeckel and Hamon, together with their popular representatives, Mr. Cotter Morison, R. Blatchford and Mark Twain, have done their utmost to make unmistakable, we are abundantly justified in saying that no such 'Determinism' ever has been, is, or will be practised in human society. Viewed practically, this genuine Determinedism is indeed a triple failure. It has been utterly unknown in the past; it is impracticable in the present; it is openly disowned in practice by its very advocates.

(1) As to the past, there is no single record in history of any human community having been held together by such principles, or of having even regarded them with toleration. In every known civilized or semi-civilized race, the sense of duty has obtained, and personal responsibility has been assumed as an unquestionable factor in everyday intercourse. In regard to savage tribes, or primitive races of antiquity, their ways and standards are really irrelevant, as intimated above. Yet the fact remains that their very superstitions and system of 'taboo,' bear sufficient witness to a self-consciousness of personal responsibility for their actions which gives the lie direct, in fact, to modern Determinedism.

(2) It is, however, only when we come to appreciate the conditions under which men exist in modern highly civilized communities, that the arrant folly and impracticable absurdity of this pseudo-philosophy become apparent. It is not enough to say that there are no practical 'Determinists.' A mere negative is not forceful enough to expose the mischievous and degrading tendency, in practical life, of such 'naturalistic' sophistries. There is in our midst one sphere, and one only, where these principles can be acted on, i.e. in dealing with lunatics. These

poor creatures are objects of genuine pity and of special care, for the very reason that they are not and cannot be held responsible for their actions. Their moral irresponsibility is acknowledged, and that is the very measure of their calamity, as also of the estimate which excludes them from ordinary society. In every other case, the notion that men are but 'conscious automata,' so 'determined' before their birth as to be 'irresponsible,' is treated in daily life as but the counsel of fools. Such an estimate is confirmed in every realm of normal human intercourse.

(i) There is no *home*, deserving the name, where such an estimate of mutual relationships is or would be tolerated for a moment. On such terms a home would necessarily become but a menagerie. Instead of the tender affections and gracious sanctities which now make home the dearest spot on earth, it would be a mere den of discords, in which 'love' and 'duty' would be as inconceivable as between the machines in a factory, or the wild animals in a tropical jungle.

(ii) Of all the superficial fallacies alleged, in which strong assertion is made to do duty for true principles, none is more common or more false than that 'Libertarians' act on 'Deterministic' principles in the *education of children*.[1] The fact that such acknowledge the influence of good or bad heredity

---

[1] As a specimen, take the following from Mr. Blatchford—'As I have said before, every church, every school, every moral lesson is a proof that preachers and teachers trust to good environment and not to free will to make children good' (*Not Guilty*, p. 187). It is rather a proof of the extent to which, assuming their sincerity, some would-be teachers can definitely hoodwink and contradict themselves. If human beings can, as this writer says elsewhere (*God and My Neighbour*, p. 19),

and environment, does not for a moment lessen, but rather emphasizes, their appeal to the moral nature of the child to make the most and best of every opportunity. The absolute certainty in the case is that there is not one single school in the land where education is conducted on the principles that no child is to be praised, or blamed, or held responsible, for anything said or done. The schoolmaster to whom such a method was proposed, would treat it as utter absurdity.

(iii) When the child grows old enough to work, is there any *master* in the country who will accept him as an *apprentice* on such terms? Is there any employer who will take on a workman under the distinct stipulation that he is not to be held responsible for anything he does? Is there any sensible workman who will hire himself to an employer on the understanding that whether wages are paid or not, whether they are fair or not, the employer cannot help himself, he is but a machine and must not be held responsible?

(iv) In the vast and complex world of *business*, amidst all the incalculable amount of financial transactions which every day makes necessary, imagine the effect of introducing into the market and applying at the bank the notion that 'no man is responsible for his own acts.' There might ensue a paradise for the thief and the swindler, the gambler and the rogue,

---

'no more sin than a steam-engine,' what is the use of talking about 'moral lessons' at all? Does the engine-driver daily deliver a moral lesson to his machine? Assuredly no wise teacher—for the very reason that he respects the moral capacities of children — thinks that he can '*make* children good' by any amount of good environment. Made goodness is a contradiction in terms, the specially constructed monstrosity of Determinedists.

but it would be of short duration, for the universal chaos would soon embrace them also.

Municipal relations and endeavours are sometimes said to be open to 'jobbery' and selfishness; would they be improved by adopting and acting on Prof. Hamon's conclusion: 'General irresponsibility, such is scientific truth'? If indeed such madness were made the civic law, Hercules' cleansing of the Augean stables would be but a trifle, in comparison with what would soon be needed to make the communal life tolerable again.

At the time when these pages are being written, a General Election is in progress. Let us turn to *Politics* and listen attentively to the address of a consistent 'Deterministic' candidate—

Ladies and gentlemen: I beg to offer myself as a candidate for your suffrages in the present election. I desire to express my entire sympathy with your local interests, as well as my profound convictions in regard to the best course to be followed in government; and I give you my deliberate assurance that if you do me the honour to elect me as your representative to the House of Commons, being a mere machine, I cannot hold myself responsible for anything I say or do.

Possibly Mark Twain and the Editor of *The Clarion* might vote for him, but would anybody else?

The picture of *a nation* so far exemplifying 'reversion to type' as to be composed of citizens no more to be held responsible 'than a tiger or a rock,'[1] is alarming enough in itself. But think of the same principles applied internationally. At present the 'armed peace' of Europe, which is said to be the best thing civilization can contribute towards national brotherhood, is costing Europe alone

---

[1] *The Illusion of Free Will*, by Prof. Hamon, p. 134.

more than £300,000,000 per year. This is colossal waste in very deed. Yet matters would be immeasurably worse if all the frightful potentialities for destruction represented by these armies and navies, were let loose to wreak their utmost havoc in all directions without any check save internecine slaughter. But why not? Nations are but aggregates of individuals. If 'no man is answerable for his actions,' assuredly no nation is. So that if, as the coiner of this phrase says he greatly fears, a German army should invade these shores, whether for greed or any other purpose, it will be but carrying out his own principles; it cannot help itself, is not to be held responsible, much less blamed, for any suffering that may ensue. As when of old, at the gates of Rome, Brennus cast his sword into the scale, and, with *vae victis* on his lips, proclaimed his moral irresponsibility, so, it seems, are the great nations and the vaster populations of to-day to find their comfort and hope in—

> The good old rule, the simple plan,
> That he should take who has the power
> And he should keep who can.

If such an Armageddon is the best that 'Determinism' can offer as the future of humanity, its total banishment from human thought would be an immeasurable boon. Any philosophical system which can only establish itself by treating the whole world of men as a lunatic asylum or a menagerie, merits but the execration of humanity.

(3) We are assured, however, that 'Determinism' has spread enormously during recent years, and that there has been not only no deterioration of moral character, but that the world is growing better. Let us hope that the latter half of this assertion is true. At present, the instances to the

contrary are numerous and woeful enough. But if 'Deterministic' principles are contributing to human improvement, at least, we are warranted in looking for examples of it. Where, then, outside the walls of the asylum, are the incarnations of these principles to be found? It is necessary to repeat plainly what we are to look for. We are to find men who believe themselves to be mere machines; no more capable of right or wrong than steam-engines; not holding themselves responsible for anything they say or do; behaving as if all praise and all blame are undeserved; utterly devoid of moral responsibility; and therefore necessarily impervious to any such conceptions as duty, high principle, unselfishness, devotion, love. For all these, beyond all controversy, are absolutely meaningless save as applied to moral beings. Where are these gross mixtures of the mummy and the monster? They are nowhere. Not one of the advocates of Determinedism acts upon his creed, or practises what he preaches. Neither himself nor any other man does he treat as the non-moral thing which his philosophy predicates. In all respectable society there is not a single 'Determinist' living. And that is the true and only explanation of the fact, if fact it be, that no deterioration of character has resulted from the flooding of the country with cheap issues which assure men that they 'cannot help' anything they do. The whole case is, indeed, as Dr. F. C. Schiller has put it—

'Of course no harm will come of a merely theoretical Determinism. To be refuted by its results a theory must be acted on. Until it is acted on its truth remains in suspense, as a claim which has not been tested or as a plaything of ideal speculation. And to show that it cannot be acted on, is to show not that Determinism is harmless but that it is false or meaningless.'[1]

---

[1] *Oxford and Cambridge Review*, 1909, p. 54.

Nothing would be easier than to show, by a myriad instances, how utterly these very advocates of moral irresponsibility contradict themselves in action. Let one suffice, as being both the latest and truly typical of the rest. The first page of Mark Twain's posthumous volume contains the assertion that ' the human being is merely a machine and nothing more.' That should be sufficiently explicit. Yet if we turn back but one page, to the preface of this strange production, what do we find? That as to these 'studies,' the writer says:—' I have just examined them again, and am still satisfied that they speak the truth.' Verily this is a marvellous 'machine'! The only pity is that the author did not live longer so as to find us its parallel on earth. A machine that compares ' truth ' with error, and is ' satisfied ' because it has ' examined ' and found certain statements true! If this is not the very incarnation of self-contradiction, what on earth can be? The same being true of all the others whose strong words are given above,[1] what follows? That the adoption of 'Determinism' is harmless? No; but that 'Determinism' is not adopted, in spite of all its vehement advocacy. Plainly it is not and cannot be acted on, even by those who most strongly urge it upon the thought of others. So demonstrably false in fact, is the Determinedism of the hour.

---

[1] Many more instances might easily be adduced. Mr. Mallock says truly concerning Mr. Herbert Spencer: ' Thus one of the few Deterministic thinkers who have deliberately attempted to interpret concrete life by Determinism, is in his own person one of the most interesting witnesses to the impossibility of interpreting it intelligibly without a covert reintroduction of the plain man's belief in freedom.'—*Reconstruction of Belief*,

The summary of Mr. H. G. Wells is thus justified:—

"I am free and freely and responsibly making the future so far as I am concerned. You others are equally free. On that theory I find my life will work, and on a theory of mechanical predestination nothing works."[1]

(3) False in Principle

Modern 'Determinism' is, however, no less false in principle. To make this clear it will be necessary to view the whole matter from four standpoints, viz. that of: (i) Religion; (ii) Moral philosophy; (iii) Psychological science; (iv) Metaphysics.

(i) *As to Religion*

It will be well first to take the testimony of religion, because it calls for least elaboration. We may be content here to define religion as the acceptance of Theism plus moral responsibility. For these two stand or fall together, as the absolutely essential foundation of Christian faith. If Theism be dismissed, there is no God. If moral responsibility be denied, there is no man. But religion demands for its very initial axiom a true God and a real man. Then religion becomes a relation between man and God. The least import of the divine is supreme power and love embodied in spiritual law. The least that can be required in the name of religion is obedience to law and response to love. But on the principles of Determinedism neither of these is possible. Obedience and love are alike unthinkable in any case save that of a free personality. An obedient clock and a loving piano are manifest absurdities. The reason of the absurdity is that

---

[1] *First and Last Things*, p. 52.

the movements of the former are the mere expression of pre-determination on the part of an external maker; the sounds which proceed from the latter are but the mechanical results of force externally applied. In both cases alike we have merely power expressing itself through an instrument. Whence it follows that if in the human case there is no moral responsibility, man also is merely the instrument of a resistless power, as truly as is the pen with which these words are written. No argument is required in such a case to show that manhood is gone, and only thinghood remains.[1] Which is tantamount to saying that religion is at an end; for a religious machine is unthinkable. If religion means, at the very least, appreciation of moral good, obedience to authority, response to love divine, then all alike are for ever impossible on these 'Deterministic' principles. A machine appreciating goodness, an obedient instrument, a loving steam-engine, are all and always inconceivable. To suggest them is to mock at reality and commit oneself to absurdity.

This is the fundamental and fatal error of Calvinism, which neither the philosophical subtleties in Jonathan Edwards, nor any collection of 'passages of Scripture,' in the least relieves. The philosophy of

---

[1] Thus, when we find this sentence, 'If God is responsible for man's existence, God is responsible for man's acts,' printed in italics (*God and My Neighbour*, p. 131), and several times repeated, as if the author were proud of it, one can but wonder at the blindness which refuses to see the manifest self-contradiction; for if God is really responsible, it can only be because man never acts at all, but is simply acted on. The same applies to other such assertions. 'No man is responsible for his own acts' (*Not Guilty*, p. 10). If he is not responsible, how can they be in any sense 'his own'? The man who is the mere consequent of resistless antecedents, no more really 'acts,' than a link in the middle of a chain.

Omar Khayyam remains hereupon impregnable from any standpoint—

> O Thou, who did'st with Pitfall and with Gin
> Beset the Road I was to wander in,
>   Thou wilt not with Predestination round
>   Enmesh me, and impute my Fall to Sin.[1]

'Sin' and 'predestination' are absolutely and for ever irreconcilable. They can no more co-exist than night with day. But Determinedism in philosophy is predestination in religion, and as the predestination of a moral being is a contradiction in terms—alike as to his every act and his final destiny—so is the religion of a non-moral being.

The three most common fallacies associated herewith only add confusion to delusion. The first is the popular and unwarranted assumption of predestination, or fore-ordination, as an element of Theism. The second is the treatment of foreknowledge as synonymous with fore-ordination.[2] The third is the pathetic if not pitiful attempt on the part of some, to set up what is superficially called 'religious Determinism.'[3] With this we shall be

---
[1] *Rubáiyát*, LVII.

[2] Both these are sufficiently illustrated in a single instance. ' Now if God is all-knowing, He knew before He made man what man *would* do. He knew that man *could* do nothing but what God had enabled him to do. That he could do nothing but what he was fore-ordained by God to do' (*God and My Neighbour*, p. 135). It would be difficult to find a more thoughtless passing in avowed argument from 'would' to 'could.'

[3] Out of many instances the following may be taken as fairly typical. ' Liberty then is by law, by obeying the deepest law. Necessity is not opposed to freedom, freedom is through necessity. As we do God's will more and more we are free' (report of sermon by Rev. G. T. Sadler in *Clarion* of June 11, 1909). To which the sufficient reply is that—(1) There can be no thinkable obedience to any law, save by a free being. (2) That 'freedom' through 'necessity' is a contradiction in terms. Compulsion cannot, under any circumstances, yield freedom.

compelled to deal more fully in a later section. It must suffice here to say that such attempts evince a laudable desire to harmonize one form of religion with certain phases of science, but they all alike fail of their purpose. If man is in any real sense 'determined,' if he is 'predestined' or necessitated, if he is a 'mere machine,' a mechanical result of heredity and environment, a pawn and nothing more in the great game of evolution, then religion is as unthinkable as the prayer of a gramophone, or the love of a wooden doll.

(ii) *As to Moral Philosophy*

So we are brought, in looking further afield, to estimate Determinedism from the standpoint of moral philosophy. When, indeed, we take at a fair valuation the principles expressed in the specimens

---

(3) That in order to do God's will at all, we must be free to act, as only a moral being can be. In Sir Oliver Lodge's words—'With freedom to obey one motive rather than another.' By no sophistry of speech can a man who is thus free be rightly said to be 'determined.' This instance will, however, be further considered.

Again, a pleader for religious Determinism says, 'The free will philosopher pathetically clings to his prerogative of blame or praise, in spite of the dictum of his Master, "Judge not." But the higher consciousness is expressed in the magnificent phrase—*Tout savoir c'est tout pardonner;* and in Mohammed's prayer—"God bless the bad; the good Thou hast already blest in making them good."' (*Muswell Hill Record*, February 28, 1908). Here, the falsity of exegesis applied to the words quoted from the New Testament, is only equalled by that of the assumption that Christ neither praised nor blamed men. In the French sentence, the last word gives away the writer's whole case. Assuredly, if a man is 'determined,' i.e. obliged to do everything he does, there is nothing whatever to 'forgive.' Whilst in the last sentence we have but another contradiction in terms. 'Made' goodness is unthinkable. Benevolent Omnipotence could no more 'make man good' than make a round square. Thus 'religious Determinism' answers itself.

above given, it would be entirely permissible to settle the matter at a stroke. If moral responsibility is to be dismissed—and 'scientific truth' involves 'general irresponsibility'—then we might as well recite poetry to a dog, or expound the binomial theorem to a lamp-post, as discuss moral philosophy in relation to human beings.

It is for ever true and incontrovertible, as Mr. Mallock has said, that 'an act wholly the result of causation, is an act morally meaningless.'[1] But this refers only to that form of Determinism which is well characterized as 'hard.' And it is necessary, as hinted above, to take into full account the other equally important and more difficult form known as 'soft.'

The exact differentiation of Prof. James is this—

'Old-fashioned Determinism was what we may call hard Determinism. It did not shrink from such words as fatality, bondage of the will, necessitation, and the like. Nowadays we have a soft Determinism which abhors harsh words, and repudiating fatality, necessity, and even predetermination, says that its real name is freedom : for freedom is only necessity understood, and bondage to the highest is identical with true freedom.'[2]

But this scarcely covers the whole area now claimed by 'soft Determinism,' seeing that its advocates sometimes do not repudiate the words 'fatality,' 'necessity,' 'predestination,' but boldly set themselves the task of manufacturing a moral philosophy out of such incompatibles, which is then said to be in all respects superior to the morality of the Indeterminist. When this attitude is found associated with such names as Fullerton, McTaggart, N. Pearson and the Hon. Bertrand Russell, not to mention others, it is manifest that contemptuous

---

[1] *The Reconstruction of Belief*, p. 279.
[2] *The Will to Believe*, p. 149.

dismissal is out of the question. Certainly those who endorse Mr. Mallock's sentence quoted above, must, in all fairness, face his next : 'An act wholly uncaused, is both morally meaningless and impossible'—which is at once the very core of the case for 'hard Determinism' and the ground upon which 'soft Determinists' erect their would-be new moral system.

Under the head of a true moral philosophy there are five distinct lines of essential thought. They are separate in conception, though one in significance ; distinct in meaning, though they stand or fall together. Self-respect, responsibility, morality, character, conduct or ethics, all must be included in any moral philosophy applicable to human beings. For our present purpose it will be best to deal first with these from the standpoint of 'hard Determinism,' and then see how they fare viewed from that of 'soft Determinism.' Something, at least will be accomplished if the valid results of the former are made unmistakable, and the conclusions of the latter are shown to be as invalid as well-intended.

In order to be quite clear in so important a matter, let us hear yet once again, from such competent lips as Mr. Mallock's, what genuine or hard Determinism really means.

'Such then is moral freedom as it presents itself to the observation of the psychologist. It is a dream—a chimera. In the language of Hobbes, it is "nonsense." As a recent writer has said, "The last word of psychology is 'Determinism'"; and on psychological grounds the doctrine of moral freedom is indefensible.'[1]

'We have seen as to man's will, that he is nothing but a mere machine who, whatever he does, deserves neither praise nor

---

[1] *Religion as a Credible Doctrine*, p. 123.

blame since whatever he does, he could not have done otherwise.'[1]

'The Determinist says, I neither forgive nor blame you: for although you have done your worst, your worst was also your best.'[2]

Now with such words before us, deliberate and typical, at least we know where we are, and that is great gain. In the light of such utterances, what becomes of the five elements of moral philosophy above specified? Let us take them *seriatim*.

(1) As to self-respect. This is more than self-consciousness of freedom, which belongs to metaphysics, and may be considered afterwards. Self-consciousness involves the actual activity of a real self. Self-respect connotes a definite estimate of the worth of such activity. Whether the standard of value be intuitional or utilitarian, the conscious activity of the self yields a double sense of value, in the result as making for the right and the good, and in the process as being able so to do. This supplies the answer to the question involved in the venerable but always incomplete axiom of Descartes, 'I think, therefore I am.' For this, after all, is but a something-nothing, until the latent query, 'I am—what?' is met. This is supremely the human question. Being, without quality, is but an inappreciable advance upon not-being. What I want to know is—'Am I man or machine?' 'More than animal or only animal?' 'Person or thing?' In each case Determinedism does not hesitate to accept the latter alternative. Thus the 'Deterministic' journalist appealing to the people, says—

'Now let us put the case in full. It is unjust to punish a man

---

[1] *Religion as a Credible Doctrine*, p. 149
[2] *Reconstruction of Belief*, p. 83.

for a *thing* he did not make. Man did not make himself, therefore it is unjust for God to punish man. It is not a question of what man is, but of whether he is or is not responsible for being that which he is. Machine or man, *it matters not*.[1] "Soul or man," reason or conscience, responsibility lies with the causer and not with the *thing* caused. And God is the cause.'[2]

And the Belgian Professor, we must not forget, affirms without hesitation: 'Man is as much an automaton as a tiger or a rock.' This, it seems, Prof. Chas. Richet also endorsed at the International Physiological Congress in Vienna, when to the question: 'What is Man?' he answered: 'Every living thing is, perchance, a chemical mechanism *and nothing more*.' Mr. Edison regards the brain as a 'mere machine,' with the addition that 'the will-power which drives the brain is possibly a form of electricity. Each man is *merely* a collection of cells.' And finally, as we have seen, Mark Twain with his dying hand points us to 'man the machine, man the impersonal engine.'[3]

In face of all this, self-respect is as impossible, and indeed as absurd to suggest, as the self-respect of a watch or a gramophone. The self-respect of an automaton is a contradiction in terms. If it be at all true that

> 'Self-reverence, self-knowledge, self-control,
> These three alone lead life to sovereign power,'

it is equally true that a thing, a machine, an automaton, offers no possibility of any one of them. And when even Prof. James writes, from the standpoint of Pragmatism:—'I ask you, quite apart from other reasons, whether any man, woman, or child, with a sense for realities, ought not to be ashamed to plead such principles as either dignity

---

[1] *Clarion*, March 9, April 13, 1906.
[2] *Not Guilty*, p. 18. Italics mine. [3] *What is Man?* p. 8.

or imputability "[1]—we are not in the least ashamed, for all the authority of his great name, to plead both. And that on his own authority, seeing that he himself commends to us[2] other words of Tennyson, in which an estimate of human nature, immeasurably higher than the above, and including both dignity and imputability, brings us—

> Nearer and ever nearer Him who wrought
> Not matter, nor the finite-infinite,
> But this main miracle, that thou art Thou,
> With power on thine own act, and on the world.

Speaking if we must and may pragmatically, every man without self-respect is a brute. And every self-respecting 'Determinist' is a pragmatical self-contradiction.

(2) Again ; as to the sense of responsibility which moral philosophy assumes. Upon this we need not dwell, because it is so frankly and utterly rejected by the genuine 'Determinist,' as we have seen above. Yet, lest it should seem that we have been dreaming, let us listen again—

'Yes, it is certain that humanity marches towards this end at which already those Determinists have arrived, who do not fear to draw the logical conclusions of their doctrine. In fact, the necessary consequence of Determinism is the irresponsibility of the individual.'[3]

'No man is answerable for his own acts,' sums up logically the whole case. In regard to which it is really sufficient to repeat that practically, there are no

---

[1] *Pragmatism*, p. 118.
[2] *The Will to Believe*, p. 143.
[3] *The Illusion of Free Will*, A. Hamon, p. 34. As a typical instance of the ever swarming self-contradictions with which the literature of 'Determinism' abounds, it may be interesting to note that on turning over two more pages of this same volume we are calmly told that ' Man is responsible, because he lives in society.'

Determinists; and that theoretically, moral philosophy without human responsibility is as unthinkable as a circle without a centre. Nor—if the words of Prof. James hereupon are to stand—is Pragmatism of any avail to help. For if 'imputability' be jettisoned, what is the use of saying that—'Instinct and utility between them can safely be trusted to carry on the social business of punishment and praise'?[1] Whatever becomes of instinct, certainly no doctrine of utility can be carried through without imputing to men responsibility for their actions. Without such imputability human society would be less moral than a community of ants or bees, and correspondingly a pragmatical impossibility. With all respect to the memory of the great psychologist, we must maintain that Pragmatism, rightly understood, tells strongly in the opposite direction.

(3) Thus we are driven to ask for an unevasive answer to the plain question—What, in the case of this 'Determinism,' becomes of morality? The true and sufficient reply is, in a word, that it is at once and for ever impossible. For if, as Mark Twain puts it, 'man is a machine,' 'an impersonal engine,' all talk about morality is but meaningless verbosity. The extent to which this creed degrades man, unblushingly, to the level of beast and thing, is shown in Mr. Blatchford's comment upon a reply by Sir Oliver Lodge—

'As to man's responsibility I should express Sir Oliver Lodge's argument thus:

'If a machine does not make *itself*, it is not answerable for its faults;

'If a tree does not make *itself*, it is not answerable for itself;

'If a dog does not make *itself*, it is not answerable for its faults; but

---
[1] *Pragmatism*, p. 118.

'If a man does not make *himself*, he *is* answerable for his faults.'[1]

In which brilliant piece of would-be satire the writer manifestly puts the machine, the tree, the dog, the man, upon precisely the same level! And although the common decencies of language compel him to say 'himself' in the case of man, yet to his philosophy 'himself' and 'itself' are evidently one and the same. So that the fact that we cannot possibly have a moral machine, or a moral tree, or a moral dog, is considered sufficient proof that we cannot have a moral man!

Returning to common sense, and to ourselves, we know that the very conception of morality assumes the appreciation of a definite distinction between right and wrong, good and evil, whatever valuation be given to these terms. But this writer says—

'I claim that men should not be classified as good and bad, as fortunate and unfortunate. As a Determinist I object to such definition. There are no good and no bad. There are only sick and well; strong and weak.'[2]

What, then, necessarily follows? Plainly this, that morality is at an end. Nor does the attempt to define the 'good' as the 'useful,' relieve the situation; for under no circumstances is morality definable by mere utility — with all respect to

---

[1] *Clarion*, April 13, 1906. Italics mine, on the pronouns—the author's on the verb.

[2] *Not Guilty*, p. 10; *Clarion*, April, 1906. As another of the myriad instances in which such writers contradict themselves, we find this on the closing pages of the same book (260, 261)—'My Friends, for the sake of good men who are better than their gods and for the sake of the good women who are the pride and glory of the world, I ask you for a verdict.' And in the same column of the same number of the same journal—'I think it is a higher morality to say do not do this for it is wrong, than to say do not do this for fear of punishment.' How there can be any right or wrong if there be no good or bad, we are left to discover.

John Stuart Mill. Morality is definable and measurable only by intention, i.e. by purpose, i.e. by personality. Its hall-mark is always and for ever triple: 'I ought; I can; I will.' These, as philosophical conceptions, are expressions of personality, of nothing else and of nothing less. As practical realities, they are matters of every day's normal consciousness. And the well-known expert in psychology is not only entirely warranted in putting into the lips of the 'Freewillists' the question, ' If our acts were predetermined, if we merely transmitted the push of the whole past, how could we be praised or blamed for anything?"[1]—but the assertion is equally justified that ' Free will means novelty, the grafting on to the past of something not involved therein.'[2] It is the presence or absence of that 'something,' be it as little definable as it may, which constitutes the difference between the moral and the non-moral.

Let us take but a single instance. By all sane men in civilized society, lying is said to be wrong, i.e. immoral; whilst telling the truth is correspondingly moral. But according to ' Determinism,' no man can ever do either the one or the other. Certainly he cannot ' lie.' For whatever he says, it is only what he could not help saying, any more than the clock can help striking whatever hour the works inside give rise to. And if a man cannot help whatever he says, there can be neither truth nor falsehood in it.[3] But someone may ask, Does not truth consist in being true to fact? And we answer, Certainly not. Morally, it consists in

---

[1] Prof. W. James—*Pragmatism*, p. 117.
[2] Ib., p. 117.
[3] See again Dr. Rudolf Otto's remark on p. 35.

being true to one's self. If I am asked what time it is, I may say that it is exactly noon, believing it to be so. But if instead, contrary to my thought, it is really 12.30 p.m., that is no lie, no breach of morals. It is simply a non-moral mistake. If, however, for some personal reason I reply that it is 1 p.m. knowing it to be but 12.30 p.m., I deliberately identify myself with what I know to be contrary to fact. That is lying. But that requires the deliberate action of a free personality. No clock on earth can ever do that, however far it may be from representing accurately the hour of the day. The same applies to justice, honesty, kindness, and their opposites, as moral qualities.

But all these, with their associated problems, 'Determinism' settles as Alexander dealt with the Gordian knot; and the result is equally false and foolish. No sophistry of words, no subtlety of thought, can create personality in a thing. There is no possibility of intention in a machine. There can never be purpose in an automaton. Morality in an engine is ridiculous. Nor on such lines, can any amount of 'instinct and utility' make morality possible. 'Instinct' is much more perfect in bees than in man. But when Dr. Callaway talks about 'moral qualities in bees,' it is an example of misused language and nothing more. As for 'utility,' there may be much more of it in a printing-machine than in a child's speaking the truth, but a moral printing-machine, however well suited to the humour or to the philosophy of Mark Twain, is, we know, an absurdity. In a word, the theory which reduces man to the non-moral stage, is not only false but degrading to the utmost. Happily it is contradicted on all hands by every day's experience and observation.

(4) If morality be at an end, of course character goes with it. But a moment's special notice is here desirable, if it be only to redeem this great word from the belittling use, or rather misuse, of it which is becoming ever more frequent in the vocabulary of 'Determinism.' There is certainly a modified and lesser sense in which, as meaning only physical or physiological quality, 'character' may be applied to plants and animals, or even machines; but such a significance is entirely distinct from moral character as relating to men. The way in which the true sense of the word is intentionally altered, and only an eviscerated significance left, thus tacitly begging the whole question of 'Determinism,' is well illustrated in the following popular statement—

'Man is a creature of heredity and environment. He is by heredity what his ancestors have made him, or what God has made him. Up to the moment of his birth he has had nothing to do with the formation of his character. As Prof. Tyndall says, "That was done for him and not by him." From the moment of his birth he is what his inherited nature and the influences into which he has been sent, without his consent, have made him.'[1]

Here the doctrine plainly is either that the newborn babe has moral qualities, or that the full-grown man has not. And the one is as false as the other. A moral baby is as inconceivable as a non-moral man. What 'character' must mean if applied at all to a baby, is clearly shown in the actual words of Prof. Tyndall—

'What have I had to do with the generation and development of that which some will consider my total being, and others a

---

[1] *God and My Neighbour*, p. 139.

most potent factor of my total being, the living, speaking organism which now addresses you? As stated at the beginning of this discourse, my *physical and intellectual textures* were woven for me, not by me. Processes in the conduct or regulation of which I had no share, have made me what I am. Here surely, if anywhere, we are as clay in the hands of the potter.'[1]

From which—aided by our italics—we may judge (i) as what the Professor says was really 'done for him, not by him'; (ii) as to the misleading employment of the word 'character' to express this, in Mr. Blatchford's garbled quotation; (iii) as to the accuracy, or rather inaccuracy, of the Professor's avowal that what he was at the time of his address was solely due to 'processes' in which he had 'no share.' That statement is either true or false. If the former, then a man is as non-moral as his hat, and has no more possibilities of real character. If the latter, then the 'share' which each man has in the processes which make him, is just that which gives him his opportunity for making character. Using this term, therefore, in its supreme and proper significance—viz. moral character—it cannot be too plainly said that 'character,' to be such, must be a new creation. The source and method of the newness may be as insoluble in its mystery as the passage from molecular motion to consciousness through the brain,[2] but it is none the less real.

---

[1] *Fragments of Science*, Vol. II, p. 362.

[2] Hereupon Prof. Tyndall truly says—'We cannot deduce motion from consciousness, or consciousness from motion, as we deduce one motion from another. When we endeavour to pass by a similar process from the phenomena of physics to those of thought, we meet a problem which transcends any conceivable explanation by the powers which we now possess. We may think over the subject again and again, but it eludes all intellectual presentation.'—*Fragments of Science*, Vol. II, pp. 394, 395.

'Character,' to be such, must ever be the incarnation of the three personal convictions, 'I ought, I can, I will.' Seeing, then, that these are the unmistakable expressions of personality, and involve something which was not in the physical antecedents, it follows that character cannot possibly be bought or sold, borrowed or received. It must be made. If it is not the direct and immediate creation of the self, it is not character. Its true significance and its only value spring out of the very making. Whatever the philosophy of this creation, which we will presently consider, speaking here pragmatically, the fact is undeniable, not only in each man's moral consciousness, but in general intercourse, observation, and acknowledgement.

No better illustrations of this principle can be desired than those furnished by its most vehement rejecters. Thus the popular writer who most of all insists that men are not under any circumstances to be praised or blamed, that no man can help what he does, that the actions of his will are mathematically fixed at birth, himself declares that—

'The glory of manhood and of womanhood is not to have something, but to be something; not to get something, but to give something—the greatness of a nation does not lie in its wealth and power, but in the character of its men and women. In our eyes the lifeboat man is a hero, and the African machine-gun soldier is a brigand and assassin.'[1]

But, however true this may be from the standpoint of moral philosophy and common sense, it is simply ridiculous from the standpoint of 'Determinism.' For on its principles the lifeboat is as much a hero as the sailor in it, and the machine-gun is as responsible for the ensuing slaughter as the man

---

[1] *Not Guilty*, p. 249; *The New Religion*, p. 13.

who fires it. If, as this writer so confidently affirms on another page of the same book, 'Everything a man does is the only thing he *could* do at the instant of his doing it,'[1] then all talk about 'character' and 'heroism' is but throwing verbal dust into the eyes of unwary readers. For as Mr. Mallock rightly says—

'Language such as this is no more absurd and irrelevant when applied to a magnum of champagne than it would be when applied to kings, statesmen, and philosophers, unless we believe that the latter possessed some faculty of self-direction—which science can discover in man no more than it can in a wine bottle.'[2]

This last phrase is, of course, but the assertion of Mr. Mallock's own Pyrrhonism, which we will examine later on. It may well be forgiven for the moment, for the sake of his plain and needed emphasis upon the truth that all references to character

'would be absolutely meaningless, if it were not for the inveterate belief that a man's significance for men resides primarily in what he makes of himself, *not* in what he has been made by an organism derived from his parents, and the various external stimuli to which it has automatically responded.'[3]

The hope of the future, no less than the dignity of the present, lies for mankind in the possibility of character. Our great dramatist's contemptuous dismissal of a 'purse' as comparative 'trash,' is endorsed by all respectable society. And the reason of the universally acknowledged preciousness of character lies precisely in that element which Determinedism asserts to be impossible, viz. in the fact that ultimately it is self-made, whatever be the mystery of its antecedents and adjuncts. On the

---

[1] p. 203. [2] *The Reconstruction of Belief*, p. 88.
[3] ibid., p. 86.

other hand, the measureless mischief, deadly danger, and blank hopelessness, of the characterlessness which false 'Determinism' postulates, is sufficiently expressed in the findings of Dr. Günther—

'In reality the world has no place for duty from the scientific point of view. The cosmic process goes on inexorably. There are no ends towards which the eternal changes are working, and there is no force that can arrest or control the rolling wheels.'[1]

(5) Out of character, beyond all question, issues conduct; from morality as a principle, ethics, as a practical rule, must be derived. The question is how this can be done in face of such avowals as Prof. Haeckel's last utterance hereupon—which is plainly in full accord with what we have seen above.

'Modern physiology shows that the will is never really free in man or in the animal, but determined by the organization of the brain; this in turn is determined in its individual character by the laws of heredity and the influence of the environment. It is only because the apparent freedom of the will has such a great practical significance in the province of religion, morality, sociology and law, that it still forms the subject of the most contradictory claims. Theoretically, Determinism, or the doctrine of the necessary character of our volitions, was established long ago.'[2]

Here we have plainly exhibited the impossibility of formulating an ethical code on 'Deterministic' principles. The whole question at issue is quietly begged in the word 'apparent'; whilst the practical necessity for such an assumption is helplessly confessed. Thus it is not only true that 'Determinism' cannot be practised, but it cannot even be consistently preached. Take, hereupon, a couple of fair specimens—

'What do we mean by the words "sin," and "vice," and

---

[1] *Darwinism and the Problems of Life*, p. 423.
[2] *Last Words on Evolution*, p. 103.

"crime"? Sin is disobedience of the laws of God. Crime is disobedience of the laws of man. Vice is disobedience of the laws of nature. Though it is wrong to disobey a good law, it may be right to disobey a bad law.'[1]

'We are now brought to this more complete definition: Crime is every conscious act which injures the liberty of action of a similar individual of the same species.'[2]

In the first of these, 'disobedience' is freely predicated of human beings. But on the principles of Determinedism, 'disobedience' is utterly inconceivable. The disobedience of a thing, an automation, a machine, is simply a contradiction in terms. The only being who can possibly 'disobey' is one who is, at the same time, able to obey. In a word, 'disobedience' connotes freedom of choice and action, which Determinedism so emphatically repudiates for human nature. The same applies to 'every conscious act' which injures another; for a thing, a steam-engine, an automaton, does not and cannot so 'act' at all—it is always and only acted on. If man is nothing but a creature of heredity and environment, to talk of his 'acts' is a misuse of words. He no more acts than does a violin in the hands of Mischa Elman, or a revolver in the grip of an assassin.

No laws of conduct, no codes of ethics whatever, can be applicable to creatures that cannot help what they do. Says our popular 'Determinist'—

'The criminal injures society, society injures the criminal. I accuse both of injurious action. I blame neither. I say that both are that which heredity and environment made them. I say neither can help it. But I say that both can be taught to help it, and that both should be taught to help it. Is there anything illogical in that?'[3]

---

[1] *Not Guilty*, p. 38.
[2] *The Illusion of Free Will*, A. Hamon, p. 63
[3] *Not Guilty*, p. 234.

Most assuredly there is, as any professing teacher of philosophy ought to know. If a man is merely 'taught,' the very term connotes his freedom to accept or reject the teaching. If he really cannot help doing what is set before him, then he is not 'taught' but compelled. 'Made to help it' is mere contradiction in terms. If he is 'made' he does not 'help it' in any sense. If he is 'made' he is compelled, that is, he does not really act at all, but is simply acted on.

According to this scheme, the only moral method is compulsion, and the only prevention of immoral conduct is acknowledged to be 'restraint.' Which is no more a true or hopeful method with moral beings, than the confinement of a dangerous lunatic in a padded cell is a guarantee of his restoration to sanity. Well indeed does Dr. Günther confess that 'Every system of ethics must prescribe something to a man : it must tell him his duty. That is evident.'[1] It is. But it is no less evident that if a man cannot help himself, and is merely a machine, every prescription of 'duty' is as absurd as would have been Nelson's famous signal at Trafalgar had it run—'England expects every gun to do its duty.' All history, all observation, all experience, testify that moral improvement has not and does not come to pass by compulsion or by restraint, but by appeal. The initial influence of heredity is never to be denied, any more than that of environment. But neither of these, nor both together, can ensure ethical progress. It may come, or it may not. It can only come when there is moral improvement, and moral improvement as

---

[1] *Darwinism and the Problems of Life*, p. 422.

the result of external forces only,[1] is sheer contradiction in terms. To write that 'man becomes what he is by the action of forces outside himself,' is palpable self-contradiction. For (i) we have here the acknowledgement that there is a 'himself' apart from the external forces. Then (ii) this very 'self' is allowed no part at all in what 'he' becomes! (iii) The very notion of 'becoming' implies the activity of the self. If the man himself is nothing but a sheer lump of passivity, not only is manhood denied,[2] but the only true expression of what happens is—not that 'he becomes' anything, but that this complex mass of passivity is made to be what it is by external forces. It is with good philosophical as well as experimental warrant, therefore, that Mr. H. G. Wells writes—

'Now each self among us, for all its fluctuations and vagueness of boundary, is invincibly persuaded of free will. That is to say, it has a persuasion of responsible control over the impulses that teem from the internal world, and tend to express themselves in act. The problem of that control and its solution is the reality of life. What am I to do is the perpetual problem of our existence.'[3]

Seeing then that such 'persuasion' cannot be denied as a fact, the only course left open to 'Determinism' is to dismiss it as illusion. That philosophical shuffle we will presently expose. Meanwhile it is enough to point out that if this 'persuasion' be illusion, so too are ethics, character, morality, responsibility,

---

[1] 'Briefly then, heredity makes and environment modifies a man's nature. And both these forces are *outside* the man.'—*Not Guilty*, p. 23. The italics are not mine, but the writer's.

[2] Right nobly says Mr. J. Ramsay Macdonald—'You cannot have things done for you and be a man of character. The man of character has a power in him which makes him an active man, not merely a passive man.'—'Character and Democracy,' in *Social Ideals* (C. H. Kelly), p. 53. See also p. 360.

[3] *First and Last Things*, p. 56.

self-respect. When these terms are cleared of confusion, and what they really connote is fairly exhibited, it becomes manifest that they can no more co-exist with Determinedism than black with white, or hot with cold. When, therefore, we think of all that is involved, of the dogmatic vehemence with which the principles of such 'Determinism' are set forth, of the unmistakable conclusions to which they drive us, we are grateful to Prof. James for the strong terms in which he describes the nature and worth of the true basis of this 'hard' pseudo-philosophy.

'The intensely reckless character of all this needs no comment. It is making the mechanical theory true *per fas aut nefas*. My conclusion is that to urge the automaton theory upon us as it is now urged, on purely *a priori* and metaphysical grounds, is an unwarrantable impertinence in the present state of psychology.'[1]

(iii) *Soft Determinism and its Pleas*

Now, however, it is necessary for a time to turn our special attention to what has been called 'soft Determinism,' in that it seeks to avoid the inferences and consequences which so plainly attach to the foregoing. In order that we may do it no injustice, let us take the definition given as above[2] from one one of its stoutest defenders—

'Every act of a man is the latest link in an immense chain of causation, in which the slightest element of uncertainty would be impossible. At a given moment there may be several courses *apparently* open to a man, but in reality there is only that course open to him which his character and his environment make the only course possible. This, put quite shortly, is the doctrine of

---

[1] *Psychology*, Vol. I, p. 454.   [2] See p. 20.

Determinism. Let us see if it is, as Libertarians declare, necessarily fatal to moral responsibility, and its allied conceptions.'[1]

It certainly seems strange, at the outset, that writers of such calibre as Dr. Callaway, Mr. J. McCabe, Mr. Bertrand Russell, Prof. McTaggart, Mr. N. Pearson, not to mention others, should be found insisting that their 'Determinism' is not only not fatal but positively helpful to morality. It must be conceded that deliberate arguments from such sources merit respectful attention. But it is also to be noted that even if their statements, to some extent at all events, are found undeniable, the result will not be that the preceding conclusions are disproved, but that there are two kinds of alleged 'Determinism,' so distinct that 'hard' and 'soft' as applied to them are by no means satisfactory terms. One at least of these two Determinisms is absolutely ruinous to manhood and to morality. That has been already demonstrated. What to think of the other, will become clearer as we proceed. No better advocates of a cause could be desired than the five writers just named. We will therefore patiently examine the main points in some of their characteristic utterances.

In the *Agnostic Annual and Ethical Review* for 1905, Dr. C. Callaway has boldly faced the question, 'Does Determinism destroy responsibility?' and we will now face the noticeable features of his answer. 'Free will,' we are told, in its assertion of human spontaneity, is but 'an arrogant pretension which an ancient metaphysic is still loudly proclaiming.' Yet further—

'This belief does not rest upon vanity alone. It is claimed to be the chief condition of morality. Determinism, it is

---

[1] *Some Problems of Existence*, N. Pearson, p. 93.

FALSE DETERMINISM

contended, destroys the sense of responsibility. This objection is a serious one, and if it is true, the advocates of Determinism will have to reconsider their position. I shall attempt to prove that it is not true.'[1]

The attempt comes to this, that 'the essence of the idea of responsibility is reciprocity'; that there is no difference in kind between animals and men in this regard; so that dogs and horses, bees and ants, may all alike be moral beings. This 'liability to respond, in man as in brutes, is the creation of social environment, and does not depend upon a belief in free will. It is absolutely essential to our existence as social beings.' How far, however, the idea of 'reciprocity' is from exhausting the conception of responsibility, may be well shown by the writer's own statement. B is held responsible for taking A's money to the bank. Then—

'B *undertakes* the required service, and audibly or tacitly *promises* to respond to the trust reposed in him. *If* he faithfully discharges his task, he is rewarded in various ways. *If* through *his own fault* the money is lost, B suffers punishment such as the disapprobation of his employer, loss of his situation, perhaps the refunding of the amount. The *wilful* appropriation of the property to his own use, would, of course, be vested with *much heavier* penalties. The essence of the matter is summed up in the definition, liability to respond.'[2]

The italics in this extract are not the author's, but will serve to show, without elaborate comment, how much more than mere 'liability to respond' is involved in such a selected instance. For certainly 'liability' carries with it two entirely distinct notions, which put a very different complexion upon the whole case. (i) The first is ability to respond, which is assumed; (ii) the second, inseparable, is the

---

[1] p. 18. [2] p. 18.

ability not to respond, which is acknowledged in the terms expressing contingency. But here we have what Mr. McCabe, writing in the same *Annual* afterwards,[1] rightly points out, in flat contradiction to the above—

'Most psychologists would, I think, agree with Prof. Stout, that man differs from other animals in having the power of self-direction and choice, and it seems to me that in this residual power we have something that ought to be emphasized by Determinists, whose language is often quite inconsistent with it, and a possible basis for the reconstruction of our moral terminology.'

Such words are refreshingly reasonable and scientific, as contrasted with the wild assertions that 'moral qualities vary in bees,' and that there may arise warfare in the 'personal desires' of insects, as truly ethical as 'the struggle in the human mind' between duty and selfishness. We are not informed as to how there can be a struggle where all is determined beforehand and externally; but it would be difficult to find a more feeble and partial expression of the true conception of responsibility than in the mere idea of 'reciprocity' which might apply just as well either to insects or to plants. It is all verily the play of *Hamlet* with Hamlet omitted. Power not to respond, which is quite as much included in responsibility as 'liability to respond,' is altogether overlooked. And by means of that overlooking, this alleged 'Determinism' shuffles out of its logical conclusion. Nothing is here suggested, therefore, to lessen the force of Sir Oliver Lodge's definition given above as to the distinctive character of man.[2]

---

[1] For 1910, p. 64.
[2] See p. 3.

Not content, however, with this evisceration of the real significance of 'responsibility,' the writer brings three allegations against the idea of spontaneity which is involved in free will. (i) The first of these is that 'a belief in spontaneity weakens moral motive,' which is said to be illustrated by the wicked careers and death-bed repentances of Constantine, Louis XI, and Louis XV; and the general inference is that if they 'had known the scientific doctrine of Determinism, and really believed that what a man sows that shall he also reap, it is inconceivable that their lives should have so grossly outraged moral principle.' From which the only possible conclusion would be that if all men only knew the full consequences of evil-doing, they would all become saints. Unfortunately, the contrary to this is not only perfectly conceivable, but it is actual every day of the year, in every human community. Even in the extreme cases alleged, if they had not 'really believed' in such consequences, they would not have thought of any kind of repentance at all. They were not lacking in any such belief, but they were mistaken in their conception of its enforcement. If 'their priests taught them that a ceremony, or at most an act of will, could wipe out in a moment the blackest list of the recording angel,' that was the fault and folly of the priests, but is assuredly no proof of Determinedism. To say that but for that mistake 'they would not have dared to flout so freely the stern and irreversible laws of nature,' is mere assertion and nothing more. That they might have dared, which is what 'spontaneity' involves, is shown by the record of every Criminal Court in the land. Nothing is more clear from actual facts than that the certainty of punishment, even capital punishment, does not make men abstain from crime, as on these principles it ought to do.[1]

The essence of responsibility does *not* consist in mere 'liability to respond,' but in the power possessed—which such a phrase connotes—either to respond or not to respond. 'Liability to respond' for a self-conscious being means, if it means anything, that I 'ought' to respond. And if there be any sense or force at all in the conviction that I 'ought,' then, without going back to Kant, it is manifest that if I ought, I can. Moreover, if I can do my duty, I can also refuse to do it. It is the consciousness of this double possibility which not only permits moral motive, but perpetually creates it.

(ii) It is, however, also affirmed that the 'belief in human spontaneity has acted injuriously in retarding the growth of justice.' For an instance is given the old-time severity of punishment as to begging. It is asserted that 'such atrocity would have been scarcely possible had men recognized that the increase in begging was the natural consequence of changing social conditions.' Whether this be true

---

[1] This writer revels in some extracts from Dr. Pusey and Mr. C. H. Spurgeon as showing that thirty years of sin may be wiped out in less than thirty minutes. But Christianity is not responsible for any sayings of individual teachers, and the Christian doctrine of forgiveness, rightly taught, does not in the very least excuse the sinfulness of sin, or make void its consequences. When Dr. Callaway adds that 'the climax of the free will doctrine is perhaps reached in the following quotation from a well-known hymn—

'Doing is a deadly thing,
Doing ends in death'—

one can only say that if he does not know better than that, he ought to abstain from printing. Such misrepresentation is nothing less than shameful—if 'shame' or 'ought' can apply to a Determinedist.

or not, it is not 'Determinism.' There is no place in its vocabulary for the 'scarcely possible.' According to its principles, those who punished begging by death, could no more help it than beggars could help begging. That they were influenced by the atmosphere of their times, is no proof either that they were 'determined' as to all they did, or that the spontaneity, with accompanying responsibility, in which they believed, made them unjust. 'The recognition of the necessity of our actions would often turn the censorious sneer into a tolerant and half sympathetic smile.' But the smile in that case would be as absurd as the sneer would have been cruel. For who either sneers or smiles at a clock when it keeps bad time?—or at an engine when it runs off the line? Yet it is but the plain truth that if 'our actions' are the mere result of 'necessity,' they are just as little open to praise or blame, and for the simple reason that they are not 'actions' at all. They are mere compulsions, as truly as the movements of the hands of the clock, and call no more for either smile or frown. Every man is in that case, as Mr. Mallock has well said, merely the 'marionette of the cosmic process.' The doctrine which suggests that justice should be done to dolls, sufficiently dismisses itself.

(iii) Still further, however, the wonder grows. 'A belief in free will tends to check benevolent effort'! It is difficult to be patient with such an outrageous contradiction of fact as these words convey, seeing that the Christian churches which believe in 'free will,' are now doing more in the way of 'benevolent effort' in one week, than all anti-Christian 'Determinism' has done in all its history. But the alleged principle is as false as the reference to fact. 'So long as vicious actions are regarded as free and spontaneous, they evoke an exaggerated sense of blame.' This is neither true in point of fact, nor a necessary result of belief in moral freedom. Moreover, it is utterly inconsistent for any avowed 'Determinist' to talk about an 'exaggerated sense of blame.' For if a man cannot help what he is doing, because his actions are necessitated, there is no more room to blame him than to blame a nail for going farther into the wood each time it is struck. Again, we are told that 'the amount of a man's will-power is not determined by himself; it is born with him, and he is no more able to increase it than he can lift himself in the air by pulling at his own collar.' Here again, the principle is false, and the illustration irrelevant. The laws of psychology are one with those of physiology in regard to the strengthening effect of use. Sandow takes just pride in reminding us that he was born feeble and delicate, and points to his system of development as the explanation of his great strength. It is not one whit less true that the exercise of will strengthens will-power, nor is anything more certain than that the amount of man's will-power, at any given period, *is* determined by himself. For it is the result either of his previous neglect, or effort, in using his hereditary endowment. 'Men were formerly blamed,' we are told, 'for being mad, as they are now censured for picking pockets.' Truly 'Determinism' reduces itself to a need for strange logic. Because we now know that insane persons are diseased, therefore all sane persons also are only diseased when they do wrong! Whence it follows that sanity and insanity are one and the same thing. The simple truth of course is, that we have learnt better to diagnose such disease as puts an end to spontaneous action, and therefore to moral responsibility. But for this very reason the actions which are not due to disease become more manifest, and therefore render the doers of them 'liable to respond.' It is upon such logic as the above, that rash statements like Dr. Callaway's, above quoted, are based—

'It is hardly too much to say that the moral improvement of the race has proceeded *pari passu* with a decline in men's belief in free will.'

Indeed it is a great deal too much to say, for it is altogether untrue. Moral improvement has increased in equal ratio with the sense of the sacredness of individuality,[1] and the consequent intensification of personal responsibility.

To speak of 'moral improvement' as having developed from the growing sense of the reign of law in the 'Deterministic' sense, is self-contradiction. One might as well attribute moral development in childhood to the child's growing sense that it no more deserves blame than its pencil, and merits no more word of appreciation for good behaviour than its boots. In the child as in the race, genuine moral improvement grows not only with the perception of laws to be obeyed, but with the inalienable sense of a personality which can and does consciously obey or disobey, whatever the consequences. It is the growing sense of the reality and competence, as

---

[1] The attempt to exalt Buddhism on the plea that 'the only great religion which is based upon the reign of law is the most just and the most humane of all,' must be left to other occasions. Both these assumptions are untrue, as may be seen by impartial study of *The Noble Eightfold Path*, by Dr. St. Clair Tisdall; *Great Religions of the East*, by Dr. Murray Mitchell; *Buddha, Mohammed, and Christ*, by Dr. Marcus Dods; also *Clarion Fallacies*, by the present writer, p. 177.

well as the mystery, of personality, which confers upon the individual the conviction of power and estimate of worth that lie at the basis of all moral philosophy.[1]

Another sentence, however, calls for notice—

'It is clearly recognized that it is not conduct but character that has to be changed. Determinism is teaching us the importance of right action as spontaneity could never do, for it connects cause with effect by iron laws, demonstrating by an unwavering experience that the consequences of conduct are as unavoidable as the succession of heat to friction.'

Such curious verbal muddles constitute the plausibility of 'Determinism.' But they melt into nothing when carefully examined. Here, for instance, 'character' is again assumed to mean nothing more than heredity and environment. But that, as shown above, is an evisceration of a great term which is neither true to experience nor justified by philosophy. Again,

---

[1] The further reference to Buddhism here is equally unavailing. 'This very doctrine of Determinism, which some suppose to be destructive of morality, is the foundation of the purest, tenderest, most catholic moral teaching the world has ever known.' For not only is the assumption of such superior characteristics quite unwarranted in comparison with Christianity, but the term 'moral' used in this connexion simply begs the whole question at issue. If necessity rules, there can be no morality, as shown above. Or if there be moral teaching in association with 'Determinism,' it is only by making the term 'moral' synonymous with useful, which is warranted neither by ordinary usage nor by philosophy. But the very quotations alleged in support of this assertion contradict it. 'Overcome anger by love.' But necessitated love is a contradiction in terms, alike unthinkable and impracticable. 'We should feel compassionate interest in the welfare of all men.' 'Should'? There is no room for 'should,' which equals 'ought,' if all men are necessitated. It would be as sensible to say that a fire 'ought' to warm a room. 'Never will I seek or receive private salvation.' Is this the utterance of necessity or spontaneity? If the former, it is a contradiction in terms. If the latter, it is a contradiction of 'Determinism.'

as to 'right action.' If a man is purely necessitated, there is no 'action' on his part at all. The whole of him is but a helpless link in an unalterable chain. Whilst 'right' can only mean 'useful to the community'; in which case, highway robbery, even with murder, is perfectly right when it is useful to a community of bandits. Furthermore, in regard to 'iron laws,' apart from the inappropriateness of the simile as applied to mental realities, spontaneity does not deny or weaken the relations of cause and effect any more than 'Determinism' does. Rather, whilst acknowledging that the consequences of conduct are inevitable, it insists upon an adequate cause for conduct, such as is not found in necessitated action. No one can talk sensibly about the good or bad conduct of a gramophone.

'But if a man's deeds are the result of unchanging law, why should we praise or blame him? Because we cannot help it. An act that confers a benefit upon us is necessarily pleasing to us; and if a robber steals my watch I must feel displeasure.'

'Cannot help it'? In that case, the blame or praise is purely impersonal, i.e. mechanical. But mechanical praise or blame is a contradiction in terms. The very essence of praise is *personal* approval. Impersonal approval is as unthinkable as a circle without a centre. Moreover, if a man is nothing but a microcosm of 'unchanging law,' then 'deeds' are altogether impossible to him. That which happens in his case is as inevitable, and as undeserving of praise or blame, as the vibration of the strings of a violin under the friction of the bow. So too if a robber is but a necessitated biped, he cannot 'act' at all. He is but an automaton, and under no circumstances can an automaton 'steal' anything, for stealing implies knowledge, intention, and volition.

'If a man is doing wrong, that is acting detrimentally to the happiness of society, I am acting justly, that is promoting the happiness of society, when I censure him. My resentment at the evil doer is a sentiment which has been produced in me by evolutionary forces for the advantage of the community. It is as much a utility as my pen, but it is a moral utility, for it promotes social welfare.'

But according to 'Determinism' there is no 'acting,' and there is no 'evil-doer.' The man from whose conduct detrimental consequences follow, no more 'acts' than does a bomb when it explodes in a populous thoroughfare with frightful results. Do we in such a case 'censure' the bomb? 'Resentment' at such consequences may be advantageous for the community, but it is not resentment at evil, for there is no evil. And if it be a 'moral utility' because it promotes social welfare, then the word 'moral' is meaninglessly redundant. The actual truth is merely that it is a social utility if it promotes social welfare. But that there ought to be another significance attaching to this great word is acknowledged in almost the next sentence, where methods of modern science are said to be 'more effective than the old-fashioned appeals to a moral nature which hardly exists.' It is certainly the true mark of a moral nature that it must be appealed to—neither more nor less. But that is not 'Determinism'; nor is it mere social utility.

'It is now scarcely necessary to argue in favour of the justice of penalty for crime. If a vicious man pleads that he sinned because he could not help it, it is a sufficient reply that society cannot help punishing him.'

On the contrary, it is no reply at all. It is a

mere meeting of mechanism by mechanism. Irresistible force is no answer to a 'plea.' It may be well, however, to note here, first, how flatly 'Determinists' contradict each other. By the side of the above words put the definite, emphatic, reiterated statement of the other popular writer above quoted. 'I do seriously mean that no man can, under any circumstances, be justly blamed for anything he may say or do.' 'All praise and blame are undeserved. *All* praise and *all* blame.' These doughty champions may be left to fight it out between themselves. Meanwhile, it must be pointed out once more that a man's sinning because he could not help himself, never could be a rational plea, because it is utter self-contradiction. Compulsory sin is unthinkable. So also is a 'vicious' man, on 'Deterministic' lines. If it means nothing more than 'detrimental to society,' then it is not vicious at all, but simply harmful, as an epidemic might be. But if it means that the harmfulness was necessitated, then certainly there is nothing 'vicious' in that, any more than there is in the pen which may be used to write a blasphemous word. If, however, it means anything more than this, then purpose, intention, volition, spontaneity come in, and 'Determinism' is at an end.

If these statements were not typical, they would not, indeed, be worth detailed analysis. But they represent fairly what is in the minds and on the lips of so many more to-day, that it is worth while to track each to its ultimate significance. As a final instance of the way in which this advocate of 'Determinism' answers himself, even in the midst of his special pleading, take his own closing words—

'Scientific Determinism teaches that our wills are not forced by an external power, but are regulated by our own consciences, and these in turn are susceptible of indefinite improvement as social evolution proceeds. The laws which hem us in will "work together for good" if they are understood and obeyed; but woe to the man or the race that defies or even ignores them.'

Certainly if 'conscience' means anything at all, it means that 'I ought' to do this or that. But a 'Deterministic' 'ought' is as utter a contradiction as a round square. It is quite true that the human sense of moral obligation is susceptible of 'indefinite improvement.' But that is not 'Determinism,' for its boast is that the improvement is so definite, that on these lines and these only can human conduct be predicted. The only sure hope of the future, we are told, is that human consciences may be made to prefer the high to the low, and the useful to the harmful. But a conscience that can be made is no conscience. A compulsory 'ought' is unthinkable. And further, as expressed above, when 'Determinism' talks about laws being 'obeyed' it cuts the ground from under its own feet. Compulsory, necessitated, mechanical 'obedience' is self-contradiction. And if man be a creature devoid of free will, a mere link between antecedents and consequences, how, in the name of all true philosophy, can such a helpless embodiment of external forces 'defy' anything? So, as ever, is Determinedism compelled to give way its case in the very endeavour to state it.

For another instance of popular appeals to the plain man to-day on behalf of 'Determinism,' no better example can be found than the thoughtful utterances of Mr. J. McCabe. All the more so because this writer shows both an acquaintance with psychology and a perception of the difficulties of

'Determinism,' together with a candour in acknowledging them, which is very seldom met with amongst its advocates. His strong statements concerning the prevalence of 'Determinism' as a philosophical and social creed, we have seen above. But after blessing it with his approval, we have the remarkably candid acknowledgement that it is 'by no means clear' that modern moral improvement is to be traced to this cause.

> 'The fact remains that all this recognition of the profound importance of environment and heredity is consistent with a belief in free will within the limits which the cultivated Libertarian sets on it to-day. Many have felt that the rigid logic of much Deterministic literature, however admirable its scientific premisses, seems to lead to conclusions which are none too easily reconciled with their own consciousness. There is also a genuine and well-founded reserve on the subject in psychological works, a sincere recognition of a profound difficulty that is too often pushed out of sight, or buried under mounds of fine scientific phrases, in much of our controversial literature. The law of causation is accepted in psychology, and the act of will is stripped of the irresponsibility of indeterminateness of the old Libertarians. Further than this we cannot go. At a point in the obscure recesses of the brain, a dark chasm in which we faintly flash the poor lanterns of our search, we lose the sequence of events.'[1]

The thoughtful modesty of this avowal is not only refreshing as contrasted with the blatant dogmatism which too often characterizes modern apostles of Determinedism, but opens the door, as we shall see later on, for a rapprochement between sincere and earnest thinkers of both schools, which is greatly to be desired.

The three writers whose contribution to the vexed problem before us we now proceed to examine, can scarcely be said to belong to the class of popular

---

[1] *R.P.A. Annual* for 1910, pp. 59–65.

writers, but as their influence affects the better educated portion of this generation, there is all the more need to do justice to their arguments.

We will take an instance first from an article by the Hon. Bertrand Russell, in *The Hibbert Journal*,[1] which alone will suffice to show how widely different are the conceptions suggested under the name of 'Determinism,' and how the fatal influence on morals is only prevented by denying or ignoring all actual determination. This writer asserts at the outset that he finds the 'grounds in favour of Determinism, overwhelming,' and goes on to insist that 'Determinism does not in any way interfere with morals,' but that free will 'would most seriously interfere, if anybody really believed in it.' He then proceeds to demonstrate this by flatly denying what other 'Determinists' so strongly affirm—

'It is said by the advocates of free will that Determinism destroys morals, since it shows that all our actions are unavoidable, and that therefore they deserve neither praise nor blame.

'It is said that praise and blame and responsibility are destroyed by Determinism.'

Indeed it is so said, and with such strong emphasis that it is impossible to mistake the meaning. But we have shown plainly above that it is avowed 'Determinists' themselves, and not merely 'advocates of free will,' who say so. No words can add to the deliberate definiteness of their assertions that all human actions are inevitable, that they are absolutely devoid of merit or demerit, and that moral responsibility is out of the question. But Mr. Russell writes—

'We apply praise or blame, then, and we attribute responsibility, where a man, having to exercise choice, has chosen wrongly, and this sense of praise or blame is not destroyed by Determinism.'

---

[1] For October, 1908, pp. 113–21.

But we have seen above that popular, 'hard Determinism' emphatically reiterates the contrary. '*All* praise, *all* blame,' under all circumstances, is declared, with the aid of italics, to be utterly unscientific and unjust. This latter attitude is manifestly the more logical, because it must be sheer self-contradiction to say that a man 'exercises choice,' or 'chooses wrongly,' if he does not choose at all; which assuredly he does not, if, in all his mental motions, he is but the embodiment of resistless antecedents.

Let us, however, listen again to Mr. Russell—

'When several alternatives present themselves, it is certain that we can both do which we choose and choose which we will; in this sense all the alternatives are possible. What Determinism maintains is that our will to choose this or that alternative is the effect of antecedents; but this does not prevent our will from being itself the cause of other effects. And the sense in which other decisions are possible, seems sufficient to distinguish some actions as right and some as wrong, some as moral and some as immoral.'

From this somewhat involved statement, and out of several similar pages, all that clear thought can make out appears to be as follows: (1) The 'softness' of this 'Determinism' does not alter the fact that there is here no real 'choice' at all. If the will to choose is inevitably decided by resistless antecedents, it is but verbal confusion and mental mockery to speak of 'choice at all.' There is here no more real 'choice' than is exhibited in a piston-rod which goes up or down according to the direction in which the steam-pressure acts upon it. If the 'will to choose' is nothing more than an 'effect of antecedents,' no matter what they are, there is no choice. For a determined choice is a plain contradiction in terms. (2) The 'other decisions' referred to are no less inconceivable; for, according to 'Determinism,' that which was decided was the only decision possible. The best decision was also the worst; for it was the only decision possible under the circumstances. (3) That which cannot but be, may be good in the sense of being useful or contributing to happiness, but it cannot be in any sense 'right' or 'moral.' (4) 'Good,' in the moral sense, is the embodiment or result of right. In Mr. Russell's own words: 'The things that are good are things which on their own account and apart from any consideration of their effects we *ought* to wish to see in existence.' But no subtlety of thought or cleverness of speech can ever identify 'ought' with the 'inevitable.' Once again Prof. James's wise words recur, that 'Determinism makes what ought to be impossible.' All that is, is obliged to be. To call that which could not but be, 'right,' is the prostitution of language. (5) 'Right' and 'wrong,' 'moral' and 'immoral,' as applied to actions, are not to be decided by the effects of the actions, but by their purpose. Moral quality derives not from what follows, but from what precedes. The 'Determinism' of popular journalism writes that 'to do harm is a crime,'[1] whereas the moral instinct of every child affirms the contrary. If a man is accidentally knocked down by a motor-car, no one thinks of attributing 'crime' to the driver, however serious the 'harm' done. It is purpose, intention, meaning, which alone confer moral quality. (6) On 'Deterministic' lines there is no possibility of intention or purpose; for all the actual present, and all the possible future, are nothing but the inevitable results

---

[1] *Clarion.*

of the past. (7) 'Determinism,' therefore, however 'soft,' does but illustrate once more the attempt to represent the play of *Macbeth* with Lady Macbeth left out. It has no room anywhere for personality; and seeing that 'right' or 'wrong,' 'moral' or 'immoral,' are and always must be personal qualities, these also are ruled out of its kategories.

There ought to be no controversy about the fact that in order to morality, there must always be a double reality. (i) A real personality, capable of receiving approval or disapproval, as both knowing right from wrong, and being able to do either; (ii) A real action, as embodying a genuine decision in which that which ought to be is either endorsed or rejected. But according to 'Determinism' both these realities are illusory. There is no self-conscious, deciding personality; there is no real action. Whether spontaneity be psychologically analysable or not, without it there is no real action at all. Where there is no action, there can be no purpose, and therefore no moral quality. In such case everything a man does is as non-moral as the revolution of a fly wheel. Hence we are not to be misled by such summaries as the following—

'Determinism, then, does not in any way interfere with morals. It is worth noticing that free will, on the contrary, would interfere most seriously, if anybody really believed in it. People never do as a matter of fact believe that any one else's actions are not determined by motives, however much they may think themselves free. Bradshaw consists entirely of predictions as to the actions of engine-drivers; but no one doubts Bradshaw on the ground that the volitions of engine-drivers are not governed by motives'—

For the main assumptions here are altogether unwarranted. (i) It is assumed that free will means motiveless action, which certainly is not true.

'Libertarians' hold as strongly as 'Determinists' that no sane man acts without a motive. (ii) But it is also here assumed that the motive acts without the man, which is even more untrue. The bald statement that actions are 'determined by motives,' is simply false. For the very conception of motive connotes personality. Motive is unthinkable apart from personality. The idea of motive as an impersonal force bringing actions to pass as the hammer drives in a nail, or of a man determined by motives as a cart's motion is determined by a horse, is sheer fatuity. People do truly 'think themselves free,' in the sense expressed by Sir Oliver Lodge: 'A free man is the master of his motives, and selects that motive which he wills to obey.'[1] But they recognize that the motives are inseparable from themselves. Certainly they never 'believe that any one else's actions' are 'determined by motives,' irrespective of personality. The writer's reference to Bradshaw here supplies all the test we need. The suggestion is that as the engine is governed by a driver, so the driver is 'governed by motives.' Both are similarly 'determined,' and according to 'hard Determinism,' both are therefore alike irresponsible and non-moral. But if 'soft Determinism' insists that the driver is moral and responsible, and the engine is not, wherein, we must ask, lies the difference? Assuredly, on pragmatic lines, when an accident occurs, all sane men hold the driver responsible and not the engine. But why? Is it not because the determination in the one case is entirely different from that in the other? The engine truly is 'governed' by the driver, and has no power to do anything but mechanically

---

[1] *Substance of Faith allied with Science*, p. 27.

follow his direction. But the driver is *not* similarly 'governed' by motives. He has something else to do than mechanically obey an antecedent push or pull. He has to decide upon the motive which deserves following, and then to embody his decision in volition. In Mr. Russell's words, 'we apply praise or blame, and we attribute responsibility, where a man having to exercise choice, has chosen wrongly.' But if it be true, as he adds, that 'this sense of praise or blame is not destroyed by Determinism,' it can only be because such 'Determinism' has become so 'soft' as to contradict itself. A determined choice is self-contradictory nonsense. And if, as usual, it be replied that for any choice there must be a cause, we will presently show grounds for pointing to the personality of the chooser as the sufficient cause, whether we can succeed in tracing it out by ultimate analysis or not.

Again, Mr. Russell goes on to say—

'In fact, no one really holds that right acts are uncaused. It would be a monstrous paradox to say that a man's decision ought not to be influenced by his belief as to what is his duty. Yet if he allows himself to decide on an act because he believes it to be his duty, his decision has a motive, i.e. a cause, and is not free in the only sense in which the Determinist must deny freedom. It would seem, therefore, that the objections to Determinism are mainly attributable to misunderstanding of its purport. Hence, finally, it is not Determinism but free will that has subversive consequences. There is, therefore, no reason to regret that the grounds in favour of Determinism are overwhelmingly strong.'[1]

Taking these five sentences as a typical summary, the reply of the advocate of moral freedom in man is that (1) as to the first sentence, he does not for a moment dream that right acts are 'uncaused.' That is a pure fiction on the part of the controversial

---

[1] p. 121.

'Determinist.' 'Uncaused volitions' are no part of moral freedom. What 'the principle of causality' really involves in this case, we shall presently consider. But (2) it is a 'monstrous paradox' for any scheme which consistently calls itself 'Determinism' to talk about either 'ought' or 'duty.' Duty is indeed that which ought to be done, but it is also that which need not be done. Whereas the very essence of Determinedism is that an action *must* be done, and that under the circumstances nothing else *can* be done. But compulsory duty is again a contradiction in terms. A man may be truly 'influenced' to an immeasurable extent, 'by his belief as to what is his duty.' But though influence may be so strong as to seem to compel, yet influence and compulsion, like the asymptotes to the parabola, may approach each other for ever, but can never meet, nor ever become synonymous. (3) 'If he allows himself to decide ... his decision has a motive.' Perfectly true; but equally true that here are both personality and contingency, neither of which conceptions can find any room in Determinedism. In the scheme which derives the present and predicts the future absolutely from the past—and nothing else is 'Determinism,' whether 'soft' or 'hard'—there is no place for an 'if,' nor is there any opportunity for a man to 'allow himself' anything. All that is, in him, and through him, was to be, so that the self becomes a mere 'epiphenomenon,' and the contingency which issues from personality is but an illusion. (4) As to 'the only sense in which the 'Determinist' must deny freedom,' if it be as represented here, that the denial of freedom only means the denial of 'uncaused volitions,' then there is no need to invoke 'Determinism,' for there are no Indeterminists. No Libertarian, however earnest, ever pleads for 'uncaused volitions.' All he demands is that justice should be done to the true nature of a volition, and the unique character of the causation to which undeniable experience unmistakably testifies therein. (5) The three concluding sentences of this statement, therefore, by Mr. Russell, may be accepted as true; but on the clear double understanding, (i) that, negatively, ' Determinism ' means nothing but the denial of uncaused volitions; and (ii) positively that, in the language of Prof. Lloyd Morgan, 'there is Determinism all along the line, but it is the self which determines,' not antecedents independent of the self.

In order, however, to do utmost justice to the 'soft Determinism' which claims to preserve responsibility and develop morality without recognition of contingency, or appeal to personality, let us now consider the attitude of two other able writers, one of whom may be said to plead for religious 'Determinism,' and the other for irreligious. In a thoughtful volume entitled *Some Problems of Existence*, Mr. Norman Pearson devotes a chapter (pp. 83-115), to ' Free Will, Determinism, and Morality,' the conclusion of which is that ' religious Determinism, therefore, is a belief from which no one need shrink, and it sacrifices nothing worth preserving of all that Libertarians are anxious to preserve.' This is indeed an excellent result if it can be honestly arrived at, but the methods suggested require careful scrutiny. Especially seeing that the preceding sentence makes this affirmation—

'Man is not moved puppet-wise as the Libertarians vainly talk, but as an intelligent and sympathetic minister, whose whole nature aspires to the goal whereto the divine power is leading him.'

This 'puppet-wise' motion is confessedly that to which the thoughtful Libertarian most strenuously objects; but he also protests that if a man is in any real sense 'determined,' it is, as pointed out above, only verbal mockery and mental confusion to call him a 'sympathetic minister,' or assume that he 'aspires,' for both these conceptions involve spontaneity. It is equally fallacious to talk about divine power 'leading' a 'determined' man. If he is only led, he is not determined. If he is determined he is not only led, he is driven. So much need is there that we should look into the matter a little more carefully. There will, of course, be no necessity to reiterate principles which have been made plain in the preceding scrutiny of Mr. Russell's positions, but in addition to those some other points may be cleared up. At the outset, then, let us mark yet once more[1] this writer's definition of 'Determinism,' and compare it with what we have already noticed.

'Every act of a man is the latest link in an immense chain of causation, in which the slightest element of uncertainty would be impossible. At a given moment there may be several courses apparently open to a man, but in reality there is only that one course open to him which his character and environment make the only course possible. This, put quite shortly, is the doctrine of Determinism.'

Now this, surely, is something very different from the representation of 'Determinism' given above, as meaning only the denial of uncaused volitions. So that, when this writer remarks, earlier, that 'the question is complicated at the outset by the fact that Libertarians are not agreed amongst themselves as to what free will means,' the compliment must be returned, not only with thanks but with emphasis. For certainly Libertarians do not so far contradict

---
[1] See pp. 20, 75 above.

each other as to affirm one moment that responsibility is impossible, and the next that it is made more emphatic than ever. This, however, we see is what avowed 'Determinists' unmistakably do. In the present case the Libertarian position is fairly represented thus—

'If the act in question is not due to the man's free choice, but is part of a predetermined order over which he has no control, then it is not properly imputable to him, and, consequently, no moral tribunal, human or divine, can hold him responsible for it. Free will, therefore, is necessary to moral responsibility and Determinism is fatal to it.'[1]

Such a statement is not only 'plausible,' but convincing, one would think, to every thoughtful mind. Let us now examine this writer's reasons against accepting it. It is said to be 'unsound,' because it rests partly on an inaccurate view of man's relations to his fellows, and partly on an untenable theory of the nature of God's dealings with man. It will be best to postpone the more exact consideration of this latter assertion, and confine our attention at present to the former.

In regard to the relations of man to man, the writer affirms that we are 'all practical Determinists' because we 'believe that conduct springs from character;' and the 'Determinist view is that conduct is the outcome of character.' There are certain universal motives by which we confidently expect that human conduct 'in general' will be ruled. Hence in engaging a servant we seek a character from which to infer his future conduct. Here the whole case for or against the alleged 'Determinism,' turns upon the little phrase which is so meekly and mildly introduced. 'In general' is true, but it is

---

[1] p. 93.

neither the whole truth nor true enough to establish Determinedism. If only 'in general,' men are ruled by their motives, then there are exceptions, and one exception is enough to wreck Determinedism. In the very words of Dr. Illingworth, which the writer vainly seeks to exploit for his purpose—'in average cases the Necessitarian contention is practically true.' But 'Determinism,' if consistent with itself, knows nothing of 'average cases.' Every case, without reference to any other, is 'determined,' and there is, therefore, no more room here to speak of an 'average,' than to say that the average man is alive, not dead. But let us note what follows—

'We have postulated that moral responsibility does not attach to conduct which cannot be properly imputed to the man himself. Consequently the question at once arises, Can any conduct which is determined by character be properly imputed to the man himself? The answer depends on whether the character is synonymous with the self. Determinism asserts that in relation to conduct the character *is* the self, and thereby rescues the moral responsibility so nearly wrecked by Libertarians.'[1]

This is an expansion of the phrase quoted above—'the outcome of character.' But it is altogether too ambiguous to permit the matter to be settled in this easy off-hand style. When, for instance, this writer repeats the usual affirmation that 'every man is born with a character of his own,' it is manifest at once, as pointed out before, that the 'character' with which a man is born, is most certainly *not* the 'character' out of which his adult acts may be said in a true sense to issue. It is strange indeed that intelligent and acute 'Determinists' should so

---

[1] pp. 94, 95. The special position attacked is that of Dr. Illingworth in his book upon *The Divine Immanence*, but we may well leave him to take care of himself in that and the other volume entitled *Personality, Human and Divine*.

persist in ignoring this unmistakable and all-pertinent distinction. If morality is in contemplation, then it is altogether a misnomer to call the physical and mental constitution with which a child is born, a 'character.' It is time that this mis-use of a most important term ceased on the part of all who desire the truth. That which comes by heredity is no more 'character,' than is the influence of environment. Hence, the position of Libertarians which Mr. Pearson seeks to ridicule, is perfectly true and well warranted. We do 'claim to fix man with moral responsibility on the ground that however much his character determines him, it is itself originally created by his own acts of choice.' To which it is no reply to say that 'this argument might possibly be tenable if the character at birth were a blank, but it is quite incompatible with the fact which the Libertarian expressly demands, that every man is born with a character of his own.'

For, on the contrary, the Libertarian expressly denies that any man is born with a character. Such a phrase is a contradiction in terms. A born 'character' is unthinkable. There need be no hesitation whatever in affirming that, so far as *moral* character is concerned, there *is* at birth only a blank sheet. Character is that which the self writes upon the blank sheet with the materials supplied by heredity and environment in combination. Seeing, then, that character, to be character, must be the work of the self, it is mere misuse of terms to talk of its being 'born with him,' or made for him, or received from heredity, or induced by environment. Both these may be channels of direction, or measures of limitation, as the quantity and quality of a fire are modified by the materials supplied or the grate in which it is confined. But they are no more character than fuel is fire. Doubtless all natural analogy fails to express the reality and activity of the self which constitutes a human personality, yet the fact remains as patent as real, as real as indescribable, that a man's character is due to himself and to himself alone, for which reason moral responsibility rightly attaches to his conduct. Conduct is not the 'outcome of character,' in the sense in which apples are the outcome of an apple-tree, or a deadly wound results from a cobra-bite. Character is the accumulation of the results of all the past actual decisions of the self; but the conduct which flows from existing character is no mere mechanical or necessary sequence even of that character, seeing that it is possible—and has been in a myriad cases an actual occurrence—that a man should contradict his former character, as Prof. James put beyond dispute in his famous Gifford lectures. As we must presently return to this matter, it will suffice here to say that ' conduct ' is, ' in general,' the self's continuation and re-endorsement of the ' character ' up to that time acquired. Hence not only the responsibility attaching to each act, but its serious import as a contribution to the future which can only under very exceptional circumstances be set aside.

The further assertion that 'human tribunals all act in practice on Deterministic principles,' equally calls for denial. No tribunal in the world treats man as 'hard Determinism' suggests, viz. as an irresponsible automaton. Nor in their assumption of responsibility from man to man because conduct proceeds from character, do tribunals at all ' adopt the view of responsibility for which Determinists contend.' If any thief were to plead in court that his conduct was but the outcome of the character with which he was born, is there a jury in the land that would hold him guiltless? Assuming only his sanity, would not every one say to him in effect that it was his duty so to rule, i.e. to make, his own character, out of his natural endowment, that the conduct issuing from it would be honest? Assuredly if, as 'Determinists' avow, the criminal is but what his parents and his environment have made him, it is they, and not he, who should be held responsible and punished accordingly.

Once more, however, let us notice the plea put forward—

'Determinism holds that conduct is determined by the influence of motives on character. To an offender who claimed immunity from punishment on the ground that his misconduct was necessitated by his character, Determinists would reply, "No doubt; but since your character and therefore your will is amenable to motives, we intend to supply motives which will operate against similar misconduct in the future." No such reply is open to any Libertarians who directly or indirectly place the will beyond the control of motives.'

Every sentence here calls for correction. In the first, it is a contradiction in terms to affirm that anything is 'determined' by 'influence.' If motives are of such a nature as to necessitate a certain character-result, then that is not 'influence' but compulsion. If, on the other hand, motives do only influence character, then there must be some other factor, somewhere and somehow, to decide what shall be the final result in character. In other words, motives no more necessarily determine character than character necessarily determines conduct. Moral character, to be such, can no more be determined from behind than projected on in front. It is no more a mere mechanical sequence of motive than conduct is a mere mechanical sequence of character. Out of many presented motives—in which presentation no character whatever is involved—one motive has to be selected from the rest, endorsed by the self's conscious identification with it, and further developed into volition, before any character can attach to the ensuing action. Conduct is but the repetition of such actions, and is not therefore, simply determined by character, and does not mechanically issue from character, but is character endorsed by self-conscious action. A man is thus responsible for conduct because he himself, and none other, is the source of the character which is continually re-affirmed in conduct.

Again: as to the offender who pleads for immunity from punishment, because his conduct was necessitated by his character; the suggested 'Deterministic' reply starts with the acknowledged injustice of punishing a man for what he could not help, but it is apparently content—'no doubt'—to do evil, i.e. 'injustice,' for the past, in order that good may come in the future. Yet even the good which is to come is certainly not Deterministic. That the will is 'amenable to motives,' i.e. follows the motive which is made strongest by the endorsement, or self-identification with it, of the conscious ego, is the definite 'Libertarian' doctrine. And the suggestion that such motives will 'operate' against future misconduct, is what every 'Libertarian' heartily acknowledges. But the only 'operation' which is deservedly called Deterministic is compulsion. Is it true, then, that punishment, whether just or unjust, necessarily and absolutely prevents the offender from repeating the offence? We know that it is not true. We know that the only case in which certain conduct can be absolutely secured, is in dealing with a machine, i.e. with a thing, and not with a person. So then this boasted judicial superiority of 'Determinism' begins with injustice, and ends with degradation. To the 'Libertarian,' confessedly, 'no such reply is open'; nor does he wish it to be open. But not for the reason assigned. It would be difficult, indeed, to find a falser statement of 'Libertarian' principles than to say that they 'directly or indirectly place the will beyond the control of motives.' The word which is omitted in this account makes all the difference in the world. It is against such mechanical control of the will by motives as leaves no room for the most certain fact in all our experience, i.e. our power to choose between motives, that the 'Libertarian' protests. To say that because Libertarians recognize this factor in character with its accompanying conduct, to them 'punishment must become absolutely purposeless, or simply vindictive'—is as gross a travesty of the truth as words can express. There is nothing vindictive in enforcing just responsibility; and there is quite as real purpose in so appealing to a moral agent—inalienably conscious of his powers of self-determination—as there can ever be in pulling the lever of a machine, or winding up an automaton. The former may be, and must be, regarded as a moral tribunal; but the latter is nothing more than mechanical. When, therefore, we are assured, as by this writer afterwards, that the 'doctrine of free will breaks down at every point where it comes into contact with the realities of existence,' we can but meet such a dogmatic assertion with an equally emphatic denial.

Nor is there any more truth in the conclusion that

'the belief in free will is at present propped up rather by groundless fears of the dangers of discarding it, than by any solid evidence in its favour.' For in the first place the 'fears' which arise from the propagation of 'Determinism' are not 'groundless.'[1] If, so far, no great practical harm has been done, it is because the 'hard Determinism' which is preached is not practised. Sane society would not tolerate it for an hour, anywhere. And although 'soft Determinism' flatly contradicts the hard variety in claiming rather to emphasize than to destroy personal responsibility, not only is that claim not made out, but there is serious room for fears that its subtleties are beyond the reach of the ordinary man, who can, however, plainly see the main position, viz. that if a man's whole being is necessitated, he never himself acts at all, therefore is never justly responsible for anything, and any villainy whatever, individual or national, may be excused upon the unanswerable plea that it could not be helped.

But further; it is the very extreme of untruth to say that the Libertarian doctrine has no 'solid evidence in its favour.' On the contrary, it has the most solid evidence conceivable, i.e. that of unmistakable and undeniable consciousness. All the efforts of Determinism to fling the confusing veil of the apparent over the real, herein, are fruitless; as we shall yet more plainly see, presently. Any philosophical scheme must be hard pressed indeed, which

---

[1] Dr. Warschauer says truly hereupon—' Just as one would not like prussic acid to lie about promiscuously where all and sundry could have access to it, lest there should be a great deal of accidental poisoning, so we are justified in viewing the broadcast dissemination of Determinist theory, not merely with the antipathy one may feel towards intellectual error, but with the apprehension excited by a moral danger.'—*Problems of Immanence*, p. 167.

is driven to seek to establish itself by treating the most real of all realities, i.e. definite experience, as an illusion. The following weighty words of an able physicist may well suffice to close our scrutiny of this writer's positions. Says Prof. Poynting, F.R.S., of Birmingham University—

'I hold that we are more certain of our power of choice and of responsibility than of any other fact, either physical or psychical. It is better to face the situation boldly and claim for our mental experience as great certainty as that which the physicist claims for his experience in the outside world. If our mental experience convinces us that we have freedom of choice, we are obliged to believe that in mind there is territory which the physicist can never annex. Some of his laws may still hold good, but somewhere or other his scheme must cease to give a true account.'[1]

It is not often that 'Determinism' is advocated by professional Christian teachers. In spite of all the influence of Calvin, and the acknowledged acumen of Jonathan Edwards, the advocates of Predestination, which is the religious form of 'Determinism,' are a diminishing and indeed insignificant minority. But a few cases naturally occur amidst the confused transitions of modern theology. The Determinism recommended is generally of the 'soft' type, and it may be instructive to examine one instance as a fair representative of others. The argument of a recent sermon is reported as follows[2]—

'Our actions are caused by laws which we did not make, but which make us live as we do. We seem to be free, but that is partly an illusion and partly true. It is partly an illusion

---

[1] *Hibbert Journal*, July, 1903, pp. 743, 746

[2] As already specified in brief footnote on p. 23, from *The Clarion* for June 11, 1909, by Rev. G. T. Sadler, B.A., LL.B. Whether the report does him justice or no, I cannot say. It is sufficient for our present purpose that the report was read by many, and illustrates the modern tendency.

because our moral acts are caused by our characters, and our characters are built up from tendencies and ideas which have come from heredity and environment. Hence we are not independent persons, and our deeds are not uncaused. The feeling that we are free is true in this sense that the cause of a moral deed is a motive within us, and not some power outside us. But this motive moves us because of what we are; because of our characters; and the character is a product of inherited instincts, appetites and passions, modified by controlling ideas which have been acquired since our birth.'

It is difficult to understand an educated mind contenting itself with these plausibilities, but the possibility of their misleading others demands that they should be examined. Taking the sentences therefore in the order in which they occur, the following comments are necessary. (1) Our actions are *not* 'caused by laws,' any more than the flow of a river is caused by its banks. Laws do *not* 'make us live as we do.' They regulate and modify our actions, but that is quite another matter. The cause of human action is human personality, which is never compelled by law but actively expresses itself through law. A little later on this same writer says that 'Liberty is by law, by obeying the deepest law.' But there must be something capable of obeying, and to say that that something, call it by what name we will, is both 'made' to act and at the same time 'obeys' law, is but psychological confusion. (2) Our sense of freedom is only an illusion to the extent to which every normal consciousness itself is an illusion. Assuming only that I am neither a cerebral freak nor a neurotic victim, my experience of freedom is as real, and as reliable, as my consciousness of being. (3) Moral acts are not 'caused by characters,' but regulated by them. When it is said that 'our characters are built up from tendencies,' the question inevitably arises, who is the builder? 'Tendencies,' *per se*, cannot build up character. Whatever my heredity and environment, no character is mine unless I, as distinct alike from both, have had a hand in its formation, i.e. have 'built it up' out of tendencies. If, as is here assumed, by 'character' we mean moral character, then it is not in the power of any heredity or environment to confer it. Even Mr. Blatchford, who is being defended by this writer, is driven to say—

'Now let us reconsider the example of our swimmer and the stream. The swimmer is *something more* than a mere heredity. He is *a man*, and he has learnt to swim. Therefore in his battle with the stream of environment *he is using* heredity and environment; for environment taught him to swim.'[1]

Of course it is not true that if a man is thrown into the water, the environment teaches him to swim; but it would be difficult for the most ardent 'Libertarian' to express more clearly the distinctive existence and action of human personality. So that (4) whilst no one says that we are independent of heredity and environment, at least the fact that we are persons, and as such entirely distinct from both, remains unmistakable and undeniable. No 'Libertarian' affirms that our deeds are 'uncaused'; but he does assert, on irrefragable evidence, that they are not caused, i.e. completely determined, by heredity and environment. As Dr. Rice succinctly puts it, 'I am myself the cause of my volitions, and no other cause is needed.'[2]

(5) 'The cause of a moral deed is a motive within us.' But a deed is not necessarily moral because it

---

[1] *Not Guilty*, p. 135. Italics mine.
[2] *Christian Faith in an Age of Science*, p. 293.

is 'caused by a motive.' If the motive within us is but a mere link in a chain of inevitable antecedents and consequents, then the ensuing deed is no more moral than the coupling together of railway trucks. Only the decision of a free and active personality can confer moral quality at all. Dr. Fisher's statement is as philosophically valid as it is consonant with the experience of every sane man—

'We can initiate action by the exercise of an agency which is neither irresistibly controlled by motives, nor determined, without any capacity for alternative action, by a proneness inherent in its nature. This freedom is not only attested in consciousness, it is evinced by that ability to resist inducements brought to bear on the mind, which we are conscious of exerting. If motives have an influence, that influence is not tantamount to Deterministic efficiency.'[1]

(6) That 'motives move us because of our characters' is only partly true. All depends upon what I, as distinct from my character, do under any given influence. Circumstances may suggest motives, existing character may strengthen or weaken them. Whether, then, such and such a motive shall prevail or not, is for me, as a deliberate scrutator of the whole case, to decide. Even that large section of experience which becomes almost or altogether automatic, began with such deliberated action. It is as vain as unnecessary to initiate an infinite regress by asking: Well then, what makes you so decide?—as it is to get behind the looking-glass in order to verify the reality of the presented image. Nothing is easier than to say that 'character is a product of inherited instincts and passions modified by controlling ideas which have been acquired since our birth'; but the irrepressible question must be faced, how can 'controlling ideas' be 'acquired'? As a ship acquires

[1] *The Grounds of Theistic and Christian Belief*, p. 4.

barnacles? Or as a tree acquires moisture? If so, assuredly all talk about moral character is meaningless. In a moral being, ideas never can become 'controlling,' without the deliberate assent of the self. 'Passion' is unthinkable as a mere 'inherited instinct.' In the degree in which it is real, it is through the conscious and definite adoption and employment by the self of an inherited instinct. That is also the only way in which any ideas tending to control character can be 'acquired' by a human personality, from the first dawning of moral consciousness until death. The preacher here goes on to say that—'Mr. Blatchford is so far right in his book, *Not Guilty*. The inward and outward conditions of a man's life, of course, make him what he is inevitably.' But, with all respect, there is no 'of course' whatever in the matter. It is quite as true that, to an unmeasured extent, a man makes 'the outward and inward conditions of his life,' as that these make him. In neither case is there any play of the inevitable. The creature who is 'inevitably made' what he is by 'conditions' of any kind, is no man at all; but a mere sub-human automaton. That may be a perfectly consistent attitude for an Agnostic writer who maintains that no man is responsible for anything he says or does, but that a Christian teacher should commit himself to the same degradation of manhood to thinghood, is strange indeed. All the more so because this same writer—who is here defended and commended—sufficiently answers himself. As regards environment, for instance, instead of a man's being inevitably 'made' thereby, his own statement, in regard to a certain Thomas who had a hereditary tendency to drink, but was helped by a 'wise friend' and a steady environment, is, that '*with a hard struggle'* he escaped the danger.'[1] But a 'hard struggle' that is inevitable, is a contradiction in terms. So again in regard to heredity. After telling us that a man is 'inevitably' what his heredity 'makes him,' the writer gives us a glimpse of his own experience. 'Talk about the difficulty of bringing up children: what is that to the trouble of educating one's ancestors? Oh, the *difficulty I have had* with mine.'[2] Is that the expression of the inevitable?

Let us hear, however, the rest of our preacher's philosophy, although sufficiently noticed above—

'We choose, but our choice is governed by all our past and by present circumstances. A will is a pair of scales, and the motives are the weights, the stronger sending the scale down. We talk of "weighing" the case.'

One does not know how to characterize such utterances from an educated source. Let it suffice, therefore, simply to point out that (1) a 'governed' choice is a contradiction in terms. If it is 'governed' it is no 'choice'; if it is a 'choice,' it is not 'governed.' (2) A 'pair of scales' never was a 'will,' and never will be. This poor little popular fallacy about a will being a 'pair of scales' has been exposed times without number.[3] But even if as a metaphor it were allowed to stand, we should still have to find *the* pair of scales which put the heavier weight into one of its own pans. Whenever this superficial formula is employed, it is conveniently forgotten that no 'pair of scales' ever weighed anything yet, or ever will do, without a weigher. 'We talk of weighing a case.' Certainly; for no case ever yet weighed itself. It is thus quite misleading to say that—

'The order of causes, then, is this: A moral act, choice

---
[1] *Not Guilty*, p. 199—italics mine.   [2] p. 251.
[3] See, for one instance, *Clarion Fallacies*, by the present writer, p. 69 (Hodder & Stoughton); also p. 6 above.

motives, character behind motives, inherited laws and tendencies, modified by later ideas and events. Such are the spiritual causes of our actions. All is law; all is inevitable by the laws of life '—

For by no possibility can a 'moral act' result from the inevitable action of resistless laws. One might as truly talk of a moral or immoral fire in the grate. If all that is 'behind motives' is an accumulation of 'inherited laws and tendencies modified by later' environment, then that is no character at all, for there is no real personal action in it. The whole is but a mechanical, accidental result. Whereas character, without a freely acting personality, is as unthinkable as a human body without life, as impossible as a solar system without a sun. In plain contradiction to the above, 'all' is *not* law where real 'choice' is concerned, as Prof. Poynting has well expressed above. Whatever else may or may not be, the human self is. And whatever else it is or is not, it is not law. Nor can it be itself, and be completely determined by law. If I am not myself, I am nothing; and as consciousness denies that, so does it equally deny that I am inevitably and helplessly under law. The 'laws of life' are the channels through which the self finds expression; but they are not the hydraulic pressure under which the self is crushed into a nonentity.

For a final instance of the way in which the avowed theory of 'Determinism' claims in the name of philosophy not only to retain, but to emphasize morality, we must examine the main positions of Prof. McTaggart, as set forth in his volume on *Some Dogmas of Religion*. The acknowledged erudition and academic standing of the writer, as Lecturer of Trinity College, Cambridge, and Hegelian specialist, invest his statements with an authority which may well constitute them the last word here on behalf of 'soft Determinism.' One must be forgiven for saying that, in spite of the deliberateness which is manifested in the carefully numbered parargaphs, fallacies abound throughout. For the moment, however, we are concerned only with the relations of this 'Determinism' to morals. Says the writer—

'It is well known that many people are and have been Determinists, and that the great majority of them, if not all, have made judgements of obligation respecting their own conduct and that of others. This is decisive.'[1]

Decisive of what? (1) That Determinists have flatly contradicted each other, as is plainly shown in what is given above. (2) That some 'Determinists' have not been consistent with their own contentions. If no man can help himself, through being completely 'determined,' it is waste of words to talk about his 'obligation' or his responsibility. But in proceeding to controvert the true principle that the 'belief in complete determination is incompatible with the validity of judgements of obligation,' the Professor adduces this curious illustration—

'In that case if A, being a Determinist, says that Nero ought not to have burned Rome, the judgement is false; whilst if B, being an Indeterminist, makes the same statement, it is true. This is clearly absurd.'[2]

Yes; but the absurdity is very easily allocated, viz. to the statement that Nero, being completely determined, 'ought' to do, or not to do, anything. For that *is* absurd, to the same extent, and for the same reason as it would be absurd to say that a locomotive 'ought' not to run over a man on the line.

---

[1] p. 150.   [2] p. 151.

Dr. McTaggart acknowledges that the 'strongest argument for free will is the argument from the judgement of moral obligation.' But as he does not deem it satisfactory, it will be necessary to ask the reader's patience for a somewhat detailed scrutiny into the reasons alleged against it.

'"Determinism" has always, as a matter of fact, been defended, and, as I believe, can be successfully defended, on the basis that judgements of obligation are valid.'[1]

Unfortunately, the 'matter of fact' here assumed, is not always the fact, as has been abundantly shown in the extracts given above.[2] The point here is whether those 'Determinists' who give up obligation, i.e. responsibility, or those who strive to retain it, are the more logical. In other words, is 'complete determination' consistent with any judgement of obligation? Let us see.

'Every judgement of obligation seems to have two presuppositions. (1) Something is such that its existence would be good or bad. (2) The person as to whom the judgement of obligation is passed, can exercise, by his will, some effect in determining the existence or non-existence of that thing. Would either of these presuppositions be necessarily false, if complete determination were true?'

---

[1] p. 152.

[2] If further proof be necessary, it may be found, *passim*, in the book, *Not Guilty*, by Mr. Blatchford, which has undoubtedly put the 'Deterministic' theory before the minds of more people in this country than any other volume has done. One more specimen will be conclusive—'*All* praise and *all* blame are undeserved. A tramp has murdered a child on the highway, has robbed her of a few coppers and thrown her body into a ditch. Do you mean to say that that tramp could not help doing that? Do you mean to say he is not to blame? Do you mean to say he is not to be punished? Yes; I say all those things, and if all those things are not true, this book is not worth the paper it is printed on' (p. 203). Unless the tramp be insane, the book is rightly estimated.

Seeing that the author is careful to explain that by 'good or bad' he 'does not mean only morally good or bad,' but anything useful or intelligible, the question becomes either confusing or irrelevant. Any machine can turn out 'useful' articles: and so can a human will, if it be but part of a machine, produce useful effects. But, in the first place, the question here is whether a 'person' is such a machine; and in the second place, if moral good be included in the meaning of 'good,' it is certain that neither a machine, nor the human will under complete determination, can have any moral effect whatever. How far the confusion extends, is manifest in the following—

'Is a volition to produce a good result, or a man who makes it, to be less approved; is the volition to produce a bad result, or the man who makes it, to be less condemned, because the volition is completely determined?'[1]

One might reply at once, and truly, that such a volition cannot possibly merit any degree of either approval or condemnation. But it is well to point out here the double ambiguity. Good and bad, we have just been told, may be either moral or non-moral. But there is a vast difference between a man's producing pleasant music or well-baked bread, and his resistance to a strong inducement to evil, or faithfully discharging a costly duty. Even apart from that, everything turns upon what 'completely determined' means. If a volition completely determined by antecedents be intended, then the 'man who makes it' is a mere verbal delusion. He does not make it. It is made for him. He cannot therefore morally be either approved or blamed at all. If, however, the volition which produces good

---
[1] p. 154.

or bad results is 'completely determined' by the man himself, then certainly he and none other is to be justly approved or condemned for it.

'Or suppose that I do will to save a man's life, but that my efforts are frustrated by ignorance due to past indolence, or to confusion caused by intoxication. In these cases I shall condemn myself, and the condemnation will be moral condemnation; for the result does, in these cases, depend upon my will. If I had willed differently in the past, I should not now be ignorant or a drunkard; I do not think that it would be denied by Indeterminists that even if the will were completely determined, moral condemnation of this sort would be possible.'[1]

But with all respect to the learned Professor, this is precisely what Indeterminists would utterly deny. For if the will were 'completely determined,' the phrase—'if I had willed differently in the past' becomes sheer self-contradiction. Both the personality and the contingency involved in this supposition are entirely incompatible with Determinedism. On its principles, whatever I have willed in the past, was absolutely inevitable under the circumstances; for which reason 'I' had no hand in it, and therefore cannot possibly be liable to 'moral condemnation.'[2]

---

[1] p. 155.
[2] In a footnote we are told that 'all villains have moral qualities.' This is doubly untrue. (1) Villains may and do become so automatic, through habit, as to be really non-moral. Unless some new and eviscerated meaning is attached to the word 'moral.' (2) If villains are 'completely determined,' there can no more be moral qualities in them than in the jemmy which a burglar employs to open a safe. A completely determined villain is no 'villain' at all. He is a mere nexus between antecedent and consequent, and for that reason can no more be moral than the connecting link between an engine and a truck that is drawn after it. A completely determined villain is, thus, a contradiction in terms. If 'will' be, as it is, the self's own power of control over the other faculties and capacities of our nature, a completely controlled power of 'control' is but verbal babble without meaning.

Again—

> 'I can see no reason whatever why the moral quality of an act should be regarded as intensified because it happened without complete determination. It seems to me that the moral quality of the act would be just the same, whilst that of the agent would vanish.'[1]

By 'complete determination' the writer of course means apart from the self. Presently we shall see that only through the action of the self can there be any genuine determination at all. Taking the phrase in his sense now, it is sufficient to reply that no 'act' so far separated from the agent as to bear a moral quality in itself, is conceivable. It cannot be conceded for a moment that because certain useful results, or the opposite, follow from an act, therefore the act itself, apart from the doer of it, is moral. An act, *per se*, is an event, a thing which can no more be moral or immoral than the rising of the sun or a railway collision. If moral quality is to attach to an act, it can only be conferred upon it by the purpose of the agent, irrespective of results. A few days ago the papers reported that a working man jumped off the railway platform in the endeavour to save his mate who had fallen over in a fit. Unfortunately both were killed by an incoming train. But the act was as truly moral as the results were injurious. To insist that such an act was completely determined beforehand, is to reduce it to the same non-moral level as the crushing by the engine wheels. And further; instead of moral quality 'vanishing' from the agent, through incomplete determination, it only becomes thinkable when the determination is so incomplete as to leave room for the agent's own decision. The 'complete

---

[1] p. 156.

determination' of an action *ab extra*, shuts out the agent altogether. Manifestly he does not act at all. He is not an agent but a dummy, a mere connecting-rod in a machine. One might as well blame a pen in a blasphemer's hands for writing evil words, as attribute moral quality to an agent who was ' completely determined ' in all his so-called actions. They were never his, and he is therefore never responsible.

Yet again—

'We regard the intellectual excellence of Shakespeare with more approval than the excellence shown by the most brilliant punster. Each of them has exceeded all other men in a particular direction, but we admire Shakespeare most because we regard excellence in his direction as more important in the general scale of values than excellence in punning. Yet it would be universally admitted that Shakespeare's genius on the one hand and the absence of equal genius in myself on the other, were facts completely determined.'[1]

May be ; but in all this there is no question of moral quality at all. This is a mere case of differing intellectual endowment, which no one disputes. What then ?—

'If excellences which are admitted to be completely determined can be judged to have different values, so that one is placed above another, then the fact that one excellence is placed above all others is quite compatible with its complete determination.'[2]

It is difficult indeed to understand how a University Professor can satisfy himself with such a shuffle as this. Non-moral qualities differ in value, although they are completely determined ; therefore moral qualities, which are highest in value, may also be completely determined ! A more manifest *non*

---
[1] p. 157. [2] p. 157.

sequitur is scarcely conceivable. Because things which are what they are by compulsion, may differ in value, therefore personal actions which as such cannot be compelled, can have moral value—the highest of all values—in spite of compulsion! The true statement is as simple as unshakable. 'Excellences' which are completely determined, have no moral value at all. To talk, therefore, about moral excellence being 'above all others,' and yet being completely determined, is palpable self-contradiction.

Again; the question arises whether the 'greatest moral excellence consists in right volition.' And the comment is as follows—

'But what, in this case, are we to say of a loving disposition, a fervent patriotism, or a passion for humanity? They are not volitions, or tendencies to volition, or habits of volition; nor can they be obtained by willing. Love and patriotism are qualities which, by the Indeterminist's own position, are as completely determined as artistic or literary excellence. Will Indeterminists be prepared to say that while justice and benevolence are moral excellences, love and patriotism are mere gifts of fortune and have no moral import at all? I think that few of them would do so, in spite of the inconsistency in which their refusal plunges them. Kant, indeed, accepted the paradox rather than the inconsistency, but he had few precursors, and he has few successors. His attempt to prove that the teaching of Jesus is on his side, can only be described as astounding.'[1]

It is not nearly so 'astounding' as many of the positions adopted in this volume. The consideration of the teaching of Jesus hereupon may be postponed. Is there any need in this case to apologize for Kant? Surely only academic casuistry can hesitate over the answer to the question propounded. In the first place, the statement of the case is inaccurate. 'A

---

[1] p. 159.

loving disposition' *is* a 'tendency to volition.' In the possession by heredity of such a disposition, there is 'no moral import at all.' The moral import comes in with the volitional use, or disuse, or abuse, of such a disposition, by the conscious self possessing it. Nor can it be conceded at all that a 'fervent patriotism' involves no volition. We may be unable so to dissect human nature as to say where in the fervent patriotism the hereditary endowment ends, and the actual volition begins. But this at least we know, that to talk of a 'fervent patriotism' as something 'completely determined,' is as absurd as to attribute it to a gramophone. In direct answer, therefore, to the question proposed, it is sufficient to say that 'justice and benevolence are,' and are only, 'moral excellences,' in that they connote right volition on the part of men who are also capable of being unjust and malevolent. Whilst 'love and patriotism,' in so far as they are 'completely determined' hereditary endowments, have truly 'no moral import at all,' any more than the colour of one's eyes or the shape of one's hands. But love and patriotism, in actual exercise, *are not*, and cannot be, 'as completely determined as artistic or literary excellence.' For they connote personal volition (apart from mental endowment) on the part of men who are capable also of being unloving and unpatriotic. They have moral import just so far only as there is involved the action of the self upon the disposition or tendency received by heredity.

We come now to the general question of responsibility. Does the 'complete determination' of volitions render men irresponsible? One would think this to be a question answered as soon as asked. But 'soft' Determinism disputes such a manifest conclusion. Three kinds of responsibility are contemplated: 'to our fellow men, to God, and to self.' We are concerned, for the moment, only with the first of these.

'With respect to the first of these, I suppose that every Determinist who need be reckoned with would admit that we are responsible to our fellow men for defects of will, and that this responsibility is only for defects of will and for their results.'[1]

From exact quotations already given, the reader can judge how many Determinists there are who need not be reckoned with, seeing that they emphatically deny what is here assumed. And with good reason. For although the phrase 'defects of will' is ambiguous, and may mean either defects of birth, or defects of personal decision, in both cases alike 'Deterministic' responsibility to our fellows is unthinkable. If there be such a thing as natural, i.e. hereditary, deficiency in will-power, how can any man be held responsible to his fellows for that? They might as well hold him responsible for being five feet high instead of six. Moreover, if the will-power he does possess is 'completely determined,' how is he in any sense responsible for what he has had, and has, nothing to do with? If his volitions were all as 'fixed at his birth as are the motions of a planet in its orbit,' it is mere mockery to talk of his responsibility to anyone for anything.

But let us proceed—

'Now I submit that my responsibility to my fellow men for my volitions consists in the fact that it is reasonable for them to reward and punish me for my volitions, and in that fact only.'[2]

But is it a fact? Is it reasonable for men to reward or punish me for my volitions? Certainly on the principles of 'Determinism' it is not; for the simple

---

[1] p. 160. [2] p. 161.

and sufficient reason that 'my' volitions are non-existent.¹ It is sheer self-contradiction to talk of 'my' volitions having been completely determined. If they have been so determined, then assuredly they are not 'mine.' For a volition, in the very nature of the case, is not a disposition or a natural endowment; it is a use of endowment, or a response to environment by a conscious self. If the volitions have been all completely determined, there is no more room for 'me' or 'my' in the volition, than there is for Paderewski in the performance of a pianola. In such a case, therefore, it is utterly unreasonable for my fellow men to reward or punish me for what I have not done. It is as unreasonable as to bind and gag and blind the captain of a ship, and then blame him for the ship's ruin on the rocks.

Once again it is pertinent to note how flatly 'Determinists' contradict each other. Says the learned Professor, 'the Determinist is not in the least inconsistent in advocating that crimes should be punished.'² But the popular advocate of the same creed declares, as above—with italics—that *all* punishment, without exception, is unjust. The Indeterminist might well wait until these champions have fought it out.

'I claim to have proved that all human actions are ruled by heredity and environment, and that therefore *all* blame and *all* punishment are unjust. Punishment has never been just.'³

But, it may be replied, that even if unjust, punishment may be useful.

'Deterrent punishment is justified for the Determinist by the fact that experience shows that the expectation of punishment

---

¹ 'But does not the free will come in when *I decide* whether to do good or bad things? No; for that has been already *decided for me* by heredity and environment.'—*Not Guilty*, p. 198.—Italics mine.

² p. 162.　　³ *Not Guilty*, pp. 209, 257.

will deter men from committing crimes which they would otherwise have committed. And other sorts of punishment are justified for him by the fact that experience also shows that a man's moral nature may in some cases be improved by influences brought to bear on him during the period of his punishment, or perhaps even by the punishment itself.'[1]

As to the first of these sentences, unfortunately, experience often shows exactly the contrary. Even the expectation of being hung, which in this country is made sure enough by fetching an escaped murderer back across the Atlantic, does not 'deter men from committing' the crime of murder. 'Determinism' thus fails as utterly in fact as it misleads in principle. As to the latter, according to it, no man ever did or ever can commit a 'crime.' A 'Deterministic' murder is unthinkable. Murder, like all real crime, involves intention, i.e. purpose. But purpose involves a free personality. The purpose of a marionette is inconceivable. The 'completely determined' criminal is no criminal at all; any more than the bullet is criminal which occasions the death of a murdered man. As to the second sentence above, it is true; but it is neither 'Determinism' nor the justification of 'Determinism.' It is indeed frank Indeterminism. If there be 'a man's moral nature,' it can only be because his nature is not completely determined. A 'completely determined moral nature' is certainly as unthinkable as a moral steam-engine. 'May in some cases be improved.' True; but why not in all? Here contingency evidently follows on the heels of a free personality. And because it is so, 'influences brought to bear on him' represent the maximum that punishment of any kind can do for a moral being. But this is not 'Determinism,' for,

---

[1] p. 162.

as we have seen emphatically stated, according to it, in the chain of causation in which man is enmeshed, 'the slightest element of uncertainty would be impossible.'

We are further told, however, that—

'A lunatic who suffers from homicidal mania is not hanged for murder, because the expectation of such a punishment would not deter a man in such a condition. It cannot, I imagine, be said that he is not punished because he has not willed the action. He has willed it as much as a sane murderer.'

Of this statement the first sentence is altogether untrue; and the second is half true, and therefore all the more misleading. So far as the lunatic is concerned, it can hardly be suggested that to hang him would deter him from further crime. As to the influence of his hanging upon others, it must be nil, for, *ex hypothesi*, being already 'completely determined,' they could not appreciate it. The true reason why such a lunatic 'is not hanged for murder' is because he has not committed—and indeed could not possibly commit—murder. There is nothing to hang him for. He not only has done no wrong, because to him, as being through disease non-moral, there is no right or wrong, but truly he has done nothing at all. For this is *the one case* in which 'Determinism' is right. He *is* completely determined, because the normal determining factor is in his case absent. Being thus completely determined, there is no 'he' to act, and therefore no responsibility for action. To say that 'he has willed it as much as a sane murderer,' is but a verbal shuffle issuing in a greater untruth. For it assumes that there is no difference between the volition of a sane man and an insane. Whereas the very phrase 'a sane murderer' points to an immeasurable difference. For it suggests by antithesis the possibility of an 'insane murderer'—which is a contradiction in terms. The truth is, that whilst the will of the lunatic is helplessly determined by the immediately preceding motive, the volition of the sane man involves a preceding deliberation, with a balancing of motives, and a selection of one motive to the exclusion of the rest, as the one through which the self is to be expressed in volition. A conscious possession of this power of deliberation and choice, is what we mean by sanity as opposed to insanity. There is no valid comparison of these, any more than night can be compared with day. Nor is there any logical argument from the abnormal to the normal. Moral philosophy rests upon the self-consciousness of the sane, not upon the diseased ignorances of the insane.

Thus we are brought finally to consider 'if any disastrous results would follow from the truth of Determinism.' This phrase, however, is also misleading. It is not merely a question whether 'Determinism' be true or untrue; but whether it be accepted as true and acted upon. Hereupon Dr. Warschauer has very wisely said that—

'In actual life, we are told, many of those who profess Determinist principles are notorious for their strenuous moral calibre, and certainly not open to the charge of laxity. Let that statement be ungrudgingly accepted; what it proves is no more than that prussic acid is entirely harmless—provided it is not taken.'[1]

It has been affirmed above, that there are no practical Determinists; let us see if academic subtlety can suggest anything to disprove the statement. It may freely be acknowledged that so long as 'Determinism' is confined to philosophical treatises, or even limited to the wild assertions of a journalism

---

[1] *Problems of Immanence*, p. 166

which is, on its own principles, irresponsible, not much harm will be done. But what if it were acted on? Prof. McTaggart asserts that—

> 'Many men and many communities have at different times and for long periods altogether accepted Determinism, and I do not think that their morality has been observed to be inferior to that of communities whose general circumstances were similar, but who rejected Determinism.'

Such a statement assumes a knowledge of history to which most of us can make no pretension. But even if it be allowed that Stoics, Mussulmans, Buddhists, and others, should be classed as Determinists, it does not help the present case. For the question which demands unequivocal answer is not whether they 'accepted Determinism,' but whether they acted upon it. If we are to understand by 'Determinism' that which its most prominent advocates to-day so confidently affirm, as illustrated in the quotations above given, i.e. that no man is to be praised or blamed or held responsible for anything he says or does, where is the man, meriting the name, or the community of men past and present, who have treated each other on these lines? There is not one on record; any more than there is one in civilization to-day. If however, we are bidden to reject such 'hard Determinism' as ultramontane, and accept 'soft Determinism' as the legitimate position, it yet remains to be proved that 'many men and many communities' have daily acted on the principle that 'every act of a man is the latest link in an immense chain of causation in which the slightest element of uncertainty is impossible.' Practical life relations leave no room for academical casuistry, so that the actual questions concerning daily conduct are virtually the same for 'soft' as for 'hard Determinism.' If all a man's acts are as completely determined as the links in a chain, it is mere sophistry of speech to talk of praise, or blame, or duty, or responsibility. Assuredly there is no historical record of any normal man, or respectable community, where these necessities and actualities of everyday human intercourse were either denied or ignored. Nor is there a home, a school, an office, a club, a corporation, a society, let alone a church —worthy of the name—where they are rejected or disdained to-day. That is the true measure of the impracticability of Determinedism.

Amongst the excellences, however, which 'soft Determinism' claims, is the greater pity of the 'Determinist' for the sinner. 'It is more natural for me than it is for the Indeterminist to look at sin, like other defects, as a calamity to the man who suffers from it.' Here, however, is only, in short compass, an intolerable assumption and an actual contradiction in terms. Certainly if sin be 'like other defects,' it is not sin at all. It was an old supposition, authoritatively corrected, that a man born blind must be somehow a sinner. The modern correlative appears to be that the sinner is merely a sufferer from some form of blindness. To which it must be said in unmistakable reply, that 'sin' which is only a 'calamity,' is a flat contradiction in terms. As much so as a hot cold, or a round square, or an active passive. In this connexion it is indeed passing strange to be told that—

'The little that we know about the life of Jesus suggests that He combined an invariable intolerance of sin with an almost invariable compassion for the sinner.'[1]

This 'almost' might be altogether omitted, for

---
[1] p. 173.

the Jerusalem over which He wept was largely composed of the Scribes and Pharisees to whom His strongest words of condemnation had been addressed. But what is the inference from this combination? The suggestion is almost outrageous. 'Little' or much, at least we know enough about His methods and doctrines to know that never did any Teacher on earth so treat men as moral beings, capable of choosing right from wrong, and responsible for such power of choice. All His appeals to men assumed that they were not, either as to character or conduct, completely determined by heredity and environment, but were capable, in response to His appeal, of modifying the former and overcoming the latter. 'Determinism,' hard or soft, has certainly nothing to gain from the life and character and work of the Christ of the Gospels. Indeed, on 'Deterministic' principles, there is no more occasion to revere the name of Jesus—or Socrates, or Buddha—than that of Charles Peace. For as Dr. Warschauer has well said: 'Think of Him simply as the product of a compelling force, unable to act otherwise than as He did, and at one stroke, all that moved us to gratitude, to admiration, all that appealed to us most deeply, is gone.'[1] How far He was, in His own consciousness, from being 'completely determined,' His unmistakable assertion unequivocally declares:—'No man taketh My life from Me; I have power to lay it down, and I have power to take it again.' Whilst it is beyond all controversy He ever treated all men as on the same plane of moral responsibility as Himself.

Yet again—

'It is said that it would be intolerable for a man to believe that perhaps he was inevitably determined to be wicked in the future.'[2]

---

[1] *Problems of Immanence*, p. 168. [2] p. 173.

But who says so? Certainly not 'Libertarians.' They would say, and with sufficient reason, that it is *impossible* for a man to believe any such thing. It is inexplicable how from such high quarters self-contradictions like these can be suggested. There never was, or will be, or could be, under any circumstances in earth or hell, a being 'inevitably determined to be wicked.' There is no more sense in such strong sounding words than in a child's prattle about its 'naughty' doll. There is some truth in the old adage that 'a bad workman quarrels with his tools,' but surely no bad workman was ever such a fool to boot as to call the chisel whose work he inevitably determines, a 'wicked' chisel. Yet the analogous absurdity runs on unblushingly through paragraph after paragraph of this special pleading for 'soft Determinism.' Thus—

'Whether virtue or wickedness comes to a man from his own uncaused caprice in the future, or from the eternal nature of the universe, it will still be virtue or wickedness.'[1]

With all respect, so long as reason remains, it will be nothing of the sort. The insinuation about 'uncaused caprice,' we will consider in due course. But as to 'virtue or wickedness,' coming to a man 'from the nature of the universe,' it is difficult to speak calmly of such a philosophical monstrosity. One might as well look for a character to fall into one's lap, like an apple from a tree. The notion of virtue or wickedness coming to a man as a lump of something from outside of himself, is so grotesque in its absurdity as to be beyond polite criticism.[2]

---

[1] p. 174.
[2] It is not the custom to appeal to the New Testament on matters of philosophy, but the words of Jesus in Mark vii. 18–23 are as irrefragable as unmistakable in this regard.

In his determination to show that morally the 'Determinist is no worse off than the Indeterminist,' the Professor makes two more points which call for notice—

'If a man desires food, or love, or anything else, the important question for him is whether he will get it or fail to get it ; anyway his success or failure can be explained as the inevitable result of what has preceded.'[1]

Here again academic subtlety stultifies itself. For to say nothing of the strangeness of a philosophy which in such a case lumps together 'food' and 'love' as if they were of the same order, and on a par with 'anything else,' one must be permitted in the name of all reality to contradict flatly the assertion thus made. So far as a man's stomach is concerned, it may not matter much how he gets it filled, so long as he does not starve. But as to 'love,' it matters everything, not nothing, whether his success is or is not the 'inevitable result' of antecedents. For if it be such a result, then when he has got it, it is absolutely worthless. All talk about successfully getting 'love' as an inevitable result, is so much pitiful nonsense. One might as well call upon a man to rejoice that a gramophone calls him a 'darling.' So that to say, 'The question as to the manner in which the result has been determined may have a theoretical interest, but is of no practical importance,' is the very opposite of the truth. It is of the very greatest 'practical importance' that love should be love ; and that it never can be as an 'inevitable result' of antecedents. Inevitable 'love' is a pitiful contradiction in terms, heart mockery and philosophical delusion in one.

Yet again. Kant, we are told, objected to the

---

[1] p. 174.

self-determined freedom of Leibnitz's Monads, that it would be 'nothing better than the freedom of a roasting-jack which also when it is once wound up, performs its motions of itself.' Upon this the Professor remarks that Kant is wrong, because—

'If a roasting-jack goes right, a joint is well cooked; if it goes wrong, it is badly cooked. If a will goes right, the man is virtuous; if it goes wrong, he is wicked.'

Verily this is a strange philosophical performance. First, the rightness of a piece of clockwork is put upon the same level as the rightness of a will which is to decide between virtue and vice! Then the will, upon which this momentous decision turns, is represented as being wound up once for all like a roasting-jack! Then finally, and to crown all, the virtuousness of a man is said to depend upon whether his will 'goes right' through being thus wound up or not! After which we are further informed that

'It must also be remembered that a man may be held to be free because he possesses, in many cases, what I have called freedom of self-direction. A roasting-jack cannot have this because it has no will.'

But (i), if the will of a man simply 'goes right' as the inevitable result of antecedents, that is neither more nor less than being wound up as the roasting-jack; in which case the latter has a will quite as much as the man. (ii) If 'in many cases' a man has freedom of self-direction, why not in all? Are there some men who are half roasting-jacks? (iii) If, in any cases, men have freedom of self-direction, then not only must roasting-jacks be ruled out of comparison, but 'Determinism' is at an end. The man who in any degree is self-determined, i.e. determined only by himself, is neither the inevitable result of antecedents, nor 'completely determined'; which is the whole matter under dispute.

We might well here conclude our scrutiny of this attempt to make 'Determinism' consistent with morality. But inasmuch as the writer deems it necessary to close his treatise with an attack upon Indeterminism, in this same regard, we have no choice but to follow him to the end. Amongst certain arguments then, against Indeterminism, we are told that—

'In the first place, Indeterminism is inconsistent with the validity of morality. Judgements of obligation are the judgements which approve or condemn the person who wills a certain thing. The approval or condemnation of the agent is essential to morality.'

With the latter sentences, no moral philosopher will quarrel, but how does the first sentence flow from them? In a strange way indeed. 'The whole fabric of morality would be upset, if our approval or condemnation of a man for his volitions had no right to last longer than the volition itself.' Perfectly true, but what is to hinder the 'Libertarian' from carrying out this canon of morality? In the view of the Professor, this—

'According to the Indeterminist the volition in each case is a perfectly indetermined choice between two motives. When the volition is over, it has ceased to exist, and it has not, on the Indeterminist theory, left a permanent cause behind it. For, according to that theory, it has no permanent cause at all. Directly Nero has ceased to think of a murder committed by him, nothing at all connected with it remains in his moral nature, except the mere abstract power of indetermined choice. How then can the Indeterminist venture to call Nero a wicked man between his crimes?'[1]

The importance of the issues at stake demands

---

[1] p. 179.

definite reply to these allegations before examining the alleged explanation of the 'Determinist.' (i) For the Indeterminist, the choice is *not* necessarily between two motives. There may be a dozen motives, all operating together, and all of different degree as well as kinds. (ii) An 'indetermined choice' is useless tautology. There can be no other choice. A 'determined' choice is a contradiction in terms. (iii) A 'perfectly indetermined choice' is perfectly untrue. There may be many and great influences brought to bear upon the choice, both from within and from without, from the past and from the present. Their joint force may approach determination, but will never actually become such, even as a bird in a small cage has its motions largely determined, but so long as it is a living bird, not wholly. (iv) A volition, if it be such, is the expression of a real and active self, which is the permanent and sufficient cause of all volitions and is 'left behind' in every case, as really as an author is left behind after writing a book. It is entirely false to represent the volition as having, according to Indeterminism, no 'permanent cause' at all. The Nero who is 'eating his dinner half an hour after ordering a murder,' is still the same Nero, and it is worse than absurd to say that 'nothing at all connected with the murder remains in his moral nature.' That could only be true if human personality consisted of a mere series of successive and incoherent thrills of consciousness. But the continuity of the ego is as real as it is undemonstrable. It is undemonstrable because it needs no demonstration. Any attempt to demonstrate it must assume it to start with, for an incoherent demonstration is unthinkable. Experience is sufficient guarantee of its reality. The Indeterminist calls Nero a 'wicked man,' because the glutton or the artist, at any moment, is the same personality as the past murderer. The person who is now consuming his dinner, or reciting an epic, is the very person, who an hour or a year ago willed the crime. So long as the human mind retains its consciousness of continuity, that is whilst sanity remains, there is neither room nor need for any metaphysical sophistry to obscure that conclusion. If we may not assume such continuity of personality, all reasoning is useless, for the being who reads this page may be another being by the time he reaches the next. Wherein, then, lies the vaunted superiority of 'Determinism' in the case before us? We learn that—

'According to it, the volitions of each man spring from his character, and are the inevitable result of that character when it finds itself in a certain situation. The approval or condemnation of the agent is based on the belief that the character, indicated by the past acts, survives in the present and is ready on appropriate occasions to manifest itself in similar acts. Nero is condemned in the present, because he has still the character which will probably cause him, when he is tired of eating, to amuse himself with another murder.'[1]

Plainly, then, what the 'Libertarian' calls personality, the 'Determinist' terms character. But we are certainly entitled to ask, How can there be a character, if personality be ignored or denied? Just as we are warranted in assuming that every personality not only has character, but has made that character for itself in the past, and inalienably retains it for the present. This, indeed, is really conceded in the very words employed by the writer here with opposite intent. 'Nero,' it seems, 'has still the

---

[1] p. 178.

character' when he afterwards eats, which he had when he murdered. Just so. But Nero is a personality whose character is not only 'indicated by the past acts,' but was *created* by those past acts, and therefore, being the very incarnation and expression of himself, remains whilst Nero remains. But we may ask further, what does our 'Determinist' mean by saying that Nero's 'character will probably cause him' to murder in the future. There is no place for 'probably' in the vocabulary of Determinedism. If Nero's character 'caused'—that is compelled—him to kill some one yesterday, it will certainly, indeed it must, cause him to do the same to-morrow. Though it must be added that if Nero's personality and Nero's character are so distinctly separable that the latter, and not the former, is the real agent, whilst it was also 'completely determined' beforehand, then Nero was and is utterly incapable of 'murder,' as much so as the knife with which a man is stabbed. He and it alike are tools, and nothing more. All which exhibits once more the eviscerating influence of 'Determinism' on human nature. To it, personality is nothing. A man is but a hollow shell of antecedents and consequences. A physical character is resistlessly riveted by heredity and environment on to an illusion, and the resulting wholly passive, never-acting, unthinkable monstrosity is called a 'moral being.' But the name no more fits the thing than the anatomy of a man is adapted to the low organization of an amoeba.

The last and most hackneyed objection to the true theory of moral freedom is that Indeterminism 'admits of no certainty of prediction.' It is a strange objection after all, seeing that 'for all practical purposes the Determinist must admit the same.' This acknowledgement we have just seen illustrated in the statement that Nero's character will 'probably' compel him after his dinner to further acts of cruelty. But a probable determination is a contradiction in terms. Its suggestion only serves to show that the theory involved will not work. Now, however, we are informed that—

'If Indeterminism is true, there is no justification whatever for making any statement as to the probability of future volitions. The Indeterminist theory assumes that in every case the choice between motives is undetermined. There cannot, then, be the slightest probability that this choice will be of one motive rather than another. There is no reason to suppose that similar circumstances will be followed by similar results, unless the circumstances determine the results, or the circumstances and the results are both determined by the same cause.'[1]

It would be difficult to find four sentences, in any attempt at philosophical statement, more fallacious. (i) The first sentence, as intimated above, completely ignores the reality and continuity of personality. 'Our only ground,' we are told, 'for supposing that a particular man will choose in a particular way' is that he has done so before. But if 'Determinism' be true, he has never chosen at all. It is but verbal mockery covering a mental shuffle, to say that a man chooses one of two or more alternatives, when he is compelled by antecedents to whatever decision is made. One might as well say that the criminal under death sentence chooses to be hanged. Until and unless the continuity of human personality be disproved, and that by the very nature of the case is utterly impossible—for there could be no experience to appeal to—it is just as natural and

---

[1] pp. 182, 183.

permissible to infer the probability of future volitions as it is impossible to forecast their certainty. It is quite true, as Dr. James Ward has said, that this freedom of personality whose results can be generally, but cannot be exactly predicted, 'lets contingency into the very heart of things,' but his further remark thereupon is as philosophically sound as pragmatically undeniable—

'It is true; I not only admit it, but contend that any other world would be meaningless. For the contingency is not that of chance but of freedom.'[1]

Such words deserve, for truth's sake, to be writ large in the annals of philosophy.

(ii) The second sentence is but the old half-truth which has already been answered to the uttermost. The choice between motives is, necessarily, undetermined by mere antecedents, physical or mental. A determined choice is an absurdity. But it is not 'undetermined' in the sense that it involves either a motiveless volition or a motiveless choice. As Prof. Lloyd Morgan says, 'it is the self which determines.' The fact that we cannot track out this self-determination amidst motives to a last analysis, no more disproves its reality, than the fact that we cannot define life turns us into corpses. Hereupon well speaks the acute student mentioned above, himself an avowed 'Determinist'—

'At a point in the obscure recesses of the brain, a dark chasm in which we faintly flash the poor lanterns of our search, we lose the sequence of events. In the human mind there is a broad vestibule in which the conflicting stimuli to action must wait and struggle for dominance. We are quite ignorant of the way in which one motive overpowers the rest.'[2]

---

[1] *Naturalism and Agnosticism*, Vol. II, p. 281.
[2] Mr. J. McCabe, *R.P.A. Annual*, 1910, p. 64.

(iii) The third sentence falls with the first. There is every 'probability' that the personality which has ever since it was conscious of itself been making its own character, will continue to act in accordance with that character, unless something which cannot be foreseen should happen to create new influences under which the free personality may act differently. (iv) This last sentence may be quite true, but it is equally irrelevant, because 'circumstances,' *per se*, are wholly impersonal, and belong to the realm concerning which there is no dispute. When an engine with the steam up stands upon the line, we have no doubt whatever that if the lever be moved in a certain way, the engine will move as it always has done under similar circumstances. But the 'if' introduces an unmistakable element of contingency. For that depends upon the will of the driver, and it neither is, nor ever can be, a matter of certainty that he will move the lever, even in obedience to a distinct signal, or command from a superior. He may; under ordinary circumstances it is probable that he will. Beyond that we can never go in prediction. Whence we conclude, as from a typical instance, that Determinedism is the true account of action in regard to things, and Indeterminism the truth and the only truth in regard to persons. But the philosophical system which demands of us that we should jettison our personality, and be content to regard ourselves as merely inert substance under hydraulic pressure, or corks upon the waters of circumstance,[1] dooms itself to be ruled out of court by all self-respecting men.

---

[1] 'Man that is born of woman is little better than a shuttlecock propelled by battledores of circumstances, even as the sparks fly upwards.' So writes *The Clarion*. The spectacle of sparks 'battledored' upwards would certainly be new, but the figures employed are instructive, as showing the trend of popular

There is no need to comment further upon the absurdity of the suggestion that 'on Indeterminist principles, it is just as likely that the majority of Londoners will burn themselves alive to-morrow, as it is that they will partake of food.'[1] If the general principle be laid down that 'when men commit suicide, or eat or hang other men, their action depends on their volition, and their volition cannot be anticipated,' it can only be carried to the extremes suggested above, by ignoring alike the reality, the continuity, and the self-created character of personality. It is quite true that to do this would 'reduce our life to a general chaos'; but by the time men are persuaded that they are no longer persons but things, life will already be such a chaos as to be not worth preserving.

The same principle is further illustrated in the closing words of the treatise we are examining. In regard to punishment, it is affirmed that even if it be justified—which it certainly could not be on 'Deterministic' principles, for it would be monstrous as well as useless to punish a pen for the bad words written by it through complete determination—'yet even here the punishment could not be carried out if the jailers decided one morning to release all the prisoners. And on the Indeterminist theory, they are just as likely to will this as they are to will anything else.' Which is absurd—for it assumes that whilst certain jailers secure the prisoners in the evening, others altogether, although inhabiting the same

---

journalism. Even in such a case, however, it is more than interesting to see how manhood revolts against thinghood, in the silent protest of the adjective. Man is 'little better.' At least that must mean a little better; and then the ancient question opens out afresh—How much better?

[1] *Some Dogmas of Religion*, p. 184.

bodies, release the prisoners in the morning. That is a reduction to chaos indeed; for it would involve that having once met a friend we are sure never to meet him again, because on another occasion another set of circumstances will have transformed the former automaton into a different one. And when it is added that—'All other non-vindictive punishments will be completely absurd. For they all depend on judgements as to the probability of future volitions'; the reply is that to the 'Libertarian' this probability is quite as valid as for the 'Determinist.'

But the unwarranted dogmatisms to which not only hard but soft 'Determinism' commits itself, are further illustrated here. We all believe that (i) a man is less likely to will to commit a crime if he knows there will ensue for him painful consequences. Also (ii) that a man 'who has been subjected to certain influences is less likely to desire to commit crime.' But the Professor then takes it upon himself to affirm that 'if Indeterminism is true, both these beliefs are absolutely baseless.' To which the 'Libertarian' is bound to reply that such an assertion is 'absolutely baseless.' There is no rational warrant for it whatever. The man who is conscious enough of freedom to acknowledge personal responsibility for his actions, is the very man who will most of all appreciate the fact that painful consequences await his doing what he knows to be wrong, and, knowing that he will himself have caused those consequences, is correspondingly less likely to will that wrong. Assuredly also he is least likely to 'desire to commit crime' if he has been 'subjected to certain influences' in the opposite direction. It is on 'Determinist' lines, which as above demonstrated ought to be truly and always called Determinedist lines, that the man is likely to be impervious alike to consequences and to influences. For in both cases, not only is 'crime' in the abstract utterly impossible, if a man's actions are 'completely determined'; but if he is brought really to believe that he is completely determined, then he may well deem the action as inevitable as the consequences, and dismiss all counteracting influences as but unavailing mockery.

Finally, as to 'vindictive punishment,' the marvellous assertion is made that it has been 'sometimes taken as the chief support of Indeterminism'! Assuredly no advocate of moral freedom worth regarding has ever committed himself to such a statement. But the closing sentences that follow are even more fallacious.

'Yet vindictive punishment does stand in a specially close relation to Indeterminism. For at least we can say that in those cases where the punishment begins before the sin ceases, vindictive punishment is not more absurd for the Determinist than it is for other people.'[1]

Indeed, it is really worse than absurd. For to the Determinedist 'sin' never begins, and never can begin; for which reason it can never cease. The man whose every action is 'completely determined' can no more 'sin' than the hands of a clock; and to punish a man for that which he was completely determined, i.e. absolutely compelled to do, would be indeed as utterly unjust as vindictive. It is not nearly enough to say that from the 'Deterministic' standpoint all vindictive punishment is 'absurd'; it is much worse. For although it would be absurd enough to smash a barometer on the ground that it was

---

[1] p. 185.

misleading, the barometer at least has no feelings. But the 'hardest' Determinist cannot deny that a man has feelings, and these make possible an amount of suffering under the 'vindictive' punishment which would be in his case as cruel as absurd. If, moreover, Determinedism admitted of moral action, such punishment would be as wicked as cruel. For the 'Libertarian,' on the other hand, there is no absurdity at all ' in those cases where the punishment begins before the sin ceases.' For him, all real sin merits punishment on the ground that it ought not to have been, and need not have been but for the man himself. The fact that it has been, is due to the personal choice of the sinner, who is therefore responsible alike for the actual wrong and for the consequences that flow from it, whether to himself or to others. As to when the punishment begins, that is utterly irrelevant. Real sin is not merely an act, but an attitude of character which does not cease when the action expressing it has become a past event. It is the work of a personality whose continuity is never broken. Whence it follows that sin never ceases until it is repented of, i.e. until the attitude which was embodied in the act is changed. But, of course, for the 'Determinist' there neither need be nor can be repentance. That which could not but be, can never occasion remorse. That which was completely determined, can never be matter for shame. Every attitude throughout a man's whole life has been but a ' link in an immense chain of causation in which the slightest element of uncertainty would be impossible.' Change in such a chain is unthinkable. To suggest repentance in such a case, would be as absurd as to bid the earth repent for too severe winters in this country. To reply that a man has a will and the earth has not, is merely a verbal shuffle, if, as is so strongly reiterated, it is true that the 'actions of a man's will are as mathematically determined at his birth as are the motions of a planet in its orbit.'

On the whole, therefore, the conclusion at which we arrive is that 'soft' Determinism has no moral advantage whatever over 'hard' Determinism. For the softest assertion it can consistently make is, as we have seen, that each man is completely determined. There is in such a theory nothing, intellectual or moral any more than physical, to differentiate it from absolute determination, or fatalism, or automatism. It must ever be philosophical mockery to credit man with a will and then insist that his will is nothing but the helpless transmitter of irresistible antecedents. The will which is but a kind of telegraph wire in the brain, is no will at all. Whether Determinism be 'hard' or 'soft,' the volition, which involves no new creation through a genuine choice, is but a misnomer. It is no more a true volition than an automaton is a true man. And the man without a will—that is a power of genuine choice between alternatives, under the control of a definite personality—is no man at all. Such a creature is but a biped, not deserving the epithet ' he,' being in fact possessed of less internal powers than not a few quadrupeds—a mummy of the philosophical schools, rather than a man amongst men. In this, at all events, the plain words of Mr. H. G. Wells merit not only endorsement but repetition—

'I regard myself as a free responsible person, amongst free responsible persons.'[1]

---

[1] *First and Last Things*, p. 52.

(iv) *As to Psychology*

We come now to consider a little more closely the witness of normal human consciousness to the falsity of the main principles of 'Determinism.' Here the fictitious distinction between soft and hard Determinism need no longer concern us, because the questions involved are independent of the difference between them. These questions are simply two: (i) Does my consciousness testify to my freedom of choice between alternatives? and (ii) Is such consciousness to be regarded as reliable?

(i) As to the former, two things are at once manifest; first, that it is a purely psychological question, in that it is solely concerned with the facts of self-consciousness; and secondly, that no individual can answer for more than one personality. The only way, therefore, to obtain any affirmation or denial of a general attitude hereupon, is to collect testimonies from competent quarters. Every sane man is, indeed, in this case, a competent source, but the deliberate assertion of careful thinkers should be of more value than the simple expression of experience, by reason of an element of critical reflection added to a definite consciousness. It would be difficult to find language more explicit than that in which such consciousness of real freedom has been acknowledged by thinkers of many schools. The varied ways, moreover, in which this conviction is expressed, are both interesting and instructive.

There is no need to dwell upon the testimony of Kant, whose renowned 'kategorical imperative' carries with it the consciousness of moral freedom. 'The law which requires personal control, implies the power of personal control.' If I ought, then I can.

And the 'hardest' Determinist cannot deny the presence of a sense of oughtness in the normal human being. But when we come to so vigorous a Necessitarian as John Stuart Mill, his acknowledgement of the actuality of this consciousness of freedom is especially emphatic.

'This feeling of being able to modify our own character, if we wish, is itself the feeling of moral freedom which we are conscious of. A person feels morally free, who feels that his habits and temptations are not his masters, but he theirs; who, even in yielding, knows that he could resist; that were he desirous of altogether throwing them off there would not be required for the purpose a stronger desire than he knows himself capable of feeling.'[1]

One knows not which is the more striking, in such a testimony, the clear accuracy with which the writer portrays the unquestionable experience of the normal individual, or the wonder that with such an acknowledgement on his lips, he should still consider himself a Necessitarian.

The names of Profs. Huxley and Tyndall were generally associated, during the last quarter of the nineteenth century, with a very pronounced doctrine of Determinism, yet neither of them ventured to question the reality of the consciousness of a moral freedom which involved and justified moral responsibility. Thus the former, besides acknowledging that it 'is a matter of experimental fact that man is a machine capable of adjusting itself within certain limits '—which is, when strictly interpreted, as Dr. Warschauer has well said, ' precisely what no machine ever was or ever will be '[2]—proceeds on the same page to say—

'I protest that if some great power would agree to make me

---

[1] *Logic*, Book VI, ch. ii.
[2] *Anti-Nunquam*, p. 55. For the possibility of applying this to certain complex machines, see p. 347 later.

always think what is true and do what is right, on condition of being turned into a sort of clock and wound up every morning before I got out of bed, I should instantly close with the offer.'

As to which deliverance, one may forgive the learned Professor the absurdity of suggesting a clock that could do 'right,' on the ground of the magnitude of the 'if,' which sufficiently expresses his own consciousness that such a transition from freedom to constraint was to him for ever impossible. 'The only freedom' he adds, 'I care about is the freedom to do right; the freedom to do wrong I am ready to part with on the cheapest terms to any one who will take it out of me.' Whether this is the more pathetic or comic, may be left undecided. The double truth which is driven home is that we know the inseparability of the freedom to do right and wrong, as well as the writer knew that the freedom to do wrong had not been, and could not be, taken from him.

Prof. Tyndall, again, in his *Fragments of Science*, has, elsewhere, left no doubt possible as to his 'Deterministic' leanings. 'Processes in the conduct or regulation of which I had no share, have made me what I am.' Yet he did not leave us the necessary task of contradicting him, but virtually contradicted himself in the same essay, when, referring to a lecture by George Dawson, he avers that 'no speculations regarding the freedom of the will could alter the fact that the words of that young man did me good.'[2] Surely the more thoroughly these last three words are analysed, the more unequivocally do they attest the consciousness of moral freedom. It would be absolutely impossible for the words of any ethical teacher, were he Demosthenes and Chrysostom in

---

[1] *Lay Sermons*, p. 296.
[2] *Fragments of Science*, Vol. II, pp. 364, 367.

one, to do good, in the Professor's sense, to any Huxleyan clock, or any machine of Mark Twain's devising.

The witness of science and philosophy is to the same effect in the lips of many of their ablest exponents. Prof. Poynting's emphatic testimony has been given above. The convictions of the eminent Principal of Birmingham University are so well known as to need no repetition here. But the avowals of one or two less known writers deserve notice. Thus, Dr. F. C. S. Schiller writes in the *Oxford and Cambridge Review*—

'The alternatives which appeal to us and are real for us, are never numerous. Our character, our circumstances, our history, our habits, our ideals and notions of what is good, do by far the greater part of the selection and immensely narrow down the field of abstract possibility. This is a simple fact of direct observation. But it is no less obvious that though all these forces determine by far the greater part, say nine-tenths of our conduct, and form a fairly rigid framework which our " freedom " presupposes, and with which and upon which it operates, yet they nevertheless do *not* determine everything, but allow scope for apparently free choices which are accompanied by a heightened and peculiar sense of power and responsibility.'[1]

Even so stout a 'Determinist' as Mr. Bertrand Russell, we have seen above, concedes as much—

'When several alternatives present themselves, it is certain that we can both do which we choose and choose which we will. In this sense all the alternatives are possible.'

The certainty here acknowledged is that of our own indefeasible consciousness, from which there can be no appeal. Prof. McTaggart also, for all his sapping and mining of Indeterminism, makes no attempt to deny the same actuality.

'To prove that we have this sense of freedom an appeal must

---

[1] September, 1907, p. 68.

be made to introspection. The fact to which the appeal is made will scarcely be denied. When I make a false accusation, or refrain from making it, when I draw my chair nearer to the fire, or leave it where it was, I have a feeling of freedom in my decision which I do not have when I am thrown from a horse, or when I abstain from leaping over St. Paul's. Now it is said this feeling of freedom is incompatible with complete determination, and the only legitimate inference is that the decision which is accompanied by the feeling of freedom is one in which I am not completely determined. I believe that we have this feeling of freedom because we are in fact free in these cases.'[1]

But in so plain and elemental a matter as self-consciousness, there is no reason why we should listen in preference to 'Determinists.' A few statements, therefore, from others no less competent or impartial, may well be borne in mind. Nothing has happened since Dr. McCosh wrote his *Intuitions of Mind*, to shake the validity of his assertion that—

'In every act of will there is an essential freedom of which the mind is conscious. The possession of a free will is thus one of the elements which go to constitute man a moral and responsible agent. This truth is revealed to us by immediate consciousness, and is not to be set aside by any other truth whatever.'[2]

Even more emphatically is the same conviction expressed by Dr. Andrew Seth—

'In the purposive I will, each man is real, and is immediately conscious of his own reality. Whatever else may or may not be real, this is real. This is the fundamental belief around which scepticism may weave its maze of doubts and logical puzzles, but from which it is eventually powerless to dislodge us, because no argument can affect an immediate certainty, a certainty moreover on which our whole view of the universe depends.'[3]

Prof. Calderwood, again, in his well-known *Handbook of Moral Philosophy*, the value of which after

---
[1] *Some Dogmas of Religion*, p. 147. [2] iv. 308.
[3] *Two Lectures on Theism*, p. 46.

thirty years remains substantially undiminished, states the case thus—

'Consciousness discovers self-determination in our activity. Consciousness of self-determination is consciousness of power exercised by me over my mental activity, and over physical organs which belong to me. Self is thus known, not merely as intelligence, but as power. I am a self-conscious, intelligent, self-determining power. I am a person, not a mere living organism, and not a mere thing. The hypothesis of constrained action of will is invalidated on the ground of inconsistency with the recognized facts of consciousness. If we cannot plead the testimony of consciousness as to the manner in which will is brought into exercise, we have its clear testimony as to the fact of the will's control over the other powers of mind.'[1]

That Dr. Illingworth should insist on this is not surprising, but there is no rational ground for discounting his witness.

'Our self-consciousness involves freedom, or the power of self-determination. My character is only the momentum which I have gained by a number of past acts of choice, that is, by my own past use of my freedom; and even so I am conscious that at the moment I *can* counteract my character, though morally certain that I have no intention so to do. This is briefly what we mean by free will; and it is a fact of immediate and universal consciousness; that is, of my own consciousness corroborated by the like experience of all other men. The sense of freedom is an immediate part of my consciousness. I cannot be conscious without it. I cannot tear it out. It lies at the very root of myself, and claims, with self-evidence, to be something *sui generis*, something unique.'[2]

As a matter of fact, our consciousness of freedom does not consist in the mere sense of willing what we do, but in the contemporaneous sense that we could wish or will otherwise, if we chose. Dr. C. D'Arcy summarizes the matter thus—

'The truth is, free will is based on man's consciousness of his

---

[1] pp. 12, 189.
[2] *Personality, Human and Divine*, cheap edition, p. 25.

moral nature. It represents not any speculative theory, but one of the great facts which every theory of things must explain or perish. It is our ordinary way of expressing the volitional side of man's selfhood. In volition everything has to be ultimately referred to self-determination. In other words, the will is free. There can be no doubt that this argument is unanswerable. Whatever depends upon consciousness, depends, ultimately, upon the self. The self is the presupposition of consciousness. There is no getting behind it. When it is shown that will to be will must be conscious, the battle against Determinism has been won. In strictness it is unnecessary to go a single step further.'[1]

The necessity to reckon with the manifest limitations of will, upon which Dr. D'Arcy proceeds to dwell, does not affect this testimony of self-consciousness. So we may further mark what Dr. Rudolf Otto points out, in his valuable work on *Naturalism and Religion*.

'The consciousness of the ego leads us naturally to the consciousness of freedom. That we will, and what it is to will, cannot really be demonstrated at all, or defended against attacks. It simply is so. It is a fundamental psychological fact which can only be proved by being experienced. And the theories opposed to freedom of the will cannot be refuted in any way except by simply saying that they are false. They do not describe what really takes place. We cannot demonstrate what will is, we can only make it clear to ourselves by performing an act of will and observing ourselves in the doing of it.'[2]

It would be easy enough to multiply deliberate judgements to the same effect from all quarters, but it will suffice to specify only one or two more, taken from writers least disposed to endorse those religious sanctions which are often said to be the ultimate source of the tendency of man in general, to accept free will as the true account of human actions. Thus, Mr. Samuel Laing, well known as a

---

[1] *Idealism and Theology*, pp. 107, 110.   [2] pp. 317, 319.

'Rationalist' author, expresses himself with refreshing plainness—

'Some philosophers have come to the conclusion that man and all animals are but mechanical automata, cleverly constructed to work in a certain way, fitting in with the preordained course of natural phenomena. But no amount of philosophic reasoning can ever make us believe that we are altogether machines, and not free agents. It runs off us like water from a duck's back, and leaves us in presence of the intuitive conviction that to a great extent "man is man and master of his fate."'

How plainly also Mr. H. G. Wells speaks to the same effect, we have already noted.

Still more interesting is the frank avowal of Mr. Joseph McCabe, who writes from the unmistakable standpoint of anti-Christian 'Determinism.' In his vigorous defence of Prof. Haeckel's Monism, he acknowledges that—

'A man can control his actions to a great extent, and will to that extent be responsible for them. On that we have the witness of consciousness. That which formerly went by the name of freedom is disproved by science. But the fact remains —and it is a scientific and a psychological fact—that we are conscious of being able to influence our character and our actions, and so we cannot deny our responsibility within limits.'[1]

Sometimes indeed a flash of poetic inspiration and expression reveals more than all the efforts of analytical philsophy. But without calling up again Browning's hero, who 'never turned his back, but marched breast forward'; or repeating, at the moment, the song that Tennyson's Enid sang to her wheel; let us appreciate the words of a less known but surely real poet, which thoroughly deserve their not infrequent quotation—

>   Out of the night that covers me,
>   Black as the pit from pole to pole,
>   I thank whatever gods there be
>   For my unconquerable soul.

---

[1] *Haeckel's Critics Answered*, pp. 60, 118.

> In the fell clutch of circumstance,
>   I have not winced nor cried aloud;
> Beneath the bludgeonings of chance
>   My head is bloody, but unbowed.
>
> Beyond this place of wrath and tears
>   Looms but the horror of the shade,
> And yet the menace of the years
>   Finds, and shall find, me unafraid.
>
> It matters not how strait the gate,
>   How charged with punishments the scroll;
> I am the master of my fate,
>   I am the captain of my soul.[1]

Seeing, then, that these expressions of experience are so unequivocal and unmistakable, as well as so true to the undeniable consciousness of mankind in general, why have they not been accepted as final? Why should they not now be regarded as a decisive answer to the question whether human will is free, or at all events free enough to constitute him both moral and responsible? The modern reply issues undoubtedly from the spread of that scientific knowledge which is apparently endeavouring more and more to bring everything in the universe, in the mental no less than in the physical realm, within the grip of what are called 'iron laws.' In view of the definite quotations sufficiently given above, it is not necessary further to define this attitude. The way in which the case is stated may be typically illustrated from Dr. Callaway—

> Science, steadily reducing one domain of nature after another to the reign of law, still finds itself confronted with one of the oldest and most inveterate of barriers, the belief in free will. It is in the citadel of free will that the last stand is being made. "In our spontaneity," we are told, "at least there remains

---

[1] Mr. W. E. Henley.

free will." This is the arrogant pretension which an ancient metaphysic is still loudly proclaiming.'[1]

Seeing that the belief in free will is ineradicable from the normal human consciousness, it is small wonder that it should be ' one of the oldest and most inveterate of barriers,' to the theory which would put an end for ever to the manhood of mankind. We are, indeed, well warranted in asking, with Dr. F. C. S. Schiller, ' Why, then, should we refuse to acknowledge this fact ? Why should we not admit it as conclusive evidence that the choices which seem real, are real ?'

It must be confessed that the replies to this query come from serious sources, and at first sight appear truly formidable. When such an authority as Prof. Sidgwick acknowledges that the verdict of consciousness is against 'Determinism,' but that it may, after all, be illusory, we are at least compelled to look this possibility of illusion in the face. Then, at once, we are transported back to Spinoza and his suggestion that the illusion may be dissected into its component parts, viz. that men are aware of their desires, but are not aware of the causes by which those desires are determined. Now a moment's clear reflection shows that this does not even touch the point at issue. It is not a mere case of our being aware of our desires, but of being aware—as we have seen even Mr. J. S. Mill acknowledge—that our desires, be they ever so strong, are subservient to us and not we to them. The very fact that I am conscious of a desire, brings with it the indefeasible consciousness that it is but a desire; and it need not be, cannot be, a volition without my own conscious and unmistakable permission.

---

[1] *Agnostic Annual*, 1905, p. 17.

How it comes to be a desire, is here irrelevant; as is also the number, or variety, or intensity, of all desires. What we do not know is no contradiction of what we do know, viz. that the motive which may truly and strongly be constituted by desire, cannot, and does not, pass into volition without the assent of the self-conscious subject.

So we come to Hume as rehabilitated by Huxley.[1] The latter indeed waxes quite scornful in his collaboration.

'The last asylum of the hard-pressed advocate of the doctrine of uncaused volition, is usually that, argue as you like, he has a profound and ineradicable consciousness of what he calls the freedom of the will. But Hume follows him even here, though only in a note, as if he thought the extinction of so transparent a sophism hardly worthy of the dignity of his text.'

It may be so, but is as such, only another instance of the blind beating the air with words which characterizes this whole controversy more than any other that has ever occupied the minds of men. If any 'sophism' in philosophy calls for 'extinction,' it is the one so calmly assumed here, i.e. that believers in free will are thereby committed to a 'doctrine of uncaused volition.' Hume's own words are here truly applicable, i.e. that 'when any opinion leads to absurdity it is certainly false.' And this absurd attribution is so false that it really ought never more to be repeated. No 'Determinist' living insists upon the necessity of a sufficient cause more than the believer in free agency, when the view of the latter is stated truly instead of being cartooned. Meanwhile, Hume's own explanation of our consciousness of freedom, is no explanation at all.

---

[1] See *Hume*, by Prof. Huxley, pp. 183–96 (Macmillan, *English Men of Letters*).

'We feel that our actions are subject to our will on most occasions, and imagine we feel that the will itself is subject to nothing, because when by a denial of it we are provoked to try, we feel that it moves easily every way and produces an image of itself even on that side of which it did not settle. We consider not that the fantastical desire of showing liberty is here the motive of our actions.'

Evidently the writer, with all his acuteness, fails to see that this very 'fantastical desire' of showing liberty, is itself a veritable illustration of the actuality of that liberty. For it could not possibly become a motive for any action, real or imaginary, without the definite assent of the self-conscious subject. And it is the reality of this act of assent of which we are as conscious as of our own being. We have, however, yet to deal with Huxley's special buttressing of Hume.

'The passionate assertion of the consciousness of their freedom which is the favourite refuge of the opponents of the doctrine of necessity, is mere futility, for nobody denies it. What they really have to do if they would upset the necessitarian argument, is to prove that they are free to associate any emotion whatever with any idea whatever: to like pain as much as pleasure, vice as much as virtue; in short to prove that whatever may be the fixity of the order of the universe of things, that of thought is given over to chance. Nobody doubts that, at any rate within certain limits, you can do as you like. But what determines your likings and dislikings? Did you make your own constitution?'

Of these five sentences, it must be plainly said that the first is false; for there are, as we have seen, plenty who do directly and emphatically deny both that men are free and that they are conscious of freedom. The second is scarcely less misleading; for those who do both feel themselves free and believe that the feeling is not illusion, are also farthest from conceding that such belief involves the giving over of the realm of thought to chance. And the remaining sentences do not at all so overwhelm them, as is here supposed. Granted that a man is free to act as he likes, is his liking determined for him? Well, the believer in freedom does not object to the 'Determinist's' reply, provided that it is rightly interpreted. 'A man's action, proceeding from his volition, is the joint result of his character and circumstances.' But it is surely imperative to ask again what is this character, and whence come the circumstances? The true reply is undoubtedly, in the words of Prof. T. H. Green, that 'a free cause, consisting in a subject which is its own object, a self-distinct and self-seeking subject,' must be 'recognized as making both character and circumstances what they are.' So that the unequivocal and unhesitating answer to the hackneyed question—'Did you make your own constitution?' is, if it be asked of a sane adult—'Yes; in great part, I did.' To an extent which can be no more denied than measured, I am my own ancestor. I am what I am to-day, because of what I made myself yesterday. My constitution to-day, both physically and morally, is not what heredity gave me to start with, nor what environment would have made of a merely animal organism. It is the result of the spontaneous action upon these of a definite personality, through all the years which followed the dawn of moral consciousness. And this no more involves an appeal to chance, than it is explicable by mere physical or necessarian causation. The confessed analytic impenetrableness of the creative activity of personality, may stand over for a moment. The point here is that the denial of necessity, on the ground of self-conscious freedom, does not involve the reduction to chaos which the Professor here assumes. The consciousness of volitional freedom is no more a reckless defiance of law, than it is a madcap feeling of vacuity. It is the recognition of reality; and the truth concerning it cannot be better stated than by Dr. Borden P. Bowne—

'There is nothing in a man's freedom to hinder his acting rationally, or to excuse him for acting irrationally; but how he will act does not find its sufficient ground in the antecedent phenomena alone, but also in the mystery of self-determination. And this is something which cannot be mechanically analysed, or deduced as a necessary resultant. It can only be experienced. The attempt to analyse it, contradicts it. The attempt to construct it, denies it. It can only be recognized as the central factor of personality, the condition of responsibility, and the basis of the moral life. Criticism cannot hope to construe it. It can only point it out as a fact, and show that the objections to it rest only on an imperfect understanding of the thought itself.'[1]

Naturally, Prof. McTaggart has something to say on this matter which must be considered. His acknowledgement of the reality of the 'feeling of freedom' we have already noticed; but his comment upon it seeks to nullify the force of the admission. First he writes—

'I believe that the freedom of self-direction is quite sufficient to explain the feeling, and that there is no necessity to accept freedom in the sense of indetermination. Whatever I do will be what I will to do in preference to the other alternatives which I recognize as being open to me. And my sense of freedom is just in proportion to the extent to which my action does depend upon my will.'[2]

This seems fairly simple, and, with a caveat, might be accepted by every one. But the issue is soon complicated—

'I maintain that my sense of freedom is quite accounted for by the fact that the action is determined by the will, and that

---

[1] *Personalism*, p. 210. [2] *Some Dogmas*, p. 147.

there is no need to hold that the determining volition is itself undetermined. The feeling of freedom first experienced, is a feeling that constraint is absent.'[1]

But any 'sense of freedom' can only be a feeling that constraint is absent. The difference suggested here is but a more subtle way, worthy of a Hegelian expert, of putting the old antithesis—does moral freedom mean that I can act as I will, or that I can will as I choose? With all respect for the man of letters, it must be said plainly that it means the latter, and not the former. And the consciousness of freedom is not sufficiently or truthfully explained by the absence of constraint from action, but by the absence of constraint from choosing. It is true that 'constraint is absent in all cases where a man only acts because he wills to do so.' But, that—to employ Prof. Huxley's expression—'is mere futility, for nobody denies it.' What the non-Determinist denies is that the man is determined, i.e. compelled, either to will at all, or to will in any one specific direction. It is this double absence of constraint, and nothing less, which constitutes his consciousness of moral freedom. The writer himself confesses that 'all our most careful examination fails to show us the whole sum of conditions which are necessary in order that a particular volition should be completely determined.' But his estimate of this failure is that—

'This by no means proves that the whole sum of conditions is not there. There is another alternative, i.e. that we have not powers of observation sufficient to discover them, and except in the case of the human will, this alternative is always adopted. It is perfectly impossible for any one to explain why a particular drop of rain falls where it does, rather than an inch away. Yet no one supposes that this event is not completely determined.'[2]

---

[1] p. 148.   [2] p. 149.

But one would have supposed that any real philosopher would see that in suggesting such a comparison he is assuming the very thing to be proved; i.e. the truthfulness of the analogy between the falling of a drop of rain, which no one whatever doubts to be wholly a physical matter, and the action of the human will, which every one knows is *not* a purely physical matter. As a matter of fact the analogy is altogether false. There is no possible comparison between a raindrop and a man. Hence, if we take these four sentences in their reverse order, that an exception should be made in the case of the human will, is exactly what ought to be; for there is nothing to compare with it, so far as we know, in the whole realm of existence. To say that 'we have not powers of observation' to discover the conditions of volition, is again a *petitio quaestionis*, for the position we are discussing is that self-consciousness does discover those conditions. The contention of the non-Determinist is that whatever be the mystery of ultimate analysis, 'the whole sum of conditions' is completed, the necessary addition to known antecedents is made, when the action of the personality, the 'free cause, consisting in a subject which is its own object,' as Prof. Green phrases it, is taken into account. It is just as true that the sum of the conditions of my volition is complete *with me*, as that it is incomplete without me. But if, with refined subtlety, it be further suggested that the freedom of such 'self-direction' yet involves that the self is determined, though the direction is not, it is enough to reply that a 'determined self' is a contradiction in terms, and merits no further regard. We may indeed lack 'powers of observation sufficient' to track out the method of its spontaneity, but that

ns actuality, than the fact that we cannot weigh it disproves the reality of the ether.

One can hardly be surprised that students who sit at the feet of this Lecturer should also raise difficulties hereupon. Two of these, perhaps, deserve notice.[1] One is that it is not necessary to pronounce the verdict of consciousness illusory in order to save the principle of universal causation, because it is an error to argue from feeling to fact. The feeling of freedom may be actual, but the fact need not be. But surely the reply must be, which fact? If the fact of freedom be other than the feeling of freedom, then certainly one cannot necessarily be inferred from the other. But we are not here contemplating abnormal conditions, such as the 'case of Mrs. A,' at the end of Huxley's physiology, or the workings of any form of mania. In the normally constituted individual the feeling *is* the fact, as regards freedom, no less truly than it is as regards being. I only know that I am, because I am conscious of my existence. That is as sufficient evidence as it is undeniable. In precisely the same realm of thought it is true that I know I am free, because I am conscious of freedom to choose. It is no disposal of such evidence to say that 'it is not a case of comparison between the reality of these two.' For such a comparison is equally rational, just, warranted, and conclusive. So then, as to whether the inference from the feeling of freedom is justified, i.e. that we are free in fact, because we are free in feeling, we must plainly ask, Why not? What inference could be more immediate? The analogy between the process of thought in both cases is so complete, that there is no rational

---

[1] Suggested by Mr. C. A. Gimblett, of Trinity College, Cambridge, in a private letter.

warrant whatever for refusing in one case the inference which is freely and universally granted in the other. If my consciousness of freedom is so illusory that, although I feel myself free, I must not believe myself free, what right have I to believe myself alive on the simple ground that I feel myself alive? Surely hereupon Prof. J. A. Thomson has only uttered the truth in saying, as above quoted, that 'if a man is to deny the reality of his mental consciousness, then there is nothing for it but to sit down and whittle a stick till death passes our way.' We are told, however, that it is not a question of denying the reality of consciousness in both cases, but of 'a particular interpretation of the verdict of consciousness.' To this the reply seems both true and sufficient that the 'verdict' of consciousness is nothing but consciousness, and that there is no more room than need for any other 'interpretation' of it. It is, so far, its own sufficient and reliable interpretation. If consciousness of existence cannot but involve being, consciousness of free existence equally involves free being. If my consciousness of freedom admits of an interpolating interpretation which amounts to a direct contradiction, so must my consciousness of existence. As I am unable to think of myself without being, so am I unable to think of myself as other than free to will as I will, and no other cause or explanation of volition is necessary.

In general, therefore, a three-fold answer may be given to the suggestion that the 'verdict of consciousness may be as illusory, as the consciousness itself, is undeniable.' (i) It is practically useless, as Mr. S. Laing points out. It not only 'runs off us like water off a duck's back,' but 'if this be but an illusion, then why not everything else, the evidence of the senses, experiments, natural law, science, morality, and religion?' Nor is this practical conviction an uninstructed dogmatism, for it is in perfect harmony with the utterance of other experts besides the late Prof. James, whose words hereupon are however surely indisputable, when he declares that—

'The whole feeling of reality, the whole sting and excitement of our voluntary life, depends on our sense that in it things are really being decided from one moment to another, and that it is not the dull rattling off of a chain that was forged innumerable ages ago.'[1]

(ii) It is psychologically unwarranted. There is no reason for referring with a touch of contempt, to 'the *mere* consciousness of freedom.' For besides the fact that, as Huxley acknowledged, such consciousness is 'our one mental certainty' which cannot be taken from us, it does not consist in the mere sense of willing what we will, but in the accompanying unanalysable conviction that we could will otherwise if we chose. The usual retort that we cannot choose otherwise than as we are compelled by antecedents, is more than a contradiction in terms. It is the last desperate resort of a predetermined theory. As Dr. Illingworth puts it—

'All attempts to explain the sense of freedom as illusory, fail. They are hypotheses, and from the very nature of the case, unverifiable hypotheses, invented to justify a foregone conclusion. Freedom must be an illusion because it ought to be an illusion, is the sum total of the necessitarian position, when stripped of all disguise.'[2]

Prof. T. H. Green has truly summed up such a psychological situation in these words—

'The evidence of consciousness fairly interpreted is final. The suggestion that consciousness may not correspond with

---

[1] *Psychology*, Vol. I, p. 453.
[2] *Divine Immanence*, cheap edition, pp. 110, 111.

reality is here at least, unmeaning. The whole question is one of consciousness, a question of the relation in which a man consciously stands to objects—those of desire—which exist only in and for consciousness. If the man is consciously determined by himself in being determined by those objects, he is so really; or rather this statement is a mere pleonasm, for the only reality in question is consciousness.'[1]

(iii) But finally, it is self-contradictory. 'The arguments which spring from the very centre of our personal consciousness can only be plausibly refuted on the assumption that that consciousness itself is fundamentally untrue.'[2] The irony of the whole situation comes out when we reflect upon three things in juxta-position. (1) It is acknowledged that our only ultimate notion of causality comes from the sense of creative power which accompanies our definite volition. (2) The great principle which has become, in some quarters at least, an established scientific fetish is that everything, without any exception whatever, must be brought under the 'iron law' of necessary causation. And yet (3) our root notion of causation is illusory. The conception of law is certainly only a scientific mirage, without the necessity of causation. Yet our only notion of causation is an illusion! What then remains of the 'iron laws' which are to sway our consciousness as really as they control our planet in its orbit? Surely they are an illusion also. In contrast with this, is not Mr. V. F. Storr justified when he writes that—

'If we are told that we are deceived, and that what we seem ourselves to do is being done in us and through us by another agency, we decline to believe it. Our awareness of ourselves as free causal agents is an ultimate fact of spiritual experience,

---

[1] *Prolegomena to Ethics*, p. 126.
[2] Illingworth's *Personality, Human and Divine*, cheap edition, p. 75.

and we refuse to hold ourselves the victims of an illusion which affects all that gives most meaning to our own personality.'[1]

Whether, therefore, it be termed Pragmatism, or aught else, Dr. F. C. S. Schiller's summary of the whole case is valid when he says that 'the conception of freedom, just as the plain man experiences and understands it, is quite rational and philosophical, and it can be refuted only by being travestied.'[2]

(iv) *As to Metaphysics*

It only remains to notice how the 'Determinism' which should be termed Determinedism, is shown to be false in the searching light of Metaphysics. The statement of the case from the psychological standpoint brings us, we see, thus far, as to a borderland—

'The question, Are we free? might be also put in the equivalent form, Can we ever will anything? and to the question as thus put, experience gives a ready answer. For we certainly do conceive purposes, and we certainly, in some of our motives, do translate those purposes in act. And therefore we may say that freedom is undoubtedly, in the only sense in which it is desired, a fact of immediate experience.'[3]

But it is now made clear that we must go further. Not only, as we have just seen, is the validity of the witness of such experience definitely challenged, but explanations of it are suggested which would seem to make some form of Determinism absolutely inevitable. 'The doctrine of Determinism,' we are told, 'is a corollary of the law of causality, and consequently a simple application of a principle established *a priori*—a truth demonstrable with

---

[1] *Development and Divine Purpose*, p. 275.
[2] *Oxford and Cambridge Review*, Michaelmas, 1907, p. 70.
[3] *Elements of Metaphysics*, A. E. Taylor, p. 365.

mathematical certainty.'[1] To appreciate the bearing of this general statement, which is really the very kernel of the whole 'Determinist' position, it is imperative that we should go behind the actual facts of experience with which psychology is concerned, into the dim and shadowy yet real region of metaphysics, where ultimately this age-long discussion must somehow and at some time, if ever, find its solution. We are indeed assured by not a few competent investigators that ' will and thought are not explicable by such categories as causality, substance, resemblance, or correspondence. Hence, truth and freedom are ultimately topics for the metaphysician.'[2] But the ordinary man is neither comforted nor encouraged by such assurance, seeing that 'Metaphysics' is a subject regarded with mingled aversion and distrust by all who are not philosophical students. The general conception doubtless is that metaphysicians are recluses who cannot express themselves clearly, discoursing upon themes that they do not really understand, to people who cannot possibly follow them. There is some truth in such a notion, because the style of most metaphysicians, so far as intelligibility and lucidity are concerned, leaves much to be desired. Yet there need be no blind plunge into a bottomless quagmire, if only perspicuity and modesty can be persuaded to go hand in hand. Assuredly, the employment of our mental faculties has its limitations, but two things may be done. Within acknowledged limits we may, by pains, secure truth and clearness. When those limits are reached, there will be little risk in going beyond if our imaginations are but in harmony with our certainties. When parallel lines

---

[1] Deussen's *Elements of Metaphysics*, p. 239.
[2] Dr. Stout's *Manual of Psychology*, p. 634.

are projected beyond our vision, there is small hazard in affirming that they will remain so, in the absence of any disturbing force.

Recall, for instance, Prof. Huxley's above-quoted estimate that there is 'no harm' in declaring 'that man is nothing but a machine,' so long as those who say so 'admit that which is matter of experimental fact, viz. that it is a machine capable of adjusting itself within certain limits.' Such a suggestion, taken at its face value, seems absurd, because it lies in the very nature of a true machine to be always 'adjusted' from without. Yet any one who has marked the action of the 'governor' of a stationary engine, or knows even what is the function of a safety valve—to say nothing of Babbage's calculating machine—cannot but acknowledge that, in such a case, we have a 'machine capable, within certain limits, of self-adjustment.' Closer inquiry, therefore, into the measure of the limits, the nature of the adjustment, the character of the ultimate source of action, becomes thus really necessary. Such necessity, as applied to the human 'machine,' demands for its consideration that we should pass beyond psychology into metaphysics. So, and only so, will it appear that the self-adjustment of the 'human machine' is entirely *sui generis*; and that only by an utterly unwarranted extension to its working, of the same principles of mechanical causation in space and time which explain the self-adjustments of a gas-engine, can any analogy be made out between the thing which an engine undoubtedly is but a man is not, and the personality which a man is, if he is man at all. We shall be brought in the end, certainly, to a conclusion which will rob Mr. Bradley's dictum, quoted above, of its terrors. It is confessedly alarming to be told that 'free will may, in philosophy, be considered obsolete, but the popular moralist will always exist by not knowing what he means.' For if the moralist be not popular, what is to become of the people? But when an equally competent metaphysician assures us, giving good reasons, that—

> 'Such a genuine but limited freedom as is really implied in the existence of morality, is not only compatible with, but actually demanded by the principles of a sound metaphysics,'[1]

the average mortal may pluck up heart of grace, and even come to regard the metaphysician as his friend rather than his foe.

The one axiom with which in all surety we may start, is that mechanical causation never was, is, or can be, a true account of the origin of human action. The word 'mechanical' in this connexion is used advisedly. For not only is it warranted by dogmatic assertions such as Prof. Haeckel's, that a true theory of the universe must 'carry back all phenomena *without exception* to the mechanism of the atom';[2] but it is the inevitable implication even in the more refined and cautious statements of metaphysical 'Determinists,' whose reiterated claim is to bring all realities of mind, no less than of matter, into the grip of 'iron laws,' where all contingency is at an end. In order to comprehend clearly the utter inadequacy of any such 'rigid mechanical determination of events by their antecedents,' as an explanation of human volition,[3] let us first see plainly what is the

---

[1] Taylor's *Elements of Metaphysics*, p. 368.
[2] *Confession of Faith of a Man of Science*, p. 19. Italics mine.
[3] Prof. McTaggart's statement hereupon really amounts to the same result as that of the hardest Determinist. 'The law of causality asserts that every event is determined by previous

real problem which has to be faced. It cannot be better put than by Prof. Deussen—

'Are the actions in which man's will is manifested, the necessary and inevitable product of the character and of the motives influencing it, or does the natural law of causality here suffer an exception, so that to a certain man in a given case, two contrary actions are possible ? That a man, apart from physical impossibilities can do what he will, of that there is no doubt; but whether he can also will otherwise than he wills, whether, in a given case from that which he wills and accordingly does, he could as easily will and so as easily do the opposite ; that is the question.'[1]

It is really but a technical putting of the popular difficulty. Even if a man be free to choose, that is, to will, how he will act, what causes him to choose or to will one course of action rather than another ? When the assertion is made in all blind confidence ' you can only choose, then, as your heredity and environment compel you to choose,' it is as sufficient as true to reply that a compelled choice is a contradiction in terms and unthinkable. But there remains a main question to be answered, and neither sledgehammer dogmatism nor verbal sophistry will dispose of it. As it was sheer mockery to cut the Gordian knot, so does it stand to reason that any attempt at the genuine untying of this knot must be prolonged, if not painful.

In answer, then, to the main question thus propounded, ' Determinism ' thinks it sufficient to reply that — (i) Volitions are determined by motives ; (ii) Motives are determined by character ;

---

events in such a way that, if the previous events are as they are, it is impossible that the subsequent event should not be as it is ' (p. 144). This is surely ' rigid ' enough for the Professor at Jena, or the Editor of *The Clarion*.

[1] *Elements of Metaphysics*, pp. 237, 238.

(iii) Character is determined by heredity and environment. Thus, 'every act of a man is the latest link in an immense chain of causation in which the slightest element of uncertainty would be impossible.' Any feeling to the contrary is only an illusion. There may be 'apparently' several courses of action open to a man's choice, but 'in reality only one is possible.' That which a man does is always 'the only thing he could do'; at the time of his volition. Such Determination is certainly rigid enough to be called mechanical, and has the recommendation of being correspondingly simple. But the unmistakable verdict of sound metaphysics is that it is as false as it is mechanical; it is as untrue to facts as it is rigid; it is as fatal to morality as it is confident in its self-sufficiency. The main items in such condemnation are as follows.

(1) These avowed principles of 'Determinism' assume that precisely the same mechanical relations exist and apply in the mental realm as in the physical. This cannot be for a moment conceded, seeing that there is no known or conceivable passage from the material to the mental; whilst the theory of psycho-physical parallelism leaves each side of the parallel actually untouched by the other, and therefore untranslatable from one to the other.

(2) There is here also a further assumption, viz. that the temporal and spatial connexions which confessedly exist between phenomena, must no less apply to the realities of personality which are confessedly behind phenomena. But whereas these connexions are all in the former case included in the physical realm, they are in the latter metaphysical, and no inference can be drawn from one to the

other. Hereupon Prof. Poynting has well and truly said—

'Above all, the choice of action which is employed in our attempt to realize an imagined future, has no correspondent, no analogy whatever, in physical actions. Our sense of responsibility when that choice is made, is utterly unlike anything in the physical world.'[1]

(3) In no real sense whatever is character 'determined' by heredity and environment. 'Real' is said advisedly here because, as above explained, character, as such, connotes moral character. Animals and things may have qualities, but not character. No heredity whatever can confer character, nor can any environment whatever compel it. So long as we are contemplating human nature, we are dealing also with another factor which, however unanalysable and by whatever name known, is as real as mysterious and patent. Character can only be made from within, in the metaphysical sense. Heredity or disposition, and environment, only become operative on character in the degree in which they are adopted as co-operative by the conscious self.

(4) Motives are not 'determined by character,' inasmuch as motives and character are really related to each other as parts are to a whole. As character is unthinkable apart from the conscious action of a personal agent, so are motives meaningless apart from moral character. A motive is not a distinctive entity which applies with the same force to different individuals, as raindrops might fall upon many and various umbrellas. That which is a strong motive to one individual, as both appealing to and already forming part of his character, would be no motive at

---

[1] *Hibbert Journal*, July, 1903, pp. 742, 743.

172 DETERMINISM: FALSE AND TRUE

all to another, any more than the smell of a public-house would be an attraction to a temperance reformer. Thus motives rather constitute character than are 'determined' by it.

(5) Volitions are not 'determined by motives.' Such a suggestion is really a contradiction in terms. A volition in which no initiation is involved, would not be an act of will at all. It would be merely a psychological *nexus* between some antecedent and its necessary consequent. A really 'determined' volition belongs to the same category of false imaginations as the superficial suggestion that 'a will is a balance,' or 'a pair of scales,' which is about as true as to say that a mummy is a man. It is often asserted with much confidence that the will 'follows the strongest motive,' but there lurks in the expression no small possibility of untruth. If the 'following' is of the same kind as that illustrated when a soldier in battle heroically follows his captain, the figure may stand. But if the intended meaning be that the will follows the strongest motive as a railway carriage follows the engine, then the metaphor is false. The truth is succinctly put by Sir Oliver Lodge in saying that 'a free man is the master of his motives, and selects that motive which he wills to obey.'[1] But the matter is so important that it merits the fuller statement of Prof. Poynting—

'An attempt is made to liken choice to physical action by saying that our acts are determined by motives, that deliberation is but the competition of all motives operating, and that ultimately we yield to the strongest as certainly as a body moves under the strongest force. Our will is like a feather fluttering through the air, swaying hither and thither by successive puffs, and finally borne off by the strongest current. Perhaps it is

---
[1] *Substance of Faith allied with Science*, p. 27.

FALSE DETERMINISM

worth while pointing out that even with this idea of motives, the analogy fails. A body does not yield to the strongest force. It moves in the direction of the resultant of all the forces from the greatest to the least, every one counting and having its full effect. But the will finally takes one course, with one aim, and the motives prompting to other courses all drop out of action.'[1]

Thus the truth is not that the will mechanically or helplessly follows the strongest motive, but that the man, the person, the self, deliberates over a real choice between motives, and permits one motive to become the means of a volition, by dismissing the other motives from regard.

(6) It thus becomes manifest that the real question after all is not whether a man has a free will, but whether the man is a free man. That is tantamount to asking whether he is a man at all. An impersonal man is a contradiction in terms; but the very soul and centre of personality is will. As 'I am' is the very least and lowest expression of conscious existence, so is 'I will' the lowest and least expression of conscious personality. Personality is not mere consciousness of unitary existence, it is also a capacity for purposive existence. It includes not merely receptivity but creative activity. The man is free to the extent to which his will expresses his purpose. 'A will which was not free would be a will which was not the translation into sensible fact of any one's purpose, and thus no will at all.'[2] As it is beyond dispute that our only and ultimate comprehension of causality springs from our own consciousness of creative will-power, so may it be affirmed that this consciousness of capacity for purposive volition, becomes more and more sure upon contemplation.

'So soon as we direct our attention inwards to the only point

---

[1] *Hibbert Journal*, p. 742.   [2] Taylor, p. 365.

where it is granted to us to set aside the forms of our intellect and seize the end in itself as the will within us, we are overcome by consciousness—a consciousness yielding to no logical argument—that the will is free. Free, not merely so far as that we can do what we will, but also so far as it depends upon ourselves alone, at every moment and under every circumstance, to will this or otherwise.'[1]

(7) This expression of self in purpose, and of purpose in will, is certainly not subject to the material categories of time and space, but is something belonging to altogether another realm. This is the reason why the Indeterminist does not shrink from the soft impeachment that according to his view 'the action of conscious beings forms a solitary exception to a principle of determination which is absolutely valid for all purely physical processes.'[2] There is no logical warrant whatever for assuming that a principle of determination which is valid for the physical realm, should be equally valid for the metaphysical. The laws or principles according to which a nail driven by a hammer enters into wood, are no more necessarily the same as those according to which the mind of the workman determines the strokes of the hammer, than the wood penetrated is the same as the brain during that molecular action which is the condition of mentality. The verdict of modern physics hereupon is unmistakable—

'It appears to me equally certain that there is no correspondence yet made out between the power of choice and any physical action, and there does not seem any likelihood that a correspondence ever will be made out. The freedom of choice then is unlike anything else in nature; it is a simple fact. Holding this view, I am bound to repudiate the physical account of nature when it claims to be a complete account. I am bound to deny

---

[1] Deussen, *Elements of Metaphysics*, p. 240.
[2] Taylor, p. 368.

that the Laplacean calculator can be successful when he takes man and the mind of man into his calculations.'[1]

(8) This unique exercise of creative power in the genuine volitions of personality, is absolutely irreconcilable with 'Determinism,' either 'soft' or 'hard.' In both these theories alike, whatever terms are employed or subtleties suggested, nature, including human nature, is a closed system ' in which the slightest element of uncertainty would be impossible.' ' This,' we are ceaselessly assured, ' is the doctrine of Determinism.' Then, in face of facts, the reply is warranted, so much the worse for ' Determinism.' For the one emergent certainty from full and fair comprehension of metaphysical realities is that wherever man is included, be the mystery of explanation what it may, there nature is *not* a closed system. The essential constitution of human nature prevents the closure. For the rest let Prof. James Ward speak plainly in words partly quoted above—

' Such a view, it may be said, is incompatible with the scientific conception of law, for that postulates necessity, whereas this lets contingency into the very heart of things. It is true; I not only admit it, but contend that any other world would be meaningless. For the contingency is not that of chance but of freedom, so far as everything that is is a law in itself, has an end for itself, and seeks the good—But were we the creatures of a blind mechanical necessity, there could be no talk of ideal standards, either of thought or conduct ; no meaning in reason at all.'[2]

(9) The only modicum of truth which can be allowed to inhere in ' Determinism,' is that a man does in general act in accordance with his character. But this is at once the mildest and least compulsory determination. It is indeed so far from helping

---

[1] Prof. Poynting, *Hibbert Journal*, p. 743.
[2] *Naturalism and Agnosticism*, Vol. II, p. 281.

Determinedism that it rather serves as means for administering to that theory its *coup de grâce*.

For (i) it is only a general formula which, though perfectly true in its text, leaves ample room in its margin for the inexplicable. The startling cases of sudden reversions of life and conduct with which observation no less than history makes us familiar, must be admitted into the region of fact as completely as the famous Gifford lectures of Prof. James demand. But although we cannot track out all the elements of the change, we are warranted in believing that if we knew the whole of a man's character—i.e. his total self—we should find that the conversion even of a Saul or a Loyola, is no contradiction to the metaphysical necessity of action according to character, seeing that character is always inseparable from and dependent on a free personality.

(ii) This necessity is, however, so far removed from the rigid mechanical causation which does not admit the slightest element of uncertainty, that it is really the guarantee of liberty and the pledge of contingency. For all that it actually connotes is that a man must be himself, and cannot be anyone else. Which is ultimately not so much a principle of necessity as the recognition of a fact ; viz. that he is himself, and acts as himself.

(iii) By this consideration Indeterminism is saved from the looseness of representation which would condemn it as irrational. We are hereby reminded that Indeterminism does not involve the notion that human volitions arise from blind chance—*e nihilo in vacuo*—and that it is not the same as the ' Libertarianism of contingent choice—by which is meant a choice which does not issue out of the total processes of mental life, in accordance with psychological laws, but springs into being of itself, as if it were fired out of a pistol.'[1] The will capable of such isolated, incoherent, unmotived, disconnected volition, would of course be nobody's will, and therefore not a will at all. There can be no mistake about the principle that 'only as issuing from my character and as the expression of my individual interests, can acts be ascribed to me as mine, and made the basis of moral disapprobation in censure of myself.'[2] But my character is as distinct as inseparable from myself. I and my character are not one. Yet as character in the abstract is unthinkable, so is a characterless self. Inseparable connexion really connotes non-fusion.

(iv) This very necessity that a volition should issue from character is the guarantee of liberty, because it must be some one's character, and therefore must be the creation of some free personality. It must be 'my' character from which my volitions proceed, but where 'me' and 'mine' obtain, there is the absolute guarantee of freedom. If I am not free, my character is not mine, but was so made apart from me that my self refuses to acknowledge it, and disclaims responsibility for it. But true 'freedom consists in self-determination, and self-determination means self-control proceeding from the self as a whole, and determining self as a whole.'[3] This is precisely what is asserted and confirmed by that consciousness to which final appeal must be made. In the words of Prof. Deussen—

'If I look inwards I find myself free and equally capable of willing an action or its opposite. In this consciousness of freedom is reached the responsibility for what I do or leave undone, the nature of which can, under certain circumstances,

---

[1] Dr. Stout's *Manual of Psychology*, p. 632.
[2] Taylor, p. 379.   [3] Stout, p. 532.

give me qualms of conscience, not to be reasoned away by any subtlety of *a priori* deduction.'[1]

The only possible alternative to this conclusion is wholly to reject personal responsibility, together with repentance, remorse, and all associated feelings, as Spinoza does, on the ground that men deceive themselves when they suppose that they are free. Then comes also, as an inevitable consequence, the rejection of personality altogether, as mere appearance and error; together with the dismissal of the notion of a human self as being unreal and self-contradictory.[2] There is no middle course. Semi-personality is unthinkable. The self cannot be half mere appearance and half reality. I, who write this, am either something or nothing. Metaphysics cannot fashion a human self out of a something-nothing alloy. If the final dictum be that ' the self seems, where not hiding itself in obscurity, a mere bundle of discrepancies,'[3] I have to choose between accepting a something which by reason of its very reality may well to my limited faculties seem to be a bundle of discrepancies, or being content to regard myself as a mere phantasm of thought, a nonentity whose only recommendation is that it has all the simplicity and intelligibility of nothingness. If the latter were really forced upon the plain man as the one and only dictum of metaphysics, it would be small wonder that he should reject metaphysics altogether as mere babble for babes. Furthermore ; if, as Mr. Bradley affirms, ' the end of metaphysics is to understand

---

[1] *Elements of Metaphysics*, p. 242.

[2] ' In whatever way the self is taken, it will prove to be appearance. The self is no doubt the highest form of experience we have, but for all that it is not the true form.'—Bradley, *Appearance and Reality*, p. 119.

[3] Bradley, p. 120.

the universe,' then there is no risk in replying that Metaphysics is at an end. Its vaulting ambition overleaps itself and lands in confusion plus delusion. The notion of understanding the universe, when the infinitesimal entity which undertakes the quest finds its very starting-point to be a mere 'bundle of discrepancies,' is positively ludicrous beyond expression. When, however, with more modesty and correspondingly more truth, the metaphysician contents himself with the projection of thought on rational lines beyond the phenomenal realm into the noumenal, he will find, indeed, the roots of reality, though little, if anything, that is finally comprehensible. But we live by the real, and there is no higher function for philosophy than to be the handmaid of reality. In this whole case, therefore, after weighing patiently and thoroughly all that Determinedism alleges as proof that 'man is determined,' we are driven to conclude, on the contrary, with Prof. Deussen, that—

'We might call that conviction of the freedom of the will an innate chapter of metaphysics, implanted, as indispensable, in every man.'[1]

---

[1] *Elements of Metaphysics*, p. 241.

II

THE TRUE DETERMINISM

II

THE TRUE DETERMINISM

(1) PHILOSOPHICAL

In the preceding pages, it has been shown that the philosophy which calls itself 'Determinism' by reason of its dogma that 'man is determined,' is trebly false. It is false in name, in fact, in principle. Above all else it is a theory of the constitution of human nature, and it represents that nature as purely passive, denying all creative activity in the hidden realm of the metaphysical, whilst in matters practical endorsing the ancient fatalism which avowed—

> 'Tis all a Chequer-board of Nights and Days,
> Where Destiny, with Men for Pieces, plays:
> Hither and thither moves, and mates, and slays,
> And one by one back in the Closet lays.[1]

We must repeat that the only fit and proper name for such a conception of human nature and human life is Determinedism, seeing that its one great thesis is that man is determined. As such, it is in five-fold contradiction with fact, it wrecks moral philosophy, it contravenes psychology, and is disowned by metaphysics. But a controversy which has extended through the ages is not at last to be settled by any mere negations, however strong. There is indeed still, as there always has been, the intuitive conviction of humanity that it is not true, based upon the pragmatic principle that it will not

---

[1] *Omar Khayyám*, XLIX.

work, as firmly as upon the verdict of consciousness. The life of the world from day to day, no less than the inner realm of individual moral consciousness,[1] proceeds always on the supposition that man is not determined. There is no practical Determinedism anywhere. Yet the theory is by no means extinct. Indeed it may be said to be growing. Some are even of opinion that 'its strongly entrenched lines have long rendered a frontal attack inconclusive.' And we have seen above that it will certainly not fail for want of lucid statement and dogmatic assertion. In this case, therefore, even more than generally, negation of error will never suffice without positive affirmation of truth. If it is not true that man is determined, what is true? If he is not a machine, not an automaton, not a link in a chain, not a mere animal, what is he? The answer which is based alike upon experience, upon psychology, upon metaphysics, is as startling as true, but, in Mr. Bradley's phrase, 'it is no worse for that.' There is a true as well as false Determinism, and the essence of it in a word is that *man is not determined because he is a determiner.* He is not a mere effect, because he is a true cause; he is not a mere link in an endless chain, because he is himself an initiator, a creator; he is not a machine, because he is a person; he is not an automaton, because he is a self-conscious being; he is not a mere sense-animal, because he is a man. Let it be frankly confessed that these are tremendous assertions; again we may say 'they are no worse for that.' Great things may be as true as small things. The unmeasured sublimity of human nature

---

[1] 'No proof of Determinism will ever be valid and overwhelming enough to prevent the freedom of the will being again and again proclaimed as a fact of inner consciousness.'—Prof. Deussen, *Elements of Metaphysics*, p. 240.

is not one whit less true, because its alternative is the indescribable pettiness of an automaton falsely and uselessly credited with a will.

There are, indeed, from the standpoint of a valid pragmatism, far too many influences in modern thought and life tending to belittle human nature. There is crying room for a philosophy, not to say a religion, which shall rescue it from self-contempt and enthrone it upon the inspirations of 'self-knowledge, self-reverence, and self-control.' That such a philosophy must be justified on lines of accurate thought, no one denies. But whereas Mr. Henley's triumphant verse—

> I am the master of my fate,
> I am the captain of my soul—

has found its justification in all history, and is ever finding it in daily observation and experience, so may it be boldly alleged that when philosophy is truly philosophical, no less than when science is genuinely scientific, there is as valid warrant in principle as in fact, for the true as distinct from the false Determinism. It is hoped that to some extent this has been already incidentally shown on negative lines. It remains to supply the corresponding positive principles which make the case as complete as reason can demand. The Determinism which merits the name, in determining to do justice to human nature, makes all rightful allowance for limitations, natural forces, heredity, environment, and all other such influences as come necessarily into consideration; but in and through them all it yet finds that the truly determining part is the human part. These all are quantities more or less known in the complex equation of a human life. There is also an unknown quantity, without which the statement of the case would be manifestly incomplete, but with which it is mathematically insoluble. For life is more than mathematics and man is more than philosophy, so that there is yet room for the true Determinism which is rock-based upon the indefeasible testimony of self-consciousness to the fact that I, and I alone, of all things or beings in the universe—not excluding the God of Christian Theism—determine my own character, my conduct, my destiny. In exposition of this we will proceed to make as clear as succinct statements permit, the main elements of the case, both philosophically and practically. In regard to the former, we are concerned with seven distinct items of positive affirmation. These include, the reality of the self; the creative activity of the self; the free self; the relation to heredity and environment; the sufficient cause; the true explanation of experience; the sufficient estimate of the future. A careful, even if brief, statement of these successive steps in a valid series, will not only yield the true Determinism, but lead the way to those moral and practical issues which crown the whole discussion with such supreme importance.

(i) *The Reality of the Self*

Our knowledge of ourselves from self-consciousness is ' our one mental certainty.' It is at once the starting-point and basis of all else. If this cannot be accepted as true and regarded as reliable, nothing else can be, and we are all mad together. The only door here open for questioning is as to the final interpretation of this consciousness. That it is, is beyond doubt. What it is ultimately, is open to discussion. We saw above that psychologically the fact of our consciousness of freedom is as valid a witness to the reality of freedom, as our consciousness of being is to the reality of existence. We have now to inquire more deeply into the significance of the latter. There are, on the whole, only two main lines of interpretation. The total contents of consciousness either testify to a real self which in unifying them proves itself to be something, or they are but the infinitesimal portions of a cosmic stream in which self is nothing because non-existent. In one plain word, there is, or is not, manifest in the revelations of consciousness, a self, an ego, a soul, a person. The name is irrelevant, it is a question—than which there is no greater—of the actuality, or not, of personality. In facing this, we pass necessarily beyond psychology into metaphysics. The facts of consciousness, in sensation and perception, are beyond all dispute. And it may be assumed that they are according to law, though not necessarily the same laws as those which rule in the physical realm. But the explanation and significance of these facts takes us into deeper and darker regions than the mere registration of successive phases of thought or feeling. There ought to be nothing alarming or repulsive in acknowledging that the inquiry must be metaphysical. There was nothing at all mystifying in the first use of the words μετὰ τὰ φυσικά by Andronicus in regard to Aristotle's treatises. There need be and ought to be no hesitation now in acknowledging that there are some realities which lie beyond the phenomenal realm, i.e. 'beyond everything in nature, and in human nature, to which we can apply the ordinary scientific methods of observation, experiment, and generalization.' As psychology deals with phenomena, so does metaphysics with noumena. We do not aim at comprehending infinity when we have recourse to metaphysics, but at throwing a little more light upon some such minute portions of the universe as inhere in human nature, when this is related to the universe and possibly to the divine Source of the universe. It was well said by Dr. Momerie that 'A science is a summation or generalization of a particular set of facts; a system of philosophy is a co-ordination of all the sciences: metaphysics is concerned with their ultimate and transcendental basis.'[1]

So far have modern studies in this direction advanced, that progress may well be reported. The older materialism is dead. No one to-day in the name of science or philosophy dare suggest that 'thought is a function of brain' after the fashion in which the secretion of bile is a function of the liver. All modern thinkers worthy of regard now follow Huxley in his repudiation of such an attitude.[2] Materialistic Monism—as Sir Oliver Lodge rightly insists Prof. Haeckel's system should be termed—is dying, if not dead.

The Professor's suggestion that thought is but a 'physiological function of the phronema' is scorned by the philosophy of his own country, no less than by leading men of science in this. The most recent and most elaborate attempt to show that mind has simply evolved from matter by chance[3]—for 'necessity' is only dynamized chance—must be pronounced

---

[1] *Personality*, p. 12.

[2] 'When the Materialists stray beyond the borders of their path, and begin to talk about there being nothing else in the universe but matter and force and necessary laws, and all the rest of their grenadiers, I decline to follow them.'—*Lay Sermons*, p. 297.

[3] *The Evolution of Mind*, Jos. McCabe (A. & C. Black).

a failure, because it offers no rational substitute for other views, notably those of Dr. Wallace, which it opposes. The veteran scientist's recent confirmation of his previously published views,[1] may be left to speak for itself. If there be any truth in Mr. Bradley's assertion that the 'popular moralist will always exist by not knowing what he means,' such an estimate applies much more truly to the popular 'Rationalist,' who, in various forms, but with unblushing confidence, still assures the people that ' the brain is the mind.'[2] For not only does all latest science insist that the brain is *not* the mind, but it also affirms that there is no known passage from brain to mind, or vice versa. Furthermore, Leibnitz's ' Pre-established harmony' is as defunct as Psychophysical parallelism is, for such purpose, useless. But the facts of human consciousness remain, and with these every doctrine of mind or morals has yet to reckon, for the inferences from them are as inevitable as far-reaching.

(1) What, then, are the facts which for all clear thinkers must surely be regarded as beyond dispute? Let us take any ordinary individual as a normal type of human experience. What does he know concerning himself? (i) That he is sure, through consciousness, of his own existence. He has no need to say with Descartes, 'I think, therefore I am.' The last three words can be discarded; for a man must be before he can think. (ii) He is conscious of persistent existence. He not only knows ' I was yesterday and I am to-day,' but ' I am the same I to-day as I was yesterday.' (iii) He is not only conscious

---

[1] *The World of Life*, just published by Chapman & Hall.
[2] *Not Guilty*, p. 95.

of the sensations and perceptions which make his 'stream of consciousness,' but he can and does distinguish himself from the stream. I who think am something other than my thought. I can think of myself as such; i.e. I can as really make myself the object of thought, as recognize that I am the thinking subject. (iv) He can distinguish himself from others, i.e. he is not only assured by his sensations of the existence of other things and beings external to himself, but is driven to infer the existence of other selves analogous to his own, from which he is yet unmistakably separate. Solipsism is a mere philosophical conceit. He knows both that he is himself, and that there are other largely similar selves. (v) He is as conscious of the ceaseless initiating activities of his self, as he is absolutely ignorant of the way in which his thought-activities arise. His mind works. Of that he has no more doubt than that he exists. The how and why of the working, are beyond his cognizance. The actuality of the activity is beyond doubt. (vi) But the ceaseless activities of his thoughts, and their utterly untraceable complexities, never for a moment suggest any kind of pluralism within his consciousness. Abnormal cases of double or multiple personality may be left out of account. So far from their study being, as Prof. James suggests, 'one of the greatest needs of psychology'—they are, at most, of secondary value, because what we seek is not an understanding of the exceptional but an appreciation of the ordinary. There is no valid inference from the abnormal to the normal. Disease can never be the true interpretation of health. The utmost that cerebral pathology can suggest in explanation of abnormal personalities is that there is a norm, as real as inscrutable, from which these depart. The exception does not cancel the rule. The average man, however mercurial or passionate, knows amidst all the restless wanderings of his thoughts, or intensity of his emotions, or tumult of his sensations, that they are all *his*. So far as physical analogy can help metaphysical conception, all his sensations, thoughts, purposes, which he knows to be his, belong to him as surely as all the stops and pipes of some vast organ belong to it and constitute the united whole. Given but an organist also, as inseparably one with his organ as the man knows himself to be with his thoughts and feelings, and the analogy would be fairly complete. (vii) But it would have to involve one other most important element. The organist would have to remain one with an ever changing organ, to an extent beyond analogical illustration. For the plainest man in the street knows that he is the same man this year as he was last year, and his powers of memory carry him back through many years to a childhood which he never dreams of disowning. One of the remarkable features of extreme old age, we know, is the facility for recalling the scenes of youth when those of yesterday are hardly remembered. But the grandfather never doubts that it is he himself who was then the grandchild. To hint that physiology explains this, is surely to ignore the fact that physiology makes it inexplicable. For the whole brain with which physiology is concerned, has in the interval been shed several times over, and the retention of cerebral convolutions is a fact of an entirely different order from the wonders of memory.

About these facts, it must be reiterated, there should be no question. Now as to their significance. What is the least that must be inferred from them?

(1) These seven phases of fact combine to give us something, not nothing. That is to say, they constitute the very essence of a person, and the seven prismatic colours of the rainbow—though not constituting an analogy—do not more surely unite to form white, than do these seven qualities of human consciousness to form genuine human personality. They answer unequivocally the main question, What besides mere consciousness is implied in personality? Nothing less than these elements can constitute a person. A person does, as a fact, exhibit nothing less than all these. In pointing out, therefore, that these are the normal constituents of average experience, we warrant a claim for personality on behalf of all normal human beings, which no abnormal instance whatever can annul.

(2) The theory which would reduce all these to nothing, i.e., in the language of Prof. Bain, to a 'fiction coined from nonentity,' cannot be stated without self-contradiction. Human personality cannot be denied without both assuming and employing it. The denier himself exemplifies what he contradicts. Illustrations may be taken at random, from any of those who have most distinguished themselves in opposing the reality of the self.

It was with good reason that Dr. Momerie declared that 'hundreds of sentences might be quoted in which the real mystery of the ego is quietly assumed, and then made to assist in its own assassination.' Hume, whom Bain, Mill, and Sully follow, declares that the 'soul is nothing but a bundle or collection of different perceptions which succeed each other with an inconceivable rapidity and are in a perpetual flux and movement. Our eyes cannot turn in their sockets without varying our perceptions.' But how can any 'our' arise out of a perpetual flux? The two conceptions are utterly and for ever irreconcilable. Bain, again, writes concerning the sense of difference that it is 'the most rudimentary property of our intellectual being.' But the application of 'our' to a mere 'physiological function of the brain,'[1] or a 'flux of perceptions,' is a travesty of speech and nothing more. As for Prof. Clifford's 'Mind-stuff,' no more valid proof that it is all 'stuff' could be suggested, than the writer's own brilliant display of a vigorous personality. Mr. Bradley, at the close of his chapter on the 'reality of the self,' tells us, as we have seen, that 'when it is not hiding itself in obscurity, it is a mere bundle of discrepancies.' Here the final sentence is—'our search has conducted us again not to reality but to mere appearance.' Yet on the very next page we read—'I will say a few words on a proposed alternative, stating this entirely in my own way, and so as to suit my own convenience.' 'Our,' 'I say,' 'I will,' 'my own'; if these are only appearances they are very real; and the attempt to extricate sunshine from cucumbers would be as hopeful as to get these out of nothing but 'a bundle of discrepancies' alternating with 'obscurity.'

---

[1] Prof. Haeckel writes (*Riddle of the Universe*, cheap edition, p. 66) that 'The ontogenesis of consciousness makes it perfectly clear that it is not an immaterial entity but a physiological function of the brain, and that it is consequently no exception to the general law of substance.' For a fair consideration of this, see the present writer's *Haeckel's Monism False*, ch. iv. It is not enough to remark here that no one has ever said that consciousness, *per se*, is an immaterial entity. Only a few pages earlier the Professor says—'Personally I have never subscribed to this hypothesis of automatic consciousness.' But it requires much more than all that he and his erudite translator have together ever written, to extract 'personally I have' out of a 'physiological function of the brain.' To 'call spirits from the vasty deep' were a trifle compared with such a task.

The late Prof. James no doubt did much to earn his reputation as a famous psychologist, but it is correspondingly difficult to understand how he came to write hereupon as he did. 'Thought itself is the thinker, and psychology need not look beyond.' Certainly if psychology were content with that, it would cease to be a branch of science, for it is manifestly self-contradictory. That thought should think is utterly unthinkable. The self-contradiction comes out only more vividly if we enlarge the statement.

'If passing thoughts be the directly verifiable existents, which no school has hitherto doubted them to be, then they are the only "knower" of which psychology need take any account. The only pathway that I can discover for bringing in the more transcendental thinker, would be to deny that we have any such *direct* knowledge of the existence of our states of consciousness as common sense supposes us to possess.'[1]

If this is the worst that the best psychology has to say against the reality of the self, surely *cadit quaestio*. It is vain to attempt to cover up the unthinkableness of the suggestion under the veil of the limitations of psychology. A true psychology cannot rest upon a false metaphysics. And it is worse than false to credit 'passing thoughts' with being a 'knower.' If a thought could know anything, the very least conclusion would have to be that passing thoughts were knowers, not a knower. Which plurality is precisely what I know that I myself am not. And the writer knows it too, for he speaks of himself as 'I.' But the whole series of 'passing thoughts' can no more constitute an 'I,' than a heap of beads unstrung can make a necklace. If 'common sense' is to be invoked—and we gladly welcome the suggestion—surely it declares that there can be no '*direct*' knowledge of states of

---

[1] *A Text-Book of Psychology*, p. 215.

consciousness unless there is a knower to know them. Whatever unfathomable mystery may attach to the conception of a transcendental ego, at least it involves no such absurdity as a thinking thought, or a single knower *identical with* a multitude of passing thoughts.

(3) It cannot be too plainly asserted that even a single sensation requires a sentient ego, as a series of sensations requires a persistent ego. Dr. Momerie's statement hereupon remains unshaken, and unshakable.

'Since the necessity for an ego is never denied without being tacitly assumed, it may be taken to be a really self-evident truth, the contradictory of which is inconceivable, that along with every sensation or feeling of any discrepancy whatever, there must exist a sentient principle capable of feeling it.'[1]

It is indeed impossible to speak intelligibly of the matter at all, without assuming both the sentient and persistent ego. For if the question be ever so elementary in regard to 'sensations,' it is absolutely meaningless until we have some answer to the query, 'Whose' sensations? Sensation *per se* is unthinkable. Feeling is no feeling without a feeler. But the persistent self, as indicated above, is such a fundamental fact of all sane consciousness, that from it the inference may be safely drawn that if I to-day must be myself in order to appreciate a certain sensation, all the sensations that go to make up the stream of my consciousness must be appreciated by the same ego to-morrow, if there is to be any coherence at all between them. A series of sensations could no more cognize itself as a series, than a single sensation could feel itself as a sensation.

(4) The unity of this self is inevitably given by

[1] *Personality*, p. 28.

its persistence. Cases of alternating or multiple personality are morbid and exceptional. They belong to pathological rather than normal psychology. Their study is much more interesting than instructive. They tell us much about an individual, but nothing about a type. The same applies to all the strange mental phenomena associated with hypnotism, mesmerism, trance experience, opium-eating sensations, unconscious cerebration, and the like. They are sports not specimens, and as such belong rather to the physician than the metaphysician. About this there is no possible controversy, that, in the proportion of a million to one, a human being is a single personality, and if he knows anything at all, knows himself to be such from childhood to the grave.

(5) So real is this persistent and unitary self that it possesses the marvellous capacity for becoming an object to itself as subject. 'The marvellous thing,' rightly says Dr. Courtney, 'about self-consciousness is, that in it the mind recognizes itself as the subject of its own states, and recognizes these states as its own. Self-consciousness is the unique property of the mind which is so real that it can appear to itself.' Here even Mr. J. S. Mill also acknowledges the fact. 'We are reduced to the alternative of believing that the mind, or ego, is something different from any series of feelings or possibilities of them, or of accepting the paradox that something which, *ex hypothesi*, is but a series of feelings, can be aware of itself as a series.'[1]

---

[1] *Examination of Sir Wm. Hamilton's Philosophy*, pp. 247, 248.
Dr. Stout suggests hereupon that 'All self-consciousness implies a division of the total self. When I think about myself, the I and myself are never quite identical. The self of which I have an idea is always distinguished from the self which has the idea' (*Manual of Psychology*, p. 545). Of this, we may say

(6) The witness of memory to the actuality of the self, is unmistakable and irrefragable. It has been well said by a competent writer that 'it is by an analysis of remembrance, that the existence of a metaphysical ego may be most clearly demonstrated.' And Dr. Courtney confirms such an estimate when he asks, 'What does any man mean by speaking of his own personality, except that he is conscious of himself as being the one identical being, who has had every kind of experience, and undergone various mental phases, and knows them all as his own?' Nothing is more common for the adult man than the recollection of scenes and events in his boyhood. But physiology combines with psychology to make plain that without a real and persistent ego, such recollection is self-contradictory to the point of absurdity. Granted that the cerebral cells are the instruments of memory, as of all thought. They will have wholly changed in the interval between childhood and manhood. To attribute to the new structure the identical molecular vibrations which thrilled the old one, is utterly unscientific. If the ego, or the something, which appreciated the psychical significance of such vibrations in childhood, is not the same as that which does so in maturity, whence can possibly arise any connexion

---

that it is verbally true and actually false. It is rather an instance of logic-chopping than a truthful representation of actuality. When I think of myself, I include the I which thinks as part of the total self about which I think. And there is no more difficulty in so doing than, if the centre of a sphere could think, there would be in its including itself as part of the sphere. The process may be beyond exact representation in words, but it is one of the most common mistakes in regard to language to imagine that, whether printed or spoken, it can exactly convey all the realities of consciousness. As a matter of fact, it does so only very inadequately at the best.

between the two? Yet if sane consciousness is to count as in any sense more reliable than insane, there is nothing to which it testifies more unequivocally than to the fact that I who write this, am the same 'I' that can distinctly remember the first formation of pothooks. Any endeavour to disprove this continuity, is tantamount to an effort to prove that I am not alive when I think about it. All talk about a 'stream of consciousness' being a mere 'function of the phronema,' gives no more account of the undeniable realities of memory, than the flow of a river at the mouth does of all the landscape scenery passed through on its banks.

(7) It is no answer whatever to ask for a definition, or description, of this necessary postulate of consciousness and memory. That it is distinct from the brain, as its mere organ, must unhesitatingly be asserted, in view of all the facts.[1] But the demand that it should be exhibited in words, is as unreasonable as to ask that an idea should be estimated in ounces. It is by all confession a metaphysical entity, and therefore, by the very nature of the case, beyond defining. We know that the bodily form is not the person, but to ask for the exhibition of the personality abstracted from the form, is no more rational or scientific than to refuse to believe in the living body without a concrete exhibition of vitality. Dr. Bowne has therefore said with equal

---

[1] 'We have definitely concluded that the facts both of brain anatomy and of brain physiology indicate that this organ of the personality is never other than its instrument, whilst the personality itself is as different and as separate from it as the violinist is separate from and not the product of his violin.'—*Brain and Personality*, by Dr. W. H. Thomson, p. 234.

truth and wisdom that 'Personality can never be construed as a product or compound. It can only be expressed as a fact. It must be possible, because it is given as actual. Whenever we attempt to go behind this fact, we are trying to explain the explanation.'[1] Although physical analogies must herein ever be imperfect, the case may be fairly likened to the working of a dynamo where the untrained eye can see nothing whatever to account for the creation of tremendous power. To deny the reality of the generation of such force because it was equally invisible and undefinable, would be no more false or irrational than to set aside all the unquestionable manifestations of personality in sensation, perception, emotion, memory, will, on the ground that we cannot comprehend what it is that feels, thinks, remembers, wills.

(8) The reality of this self is the necessary and reliable beginning of all Metaphysics. Nothing, of course, is easier for the average man than to contemn Metaphysics in general. But there is no more common sense in such scorn than in the contempt which a plough-boy might evince for a page of Newton's *Principia*. His scorn would simply be the measure of his ignorance. And there can be no ignorance on earth greater than that which does not know that there is something under or behind phenomena— that reality lies beyond appearance. To speak of the 'substance' of the ego might prove bewildering indeed to many ; but it is quite open to any thoughtful man to say that 'a substance, in philosophy, is a thing that exists *per se*, or of itself, and is thus distinct from an attribute or a thought which exists

---

[1] *Personalism*, p. 264.

in dependence upon some substance.'¹ It ought to be, we repeat, if it is not, beyond all rational controversy that thought itself cannot think, any more than feeling can feel. If there is to be love, there must be a lover; and if self-consciousness is anything more than an everlasting delusion, there must be a self to be conscious of itself. The metaphysicians who have asserted that this foundation is immovable have not erred, even though they may have sometimes darkened counsel by words in building upon it. There is no rational warrant whatever for asserting that the ego cannot exist because it is transcendental. There are overwhelming reasons for assuming that it does exist, however poor may be the best human language to describe it.

(9) This much is for ever certain, that without it all philosophy is at an end. 'There are three factors,' says Dr. Rudolf Otto, 'which may be established in regard to the psychical in spite of all naturalistic opposition; they are, self-consciousness, the unity of consciousness, and the consciousness of the ego.'² Whether we can focus these three or not into one distinctive something which the mind can hold, this ego is the most certain reality, without which the simplest personal life would be impossible. Here poetry and philosophy embrace each other.

> The baby new to earth and sky,
>   What time his tender palm is prest
>   Against the circle of the breast,
> Has never thought that—'This is I.'
>
> But as he grows he gathers much,
>   And learns the use of 'I' and 'me,'
>   And finds 'I am not what I see,
> And other than the things I touch.'

---

[1] Harris, *Pro Fide*, p. 159.
[2] *Naturalism and Religion*, pp. 313, 316.

> So rounds he to a separate mind
>   From whence clear memory may begin,
>   As thro' the frame that binds him in
> His isolation grows defined.[1]

It will do us no rational harm to give up in despair any attempt to abstract the 'ego' from its activities, or to describe the reality of personality apart from a living person. But without such an 'ego' there is no more possibility of a philosophy of human nature, and therefore of the universe which has to be viewed, if at all, from the human standpoint, than a study of harmony is possible without the vibrations of the atmosphere, or a scientific theory of light without the molecular vibrations of the unknown ether. The analogy is necessarily imperfect, but the fact is manifest. 'I am I,' is the unfathomable, unmistakable, sufficient, absolute essential of all philosophy.

(ii) *The Creative Activity of the Self*

In considering the case for the true Determinism, we have next to note that the reality of the self, as a transcendental entity, is by no means the whole truth of human experience, for there is in every normal individual that which confirms the assertion of Prof. Ward in his brilliant Gifford Lectures. 'Every man knows the difference between feeling and doing, between ideal reverie and intense thought, between impotent and aimless drifting and unswerving tenacity of purpose; between being the slave of every passion, or the master of himself.'[2] The simplest analysis of daily experience not only appreciates

---

[1] *In Memoriam*, XLV.   [2] Vol. II, 52.

the difference between passivity and activity in consciousness, but makes clear that the latter is as real as the former. Besides which, as Dr. Ward adds: 'What he finds in his own experience—this fundamental contrast between passivity and activity—he believes to be shared by his fellow men.' Whether the lower creatures have anything approaching this, need not here concern us; the main question is as to the reality and significance of this self-consciousness of something more than mere receptivity. One would think, both from experience and observation, that this sense of activity within, this undeniable consciousness of power to manipulate mentally every impression received from without, was clear enough and strong enough and effective enough to require no discussion, either as to its reality or its significance. Since, however, it is the characteristic of the Naturalism which involves false Determinism to assume that the whole kosmos is 'inert as a whole and inert in every part'—a closed system to which nothing can be added, and from which nothing can be subtracted—it goes without saying that the reality of the human mind's consciousness of activity will be challenged as surely as the sense of freedom. Ultimately, of course these two are one and the same; and they will be challenged because they must be. Dr. Illingworth's estimate of the method, as above given, is thoroughly warranted. 'Freedom must be an illusion, because it ought to be an illusion, is the sum total of the necessitarian position when stripped of all disguise.'

Let us repeat that if Huxley's account of things is to be taken for true, viz. that 'we are but parts of the great series of causes and effects which in an unbroken continuity composes that which is, and has been, and shall be, the sum of existence'—it is evident that there can be no room for the insertion in this 'unbroken continuity' of even a knife-edge amount of creative activity. All the motions of the minds of men are as inevitably predetermined as are the motions of a clock that has been wound up and is allowed to run down. Freedom, in such a case, would be as unthinkable for the man as for the clock. We have noted how, in the Professor's own sighing for such a machine-like construction, already mentioned, as should enable him to do 'right,' he expressly puts it as a mere hypothesis, and leaves it as hopelessly impossible. But according to the attitude of the Naturalism he recommended, it is precisely what ought to be possible. So that the Naturalism which would preclude all spontaneity of activity, stands doubly condemned. It is impossible, in the sense of being inconceivable; for no subtlety of thought or sophistry of speech can ever extract right or wrong as moral qualities from a mechanical system. And it is false, as being directly contrary to the most certain of all facts in normal human experience.

It becomes necessary, therefore, in the interests of true Determinism to call brief but definite attention here to four points: (i) The clear significance of this creative activity of the self. (ii) The unmistakableness of the witness of consciousness to that effect. (iii) The uselessness of denying it. (iv) The plain emergence of the germ of true Determinism.

(i) It cannot be too strongly affirmed that the general experience of all normal men bears out the poet's estimate, when he insists that he knows himself to be something more than an automaton, or a machine determined *ab extra,* or 'clay in the hands of the Potter,'

> Not only cunning casts in clay:
> Let science prove we are, and then
> What matters science unto men,
> At least to me? I would not stay.[1]

The consciousness of power on one's 'own act and on the world,' is the very breath of our inner life from hour to hour, throughout every day. Whence does it come, and what does it mean? Well, it means at the very least that the world within is not the world without. The child and the practical man no doubt think of the outer world—for want of thought—say, on a summer's day, as being composed of green fields, with blue flowers in the hedges and a red-brick house in the distance, with the sound of the song of the lark overhead, or may be the music of a passing band to heighten the impression. Tell them that there are none of these things where they look at or listen for them, and you will be but deemed mad for your information. Yet it is even so. If your dog should be with you, he may be appealed to as an impartial witness. For certainly to him there are no green fields, or blue sky, or red pillar-box or singing birds, whilst his opinion about instrumental music is generally very definitely expressed. If they are not there to him, and they are there to you, there is but one possible inference when the matter is thought out. Out of the material supplied by an external world you have internally made your external world, and the dog has made his. If his life be, as James Mill said, 'a mere succession of smells,' even then there is to a certain extent a necessity for activity in canine

---

[1] *In Memoriam,* CXX.

psychology. But by how much the man's cerebral organization, together with the sensations and perceptions depending on it which constitute his whole inner and outer world, are more complex and comprehensive than a dog's, by so much does he also excel in creative mental activity.[1]

Furthermore, the much-described 'laws of association of ideas' are certainly not mere 'laws of a mental chemistry,' but of mental behaviour. 'Their separating and uniting, their grouping into units, their "syntheses," are not automatic permutations and combinations, but express the *activity* of a thinking intelligence.'[2] In a word, the inner perceptive world is always a created world. It is what it is, not because of impressions just received from without, but because of what the mind itself does with those impressions. This much is beyond controversy now, thanks to the spread of modern scientific knowledge. But surely some other realities cluster round and accompany it. If it be thus true, as it undoubtedly is, that consciousness itself creates its own world,

---

[1] The whole case could not be put more clearly and succinctly than by Dr. Otto in his *Naturalism and Religion*, p. 305. As to the beautifulness or otherwise of the landscape or the city which impresses the plain man—' These qualities are not actually present in the things themselves, they are rather the particular response which our consciousness makes to stimuli. What outside of us is nothing more than a complex process of movement according to mathematical conditions, blossoms within us to a world of sound, tone, and music. The world we know is in the most real sense the product of consciousness itself. Consciousness is certainly dependent on the impressions stamped on it from outside. But it is by no means a *tabula rasa*, or a merely passive mirror of the outer world, for it translates the stimulus thus received into quite a different language and builds up from it a new reality which is quite unlike the mathematic and qualityless reality without.'

[2] Dr. Otto, p. 312, where his illustration by means of squares is peculiarly forcible.

and that 'the spirit is never passive,' then one mainstay of false Determinism is knocked away from its very foundation; i.e. the conception of man in his whole mental constitution as a mere incarnation of passivity, a mere transmitter of motion, whether molecular or otherwise, received from without. Let us mark once more what in these days is issued to the people hereupon. 'Your mind is a machine, nothing more. You have no command over it. It has no command over itself. It is worked *solely from the outside.* That is the law of its make, as it is the law of all machines.'[1] It is certainly amazing at this time of day to find one deemed worthy of an English Doctorate deliberately printing, and with all the emphasis of italics, that

'A man's brain is so constructed that *it can originate nothing whatever.* It can only use material obtained *outside.* It is merely a machine, and it works automatically, not by will power. *It has no command over itself, its owner has no command over it.*'

But what is this power to 'use' material obtained outside, if not a power of original action? And if an 'owner' has no command over the machine at all, in what sense can he be an owner? It is humorous enough, in good sooth, to be told that a man's mind is a machine, and that he is a machine, nothing more. Yet somehow one machine happens to 'own' another machine, and 'use' it by methods and for purposes compared with which earth's most complicated inventions are but crude and clumsy exhibitions of simplicity! This is really a case not of *solvitur ambulando* but *solvitur risu.* A laughing machine could not but be a new creation.

Coming back to sobriety, i.e. to consciousness and

---

[1] Mark Twain's *What is Man?* pp. 10, 12. The italics are his.

truth, Dr. Otto may well summarize for us at once the reality and significance of what we know to be actual in our own experience. 'We are really agents, not mere points of transit for phenomena foreign to ourselves, but starting-points of phenomena peculiar to us, actual causes, beings who are able to initiate activity, to control things, and to set them in motion.'[1] It is this 'peculiar creative character' of consciousness which not only makes a man, but makes him a true Determinist, because a real creator, even in his humblest experiences. He is not a mere connecting link, inert and helpless, between some antecedent and its consequent, but the living answer in himself, in a real though inexpressible sense, to old Omar Khayyám's question—

> And strange to tell, among the Earthen Lot
> Some could articulate, while others not:
> And suddenly one more impatient cried—
> 'Who *is* the Potter, pray, and who the Pot?'[2]

For he knows assuredly in himself that he is not merely 'the Pot,' he '*is* the Potter,' to an extent which can no more be denied than it can be measured. In a word, he knows himself to be not a 'pot' at all, but a person; and Dr. Rashdall has only stated the truth clearly in saying that 'the most essential of all attributes of personality is not merely a feeling, but a willing and originating consciousness. The self is conscious of being an '$ἀρχή$',[3] i.e. a starting-point *de novo*. The same truth is even more forcibly expressed by Mr. V. F. Storr—

'We ourselves, if the verdict of our self-knowledge and experience can be trusted, are in our limited degree, true creative

---

[1] *Naturalism and Religion*, p. 317.
[2] *Rubáiyát*, LX.
[3] *Personal Idealism*, edited by H. Sturt, p. 372.

causes. Physically regarded, we are effects of antecedent conditions; regarded spiritually, we may in part be so, but there does come a point in our analysis of moral personality where we are obliged to stop in our regress, and to confess that we cannot be entirely interpreted in terms of antecedent conditions, but have the power of true self-determination and can originate change."[1]

The clearness and unmistakableness of this verdict of consciousness ought to have prevented the suggestion of any theory that man is a 'conscious automaton,' with all deference to the usual acuteness of Prof. Huxley.[2] The very terms employed are but a futile attempt to blend actual incompatibilities. Consciousness we know, and automatism we know, but 'conscious automatism' is a hopeless self-contradiction. Consciousness, so far as we know it, absolutely refuses to be considered such a mere stream of passivity as automatic construction necessarily involves. Whilst the very conception of an automaton suggests not only mechanism but the absence of everything else. An automaton is said to 'work,' but what is meant is simply that all its motions have been arranged for it and determined beforehand. No person of intelligence ever suggests that an automaton either acts or thinks. Thinking and acting involve perception and volition. But what is knowledge? Certainly not, as we have seen, mere receptivity. Knowledge is the active formation by the self of ideas from 'raw material,' however supplied, and volition is but the similar activity of the self with a purpose in view. One process is constructive, the other teleological. To attribute either, let alone

---

[1] *Development and Divine Purpose*, p. 278.
[2] In his *Gifford Lectures*, Dr. Jas. Ward has dealt with this fairly and finally. *See* Vol. II, Lecture XII, pp. 34–64.

both, of these to an automaton, is but the prostitution of language. Yet without both of these, not only is personality inconceivable, but consciousness is a lie. Huxley's suggestion that, though automata, we are free to do as we like, is quite inappropriate, because an automaton is as incapable of liking as of willing. And that for the simple reason that liking as really, though maybe not so strongly, as willing, involves mental activity. A child likes a mechanical toy, but even the child knows better than to imagine that the toy likes its owner. Nor does Spinoza's well-known attempt to dispose of freedom help the Naturalist case in the least. 'That men are aware of their desires, but ignorant of the causes by which those desires are determined'—is really a *petitio quaestionis*. For a determined desire is not only unthinkable in itself, but is the very point at issue. No antecedent, and no number of antecedents, can 'cause' or 'determine,' i.e. compel a desire.[1] There is an element of self-activity in a genuine desire which cannot by any possibility be eliminated. The spontaneity of a true desire is inalienable. Any attempt to dissect out this active element of the self from desire, is doomed to precisely the same result as an attempt to dissect out vitality from a human body. Only a corpse is left behind in the latter case, and in the former only a sensation. It is small wonder, therefore, that Dr. Ward should say, 'Paradoxical though it may seem, yet even the illusion of activity and spontaneity is certain evidence that activity and spontaneity somehow exist;

---

[1] It may be suggested that there are many automatic desires such as hunger—a desire for food, &c. But these are only physical sensations, not 'desires' in Spinoza's sense. To be accurate, appetite or any other craving which arises from physical sources, should not be termed a 'desire' at all, but an organic function.

and since by common consent they are not found in the physical world, they must be in the psychical.'[1] Here then, is the germ, the *fons et origo* of true Determinism. The main, unmistakable, undeniable, feature of experience is activity. This is the initial stage of that real self-determining which alone deserves to be called Determinism. Whether it can be reconciled with the 'conservation of momentum' or not, is for the moment irrelevant. It is fact, and fact it remains. It is the supreme and inalienable characteristic of the human self. As such it marks man out as not only superior to all other or lower animals, but unique in the known universe. Dr. Andrew Seth has put this wondrous characteristic with admirable succinctness—'Man does what science, occupied only with the law of events, and speculative metaphysics when it surrenders itself to the exclusive guidance of the intellect, alike find unintelligible and are forced to pronounce impossible—he acts.'[2] His being acted on from without, is but the opportunity for his own real action within. His external manifested actions are but the index to his internal actions, and upon the freedom of the latter depends necessarily the character of the former.

(iii) *The Free Self*

The whole matter with which we are here concerned is popularly known as the 'free-will controversy.' Such a phrase, however, is correct only in so far as it intimates that the final question of all is concerning freedom. If the testimony of consciousness in regard to a real and an active self were

---

[1] Vol. II, p. 49.
[2] See *Personal Idealism*, p. 345.

accepted, freedom is involved, and the discussion is ended. But the theme is confessedly so complex and elusive that although it would seem as if everything pertinent had already been said upon all sides, there is need for more, in the hope that repeated and prolonged consideration may do for this perplexing subject something like that which photography has done for astronomy. As the carefully directed and long-continued exposure of the camera's sensitized plate reveals what the keenest glance of the strongest eye could never apprehend, so by persistency of view and repetition of main points, it is possible that the truth in regard to some of the deeper and therefore more obscure portions of human nature may yet be established. There are really two plain questions, whether the answers be plain or not. We need to know as definitely as possible (1) what it is that is free; and (2) what the freedom really means.

(1) As to the first of these, in spite of the immeasurable strength of popular convention in oft-repeated phraseology, it must be definitely affirmed that the well-worn phrase is both unwarranted and misleading. The real question at issue is not that of the freedom of the will. Unless we are to be at liberty to play fast and loose with words on occasions where we need most of all to be careful and exact, there can be no controversy about 'free will,' because will that is not free is no will at all. Will cannot be will without being free. There may in human mentality be motion, energy, result, as in the working of a piston-rod in an engine, without freedom, but not will. Mr. Taylor's words above-noticed deserve repetition—'A will which was not free would be a will which was not a translation into sensible fact of any

one's purpose, and thus no will at all.'[1] So too, Dr. D'Arcy—'Freedom is then the characteristic of will.' Even Hegel here is as intelligible as true, 'Freedom constitutes the substance and essential character of will. Will without freedom is an empty word, and freedom becomes actual only as will.' If, then, all further inquiry as to the 'freedom of the will' could be definitely and for ever discarded, there would be no small gain. Unfortunately the popular clinging to meaningless phrases is not only manifest and persistent, but is encouraged by pseudo-philosophers who set up as teachers.[2] Only slowly, therefore, can we hope that the truth will become clear, viz. that the subject for freedom, in this whole matter is not the will but the man, not the faculty but the self. There is no harm in defining will as Prof. Calderwood did, if it is taken intelligently—'Will is a power of control over the other faculties and capacities of our nature by means of which we are enabled to determine personal activity.'[3] It is 'I' who determine by means of will, not will that

---

[1] *Elements of Metaphysics*, p. 365.

[2] Thus Mr. Blatchford writes, with his usual confidence—'Christians speak of the will as if it were a kind of separate soul, a little cherub who sits up aloft and gives the man his course. Let us accept this idea of the will. Let us suppose that a separate will or faculty called the will governs the mind. That means that the little cherub governs the man. Can a man be justly blamed for the acts of the cherub?' (*God and My Neighbour*, p. 133). If uneducated Christians in popular addresses do so speak, it is no more sensible, or indeed honest, to attack Christian philosophy from such a source, than to take the idea of Socialism which this writer advocates from the wild demands of some continental anarchist. Neither the Bible nor Christian philosophy teaches any such thing as a cherub-will, nor gives the least warrant for such stupidities as are here printed, e.g. 'If God put a "will" on Adam's back, and the will followed the beckoning finger of Eve, whose fault was that?'

[3] *Moral Philosophy*, p. 165.

determines by means of me. Prof. Green's avowal hereupon merits careful regard: 'The will, then, is not some distinct part of a man, separable from intellect and desire, nor the combination of them. It is simply the man himself, and only so the source of action.'[1] But it is necessary to be perfectly clear in this matter, because only so can the truth hinted at above be appreciated, i.e. that the activity of the real self involves also the freedom of the self. Self and will are only separable in thought; in actual volition they are one. Volition is but the teleological expression of the self, i.e. the activity of the self making occasion for its own expression. Such activity connotes freedom, for without freedom there can be no real action, though there may be motion. Certainly no locomotive acts, whithersoever it may move. There is thus a lurking ambiguity which should be exposed in the phrase so often employed, that the will is 'self-determined.' Because it is never true that the will is determined by itself, but always that the human self determines the will.[2] A will is assuredly not a 'cherub that sits up aloft'; it is but the power of control through which the real and active self expresses its aims or seeks to realize its purposes. In that sense we may endorse Prof. Green's words that 'the will is simply the man. Any act of will is the expression of the man as he at the moment is.' In each volition, therefore, man is a true Determinist, for it is he, and he alone, who determines

---

[1] *Prolegomena to Ethics*, p. xxii.
[2] The student who would see this philosophical truth worked out with succinct thoroughness, should procure a little booklet by Dr. Warschauer entitled *Das Willensproblem* (Jena, Verlag von Otto Rassman), in which the thesis that 'Der Wille gehorcht; der Mensch ist frei,' is conclusively set forth.

what the volition shall be, and, so far, the following consequences. Thus the thorough analysis of the facts points us to the philosophy of a true Determinism.

(2) We are now in a position to inquire, with some hope of reliable answer, as to what freedom really means. It will be necessary to clear the way by means of negatives. (i) Mr. Taylor writes that ' to be free, in whatever sense you may use the word, means to be free *from something*.' But surely the only ' something ' from which the term ' free ' connotes deliverance, is constraint, i.e. determination. The source whence the determination is threatened is irrelevant. In the present case there is, however, a plain division into external and internal sources. The ' soft Determinism ' which we have yet seen to be false Determinism, promises freedom from external, i.e. physical constraint. It can do no more. But what a man needs, in order to be a man, is what true Determinism claims for him, i.e. freedom from internal or psychical constraint. It is no real freedom either to assure a man that he is not physically hemmed in by bolts and bars, or that he will not be prevented in any way from doing what he likes, when what he likes, or can like, has been determined for him by antecedents beyond his control. Such freedom simply assures him that he is at liberty to expend a worthless cheque. In response to which—' Thank you for nothing '—will evince sufficient gratitude. The real freedom of true Determinism bids him like what he likes, and choose what he himself prefers. There may be limitations, hindrances, conditions to such freedom, as there are to the freedom of a bird in a cage. But in the cage, be it larger or smaller, the bird is free. Whereas the opposed ' liberty ' of false Determinism means not

only a real cage, but the bird glued to the perch with its head and wings fastened by wires in all directions, so that it may rejoice in the freedom of being an unalterable part of a 'closed system,' in any part of which uncertainty is impossible. This is really what the charm of the 'spontaneity' which is endorsed by the great names of Spinoza and Hegel amounts to. It is a little too much, with all deference to Mr. Picton's memory, to ask either man or bird to be 'satisfied with the freedom of conscious spontaneity, a condition in which we do just as we want to do, though our will is a link in an endless series of untraceable sequence.' Surely in the ultimate this is but pitiful mockery. A will which is but a 'link' is no will at all; and conscious spontaneity which is but part of an endless and resistless series, is no spontaneity at all. From such mocking phantasmagoria true Determinism assures us we are actually free.

(ii) But the liberty which is real is not therefore the much-condemned 'liberty of indifference' which is the same as chance. Dr. Ward's illuminating sentence has been already quoted, but calls for repetition. True liberty does and must 'let contingency into the very heart of things.' But 'the contingency is not that of chance,' because it is that of freedom. We must often acknowledge that there is a point beyond which our analysis cannot penetrate, especially when we ask for the reason or explanation of a choice by a free self. But the assumption that there is nothing beyond our vision, is unwarranted. The fact that I cannot always give myself, let alone others, a clear explanation of my volitions, is no ground whatever for asserting either that my volitions are motiveless, or that my selection of motives has been purely accidental, or that such selection must have been determined. The fact that each of these three alternatives is really unthinkable, drives us back upon a fourth, viz. that the motive whence my volition springs has been made into a *vera causa* only, but surely, by the undeniable, though inexplicable, activity of a free self.

(iii) There is room here also for another caveat. The need for it will be best expressed in Mr. Taylor's words—

'It is no doubt true that I am often aware in resolving on another course of action that I could, if I pleased, act differently. But before I could please, I should have to become a different man. While I am the man I am, it is a manifest absurdity to hold that I can indifferently express in my behaviour, the purposes which constitute my individuality, or their opposites.'[1]

Now experience contradicts this as directly as psychology renders it unnecessary. A man is something more than his moods. But a mood is quite sufficient to explain how I 'could please,' being the same man, both to be patient one hour and impatient the next; or even to do some dark deed one week, which I should certainly not have done another week. 'While I am the man I am,' i.e. a free agent, it is quite open to me, in the mysteries of experience, to preserve self-control one day, and the next yield to drink, or passion, or other solicitations of circumstances. We say truly of a certain action of a known friend 'it is not like him'; yet there is no 'different man' on whom to fasten responsibility. When the prodigal 'came to himself,' he did not come to a 'different man,' but to a different appreciation of himself and of his active powers, with corresponding opportunities and duties.

---

[1] *Metaphysics*, p. 377.

(iv) The true freedom which is given in experience also involves that the self is not the slave of motives, whatever be their reality and influence. Here it would sometimes seem as if the true Determinist, whether he is called a Libertarian or an Indeterminist, has been so far frightened by the threats of false Determinists as to what would happen if he dared to suggest an unmotived and—it is asserted—therefore, uncaused volition, that he has been led to make rather too much than too little of motives, and their relation to volition. He freely acknowledges that an unmotived volition is unthinkable. The self cannot will for nothing. A volition without some reason for it is inconceivable. Every real volition is, in thought, though not necessarily in time, preceded by a motive which is a proleptic result. Motive really expresses the teleological determination of the volition, and therefore is as necessary to volition as being is to thinking. But having gone thus far, it is necessary to proceed carefully. The very conception of a motive implies energizing influence, and in this respect it is more than mere desire. It may be synonymous with a wish, but before the solicitation of desire can become a sufficiently definite wish to act as a motive, something not inherent in it must be added to it. This is what Prof. Green rightly indicates when he says that desires ' do not become motives until the self has identified itself with one or the other.' This is precisely the addition of energy from the active self which is required to transform a wish into a motive. There seems no need here of the shyness with which Prof. Upton regards this statement, for it is entirely true and philosophically essential.

But it is necessary to take cautiously the usual

statement of the case. Thus Prof. Romanes says: 'Although it is true that volitions are caused by motives, yet it is the mind which conditions the motives and therefore its own volitions.' When we ask what it means that the mind 'conditions the motives'—and then that volitions are 'caused by motives,' the general answer is that the mind, or self, makes one motive the strongest and so compels volition. But this requires more thought, as Mr. Taylor has excellently shown.[1] 'Strongest' in this connexion is a dangerous term because of its physical suggestion, which may well suit the purpose of the Naturalist but is not according to truth. For a motive is not and can never be something in itself, independent of the character of the self. That which is a motive to one man is the very opposite to another. 'An alternative is not a motive at all, except in relation to the already existing but not fully defined purpose of some agent; and whether it is a "strong" or a "weak" motive depends likewise on the character of the agent's purpose.' Thus, it is the self alone which transmutes desires into motives, and selects, amongst motives, one which by conscious attention it makes 'strongest,' and so finally the spring of volition.[2]

---

[1] See p. 373 of his *Elements of Metaphysics*.

[2] Sir Oliver Lodge's statement of the case is also well balanced and succinct. 'The free man is he who can control himself, who does not obey every idea as it occurs to him, but weighs and determines for himself, and is not at the mercy of external influences. This is the real meaning of choice and free will. It does not mean that actions are capricious and undetermined; but that they are determined by nothing less than the totality of things. They are not determined by the external world alone, so that they can be calculated and predicted from outside; they are determined by self and external world together. A free man is the master of his motives and selects that motive which he wills to obey.'—*Substance of Faith*, p. 27.

Thus Prof. Upton's representation is correct that man 'in the critical moment of temptation is not merely a theatre on which conflicting motives contend, but is himself able, by having his power of attention at his own free disposal, so to act upon his own ideas or emotional states as to make one or the other the dominant one.'[1] That which is clear as well as that which is not clear herein, will be best exhibited if we consider carefully the normal order of events in any ordinary action. We find this series. (1) Suggestion from external circumstance. (2) Response of real and active self giving rise to various solicitations of desire. (3) Certain desires become, through identification with the self, conflicting motives. (4) Deliberation and consideration of these motives by the self. (5) Selection of some motive from alternatives for emphasis by attention, and consequent rejection or inhibition of others.[2] (6) Emergency of a 'strongest' motive, embodying endorsement by the self as an intention. (7) Permitted passage of motive embodying intention into actual volition. (8) Volition expressed in action. The only point in this series where we encounter the impenetrable is at (5). This step may often mock at our attempted analysis. For there must be some answer to the inevitable question as to why and how any one particular motive is so selected rather than some other. As to the 'how,' frankly we do not know; any more than we know how, by any conceivable process of molecular vibration or cerebration, desire is energized into motive, and motive into volition. As to the 'why,' it is, after all, an evasion to say

---

[1] *Hibbert Lectures*, 1893, p. 309.
[2] 'Effort of attention is thus the essential phenomenon of will.' See pp. 450–452 of Prof. James' *Text-Book of Psychology*.

so easily that the selection of some one particular motive for attention by the self, is the necessary consequence of the character of the self. For in the first place a necessarily acting self would be no self, even as a necessary, i.e. compelled, action is in itself unthinkable. But in the next place, supposing the character of the self to be supremely influential, without being absolutely compulsory, yet whence comes this potent character? If it be simply and wholly due to heredity and environment, then there is no freedom. And if there is no freedom, certainly there is no real selection. On the other hand, if there is real selection, there must be freedom. That is to say, the character must have been formed from heredity and environment, as from 'raw material,' by the self, which is, according to true Determinism, what has really happened. But it must be acknowledged that in such a case the action of the self is left without any adequate explanation. To this, however, as the final crux, we must presently return.

(v) It is enough here to mark that as the self is not the slave of motives, no more is it the slave of character. Here, indeed, Modern Absolute Idealism lands us in an *impasse*. 'The will,' we are told, ' is the man himself.' Also the will is ' governed by motives.' In that case the man, the self, is governed by motives. But that which is governed is certainly not free. Therefore the self, the man, the will, is not free. But, then, 'soft Determinism' insists that the man is free because he has control over his motives, and therefore is only governed in the sense of being self-determined. We are also assured, however, that motives are determined by character, and that the character is the man.[1] So, then, the will,

---

Green's *Prolegomena*, p. xviii.

that is the man, is governed by motives? And yet the motives are governed by the character, that is, by the man. That the man is governed by the man may be true, but is not much of a philosophical discovery. However, although Absolute Idealism does not recognize the existence of a causal self, we may be well content with Prof. Green's summarizing sentence hereupon, as the answer to Dr. Martineau's very pertinent question: 'Is there not a causal self, over and above the caused self, or rather the caused states and contents of the self, left as a deposit from previous behaviour?'—to which we must presently return. Now, however, we echo the reply that 'the feeling, thought, and desire, with which an act conflicts, are influences that a man is aware of, influences to which he is susceptible, but they are not *he*.'[1] After all, we can get behind character, but we cannot get behind 'he.'

(3) So from negatives we pass to what must be said positively concerning the freedom of the self. When the true Determinist insists that the reality of this freedom is given in consciousness, he first faces frankly and unhesitatingly denounces, as a contradiction in terms, the usual sophistry of false Determinism, whether popularly or critically expressed. The superficial appeal to the people, as we have seen, is: 'You have power to choose, then, but you can only choose as your heredity and environment compel you to choose.'[2] The Hegelian expert asks, more subtly: 'Why should the belief that if I choose to shut the door, my choice to shut it was completely determined beforehand, make it unreasonable of me to choose to shut it?'[3] To both of

---

[1] *Green's Prolegomena*, p. 179. [2] *God and My Neighbour*, p. 146.
[3] Prof. McTaggart, *Some Dogmas of Religion*, p. 170.

which the answer must be repeated, i.e. that a 'determined,' i.e. a compelled, choice is at once and for ever unthinkable. Compulsion we know, and a choice we know; but a compelled choice is a meaningless jangle of words. A choice 'completely determined beforehand' is no more thinkable than a round square. So that the belief in such a thing would be in itself unreasonable; for whilst leaving a man perfectly at liberty to shut a door, it would leave him no liberty at all to choose to shut it, any more than the door itself, if not shut, would choose to be left open.

We next echo and answer Prof. Upton's question: 'The Libertarian wishes to know from the Absolute Idealist whether the self has any power of alternative choice, in identifying itself with one solicitation of desire rather than with another?' The true answer —though not such as the Absolute Idealist would give—is an unhesitating affirmative. It is this conscious power of alternative choice which is so unmistakable in normal human consciousness. I am sure that between suggested alternatives I can and do choose, i.e. I originate the series above expressed, at the point indicated; and further, when I have chosen, I am sure that I *could* have chosen otherwise. This, moreover, in point-blank contradiction to the bald confidence with which false Determinism asserts that 'whatever a man does, it is the only thing that he could possibly do at that time.'[1] The reason of the fact that I did not do such and such a thing, is that I *would* not, *not* that I *could* not; and the 'would not' was a definite exercise of causal power by the self, more or less in accordance with character,

---

[1] *Not Guilty*, p. 203.

the character itself being due to habits which were the embodiment of volitions due to previous real repetitions of choice. Whence came each individual choice may remain unknown. At the utmost it is a case of hidden causation rather than causelessness. But the main point is impartially put by Mr. J. S. Mill: 'A person feels morally free who feels that his habits and temptations are not his masters, but he theirs; who even in willing, knows that he could resist.' And it is corroborated by Prof. Romanes in his remark that the 'question of moral responsibility depends upon the question as to whether a man's action in the past might have been other than it was, notwithstanding that all the conditions under which he was placed remained the same.'[1] That, and *that only*, is real freedom, however it may be expressed. It will stand very well in Prof. Mackenzie's phrase: 'To be free means that one is determined by nothing but one's self.'[2] *This, and this only, is true Determinism*. I, the man, the self, by virtue of my personality, determine for myself, my actions, whatever may be the preceding conditions or intermediate steps between suggestion and action. Such self-determination may be unique.[3] There is no reason why it should not be. It is not more unique than is man himself, as

---

[1] *Mind and Motion and Monism*, p. 145.

[2] *Manual of Ethics*, p. 94.

[3] 'A theory of the will is completed only by maintaining that this power is distinct in nature from any other known to us, and that freedom of action in adopting valuable alternatives, is the law of its exercise.'—Calderwood's *Handbook of Moral Philosophy*, p. 190.

Prof. Poynting's weighty words quoted on p. 174 should be recalled. 'Freedom of choice is unlike anything else in nature; Every time an intention is formed in the mind and a deliberate choice is made, we have an event unlike any previous event.'

a product of evolution. It may be mysterious. There is no reason why it should not be. Not a word of Dr. Otto's summary is open to challenge—

'We cannot demonstrate what will is, we can only make it clear to ourselves by performing an act of will and observing ourselves in the doing of it. What is personality? We all feel it. We respect it from the depths of our soul whenever we meet it. We bow down before it unconditionally. But what it is no philosophy has ever yet been able definitely to state.'[1]

Prof. Upton, also, is warranted by the spread of modern scientific knowledge, which reveals above all else our ignorance of ultimate realities in everything, when he asserts that 'it is therefore wholly futile to seek to invalidate man's consciousness of freedom of choice in moments of temptation, on the ground of its inconceivability.' It is not one whit more inconceivable, *per se*, than is the child's consciousness of its own existence. What we do know is that in all our daily experience, ceaselessly recurring and indubitable instances prove that 'there are mental states, or acts, which cannot be deduced from the antecedent mental states. By their very nature they lie beyond scientific explanation.'[2] Such impossibility of explanation is but a testimony to their reality. Speaking on behalf of true Determinism, Dr. Illingworth has, therefore, not said too strongly that 'Freedom is a point upon which we can allow no shuffling or juggling in argument. It is unique, but it is self-evident; and every attempt to explain it away can be shown to involve a *petitio principii* or begging of the question.'[3]

---

[1] Dr. Rudolf Otto, *Naturalism and Religion*, pp. 320, 325.
[2] Bowne's *Personalism*, p. 322.
[3] *Personality*, cheap edition, p. 55.

(iv) *The Sufficient Cause*

It is impossible, however, to discuss the question of the actual freedom of the self without reference to the plea which above all else is made by false Determinism in regard to the universality of natural causation. We have noted above how scornfully its advocates dismiss the notion of any real freedom. The unpardonable sin in the eyes of modern Naturalism is a breach of 'law,' and the reign of 'iron laws' everywhere is said to find its most irrefragable embodiment in the principle of causation. When, therefore, it seems that the conception of a free human self ignores or defies this principle, nothing more is needed for its wholesale condemnation. But how unwarranted is this whole proceeding may be shown without any such appeal to confusing technicalities as sometimes only too reasonably evokes ' the bitter cry of the plain man.'

However it may be expressed, in some form or other, the supreme argument against true Determinism is connected with the principle of natural causation, as expressed in the grip and the extent of law. The typical form of expression is that quoted from Dr. Callaway—' Science steadily reducing one domain of nature after another to the reign of law, still finds itself confronted with one of the solidest and most inveterate of barriers, the belief in free will.' With more or less of blustering dogmatism from some quarters and subtle dialectic from others, the case is represented as a necessary attack in the name of modern science upon the obscurantist philosophy associated with religion. The relation to religion may be postponed whilst we definitely estimate the assumptions made in the name of science, and show that they are no more scientific than philosophical. 'The main argument against Indeterminism,' writes Prof. McTaggart, 'is that which proceeds by establishing the universal validity of the law of causation, and so showing that volitions, like all other events, must be completely determined.'[1] In addition to what has been already pointed out, it is sufficient to reply to such a statement that it answers itself; in that a 'completely determined volition' is a contradiction in terms, as unthinkable as a completely round square. But taken along with other similar statements, it calls for further consideration. Mr. Bertrand Russell puts it thus—

'The principle of causation, that every event is determined by previous events and can theoretically be predicted when enough previous events are known, appears to apply just as much to human actions as to other events. What Determinism maintains is that our will to choose this or that is the effect of antecedents, but this does not prevent our will from being itself a cause of other effects.'[2]

The significance of this last clause we will further consider in a moment. Further quotation is unnecessary to show that the attitude of Naturalistic Determinism here involves two main principles, viz. (1) The universal validity of the law of causation. (2) Its application to all phenomena alike, whether physical or mental. The second of these is, of course, included in the first, but demands separate consideration by way of emphasis.

(1) The supreme axiom of science is the universality of causation. The laws of nature, we are told, as a most elementary and absolutely established fact, work everywhere and always, holding literally

---

[1] *Some Dogmas of Religion*, p. 177.
[2] *Hibbert Journal*, October, 1909, pp. 115, 118.

everything in their grasp. Like some other principles, the conservation of energy to wit, it seems so simple and sure as not to need consideration, until it is thought about. Then many and serious modifications are seen to be quite inevitable. Its insatiable demand is indeed unmistakable. 'It means,' as Dr. B. Bowne says, 'to explain all the higher forms of experience, including life and society, in terms of matter and force, working in space and time under the forms of motion.'[1] Similarly Comte declared that 'all phenomena without exception are governed by invariable laws, with which no volitions, either natural or supernatural, interfere.' Such lucidity, it must be acknowledged, is in this case, definite gain. We know what we have to deal with, and therefore, to that extent, how to deal with it.

(i) The first assumption here is that this universal validity of the law of causation, i.e. the causal determination of an event by its antecedents, is a concrete reality in time and space; which certainly we have no warrant to affirm, for it is not only not proved, but not even provable. It is merely a theoretical hypothesis rendered permissible by such observations as our limited faculties are able to make.

(ii) But the very law of causation itself which is here invested with universal validity, is nothing more than a working hypothesis which is only rendered workable by self-contradiction on the part of Naturalism. For if 'no volition, natural or supernatural, can interfere' with laws because they are invariable, how is their invariability demonstrated, and whence is it derived? It cannot be the former, for that would require, by way of proof, very much more than Naturalism has to offer. It

---
[1] *Personalism*, p. 222.

would require to go both backwards and forwards to infinity to establish a demonstration of absolute invariability. Whilst as to the origin for such, even an infinite regress would not supply it, without a genuine First Cause somehow and somewhere. Without such a dynamic as only a true First Cause can supply and maintain, law itself is but a loud-sounding delusion. For it would have nothing to support it save accidental antecedents with sequences which were not consequences. In a word, law without dynamical causation is unthinkable.

(iii) But law, as involving causation, is the expression and embodiment of volition. So that volition =causation=determination. As law is determined sequence, if any antecedent is to have any consequent, so the true determinant is volition. And to talk about law whilst ignoring volition, is but to beat the air with meaningless words.[1] But when law is rightly regarded as the result of volition, there is no longer any warrant for dogmatic denial of 'interference' by 'volition, either natural or supernatural.' For certainly, the volition without which the origin of law is unthinkable, is equally necessary for the maintenance of law; and such maintenance, whilst excluding the notion of interference, plainly precludes also that of invariability. The power that can originate can vary infinitely. And as the only true conception of law is dynamic determination, there is no prescribed limit to the determination beyond that which is supplied by the dynamic, which is confessedly infinite.

(iv) Indeed, no small portion of ordinary parlance

---

[1] 'To substitute law for cause is puerile thinking, as much as it would be to substitute method for intention, and is indeed a closely analogous blunder.'—Wm. Arthur, Fernley Lecture, *Difference between Physical and Moral Law*, p. 23.

about the 'invariable laws of nature' according to modern science, is simply high falutin. Science, properly understood, knows nothing about either law or invariability.[1] The function of science is the accurate registration of phenomena; and all that it has power to say, even in that sphere, is that within its very limited purview certain antecedents are uniformly followed by certain consequences. We have thus a vast number of series of phenomena which are, so far as we know, unvarying, and by us unalterable. But that is a very different statement from the magisterial pomposity with which a sweep of the hand of Naturalism settles the possibilities of the illimitable universe.

(v) Of this last performance no better exhibition can be imagined than the sentences above quoted: 'All phenomena without exception,' it is affirmed, are governed in precisely the same way; 'Causality applies to human actions just as much as to other events;' 'Volitions, like all other events, must be completely determined'; and so on. But with all respect, such utterances are as unscientific as they are dogmatic. Science knows nothing whatever of any 'must be.' Nor does philosophy warrant any such Papal decision. Whilst as to metaphysics, its verdict is exactly the contrary to what is here so solemnly asserted. For its very first protest is against the confusion which here does duty for argument, and against the wholesale begging of the question which assumes the very thing to be

---

[1] 'There is no longer anything dynamic whatever in science, whether observational or theoretical, but simply a study of the way in which phenomena hang altogether in the observed order of law. Of course this does not deny the idea of causation, but simply locates it in another realm.'—Bowne, *Personalism*, p. 171.

proved, viz. that human volitions are like all other events.

(2) This brings us, however, to the second query above specified, as the inner part of the first, viz. how Naturalism justifies such an assumption of the universal validity of the law of causation as puts physical and mental phenomena into precisely the same kategory; and then, from certain acknowledged principles as to the former, proceeds unhesitatingly to infer the same in regard to the latter. As this is an element of prime importance in the whole case, it is necessary to say with equal carefulness and emphasis, that such a proceeding is worse than false, it is both philosophically invalid and practically absurd.[1] Well does Dr. Otto ask 'what reason is there for regarding occurrences in the realm of physics as a *norm* for the psychical?'—and go on to point to the 'primary and fundamental fact, not indeed capable of explanation, but all the more

---

[1] The Rev. W. Arthur, in his valuable Fernley lecture on *The Difference between Physical and Moral Law*, has added a well-deserved touch of scorn to his protest. 'I must confess that with me it is to this hour a case not proven, that any man could in the silence of his own soul ever say to himself with intelligent conviction, I do believe that discernment, judgement, and choice, that forethought, afterthought and conception, that affection, imagination, and conscience, are governed by laws of one and the same order as weight and measure, taste and odour, colour and form. Fully as is the human intelligence capable of rebellion against the lessons of experience, and of contempt for the registered knowledge of the race, I have my own doubts whether it ever goes so far in that direction as to enable a man to sit down on a cliff by the sea-shore, and, with all his thoughts alive say to himself, 'Those children on the beach are to be governed by laws of one and the same order as the pebbles among which they play.' Or to stand on a ship's deck and say the crew are to be governed by laws of one and the same order as the tackling and the spars. Or to go into a great laboratory and say the students are to be governed by laws of one and the same order as the retorts and the powders' (p. 14).

TRUE DETERMINISM

worthy of attention on that account, that there is an absolute difference between physical occurrences and mental behaviour, between physical and mental causality.'[1]

There are really five main points meriting attention.

(i) In the name of metaphysics as well as of common sense, a definite distinction must be formed between mechanical causality and volitional causality. The former, in point of fact, does not deserve the name at all, but it may be used for the moment as a convenient term for the description of the most common of all relations between ordinarily observed phenomena. It has been well and truly said that in interaction and causal sequence we really see no causality, but only change according to rule, for which we affirm and seek causality.'[2] It seems sweetly simple, and is doubtless sufficient for popular notions, in striking a match to say that the motion is the cause of friction, and the friction is the cause of heat; but deeper thought soon shows that we are making a much larger affirmation than is warranted.[3] All that we see is all that we know, viz. that heat is a uniform sequel to or accompaniment of friction, as friction is of motion upon a rough surface. There is in such series of phenomena neither exhibition of nor room for causality.[4] The name usually employed

---

[1] *Naturalism and Religion*, p. 311. Professor Poynting's emphatic testimony to the same effect has been quoted above. See pp. 107, 174.

[2] Bowne, *Personalism*, p. 173.

[3] 'It is possible, antecedent to reflection, that the cause is found in the things of perception, but it is equally possible that these things are only phenomenal process of an energy beyond them and manifesting itself in them, in which case the causality is no longer in them, but elsewhere.'—Bowne, *Personalism*, p. 173.

[4] 'Where, as in abstract physics, we are restricted to the continuous changes of an energy that has neither beginning nor

for all such happenings is far too great for the occasion. When a boy does his sums upon a slate, there would be no more science than sense in affirming that the pencil was the cause of the marks upon the slate. But the causelessness of the action of the pencil—seeing that it is completely determined *ab extra*—would be perfectly typical of that which is ceaselessly going on around us throughout the whole phenomenal world. 'Causality,' said Kant, with good authority, 'is intelligence endowed with will.' But there is in nature, according to naturalistic Determinism, neither intelligence nor will. There is merely an unvarying succession of completely determined events following upon preceding events. In such case it is vain to talk about causation in nature at all. There can be no causation where there is no volition. In what is termed physical causation, every event is but the completely determined result of the preceding event, so that if the notion of an initiating infinite volition be excluded, all natural phenomena are simply facts for which the only cause is an infinite regress—which is, of course, no cause at all.

(ii) Further: Mr. Herbert Spencer has definitely shown that our idea of causation not merely requires a mind for its occurrence, but that in every mind where it does occur it has been directly formed out of experience of effort in giving rise to a volition. From the unquestionable results of such causal effort on our own part, we infer the necessity of a causal

end, transforming itself indefinitely within the two endless *continua* of space and time, there is no place for causality, but only for varying facts due to varying relations of position, speed, &c., between the moving masses. The world for physics is one vast continuous fact taking the form of change.'—*Personal Idealism*, p. 174.

explanation for all phenomena. In so far, then, as these phenomena are only effects, they are but the result of an adequate pre-determining volition.

(iii) The volitional causality of which we are self-conscious being real causality, the human mind becomes necessarily in itself a true, that is, a first cause, and so a volition is more than a phenomenon, and if it be called an event, it is certainly unlike all other events. Prof. Romanes' statement hereupon merits undiminished regard. 'If it thus belongs to the essence of our idea of causation that finality must be reached somewhere, I do not know where this is so likely to be reached as at that principle wherein the idea takes its rise, viz. mind. But if so, the statement that any particular acts of mind are uncaused, ceases to present any character of self-evident absurdity.'[1] A volition is thus in every case an initiation, a fresh starting-point. It not only faces the future teleologically, it creates the future. In other terms, it determines the future, and is thus in human affairs the true and only Determinism with which moral philosophy is concerned.

(iv) The usual objection here raised is not nearly so formidable as it seems, or is often assumed, to be. 'How often,' well says Dr. J. Ward, 'in the history of science have false and hasty assumptions been called axioms, only because they were simple and could not be proved,' and we may add—or disproved. The notion that the principle of the 'conservation of energy' was a fatal bar to any such suggestion as a new creating force in a human volition, ought now to take its place amongst exploded fallacies. In the same brilliant lecture from

---

[1] *Mind and Motion and Monism*, p. 153

which the words just quoted are taken,[1] the Professor has also given good reasons for saying that—

'Those who insist that the quantity of energy in the universe must be constant, appear to me in the same position as one who should maintain that the quantity of water in a vast lake must be constant merely because the surface was always level, though he could never reach its shores or fathom its depths.'

Thus, in the first place, any dogmatic statement of the incompatibility of the principle of the conservation of energy with human freedom, on the ground that the amount of energy in the material universe is constant, is quite unwarranted, because there is no valid reason for this last affirmation.[2] It is not known to be constant. No attempt has been made to prove it—no human attempt could possibly come near proving it. Dr. Ward rightly asserts that 'it is plainly impossible to prove that this phenomenal energy in the universe is fixed in amount.' But that is not all. 'This so-called principle of the constancy of energy has not even the hypothetical necessity of a regulative principle of physics.'[3] All that it really amounts to is that if a certain measured quantity of physical energy be

[1] *Gifford Lectures*, for 1896, Lecture XIII.

[2] 'This statement is far from being the record of an established fact. What physicist has ever established an equation between the whole energy of the universe at any time, including the energies of all the stars of heaven and all the souls of all living bodies, and its energy at a subsequent moment of time?'—Mr. W. R. Boyce Gibson, in *Personal Idealism*, p. 151.

[3] This further sentence from the same thoughtful writer should be added. 'Now when the constancy of energy is understood in this strictly economical and scientific sense, the interpretation cannot in any way demand the exclusion of mind from among the possible determinants of material changes, without making the assumption that the truth of the principle within the closed circle of material agency, sufficiently justifies the inference that material things must *under all circumstances* form a circle closed on all sides' (p. 153).

transformed, its amount after transformation will be the same as before. That is a very useful and well-warranted postulate of physics; but it has no force whatever against the initiation of energy from such a genuine starting-point as a human volition. Mr. Gibson has good grounds, therefore, for concluding that 'the doctrine of the conservation of energy can offer no decisive objection to the theory that mind controls matter by actually increasing or diminishing the amount of energy in the universe.'[1]

(v) Dr. Ward puts the case so explicitly as to throw emphasis upon another matter of definite importance. We have noted above how Prof. W. K. Clifford in one of his lectures, said, with his usual dogmatic tone, 'If anybody says that the will influences matter, the statement is not untrue, it is nonsense.' Seeing, however, that five minutes' reflection on one minute's experiment, is at any time enough to convince every open mind that this assertion is as false as it is confident, correspondingly refreshing from a philosopher of first rank is the deliberate assurance that 'these two things seem certain, that mind does somehow direct the movements of matter, and that the constancy of the phenomenal energy of the universe is neither a fact established by indication nor a necessity of thought.'[2] There we may well leave this alleged objection.

---

[1] *Personal Idealism*, p. 154.

[2] *Naturalism and Agnosticism*, pp. 11, 78. If the word 'nonsense' must be used at all in this discussion, it would appear to be in such a connexion as Dr. Bowne illustrates when he says—'To tell us that this life as lived is a case of matter and motion, is nonsense. To tell us that this life is explained by matter and motion, is equally nonsense.' But it is irrefragable truth that 'whether our thoughts and purposes have any influence upon our physical states, is to be determined by experience only' (*Personalism*, pp. 317, 318). How then, can any man, in the name of philosophy, ridicule its direct testimony?

In the light of the foregoing, let us attempt to summarize what true Determinism involves, as protesting against the modern greedy grasp of 'iron laws' relative to cause and effect. When, in the name of experience and of valid philosophy combined, it is asserted that man is free as to his volitions, what is definitely intended? Certainly the following.

(i) Such real freedom distinguishes volitional causality from what is observed elsewhere in nature, which may be called mechanical or necessary causality, though it is really no causality at all, but simply the transmission of influence from one effect to another.

(ii) It regards each sane human mind as a real, that is a first, cause. 'The cycle of inner mental life does not consist throughout of a rigid mechanism working necessarily, but along with unlimited freedom of will which also possesses a limited power of unconditional commencement.'[1]

(iii) This apprehension of the true cause of human volition, at once satisfies the scientific principle of causation, and gives metaphysics the sufficient cause which it also demands. It bids us, indeed, cease to speak and write about 'free will'; but it gives us the truer and better concept of the free man. It is the free self which speaks from the very heart of human consciousness as in the above-quoted words of Dr. Rice, 'I am myself the cause of my volitions, and no other cause is needed.'[2] Beyond or behind that it is neither necessary nor possible to go.

(iv) The present is thus explained both with and without the past. To an extent which cannot be measured any more than it can be questioned, the present is conditioned by the past. But it is not

---
[1] *Lotze*, quoted by Ward, Vol. II, p. 83.
[2] *Christian Faith in an Age of Science*, p. 293.

determined. The past itself was not determined for me, but has been to an immeasurable extent created by me. And still more, as long as my manhood remains, be the influences of the past what they may, I determine the present, and so far influence the future.

(v) This 'I,' which is at once the symbol and substance of personality, does not admit of analysis, any more than of denial. 'Personality can never be construed as a product or compound.' It can only be experienced as a fact.[1] It is worse than useless to try to explain the figure in front of a mirror by feeling about behind the mirror.

(vi) The self-consciousness which is the essence of personality is as unshakable as unanalysable. A person is a being who is 'distinctly conscious of his own activity as a causal self every hour in his life.' The consciousness of existence, moment by moment, is not one whit more indubitable than the consciousness of causal power. The canary in the cage learns by experience that it cannot fly beyond the bars, but the experience that it can fly which way it is disposed within the cage, is quite as reliable as it is real. If it does not know that it can hop upon which perch it chooses, it knows nothing. Probably it does not know. Its cerebral limitations, permitting no abstract thought, doom it to a genuine pragmatism. But the possession of a human faculty for the apprehension of the abstract, after all, only means a larger

---

[1] *Personalism*, Dr. Bowne, p. 264.

[2] Prof. Upton's *Hibbert Lectures*, p. 312. He goes on to say that when Mr. Bradley, following Mr. J. S. Mill, asserts that voluntary attention to an idea only means that the idea happens to be more vivid than other attendant ideas—'It would be difficult, I think, to find a more flagrant case in which the clear deliverance of consciousness has been unconsciously perverted to meet the exigencies of a preconceived philosophical theory.' Such a stricture is abundantly justified.

cage. It does not mean that because consciousness is so much more clear and intense in its reality, it must be correspondingly unreliable.

(vii) Rather may we certainly affirm that the philosophy which calls upon a man to deny that which he knows best, most surely, and most immediately, may be dismissed as no less untrue than unworthy. The only warrant for suggesting that such clear consciousness of causal freedom is illusory, we are driven to repeat, is the maintenance of a preconceived system of philosophy. The only philosophy of the human mind that deserves the name, is inductive. But the induction which commences by rejecting the most patent as well as potent of realities, blocks the way to any further progress and so becomes wholly futile. As no science of psychology can be constructed upon the denial of the ascertained phenomenal relations of mind and brain, so can no mental philosophy be built up upon the denial of the clearest and surest factor in metaphysics.

(viii) The true Determinism, however, which is founded as a philosophy upon the undeniability of experience, neither needs nor cares to deny the real crux of the whole difficulty which is inseparable from the genuine freedom of the casual self. It is hardly necessary to point it out, because it appears everywhere. In his admirable summary of the case, Dr. Warschauer says—

'Every choice is certainly the result of an efficient cause, but the fact of this being so interferes in no wise with the reality of liberty, nor does it contradict the universality of the law of causality. For the efficient cause is the man himself, and the fact that he can choose is attested in the very act of choice.'[1]

Which is as true as succinct.

---
[1] *Problems of Immanence*, ch. ix.

We have, however, still to meet the obvious reply of the false Determinist, which is at once—in Prof. McTaggart's formula—that according to this theory 'our choice between motives is not determined by anything at all.' Assuming that the man himself *is* the efficient cause of a choice, yet the choice must be at least between two alternatives. Why, then, does the man choose one alternative rather than another? A choice for no reason is as unthinkable as Buridan's ass was immovable. But if he chooses for some reason, does not that reason determine the choice? When, indeed, it is said that a man's character ultimately decides his choice, and so the psychological situation is saved—as Prof. Green taught—the reply must obviously be that in this case freedom is lost. If a man's character determines his choice, then manifestly he has no choice at all. If, however, the Indeterminist insists, and truly, that the man may act against his previous character, and certainly makes his own character, the same question still remains. Dr. D'Arcy says, 'In the main, character consists of habits. It is, therefore, the child of will. It is self-created.'[1] But for each separate act, which contributes to a self-created habit, there must be some reason, some motive. Why does the free self choose one line of action rather than another?

---

[1] *Idealism and Theology*, p. 109. Dr. Fairbairn, with his wonted perspicuity, puts it thus—'If motives determine action, the fable of Buridan's ass ceases to be fabulous. It is possible to conceive alternatives where the motives are so equally balanced that the will would be compelled to remain in a state of complete equilibrium, incapable of inclining either to the right hand or to the left. But while will is not necessitated by motives, motives are necessary to choice. For it is the very essence of rational freedom to demand a reason why it should act. If there were no reason, choice could not be rational; it would be an accident or a chance.'—*Philosophy of the Christian Religion*, p. 77.

The only choice left us here appears to be between an antinomy and an infinite regress, which is a veritable Scylla or Charybdis. If the self be ever so free to choose, choice without a reason—or cause, or preference—for that choice, is unthinkable. If the reason be sufficient, it is determining. So we come to the antinomy of a free and yet determined choice, which seems self-contradiction. If, however, it be suggested that self exercises control over the reason which controls the choice, then there must be a reason for such control, and so on *ad infinitum*. Dr. Bowne says with much force that 'in every mechanical doctrine of causality, every present change finds its causality in an infinite regress which can never be completed, and in which thought perishes. In volitional causality we trace the act to the personal purpose and volition, and there the regress ceases.'[1] But does it cease? Must not the 'personal purpose' look definitely in some direction? If so, why not in another direction? There cannot be purpose without a motive for it. Whence, then, comes that motive, and how does it become the sufficient motive for the purpose?

(ix) Dr. Fairbairn remarks, truly enough, 'that the reality of freedom lies deeper than argument.' But we must have a reason even for being content with that which cannot be rationally made clear. In the present case, it would seem to be this, that whilst philosophy can be baffled, consciousness cannot be denied. The very worst that can be said against the true Determinism which constitutes the essence of our free personality is, in Mr. McCabe's candid phrase, that 'at a point in the obscure recesses of the brain we lose the sequence of events.'

---

[1] *Personalism*, p. 191.

Only 'brain,' here, is not deep enough. Rather is it true that in the still more obscure recesses of consciousness, whether subliminal or otherwise, we fail to discover the reciprocal action of self and motives one upon another.

Seeing, however, that we can by no means define the self, it is small matter for marvel that we cannot trace its action. I know that I am, without knowing ultimately how I am what I am. I know that I will, and that through an immaterial volition I act directly on matter, both within and without my body, but how, I know not, nor can any man tell me. I know that my volition follows a final motive, but that I am responsible for both its finality and its efficiency, because I myself and none other so determined it. My motive is nothing without *me*. My finally permitted motive is the expression of myself in purpose. But how I come to consent to that motive's prevalence whilst others are rejected, is a matter beyond further analysis. I know that my character counts in such a selection of prevalent motive. Yet I know that it *is* a selection, and that not even my character can determine it without me. My character, indeed, is in itself but the result of my consciously free self's use of what was received in heredity and has come from environment. But I and my character are not synonyms. I am more, and other, than my character. That which is mine is necessarily distinct from me. I am the causal self, my character is the caused self. From out the impenetrable heart of the mystery of human consciousness I emerge, a real, free, and active self. In and through all the activities of thought-life from day to day, I remain the efficient and sufficient cause of my volitions by means of permitted or created or intensified motives. I and I alone, in heaven or earth, am the determiner of my growing character, the captain of my soul, the master of my fate.

(v) *The Relation to Heredity and Environment*

The strongest element of the appeal of Determinedism to the ordinary mind comes through reference to heredity and environment. These are markedly distinct in thought, but for the purpose of showing that the average man is so completely determined that he cannot help himself, the two are always linked together because they are in their practical working inseparable. 'Heredity makes the man, and environment modifies him,'[1] is the current superficiality which plumes itself as an oracularly simple settlement of an age-long problem.

---

[1] *Not Guilty*, R. Blatchford, p. 127; with the modest comment that this settles all 'the confusion of mind into which educated men fall when they deal with this simple subject.' Where the simplicity really lies is manifest enough to every student. Elsewhere (*Clarion*, March 3, 1911), this writer says that his books on these themes are 'plain and careful demonstrations of the obvious. I cut and shovelled away the pedantic débris and showed the old truths so that all might see them. I translated the language of the pedants and the sophists into plain Saxon English.' It would be impolite to say what is indeed most of all 'obvious' here. But such a mood seems inseparable from arrant dogmatism in the modern popular advocacy of Determinedism. Thus Prof. Hamon sums all up by the assurance that 'only backward minds, expressed by vague metaphysics, defend the inconceivability which we call freedom of the will. Scientifically, man is the inevitable product of the surroundings in which he lives and in which his ancestors lived. He is not responsible for his actions, for he could not help wishing them, the conditions once given.'—*The Illusion of Free Will*, p. 115.

TRUE DETERMINISM

The man in the street is naturally caught by the glib confidence of Mark Twain's posthumous deliverance, that 'a man's temperament and training will decide what he shall do, and he will do it. He cannot help himself, he has no authority over the matter.'[1] One can hardly expect the average reader to appreciate the self-contradiction of talking about a man's 'doing' anything, when he cannot help himself. As if the pen that writes these words, really did anything! Unfortunately, however, these popular dogmatisms, which have become of late increasingly frequent, find no small support from some quarters which loudly claim to be scientific. Dr. Maudsley, for instance, declared that 'there is a destiny made for a man by his ancestors, and no one can elude, were he able even to attempt it, the tyranny of his organization.' Prof. Tyndall's words, above quoted, not only reached the men of his own generation, but produced an effect which has never been wholly dissipated. 'My physical and intellectual structures were woven for me, not by me. Processes in the conduct or regulation of which I had no share, have made me what I am. Here surely, if anywhere, we are as clay in the hands of the potter.'[2] But such a statement is only a half truth which begs the question. The very matter which Determinedism ought to prove, but certainly does not and cannot prove, is that 'processes *per se*,' of any sort, 'have made me what I am.' Such a representation is as a violin solo with the violinist left wholly out of account. But the further words of this eminent scientist may well here be given as expressing succinctly what is still, with the added

---

[1] *What is Man?* p. 140.
[2] *Fragments of Science*, Vol. II, p. 362.

emphasis of later biological and physiological research, the attitude which largely obtains to-day—

'If, then, our organisms, with all their tendencies and capacities, are given to us without our being consulted; and if, while capable of acting within certain limits in accordance with our wishes we are not masters of the circumstances in which motives and wishes originate; and if, finally, our motives and wishes determine our actions, in what sense can these actions be said to be the result of free will?'[1]

Now the first comment that has to be made upon this attitude, is that it is in this case utterly unscientific to be only scientific. For we have to face realities which are beyond science, and it would be as scientific to leave out all thought of ether in physical matters because it cannot be located or defined, as it would in matters human to dismiss metaphysical considerations, because they cannot be weighed in the balances of our laboratories or precisely set forth in psychological definitions. The quest upon which we are here engaged, starts from the fact that we are dealing with human beings. And the very fact that we are capable of such a quest is sufficient proof that in man brain connotes more than it does in animals. To write as the popular journalist does that 'the brain is the mind' is simply stupid.[2] That the brain is the

---

[1] p. 364. All the specious modern propagandism of false Determinism during recent years is but an echo of this, e.g. 'From the moment of his birth, man is what his inherited nature and the influences into which he has been sent without his consent have made him.' 'Man is what he is by the act of God, or the results of heredity and environment. In either case he is not to blame. Take away from a man all that heredity and environment have given him and there will be nothing left,' &c.—*God and My Neighbour*, pp. 139, 144.

[2] *Not Guilty*, p. 95. It is not improved by later deliverances, e.g. 'When I think, I become unconscious of my personality and of my surroundings. I am not a "self," I am a brain isolated in space' (*Clarion*, March 3, 1911). How an isolated brain can think at all, we are not told.

organ of mind no one wishes to deny. The cardinal fact is that the brain of man is the means of mind in a unique sense. The difference between mind in man and its analogue in animals, is psychologically immeasurable. For it lies, as Dr. Otto has well said, 'not in the fact that man has a few more capacities than an animal, but in the difference in principle, that the psychical in man can be developed to spirit and that this is impossible anywhere else.'[1]

On the ground of experience, the development of the psychical in human nature may be said, in spite of all controversy, to involve not merely consciousness, but consciousness of a unique self. This self is not only receptive from without, but creative from within, and is distinguished no less by reality of volition than by actuality of perception. These qualities united give human personality. To start any questions concerning heredity and environment with less than this, is to be untrue to fact and therefore unscientific. Mr. V. F. Storr has not in any degree exceeded facts in affirming that—

'Physically regarded we are effects of antecedent conditions; regarded spiritually, we may in part be so, but there does come a point in our analysis of moral personality where we are obliged to stop in our regress, and to confess that we cannot be entirely interpreted in terms of antecedent conditions but have the power of true self-determination and can originate change.'[2]

It being clearly understood, therefore, that we are dealing with human heredity and environment, there are four inquiries to be met. (1) What is heredity? (2) What is man, more than heredity? (3) What

---

[1] *Naturalism and Religion*, p. 332. So again, 'Psychical capacity is nothing more than raw material. It is in the possibility of raising this to the level of spirit, of using the raw material to its purpose, that the absolute difference, the impassable gulf between man and animals, lies.'

[2] *Development and Divine Purpose*, p. 278.

is environment? (4) What can man be or do, under the influences of heredity and environment?

(1) Upon the first of these it is not necessary to deal to any detailed extent. First, because there is no ground of dispute as to the biological factors of the case.[1] Secondly, because not only is the whole subject of heredity, even biologically considered, so complicated as to leave us almost without any hope of apprehending, let alone controlling, it—Mendelism has at present no certain application to the human species—but the elements involved in the propagation of the human race, mark it off as quite distinct in most important elements from all that we know concerning the lower animals. When, indeed, justice is done to the wondrous constitution and powers of the human spirit, it is easy to understand how the keen controversy of old between Creationism and Traducianism could arise and be prolonged. If the former is now given up by general consent, it is not because life's mystery is solved by the latter. Nor is it true, as sometimes assumed, that the germ-plasm theory of Weismann has so completely triumphed as to oust alike Galton's Stirp Theory, Darwin's Pangenesis, or H. Spencer's theory of physiological units, to say nothing of Delage and Hertwig. The doctrine of the transmission of acquired characters has fallen temporarily into disrepute. Not only, however, does Eimer remain largely unanswered, but there are certain facts of common observation which serve to show that something more than 'stock' does definitely

---

[1] An excellent summary of these will be found in Dr. S. Herbert's *The First Principles of Heredity*, recently published by A. & C. Black, with many helpful illustrations and diagrams. Also, in a still more succinct form in Mr. Doncaster's little volume—*Heredity in the Light of Recent Research* (Cambridge University Press).

come into play, in what is transmitted from parent to child. We must here be content to say that such transmission includes the whole being; the body and mind of the child with all their potentialities, are undoubtedly derived from the parents. Not, of course, from the father only, or from the mother only, but from that mysterious blending of two natures which science is utterly baffled to trace out. So complete thus appears to be the dependence of the human offspring upon heredity, that the second query above proposed becomes inevitable.

(2) What is in man, if anything, more than his heredity? If heredity gives *everything* that is found in each man's experience, except an inevitable effect of environment, of course, freedom of any kind is at an end, and Determinedism is demonstrated. 'Given a particular nature,' says the popular advocate, 'and given particular influences, the result will be as mathematically inevitable as the speed and orbit of a planet.'[1] Which is as simple and dogmatic as any Determinedist can desire. The fact that such an oracular deliverance completely begs the whole question, does not apparently trouble the writer in the least. It is here, however, that the first strong stand has to be made by the true Determinist. There is assuredly no controversy possible concerning the fact that a planet is a thing, devoid in itself alike of life and consciousness. If, then, the analogy so triumphantly proclaimed is to hold good in the exactitude asserted, it can only be upon the unqualified assumption that man, too, is just a thing, neither living nor conscious. If we do not know that to be false, we know absolutely nothing, and all our words, written or spoken, are but sawing the wind. But be the

---
[1] *God and My Neighbour*, pp. 138, 139.

psychological and metaphysical problems of personality as baffling as they may, Dr. Otto is quite justified in saying that 'it is by no means the case that in order to discover the truth, we must start from a position of scepticism, instead of from calm confidence in ourselves and in our conviction that we possess in direct experience the best guarantee of truth.'[1] Is it not beyond controversy that we possess in ourselves the direct experience of personality? At all events no man can deny that without affirming it. For only a person can deny anything. Moreover, the very difference between truth and error, which is supposed to be the aim of all discussions between those who advocate Determinedism and their opponents, implies that a man must be a real, that is a free, personality, in order to enter upon it. If Naturalism be in the right, thought is not free—any more than there is free thought in the swing of a planet round its orbit—and if thought be not free, there can neither be truth nor error. So then the man of whom we think, in order to be a man, must be and is a person. That is fundamental and absolute. If it were not, these pages could never have been written, nor could they ever be read.

But the next step is no less firm, viz. that a person is always a creature of three dimensions, and never of two only. Never can there be with truth any such statement of the human equation as that heredity + environment = personality. There is on the right side an unknown but most real x, which renders such an equation for ever insoluble. So unmistakable and intractable is this human surd, that those who deny it cannot but confirm it in their

---

[1] *Naturalism and Religion*, p. 295.

very denial. Only a person can possibly deny that he is a person. No other animal can possibly disclaim personality. If actual demonstration to this effect be desired, it can be supplied without limit from the works of those who set themselves to show, as Mark Twain has recently done, that 'man is merely a machine and an impersonal engine.' We have only to listen—

Young Man. 'You really think that man is a mere machine?'
Old Man. 'I do.'
Y.M. 'And that *his* mind works automatically, and is independent of *his* control, carries on thought on *its* own hook?'
O.M. 'Yes.'

And yet the writer does not see that in his very employment of the pronouns which we here italicize, he contradicts himself as flatly as thought and language together permit. If it be anything better than the babble of a lunatic to speak of 'his mind,' then there must be a 'he' to match. And all the humorists in the world cannot make us smilingly acknowledge an impersonal 'he.' Every child is philosopher enough to know that to speak of an engine or a doll as 'he' or 'she,' is mere pretence and nothing more. Perhaps, seeing the importance of this matter, even for the least instructed, it may be well to take one other instance from the collection of superficial dogmatisms which has been issued on purpose to convert modern society to Determinedism.

'Now let us consider the example of the swimmer and the stream. The swimmer is something more than a mere heredity. He is a man, and he has learnt to swim. Therefore in his battle with the stream of environment he is using heredity and environment. For environment taught him to swim.'[1]

---

[1] *Not Guilty*, R. Blatchford, p. 135

The last sentence suggests a refreshingly simple way of life-saving which should economize all the Humane Society's medals in the future. When a man falls into the water, all we have to do is to let him alone, for the water will teach him to swim. It is a pity this was not made known to humanity earlier. As for the rest of this oracle of Determinedism, one can but be grateful. A franker statement of true Determinism it would be difficult to find. A man is 'something more than a mere heredity.' He is, indeed——'I thank thee, Jew, for teaching me that word.' But 'he,' it is also to be observed, 'battles with the stream of environment.' It would be interesting, if we keep this writer's previous figure well in mind, to know how a planet with mathematically fixed motions, 'battles with' its environment, as it is driven round its ellipse. But if man = heredity + 'something,' is it the heredity or the 'something' which initiates the battling? Still more noticeable, however, is the avowal that man, this same heredity + something, 'is using heredity and environment.' Here again it is necessary to ask, Is it the heredity, or the something, which is 'using' these two factors for a purpose? Perhaps this pseudo-philosopher would not even decline the task of proving that heredity is using heredity. We are rather driven to the inevitable conclusion that something, which is not heredity, 'is using heredity and environment.' Which is the indubitable truth. But the issues do not favour Determinedism. The 'something' of which I am conscious, in addition to my heredity, is my personality. Whether it be called a self, or a soul, or an ego, or an individuality, or a something, is quite irrelevant. It is I myself. And unless all thought be mere delirium, and all language parrot-chatter, when I *use* anything I am both distinct from it, and, as far as it is concerned, free. No sophistry of thought or speech can identify me with the pen which I use in order to write this, or make my actions to be completely determined by it. To those, therefore, who strenuously deny the autonomy and freedom of the human spirit, we are indebted for bringing us thus far on our quest. Heredity gives the child the initial body and brain in which, far too deeply hid for all our scrutiny to analyse, lie the potentialities of physical growth and mental development. The mental development becomes unique. Mind in animals there may be; but it is far from the same as mind in man. Nor is the difference merely quantitative but definitely qualitative.[1]

Out of the human heredity develops—we neither know, nor need to know, how—personality, concerning which whatever we do not know, two things, at least, we do know. First, in Dr. Otto's above-quoted phrase, that 'it is the most certain reality, without which the simplest psycho-physical life would be impossible.' Secondly, that out of and with the personality develops, through gradual but unmistakable self-realization, an individuality which 'is absolutely bounded off from the whole world and all existence, as a self-contained and independent world in itself.'[2] This is confessedly the very core of human existence.

---

[1] Prof. Haeckel intimates (*Riddle of the Universe*, cheap edition, p. 72) that if a man will keep a fine dog for a year, he will be convinced of the similarity—as regards any claim to immortality—between the human and the canine mind. Let any one do it honestly and thoroughly, as I have done with several fine dogs for years, and the overwhelming contradiction may be left to make itself felt.

[2] *Naturalism and Religion*, pp. 316, 336.

252 DETERMINISM: FALSE AND TRUE

This individual self, as distinct from mere heredity, as I am from my body, is at once the very mystery of mysteries, and reality of realities, of our human nature. We are entitled to regard this as absolute certainty, not merely on the ground of our own consciousness of individuality, but because philosophy is impossible on any other lines; whilst ordinary fact testifies quite as clearly as profound reflection, to the utter impossibility of truly representing or fairly construing human nature in less than three dimensions. The case for a *man* as a creature of two dimensions only, heredity and environment, never has been stated and never can be. The attempt to state it necessarily contradicts it. It is, however, true to the uttermost, so far as we can analyse ourselves and watch our children, to affirm that—

'No psyche is simply derivable from other psyches. What the child receives from its parents by heredity, are factors which taken together amount to more than the mere sum of them. The synthesis of these is at once the creation of something new and peculiar, and what has been handed down is merely the building material.'[1]

In face of all the facts, it is not too much to say that by how much, through the intervening mind of the architect, a noble pile, whether cathedral or city hall, differs from the stones and beams gathered for its construction, by so much, through the unanalysable but actual work of the individual self, does the character evinced by the child after the years have afforded opportunity for self-realization and self-determination differ from the constitution received from parents. That such a process involves real freedom, and connotes the true Determinism which

---

[1] Otto, *Naturalism and Religion*, p. 327.

is at once the glory and the danger of human nature, requires no demonstration.[1]

How actual this freedom is, once again we may learn from those who deny it. On one page, the valiant champion for Determinedism affirms that 'Heredity and environment have decided the action of the will before the time has come for the will to act.' But a few pages later the same writer exclaims, 'Talk about the trouble of bringing up one's children; what is that to the trouble of educating one's ancestors? O, the difficulty I have had with mine!'[2] So that the ancestors who, through heredity, fix the action of a man's will before he is born, have yet to be reconciled with and directed by the man himself as to how to determine their determination. In other words, heredity makes the man, but only when the man himself determines what the make shall be. Which is the only true Determinism.

(3) It is, however, often said in reply, by the thorough-going Determinedist, that what heredity leaves open in the complete predetermination of the human will, environment comes in to decide. It becomes necessary, therefore, to consider for a moment what environment is, in clear distinction from what it is not, as well as to estimate its influence for good or ill. The confusion which yet prevails hereupon and is fostered by the modern atmosphere

---

[1] Dr. Fairbairn's putting of the case merits mention for its succinct lucidity: 'What a man inherits leaves him still a free man. The judgement he has to bear is for his own act, not for the acts of his ancestry, even though they may have created in him tendencies which are not easily resisted. These tendencies do not cancel freedom, they only condition it; they define the limits of responsibility, but while they may qualify they do not annul it, for its ground stands unbroken.'—*The Philosophy of the Christian Religion*, p. 77.

[2] *Not Guilty*, pp. 181, 251.

will best be illustrated from the same popular source just quoted, for the statement is typical of many others.

'When we speak of a man's environment, we mean his surroundings, his *experiences*, all that he sees, hears, *feels*, and *learns* from the instant that the lamp of life is kindled to the instant when the light goes out. We mean his mother's milk, the home and the state of life into which he is born. We mean the games he plays, the *work he does*, the sights he sees, the sounds he hears. We mean all his *hopes* and *fears*, his *victories* and defeats, all the *harm* he *does*, and all the *help* he *gives*—everything he *does* and suffers under the sun. We must remember that everything that happens to a man, everything that influences him, is part of his environment. Everything outside our skin belongs to our environment. *Education* is environment; *religion* is environment; *honour* and dishonour are environment; *love* is environment.'[1]

The words italicized—not by the author—will sufficiently serve to emphasize the fallacies of such pseudo-philosophy. Not only is it in itself untrue that all these are mere environment, but they plainly fail to stand the double test which the statement itself proposes. 'Everything that happens to a man'—'everything outside our skin.' To apply these to the terms specially pointed out, is to see the absurdity of the jumble which is offered as definition. Experience, work, victory, education, religion, honour, love, as things that 'happen to a man' from 'outside his skin,' are suggestions which would be positively comic, were the subject less grave. The whole case is well summarized in the true words of Prof. J. S. Mackenzie—

[1] *Not Guilty*, pp. 87, 88. It is, of course, true that the opportunity to get education and the forms of religion may be environment, as may also be the being honoured or loved by others. But if this is all that is intended, a self-proclaimed teacher should say so. The previously alleged instances here warrant our taking them subjectively rather than objectively.

'It is misleading to speak as if character and circumstances were two co-ordinate factors in human life, since it depends largely on character whether anything is to be reckoned a circumstance or not. Probably by far the greatest part of any man's present circumstances is simply the expression of what his past character has been. Two men living to all appearance in the same general conditions may in reality be in wholly different circumstances.'[1]

Daily experience and observation abundantly confirm this estimate. In other words, a man's environment is largely determined from within, as an unmistakable result of the reality and activity and freedom of that self which is more than a mere heredity and other than any surrounding circumstances. Even in regard to infra-human organisms, latest science warns us that the sometimes-assumed omnipotence of environment may be quite misleading.[2] But as regards human nature, the case is rendered unique beyond compare by that actuality and activity of the self-conscious ego which makes the whole problem of environment everlastingly a double one. It is a mere truism to say that 'environment is very powerful for good or evil.'[3] We all know that. The question which waits for answer is as to *how* powerful,

---

[1] *Manual of Ethics*, p. 87. The supreme example of this truth is in the New Testament. 'The prince of the world cometh; and he hath nothing in Me' (John xiv. 30). But our great poet has luridly shown up the dark side : 'Which way I turn, myself am hell.'

[2] The greatest stress of philanthropy is now laid upon Eugenics. 'Those who maintain that a change of environment alone, however favourable, will have permanent effects on succeeding generations, basing as they do their belief on the presumed inheritance of acquired characters, have little grounds for such an assumption. Whatever environment may do for the individual, its effects are not embodied as part and parcel of the heritage of the progeny.' (*First Principles of Heredity*, Dr. Herbert, p. 175.) But the whole complexity is still *sub judice*.

[3] *God and My Neighbour*, p. 141.

for good or ill, the influence of environment may be. One incontrovertible part, at least, of the answer is that very much depends upon the person influenced, according as he yields to or strives against the natural effect of his environment

It is customary to illustrate this influence, and indeed suggest its omnipotence, by appeal to the extremes of social life in our modern midst. No one can deny either the bright or the dark side of the picture presented. Nor, it must be frankly confessed, can any one measure the effects upon the sensitive human organism of a pure and happy childhood, followed by comfortable circumstances, as compared with a birth in the slums leading on to the death in life of a victim of modern sweating. But whether we learn most from extremes, or from ordinary circumstances, the principles remain the same : viz. that it is equally false to deny the influence of environment, or to assert its omnipotence. Though they may be both immeasurable, yet the influence of a man on his environment is every whit as real as the influence of his environment on the man. Whether the whole philosophy of the case can be made clear or not, experience and observation alike testify that it is, after all, the man himself who determines what shall be the effect of his environment upon him. To an extent which can no more be questioned than measured, he can determine what the environment itself shall be.[1] And when, under the pressure of

---

[1] Of all the false and foolish things of which the popular advocacy of Determinedism is capable, one of the most noteworthy instances is found in the assertion of *God and My Neighbour* (p. 140), that 'No man can select his environment.' Whereas there is no man living, outside of an asylum or a prison—and to a considerable degree inside—who does not, to a greater or less extent, select his environment every hour of the day.

social life, he finds himself in an environment from which it is very difficult to escape, it is still open to him to assert his manhood by refusing to succumb to the pressure thus brought to bear upon him.

It is useless to repeat the see-saw philosophy which is so commonly adopted in this matter by the advocates of Determinedism. If a man in a bad environment overcomes it and turns it into good, that is said to be the work of his heredity. On the other hand, if a man with every initial advantage that heredity can offer falls into evil ways, that is put down to the overwhelming influence of environment. But neither case is demonstrated, or indeed demonstrable. For it overlooks altogether the one element in the case of which, as pointed out above, we are quite sure, in what else soever we may be perplexed, viz. that a man is a man, be his heredity and environment what they may.[1] Being a man, he is a person; and a person is never—as clay in the hands of the potter—a mere passive receiver of environmental influences or transmitter of hereditary tendencies. Even these have to be made his own, by himself, before they can do anything within him for good or ill. The exact extent to which influences and tendencies may affect personality, is beyond us to calculate. We can do but two things in regard to it. We may and must acknowledge that it varies greatly, very greatly, in individuals. But we also may and

---

[1] That there are many sad and difficult problems in human nature is undeniable, but true Determinism never sinks so low in its estimate of human nature as Determinedism. Thus, 'many of our wrongdoers are ignorant, or diseased, or insane or mentally deformed. But there are some who are base and savage by nature. These should be regarded as we regard base or savage animals; as creatures of a lower order, dangerous, but not deserving blame nor hatred.'—*Not Guilty*, p. 19.

R

must insist that so long as sanity remains, there is that in every individual to which appeal may be made, differentiating him definitely and for ever from a mere complex mass of tissue, or a peculiarly twisted telegraph-wire.

(4) To the final question, therefore, what can a man be or do under the influences of heredity and environment, only a general, yet none the less valid, answer can be given. Whether we say with Ribot that 'heredity has actually more power over our mental constitution and our character than all external influences, physically or morally'; or with Dr. Warschauer, and the late Dr. Barnardo, that 'environment is a greater power than heredity'; there is one certainty which emerges in regard to each of them when thought of singly, or in regard to both when viewed as working together. It is that whilst they are acknowledged influences, potent and immeasurable, they are not determinations, and never can be, so long as man is man. Although it may be true that 'a thousand hands instead of one strike the blow which makes a man a murderer,' yet it is also true that but for the man himself the thousand hands would never have struck at all. 'Even though his choice,' truly says Prof. Romanes, ' be influenced by his physical and social environment, it does not follow that this influence is of a kind to neutralize or destroy the causal nature of his own volition.'[1] Such a sentence should be writ large, because that, and that only, is the main point upon which all else turns. The true relation of a man—who is only such by virtue of his capacity for causal volition—to his heredity and environment, is,

---

[1] *Mind and Motion and Monism*, p. 158.

indeed, well expressed by the leading prophet of popular Determinedism. A certain 'Thomas has the same hereditary inclination to drink as John who is a drunkard, and derived it from the same source. But he worked in an office where all the clerks were steady and a wise friend warned him; so that *with a hard struggle* he escaped the danger.'[1] Which illustrates, for the thousandth time, the inability of Determinedism to plead its own cause. Here it represents a man overcoming his dangerous heredity through the help of his environment, and yet, only 'with a hard struggle.' Was this, then, 'completely determined?' Certainly, *ex hypothesi*, not by the heredity. With equal certainty, not alone by environment. For how, in the name of common sense, could it possibly be environment, before it existed? And how in the light of any true philosophy could a 'hard struggle' be 'determined,' without involving point-blank contradiction in terms? So does false Determinism when driven into a final corner, ever testify to the actuality of true Determinism.

If any further witnesses be necessary, they may be found in the realm of fact, where, by the myriad, instances are forthcoming of men and women who have done everything that Determinedism says they cannot do. In his brilliant—and dazzling—Gifford lectures, Prof. James gathered specimens of 'conversion' which both for quantity and quality ought to have given the *coup de grâce* to Determinedism, were it not that a 'completely determined' theory possesses an almost inextinguishable vitality.[2]

---

[1] *Not Guilty*, p. 125. Italics ours.

[2] Those to whom this volume may be inaccessible, will find an equally impressive and valid collection of analogous instances in Mr. H. Begbie's *Broken Earthenware*—which fully merit the attention of every philosopher. The real question in every

Whereas men are told, in the name of modern science, that they cannot help themselves; that they cannot resist heredity; that they cannot overcome environment; that whatever they do it is the only thing they can do, so that every man's worst is at the same time his best,—every one of these pseudo-philosophical maxims is flatly and vividly contradicted in the actual lives and conduct and character of unnumbered hosts. If Dr. Holmes points us to the gruesome story of Elsie Venner, we remind him of the actual history and noble character of Marcus Aurelius, who, on Determinedist principles, ought certainly to have been a vicious tyrant If assassins of the Guiteau type are said to be not only inevitable but unalterable, how is the marvellous reversal of Jerry McAulay's long career of crime to be explained? If Charles Peace was a 'completely determined' villain, how came John Bunyan to be the author of *Pilgrim's Progress*?[1] If Napoleon was

---

case is the same and must not be evaded, viz. did the change of environment or the influence, say of the Salvation Army officer, produce the vast change in feeling and conduct *without any* definite effort or choice or decision on the part of the former wastrel? If so, why was not every other man or woman under the same circumstances, similarly 'converted'? Some of them only scorned the appeal thus made to them. The ascription of this totally different result to a mere difference in heredity, which caused, i.e. compelled, *some* to resist what others were unable to resist, is so manifestly a see-saw shift of a predetermined theory, that it must surely yield to the total inexpressible but inalienable testimony of self-consciousness as to our power to welcome or reject appeal.

[1] An attempt is made in the book *Not Guilty* to show that John Bunyan also was a mere creature of environment. 'Bad environment got John Bunyan down, good environment lifted him up. The manhood was the same at both periods. It was the environment that changed. If ever there was an example of the power of environment to save or sink a man, that example is John Bunyan, tinker and poet.' The writer evidently does

made before he was born the irreversible incarnation of ruthless ambition, how came Ignatius Loyola to turn from soldier to saint? If Nero was a helpless creature of heredity and environment, how came the young Jewish Rabbi upon whom these both pressed with all possible force, to revert from Saul, the popular persecutor of Christians, to Paul the persecuted and martyred apostle of Jesus Christ?

The relation of these reversals of character to religion, may be for a moment postponed. We need here neither deny nor affirm the potent objectivity of the grace of God. Perhaps the whole truth will be best told if we venture upon a small but significant correction of a statement by Prof. James which,

---

not see that in this, as ever, he is begging the whole question under discussion, and calmly assuming that John Bunyan was a mere man of receptivity, i.e. a thing, and not a person. This we must once more repeat is as contrary to fact as to consciousness. If this man was simply 'made' good—waiving for a moment such a contradiction in terms—by good environment, then wherever there is a man in a good environment, he, too, must be similarly 'made good,' which every one knows to be false. This writer himself acknowledges as much on the next page— 'There remains the college. Now men may learn good at colleges, and they may learn bad. Is not that so?' Certainly it is; but it flatly contradicts the omnipotent-environment theory. For colleges are either good or bad environment. If the former, then no man can 'learn bad' there. If the latter, no man can 'learn good.' The plain truth is that the best environment can do nothing towards making any man good, without himself. The best environment for a person is but an appeal, and the effect of the environment depends upon his response to that appeal. That we cannot ultimately analyse the method of the action of such personality, may be conceded. As Prof. James puts it—'How anything operates in this region is still unexplained.' But mystery and reality go ever hand in hand; and it is far better to leave the man with the reality of his manhood in the region of uncertainty which is beyond us, than to insist upon a certainty alike false and degrading, i.e. that a man must be less than a person, and consequently no more capable of self-direction than a thing.

surely, on further thought, he would have allowed. He tells us that—

'Psychology and religion are in perfect harmony up to this point, that both admit that there are the forces seemingly outside of the conscious individual that bring redemption into his life. Nevertheless, psychology, defining these forces as "sub-conscious," and speaking of their effects as due to "incubation" or "cerebration," implies that they do not transcend the individual's personality; and hereon show divergence from Christian theology, which insists that they are supernatural operations of the Deity.'[1]

But the truth, gleaned from careful philosophy, and confirmed by appreciation of all human facts, is not that external forces 'bring' redemption, i.e. always and necessarily, but that they *may* bring, i.e. they do sometimes; sometimes they do not. And Christian theology, at all events in the form with which we have to deal to-day—which is not Calvinistic—does not insist that the forces which bring redemption are the 'operations of Deity,' but that they are divine co-operations; and that in the co-operation the free and real action of the human is always and equally as necessary as the divine. This is the only true Determinism, because it is ever doubly true. It fully acknowledges the influence of tendencies and circumstances, but it denies compulsions. Such an attitude is in equal accord with convictions of consciousness and facts of observation. The whole situation is, therefore, well expressed in the conclusion that 'the most that we can say is that we know that we are free, but that our freedom is modified by heredity and environment, and by the fountain of personality from which we have sprung, but of which we know little.'[2]

---
[1] *Varieties of Religious Experience*, p. 211.
[2] *Heredity and Christian Problems*, Amory H. Bradford, p. 101.

(vi) *True Determinism the only Valid Explanation of Present Experience*

We have already seen that consciousness, fairly heeded, denies that a man is completely determined, and that there are no valid grounds for denying that denial. But the whole truth concerning human experience is far from being expressed by any such negation. The actuality of personal experience is beyond dispute. It is nothing less than absurd to talk of our 'experiences' as 'environment,' after the fashion of the popular writer above quoted. For experience is precisely what environment never was, is, or can be, until we make it such by the causal activity of the individual mind. A golden sunset is no experience either to a blind man or one who keeps his eyes shut. Human experience, indeed, is always necessarily twofold. As subject and object mutually imply each other, so does the world of experience always necessarily include both the experiencer and the experienced. The one is unthinkable without the other, so that the two are as inseparable as the two sides of a sheet of paper, which can never by any possibility be made thin enough to have but one side. The object may indeed be vastly greater than the subject,[1] but the subject is the initial reality, and as the eye contemplating a mountain in the distance can form an exact miniature

---

[1] Prof. James puts the case with his usual lucidity, thus—'What we think of may be enormous, the cosmic times and spaces, for example; whereas the inner state may be the most fugitive and paltry activity of mind. Yet the cosmic objects, so far as the experience yields them, are but ideal pictures of something whose existence we do not inwardly possess, but only point at outwardly, while the inner state is our very experience itself, its reality and that of our experience are one.'—*Varieties*, &c., p. 499.

a million times less in size, so on a more transcendent scale can the subject contemplate an object whose immense or infinitesimal dimensions are irrelevant, in being amenable to the limitations of time and space. The objective is always something—even when object as well as subject is wholly within the inner world of consciousness; but what it is depends, at least in part, upon the subject. It is out of the endless and the immeasurable, no less than from the momentary and the sensational, that experience is made up. Human experience, in a word, is articulated consciousness, the articulation being accomplished by the personality.[1]

Here Mr. Mill's representation of the doctrine of liberty as against necessity, calls for correction. He states that the 'negative opinion'—that is the opinion which denies the application of causality 'in the same strict sense to human actions as to other phenomena'—'maintains that will is not determined like other phenomena by antecedents, but determines itself.' It is a remarkably loose as well as false representation from a writer so acute.[2] 'Libertarians,' if that name be conceded for the moment, do not maintain any such self-contradiction. The will of a will is unthinkable. For a volition to determine itself, would require that it should act

---

[1] In regard to the relation of brain to mind and therefore to experience, the deliberate statement of such an expert as Dr. Thomson—well supported by scientific principles and facts—in his work upon *Brain and Personality*, merits attention. 'It is not with his whole brain that a man knows, thinks, or devises, but he does so in limited areas of one hemisphere thereof only, which he himself has educated for the performance. The question then follows, How came these brain places to be thus chosen and not others precisely like them in original organization? That this great creative choice proceeds from no source in the brain itself, is demonstrated by the following considerations.'—p. 178.

[2] *Logic*, Book VI, ch. ii.

before it came into being, which is a strange suggestion from an avowed logician. The difference between mechanical causality and volitional having been sufficiently made clear above, it only remains to add that what true Determinism maintains, as against Determinedism, is, that the self determines the will, by means of motives, as part of its native activity.[1] On the same principles we see that the self determines its own experience; and there is no other rationale of human experience which is philosophically justifiable, save such determination. That the whole process is immeasurably complex, and ultimately beyond our utmost analysis, must be acknowledged.[2]

But under all the circumstances, such defiance of analysis is only reasonable. Seeing that the commonest processes of life in the simplest cell remain an enigma which utterly baffles our modern knowledge, it would be preposterous to demand the elimination of all mystery in those unspeakably more complicated processes of brain and of mind in correlation, which

---

[1] Hereupon Prof. Romanes well says—'Although it is true that volitions are caused by motives, yet it is the mind which conditions the motives and therefore its own volitions. It is not true that the mind is always the passive slave of causes, known to it as motives. The human mind is itself a causal agent.'—*Mind and Motion and Monism*, p. 140.

[2] Dr. Otto's summary is instructive. 'There are three things to be borne in mind. First, the origin, the "whence," of the psychical is wholly hidden from us, and notwithstanding the theory of evolution and descent, it remains an insoluble riddle. And, secondly, however closely it is associated with and tied down to the process of bodily development, it is never, at any stage of its development, really a function of it in actual and exact correspondence and dependence. And finally, the further it advances in its self-realization, the further the relation of dependence recedes into the background and the more do the independence and autonomy of the psychical process become prominent.'—*Naturalism and Religion*, p. 299.

are essential to human experience. The unfaltering contention of the advocate for human freedom is not that these are all free in the sense of being causeless, as Mill strangely and unwarrantably intimates, but that they are not subject to causality 'in the same strict sense,' that is, mechanically, as other phenomena, although they are valid effects of a true cause, i.e. the real and active self. There is, it may well be said, no analogue of this in the phenomenal realm, for there all are but effects; the alleged causes are not causes at all, but only preceding effects whose utmost approach to efficiency is transmission. But Miss Benson is perfectly warranted in her protest that—

'When we cannot eliminate an element of our experience which is at the same time the basis of a necessary principle of practical action, it would be no more logical to reject it because it does not harmonize with our other general conceptions, than it would be to reject any phenomenon which stood the test of experience because it did not appear to be an instance of any known law.'[1]

Mr. Mill frankly gives up the term 'necessity', and that in strong language, as applying to human experience and character.[2] But then his own doctrine of

---

[1] *The Venture of Rational Faith*, p. 74. To which may be well added the verdict of Prof. James—'In spite of the appeal which the impersonality of the scientific attitude makes to a certain magnanimity of temper, I believe it to be shallow, and I can now state my reason in comparatively few words. That reason is that so long as we deal with the cosmic and the general, we deal only with the symbols of reality, but as soon as we deal with private and personal phenomena, as such, we deal with realities in the completest sense of the term.'—*Varieties*, &c., p. 498.

[2] 'The application of so improper a term as "necessity" to the doctrine of cause and effect in the matter of human character, seems to me one of the most signal instances in philosophy of the abuse of terms. The subject will never be generally understood until that objectionable term is dropped.'—*Logic*, Book VI, ch. ii, p. 3.

cause and effect is really that of non-causation. That 'there is nothing in causation but invariable, certain, and unconditional sequence,' is said to be what the best philosophical authorities now hold. 'The feeling of some more intimate connexion, of some peculiar tie or mysterious constraint exercised by the antecedent over the consequent,' is said to be neither true of human actions nor of inanimate objects. But such an assertion, no matter by what authorities, is neither more nor less than a wholesale *petitio principii*. For it assumes a perfect analogy between 'human actions and inanimate objects.' Such a proceeding entirely ignores the most real and potent factor in the whole question, i.e. the personality which, by general consent, human beings possess and inanimate objects do not. But any doctrine which rests upon a complete ignoring of unquestionable fact, is self-condemned. If 'the best philosophical authorities' choose to ignore the unfathomable chasm between a person and a thing, it only shows that they are falsely estimated. Meanwhile, can any authority to-day seriously dispute what Professor Andrew Seth affirms, viz. that 'inexplicable in a sense as man's personal agency is, nay, the one perpetual miracle, it is nevertheless our surest datum and our only clue to the mystery of existence.'[1] We are warranted in affirming with all emphasis that human experience includes real as against pseudo-causation. It is a truism that our only valid conception of causation at all is derived from our own consciousness, that is from our indefeasible awareness in our experience of 'some more intimate connexion, some peculiar tie or mysterious constraint

---

[1] See *Personal Idealism*, edited by H. Sturt, p. 345.

exercised by the antecedent,' when dynamized by the self, ' over the consequent.'¹

Effects in experience, resulting from such a cause, are not mere sequences, any more than they are 'epiphenomenal' concomitants of a psycho-physical parallelism. They are veritably new creations, results of a true cause, exemplifications of genuine causation. Be my objective environment what it may, even in sensation, still more in perception, above all in volition, *I* am the cause of my experience, *I* am the true Determinist of my whole inner world. To cite Prof. James once more : ' It is absurd for science to say that the egotistical elements of experience should be suppressed. The axis of reality runs solely through the egotistic places—they are strung upon it like so many beads.'² In her fascinating volume, *The World I live in*, Helen Keller, the blind, deaf, and dumb patient, has given us a wondrous kinematograph of the transition from ' a child in her seventh year with each of the avenues of incoming and outgoing speech closed to her,' to a young woman, ' a graduate with honours of Radcliffe College, versed in the sciences taught there, along with extensive reading in Latin, Greek, French, German and English classics, passionately fond of poetry and of history, a writer of the purest English style, and an author of no mean order.' Can any language describe or imagination conceive the quantity and quality of what we call personal effort in such an experience ? Even now her inner world differs inexpressibly and inconceivably from that of the average member of

---

¹ ' Experience certifies only volitional causality as real, and our thought of causality must be either that or nothing.'—Bowne, *Personalism*, p. 215.

² *Varieties*, p. 499.

human society. But the one outstanding feature of her wondrous experience assuredly is, that it is her own creation. Heredity did not fix it before she was born, for her heredity has never known such an experience. Environment has not made it, for she had no environment save that which she herself made out of the raw material—pathetically raw, indeed, seeing that her first conception of water was the tracing of letters that spelt the word on the palm of the hand whilst wet—supplied by a sympathetic teacher. As a testimony to the perpetual miracle of personality it is perhaps beyond compare, unique in history. It is not too much to say that it is absolutely inexplicable on any theory of materialistic Monism or naturalistic Determinedism.

Yet the main principle of which it is so vivid an illustration, finds ceaseless and vigorous scope in every normal individual. Never in our waking hours, least of all in our best hours, either of sensation, or of perception, let alone of volition, is our experience a mere agglutinated heap of consciousness. It is no more so than the pearl necklace or diamond tiara of some lady of fashion, is a mere heap of jewels. Certainly they came not where they are without selection, arrangement, connexion. Poor similes, confessedly, of the mental associations, selections, determinations, which go on in the inner life even of a slum dweller during the course of a single day. Yet they may point to reality, as a dewdrop may mirror the sun. The diamonds in the necklace are no more really shaped, collected, arranged, connected, by human skill, than are the heterogeneous sensations, perceptions, volitions, of human consciousness, determined by the causal self into the harmonious, continuous, persistent whole, which constitutes human experience day by day. No one doubts that experience varies vastly between individuals, as a cottage differs from a mansion or a cathedral, according to the plans and stones supplied to the builders. But whether it be a palace or a mud hut, builder there must be. Whilst the material supplied limits or conditions or decides the colour and strength of the structure, it is the architect who determines what shall be the form and worth and significance of the whole. So the true Determinism is such a conception of the facts of philosophy of human nature as acknowledges that, whatever the heredity and environment, the true constructor of human experience is, in every single case, the causal self. Iago was right—

> 'Tis in ourselves that we are thus and thus:
> Our organisms are our gardens, to the which our
>   wills are gardeners.

(vii) *The Sufficient Estimate of the Future*

One of the strongest pleas urged on behalf of the false Determinism which regards every man as completely determined in all his actions, is that only on such principles can there be any reliable prediction of the future actions of men and women. It is manifest that if human society is to hold together, there must be to some extent a power to forecast the future; that is, a well-warranted degree of expectation as to the way in which our fellow men will act under given circumstances. This is said to be guaranteed by Determinedism, whilst the ' Libertarian ' view is reproached with being useless in theory and disproved in fact. Such an attitude merits a moment's careful consideration. It is put as vividly as typically by Prof. McTaggart, in his work already referred to.

'According to the Indeterminist theory our choice between motives is not determined by anything at all. And thus it follows that all ground for predicting the action of any man, so far as it depends on his volition, vanishes altogether. One result of this is that the Indeterminist is quite inconsistent in expecting one line of conduct from one man and another from another. It is just as probable that an English general to-day should eat his prisoners as it was that a Maori chief should do so a hundred years ago. If the Indeterminist is right, we have no reason to expect any line of conduct from any one, rather than any other line of conduct which is physically possible. It is just as likely that the majority of Londoners will burn themselves alive to-morrow, as it is that they will partake of food.'[1]

It is well and truly added that such a disposition as this 'would reduce real life to chaos,' but it is equally true that the Indeterminist, in the sense in which that term is here employed, has no more fear of such a chaos than he has of waking up some morning to find himself transformed into Huxley's clock or Mark Twain's machine. It is not necessary to repeat the exposition of preceding pages, to show that both these intended assaults upon the principle of personal freedom fail of their purpose. It is simply untrue that those who deny Determinedism are without warrant, in expecting an English gentleman to-day to behave differently from a cannibal chief in other times and places. The assumption required to support this suggestion would be that human personality is a blank abstraction, exactly the same for all human individuals in all ages and under all circumstances. Which is equally absurd and unwarranted. The philosophical assertion, irrefragably

---

[1] *Some Dogmas of Religion*, p. 183.

based on consciousness, that every human individual is at least a person, as distinct from a thing, yields no ground whatever for assuming that all persons are alike. For personality is no separate entity which can be abstracted from character and be exhibited *in vacuo*. Every person has a character, though how the character is formed by the personality out of the material supplied by heredity and environment, we cannot exhaustively show, any more than we can doubt that to an unknown extent the character is influenced and limited by these joint factors The English gentleman of to-day is no less a person because he was born of English parents in the nineteenth century; and the influence on his character of such parentage and such surroundings, though never amounting to the complete determination which would rob him of his personality altogether, is yet quite sufficient to bring the action of that personality within limits altogether different from those which operate in the case of a savage. No sensible doctrine of human freedom has ever taught that the freedom was unlimited. It is the freedom, as already acknowledged, of a bird in a cage. But the cage may vary greatly, in shape and size, without depriving its inmate of a manifest measure of real freedom. The German officer of to-day is, occasionally, quite capable of treating his subordinates savagely, though he is prevented by public sentiment—which ultimately finds expression in physical results—from making a meal of them. It is, however, an utter absurdity to suggest that because we hold him responsible, as a free agent, for the harshness which is possible to him, therefore it is equally likely that he will kill and eat those in his power.

The same applies, *a fortiori*, to the yet larger insinuation that if we credit human nature with the freedom which is inseparable from real personality, we must never expect any specific conduct from any one. This again completely ignores the actuality of the character through which alone any human personality can and does express itself, together with the fact that persons can both definitely formulate principles and steadily act upon them. One would think from such suggestions as these quoted, that in insisting upon the reality and activity of the self, all else that goes to make the concrete man amounted to nothing. There is no warrant for such an inane supposition, in the true doctrine of human freedom. No one save an idiot or a fanatic would burn himself alive; but the characteristics of the 'majority of Londoners' are not such as to warrant any expectation that they will behave like idiots to-morrow. Sufficient guarantees for that we have in their behaviour to-day. It is but the desperate resort of a completely determined theory to suggest that because men are men, they cannot be expected to behave other than lunatics. It is not only philosophically unsound, but contrary to all that we know to be true, both in ourselves and in others, to assert that the only hope we can cherish as to the future reasonable action of our fellow men, depends upon our first depriving them of power to act at all. The difficulty of answering the ultimate question as to how 'our choice between motives' arises, has been acknowledged above. But the mystery is, after all, much more credible than a point-blank self-contradiction. This latter certainly characterizes the theory which insists that in order to be sure of continuity of character, our 'choice between motives' must be completely determined beforehand. That is to make language a meaningless babble, for neither choice nor character is thinkable in such a case. That we do not know precisely how the self ultimately chooses between motives may well be true, but that does not make the choice characterless, or reduce all other choices of the same personality to a mere succession of chance volitions.

The main principle of the alleged 'inconsistency involved in the position of the Indeterminist' is thus shown to be mistaken. There is no ground at all for the assertion that according to the doctrine of human freedom 'there is no justification whatever for making any statement as to the probability of future evils.' The Indeterminist theory does not assume that 'in every case, the choice between motives is undetermined.' What it does insist upon is that the choice, if it is to be choice, must be free in the sense that it is not determined by anything save the real, active, causal self. That yields no reason for affirming that 'there cannot be, then, the slightest probability that this choice will be one motive rather than another.' The assumption here again is that the self, to be a self, must be utterly characterless, which is wholly without warrant. The choice will be according to character, but the character will be both self-determined before the moment of choice, and at the moment confirmed, or resisted, by the self.

The question is asked, 'Why should we suppose that similar circumstances will in future be followed by similar results?' But the answer which follows is such as could only come from a completely determined theory. 'There is no reason to do so unless the circumstances determine the results, or the circumstances and the results are both determined by the same cause.' Hereupon two definite notes must be made. (1) If circumstances completely determine results, then it is not a case of 'supposing' what may happen. The only consistent language would be that we are absolutely sure—in human affairs, be it observed—that under similar circumstances similar results must and will always follow. And that is certainly contrary to all observation in the past, either in regard to ourselves or others.[1] (2) When from absolute certainty we turn to high probability, such may be predicted with good reason whenever the person, retaining his character, acts under given circumstances. For although results may largely depend upon circumstances, the circumstances themselves depend upon character, as to whether they shall have any influence or not.

It will doubtless be remembered that Mr. J. S. Mill in his *Logic*, whilst giving up the term 'necessity,' yet regards it when applied to this prediction of future actions, as 'a mere interpretation of universal experience, a statement in words of what every one is entirely convinced of.' It comes to this— 'that if we knew the person thoroughly, and knew all the inducements which are acting upon him, we could foretell his conduct with as much certainty as we can predict any physical event.'[2] But there are two distinct objections to such a statement.

---

[1] 'We have repeatedly seen that the question of moral responsibility depends upon the question as to whether a man's action in the past might have been other than it was, notwithstanding that all conditions under which he was placed remained the same.'—Romanes, *Mind and Motion and Monism*, p. 145. It is no less true that an absolutely certain prediction of invariably similar results from similar circumstances, would connote moral irresponsibility.

[2] Book VI, ch. ii.

(1) The knowledge assumed is precisely that which could never be obtained. Prof. McTaggart himself acknowledges that 'for all practical purposes the Determinist must admit the same uncertainty of prediction as the Indeterminist, since only an omniscient person could be quite certain what causes were at work and with what strength.' What then, one may well ask, is the use of a theory which could never be applied ? What it comes to is simply that we are sure that we never can be sure of any future action. Which does indeed leave ample scope for true human freedom. But again; (2) even if we did know the person thoroughly, and all the inducements that act upon him, the inference suggested by Mr. Mill is not warranted. For the simple but sufficient reason that no amount of knowledge whatever on our part could make the process of human volition to be of the same order as ' any physical event.' Whatever we do not know about the action of the causal self in volition, we do know this, that it is not a physical event. With equal clearness and scientific warrant, Prof. Poynting says hereupon, as partly noted above—

'Holding the view that freedom of choice is unlike anything else in nature—that it is a simple fact—I am bound to repudiate the physical account of nature, when it claims to be a complete account. I am bound to deny that the Laplacean calculator can be successful in any avowed prediction of the future when he takes man and the mind of man into his calculations. If he is watching the dance of atoms in the brain, he will see every now and then changes of direction of motion not calculated in his system of transformations of energy, not provided for in his forecast.'[1]

The theory of Determinedism in regard to the future, is thus equally untrue and useless. It is untrue

---

[1] *Hibbert Journal*, July, 1903, pp. 744, 745.

in suggesting that the actions of man can, under any circumstances whatever, be put into the same category of future expectations as physical events. Nothing could justify such a proceeding except the reduction of human nature to pure mechanism, which is sufficiently contradicted by consciousness, as well as by valid psychology. Moreover, Mr. Mill's assertion, which is fairly typical, that ' our volitions and actions are invariably consequents of our antecedent states of mind,' will not bear inspection. He declares such a view to be neither degrading nor contradicted by consciousness. But we are constrained to affirm that it is both. For if ' states of mind ' be taken to exclude the causal personality, then manhood is exchanged for thinghood. If, however, personality be included in such a phrase, then the term ' invariable ' is too strong. Our actions and volitions are undoubtedly the consequent of the preceding causal activity of the self, but they are not invariable. They may vary. It is at least possible that the self may will differently on two occasions under the same conditions. And this does not involve either chance or chaos, but simply freedom, in that the depths of personality are beyond our sounding. Personality whose every decision could be fathomed, would be as real a self-contradiction as a free man whose every motion was restrained.

What is known about the future of human actions, and all that is known, as well as all that needs to be known, is probability in varying degrees—but never certainty ; together with a general power of prediction which is as useful as it is indefinite. Absolute certainty in prediction would simply show that we were dealing with physical—not human—phenomena, whose sequences had been proved before to be, so far as our knowledge goes, invariable. But when the region of the human is entered, the merely physical is left behind. Thenceforward, probability of various degrees is all that is left to us in philosophy, and all that is ever known in fact. The suggestion that statistics show a mechanical regularity of human actions, as in marriages, suicides, &c., only betrays want of sufficient thought. All appeal to the facts of averages prove nothing beyond the fact of the average. For average facts are really no facts at all. They are merely abstractions from facts. An average which was all fact, would be no average. The very term connotes the unlikeness of individual cases. The 'average' Englishman, for instance, who is said to marry at a certain age, is a pure nonentity. There never was such a man. The term is but a deluding appearance of certainty, obtained by ignoring the actual reality of uncertainty. Whatever statistics may show in regard to the community as a whole, they are utterly valueless as to the life, or character, or conduct, of any single individual. But it is with this latter that we are here solely concerned. Prof. McTaggart's acknowledgement, therefore, that in this respect Determinedism gives no more certainty as to individual action than true Determinism does, is well founded. All that we know, or can know, about human action in the future is probability.

Mr. Mallock, however, with his usual adroitness, has endeavoured to twist even this round into the service of false Determinism. In his volume on *Religion as a Credible Doctrine*, after a dismissal of human freedom on psychological grounds pronounced enough to satisfy the most utter automatist, he makes final appeal to a Christian objector from the doctrine of Christ Himself—

'"If the men of Sodom," said Christ, "had been able to hear Me, the men of Sodom would long ago have repented." An external circumstance being present, they would have resolved in a certain way. They failed to do so only because the circumstance was absent. No statement of the doctrine of Determinism can be more distinct than this.'[1]

It is but a melancholy instance of the way in which a special pleader for a completely determined theory will turn in any direction, and clutch at anything to support his thesis. Let any reader of the New Testament who can, think of the Christ of the New Testament as a Determinist in Mr. Mallock's sense, i.e. in his own words, that Christ regarded man ' as but a part and parcel of one single inexorable process, and no more responsible for his thoughts or actions than for those of his grandfather, or for the colour of his eyes, or for the temperature of the earth ' ! If such a suggestion be preposterous, not to say blasphemous, how can the professed finding of it in the reference to Sodom be justified ? The plain truth, which no one but a theory-monger would miss, is that no thought whatever of anything approaching Determinedism was in the Speaker's mind, or is honestly in His words. It is a general statement of probability, and nothing more. Even if the devout believer should feel bound to regard it as a case of Divine knowledge of conditional events, the one word 'would have *repented*' sufficiently involves moral free agency. As is usually the case in these picked passages, if the quotation be only fairly continued, it explains itself ; and assuredly in this case, also puts an end to Determinedism. ' Howbeit I say unto you, that it will be more tolerable

---

[1] p. 118.

for the land of Sodom in the day of judgement than for thee.' 'More tolerable in the day of judgement'—when according to Determinedism man is 'no more responsible for his thoughts or actions,' than the ground on which he treads! Once and for all it may be said that the New Testament should be the last resort of any pleader for false Determinism. Certainly whenever he appeals to it, it will make the last of his appeal.

That a high degree of probability in regard to human actions is both necessary and possible for human intercourse, does not call for controversy. It is too manifest to permit of contradiction; and there is certainly nothing in the true doctrine of human freedom to prevent it. The reality, activity, and causal power of personality, does not diminish, let alone destroy, the reality and influence and potency of character. But the 'force of character' is not a mechanical force in a closed physical system; as it would have to be if human conduct is to be as certainly predicted as an eclipse of the sun, or the freezing of water below 32° Fahrenheit. After all, in this whole strongly urged plea on behalf of false Determinism, we have nothing but a variation of its main principles, viz. jettison personality, and then make assertions, inferences, claims, concerning human nature. As if there could be any human nature without personality, including all its contents and significance! Such a proceeding is of the same order as if one should empty every egg in a hen's nest, and then discuss with the mother bird the nature and destiny of the coming chickens. Beyond all doubt so long as human life remains there will be influences in the future of each man as real and as potent as those of heredity in the past, or environment in the present. But the same truth obtains in regard to the first of these, as in regard to all the rest. They are all influences, not compulsions. Heredity and environment do not constitute the self, or make character. The tensions of temperament and the pressure of circumstances, will not make character in the future. It will be still possible for men both ' to rise on stepping-stones of their dead selves ' to nobler things, and to fall from pinnacles of noble position to wrong and infamy. Both processes have always been, are being, and will be, illustrated in actual human lives. True Determinism sees in such actualities an unmistakable reminder at once of the dignity, the responsibility, the danger, the opportunity, of manhood, and proceeds thereupon to formulate the utmost pressure that can be brought to bear upon a moral being, i.e. an appeal to be and to do ' the utmost for the highest.'

(2) Practical Considerations

(i) *True Determinism the only Valid Foundation of Morals*

We have seen above how false is the doctrine of Determinedism in regard to moral responsibility. That is to say, it has been clearly shown that if that ' hard Determinism ' be taken for true, moral philosophy is at an end, or rather can never obtain a beginning. A moral automaton is for ever inconceivable. Some specially hardy advocates of this debasing doctrine, we find, do not even shrink from jettisoning moral responsibility altogether. Others, whilst still indulging in lofty talk about morality, are driven to confess that all praise and blame and sense of responsibility is unwarranted. Others again, less logical but more self-respecting, endeavour to save the situation by means of the ' soft Determinism ' which urges that morality is untouched by their philosophy, and responsibility unaffected. This latter class of writers generally endeavour also to make their case stronger by assuming an aggressive attitude, and boldly asserting that morality can only exist or be defended on their principles.[1]

The usual and all-comprehending principle upon which this attitude rests is, of course, the law of causality which, according to Prof. McTaggart, ' asserts that every event is determined by previous events in such a way that if the previous events are as they are it is impossible that the subsequent event should not be as it is.'[2] Still more fully we are told on the next page that—

' Determinists maintain that our volitions are as completely determined as all other events. From this it is generally, and I think correctly, held to follow that it would be ideally possible to deduce the whole of the future course of events from the present state of reality, though, of course, a mind enormously more powerful than ours would be required to do it.'

The reference to the possibility of prediction has

---

[1] Prof. McTaggart roundly asserts, for instance, that ' Indeterminism is inconsistent with the validity of morality.'—p. 177. Whilst Mr. Pearson writes that—' Determinism asserts that in relation to conduct the character is the self, and thereby rescues the moral responsibility so nearly wrecked by Mr. Illingworth.'—*Some Problems of Existence*, p. 95. And again, ' Determinism, so far from impugning moral responsibility for conduct as between man and man, emphatically affirms it, and any danger which threatens the belief comes rather from the Libertarians than from their opponents.'—p. 97. In the same strain Mr. Bertrand Russell, in his *Philosophical Essays*, expresses his desire to prove that ' it is free will, not Determinism, which has subversive consequences for the moral life.'

[2] p. 144.

been sufficiently discussed above, but the first sentence here calls for comment, even at the risk of repetition; for it is the very core of the whole case, the pivot upon which all else turns. Thus Mr. Pearson waxes scornful in his reference to it.

'The Libertarian claim is only possible on the assumption that the self is an originating or uncaused cause of action—in other words a standing exception to the causation which prevails throughout the rest of nature. The only fact in favour of this assumption is our feeling of being free in our acts of volition, a feeling which it is admitted may be quite illusory, while the probabilities against it are almost overwhelming.' [1]

But the writer's wish leads his thought astray. It is certainly not admitted, by numbers of the most able thinkers, that the consciousness of freedom 'may be quite illusory.' To specify only one, Dr. Momerie gives every evidence of being at least quite as competent a writer on these matters as Mr. Pearson, but he emphatically declares—

'It seems to me that all the attempts which have been made to disprove our consciousness of freedom have failed, as signally as those which have sought to disprove our consciousness of our own permanence. For my own part, at any rate, I am conscious of myself as a being capable not only of feeling and of receiving ideas that are presented to me, but capable also of a voluntary exercise of attention, and a voluntary origination of a train of thought, or a course of conduct.' [2]

And there are no more 'overwhelming probabilities' against such a feeling being an experience of what is really true, than there are against the validity of the consciousness of one's own existence from moment to moment.

Still more important is it to mark the one point which arouses the philosophical ire, not only of these writers but of all Necessitarians or Determinedists.

---

[1] *Some Problems of Existence*, p. 91.   [2] *Personality*, p 89.

'Volitions as completely determined as all other events'—'the causation which prevails throughout the rest of nature.' Such phrases, repeated *ad nauseam* would sweep away all opposing argument, as Dr. Momerie rightly says, 'by assuming the very point to be proved, viz. that man *is* moved in the same way as a material object.' But really it ought not to require a profound psychologist, or metaphysician, to show that a human being is *not* on a par with ' the rest of nature '; as also that a volition is *not* ' like all other events.' To deny these ' facts ' is not only to assume what demands tremendous proof, but virtually to put oneself beyond argument. Reasoning is lost upon the advocate of any theory who denies that reason, as found in man, is *sui generis*. It is a plain statement of philosophy against which there can be, on the ground of unintelligibility, no 'bitter cry of the plain man' that—

'Man, since he is the interpreter of Nature, might, *a priori*, be conceived as something more, something other, than a mere part of her process, and hence it might be expected beforehand that his actions and Nature's would not be amenable to the same canons.'[1]

This at least must be maintained, amid all the welter of modern words, that man is the only moral being. Not even the boldest advocate of 'mental evolution in animals' suggests that the 'placental mammals' to whose level Haeckel says we are now reduced, are or can be regarded as moral agents. When, therefore, we find those who so strongly insist upon Determinedism equally anxious to preserve the attribution of this supreme quality to human nature, it becomes especially necessary that its implications should be considered with the utmost

---

[1] *Personality*, p. 97.

TRUE DETERMINISM

care. If it be conceded as beyond dispute that a man is a moral being, we must know what morality involves. That does not mean that any special standard of morals need be adopted. We are here concerned not with the contents of morality, but with the capacity for it. It will be quite sufficient for the moment to say that the right is that which ought to be done in order to accomplish the good. The special capacity of human nature with a view to the moral life can scarcely be expressed in a better form than that which we may here repeat, from Sir Oliver Lodge—

'The distinctive character of man is that he has a sense of responsibility for his acts, having acquired the power of choosing between good and evil, with freedom to obey one motive rather than another. Creatures far below the human level are irresponsible. They feel no shame and suffer no remorse. They are said to have no conscience.' [1]

This is unquestionably a fair general statement of the foundation of morality in men and women. The main features of such an estimate are equally true to philosophy and to fact, and will lead us ultimately to the only true Determinism.

(1) The first element of the case is that if moral responsibility is held to attach to conduct, that conduct must be attributed to the man himself. About this there can be really no controversy.[2] Prof. McTaggart rightly says that 'The approval or condemnation of the agent is essential to morality.'[3] It is however important to mark it well, because it is rather the fashion of Determinedists to talk about

---

[1] *Substance of Faith allied with Science*, see p. 3 above.
[2] 'We have postulated that moral responsibility does not attach to conduct which cannot be properly imputed to the man himself.'—Pearson, op. cit., p. 94.
[3] p. 178.

blaming or praising 'acts,' wholly apart from the agent. 'The philosophical Determinist would denounce the offender's conduct, but would not denounce the offender,' says the author of *God and My Neighbour*. 'We Determinists do not denounce men, we denounce acts.'[1] Mr. Pearson, also, in trying to deal with the real difficulty that 'it is idle to hold up to man any moral ideal, if he has no free power to choose either the right or the wrong,' says that the answer is simple. 'Praise and blame are but shifted from the agent to the act.'[2] We must, however, be permitted to repeat that it ought to be manifest, even to a tyro in these matters, that it is altogether absurd to blame an act apart from its doer. For on the writer's own showing, an act separated from the agent is utterly incapable of moral quality. In strict truth such an act is unthinkable—as much so as is the writing of these words by a pen, apart from the writer. Whether the writing is represented by paper, or ink, or pen, or all combined, it is in itself, apart from a writer, inconceivable, and if contemplated at all, absolutely non-moral. It may be pretty or ugly, it may have cheering or depressing sentiments, it may tend to happiness or the opposite. All such considerations are irrelevant. To denounce an act is to denounce a thing, and the attribution of moral qualities to things is philosophic absurdity. That an act may have harmful consequences, or may tend to produce painful results, on any scale, does not affect the case in the least. The act is not responsible for any one of them. To tell the whole truth, an act is not even a thing. Apart from the doer of it, it is nothing, and assuredly moral responsibility cannot be attributed to nothing.

---

[1] p. 141. [2] *Some Problems of Existence*, p. 101.

(2) But it is rightly attributed to the man himself, because of the definite and necessary understanding that he himself is its true cause. Even in the formation of his character, as above shown, he is an active participator, not a mere passive receiver. Still more plainly in regard to all his visible actions is he responsible, because they are the very expression of himself. Here Mr. Pearson speaks truly in saying that, ' only out of action could morality be evolved.' Mere receptivity can never be moral. Inertness yields no opportunity for showing moral quality. ' On the principles of scientific Determinism,' says Mr. Mallock, 'there is nothing original in the universe.' In that case there is nothing moral. The whole phenomena of being come to be nothing more than a series of effects, and no effect whatever can be held responsible for being the consequence of its cause. But experience testifies unequivocally—and philosophy has nothing to say to the contrary—that man is a creator. Every volition is a new creation, i.e. it is a real action. It may follow upon a motive, but a motive is not necessarily the cause of a volition. It is a suggestive direction, but requires the intervening activity of the self to transform it into volition. It is for the exercise of that intervening activity which is the energetic expression of self, that the self, the man, the agent, is rightly held responsible. But for him the action would not have taken place. The fact that it has taken place is, therefore, due to him and justly attributed to him, whatever its consequences.

(3) There is, however, another element in the case definitely and equally essential. The action which is to merit moral quality must not only be actual, but intentional. It must be teleological as

well as effective, and must embody purpose no less than energy. Prof. Mackenzie rightly says in his *Manual of Ethics*, that ' in conduct on which a moral judgement can be passed, a man is never moved solely by feeling,'[1] that is, by the sensational influence of the moment. 'Moral activity or conduct is purposeful action, and action with a purpose is not simply moved by feeling, it is moved rather by the thought of some end to be attained.' And in regard to all the stress laid upon the necessity for motives, whilst it is fully acknowledged that a motiveless volition is unthinkable, yet it is most necessary to point out that the moral quality of an action does not consist in the fact that there must be motives to give occasion for volition, but in the quality of the particular motive which is enabled by the self to pass into volition. In the words of Prof. Romanes, 'Although in any event man is necessarily bound to adopt means in order to secure his ends, the moral quality of his choice has reference only to the ends which he chooses, not at all to the fact that he has to employ means for the purpose of attaining them.'[2] Thus we obtain the three prime essentials to morality, i.e. an agent, an action, a purpose. Without all of these, morality is as unthinkable as a triangle with less than three sides.

(4) These constitute, however, only the subjective features of the case. There are also three other and objective features of equal importance, which must be fairly estimated before a full-orbed morality can be predicated. Kant's 'kategorical imperative' naturally finds no favour with Determinedists, though they

---

[1] p. 63. [2] *Mind and Motion and Monism*, p. 158.

do not all denounce it so virulently as Prof. Haeckel.¹ But the estimate which Necessitarianism forms concerning the conception of duty, is conveyed in the reference by Bentham, in his *Deontology*, to the term 'ought,' which we have noticed above. The full statement stands thus—

'It is very idle to talk about duties. The word itself has in it something disagreeable and repulsive. The talisman of arrogance, indolence, and ignorance, is to be found in a single word, an authoritative imposture. It is the word "ought." If the use of the word be admissible at all, it "ought" to be banished from the vocabulary of morals.'

Which, assuredly, is definite enough and dogmatic enough. Only it provokes at once and inevitably the question, what is left of morality when 'morals' are to this extent eviscerated? Optional morality is a sheer contradiction in terms. If an action 'ought' not to be done, however useful and beneficent it may be, it falls short of morality. The Utilitarian or the Hedonist can only advocate or defend their respective theories by investing with authority— i.e. with oughtness—the useful or the pleasurable. It would indeed be alike true to philosophy and sufficient in fact, to define man as the one creature on earth who ought to do his duty. The man who has no sense of duty, or no respect for the oughtness of right, is rightly regarded as rather a monstrosity than a man. Dr. W. B. Carpenter had good warrant for saying, in his *Mental Physiology*, that he could not anticipate the time 'when the words, "ought, duty, responsibility, choice, self-control" and the like will cease to have the meaning we at present attach

---

¹ 'The cupola of his great cathedral of faith was crowned by Kant with his curious ideal—the famous "kategorical imperative." Modern anthropology has ruthlessly dissipated that pretty dream.'—*Riddle of the Universe*, cheap edition, p. 123.

to them, and when we shall really treat each other as automata who cannot help doing whatever our heredity and environment have necessitated.' It is utterly and pitifully useless for popular Determinedists to preach that no man can help what he does and therefore no one is responsible. No one believes them. No one attempts to act upon such moral dementia. All civilization, we may say with truth, endorses to-day the sacredness of duty. And men will continue to endorse it, as long as reason, let alone morality, remains to them. The man, who has no sense of ought, is only fit for the asylum. A prison is too good for him.

(5) Again; the duty which ought to be done, *can* be done. It is never a man's duty to undertake the impossible. Nor does any 'ought' attach to that which is manifestly beyond his power. No man ought to try to make a world. But if, under any circumstances, 'England expects every man to do his duty,' then with the same words every man is reminded that his duty is within his power. There is also another double assumption in every such phrase, viz. that a man may fail to do his duty, and that he cannot be made to do it. England knows only too many cases in which every man has not done his duty. England has no power to decide that every man shall do his duty. England can only expect, that is appeal and hope, that every man will do it. But all this is as far from Determinedism as a man is from a marionette. Inasmuch as this whole matter comes well within the province of a professor of moral philosophy, it may be well to let one of acknowledged competence speak hereupon. Thus Prof. Mackenzie:

'There is involved in the moral consciousness the conviction that we ought to act in one way rather than any other, that one manner of action is good or right, and another bad or evil. Now, as Kant urged, there would be no meaning in the "ought," if it were not accompanied by a "can." But if a man's will were absolutely determined by his circumstances, it would be strictly impossible for him to become anything but that which he does become, consequently it would be impossible that he ought to be anything different. There would thus be no ought at all. The moral imperatives would cease to have any meaning. If, then, there is to be any meaning in the moral imperative, the will must not be absolutely determined by circumstance, but must, in some sense, be free.'[1]

Once again we cannot but recall Prof. James's profound saying, which really covers and concludes the whole case—'Determinism, in denying that anything else can be in the stead of what ought not to be, virtually defines the universe as a place in which what ought to be is impossible.' Which is chaos enough to constitute the end of any such philosophy. That which ought to be, is that which can be, or can not be. And if this is true for the present, it is also true concerning that which was once the present but has now become the past. That which has been, need not have been, but might have been something else. In Prof. Romanes' words, 'the question of moral responsibility depends upon the question as to whether a man's action in the past might have been other than it was, notwithstanding that all the conditions under which he was placed remained the same.'[2] If that which a man did yesterday was the only thing he could do,

---

[1] *Manual of Ethics*, p. 91.

[2] *Mind and Motion and Monism*, p. 145. Or thus again—'The question of moral responsibility can only obtain in cases where two or more lines of conduct were alike possible, so far as the external system of causation is concerned; or where the will was equally free to choose between two or more courses of bodily action.'—p. 149.

then there is no possible moral quality about it. It is but mockery to call it his worst, seeing that it was at the same time his best. When the best is the same as the worst, morals are at an end. That which could not but be, can never be either bad or good.

It is necessary here to look another objection to true Determinism fully in the face. It is put incisively, as usual, by Mr. Mallock—

'Since no act of will can take place at all, unless there is some object of desire to the gaining of which the act refers, it follows that if a man is so situated at any moment that one such object and only one is presented to him, one act of will and one alone is possible to him, i.e. the will to do that by which this one object is to be gained.' [1]

Being apparently under the impression that here, at least, he has all the opposition to psychological Determinedism beneath his feet, the writer proceeds, as he thinks, to grind it to powder beneath his heel by the further avowal that nothing can alter

'The simple and fundamental fact that the bondage of our wills in every act of willing, to the sole desire, or the strongest desire of the moment, is absolute, necessary, invariable. It admits of exceptions no more than does the law of gravitation itself.'

But this sledge-hammer crushing is really waste of energy, and uncalled for. In the first place, no desire can become either the 'sole desire' or the 'strongest desire' of the moment without the free decision of the self as expressed in attention, deliberation, and exclusion of all other desires. In the second place, it is altogether a misuse of language to talk about any 'bondage of our wills' to the sole desire, for the simple but sufficient reason that the volition, the act of willing, is but the final stage of the

---

[1] *Religion as a Credible Doctrine*, p. 97.

whole psychological process by which a suggestion becomes an act. One might as well speak of our limbs in walking being in bondage to the brain. The course of procedure is not difficult to follow. We have first, a suggestion, or mixture of suggestions, from without. These become motives, or not, according to the character of the individual and his attention to or disregard of them. If a certain motive is allowed by the free agent's endorsement to develop, it becomes the strongest desire, which is the natural and necessary transition-stage leading on to volition. There is no bondage anywhere, but merely a series of steps through which the real, active, free, causal self definitely acts. Motive is but suggestion sifted by character. Desire is motive endorsed by self. Volition is dynamized desire.

But another more subtle fallacy yet lurks in this representation of a somewhat common attitude. We are told that 'no act of will can take place at all, unless there is some object of desire to the gaining of which the act refers.' Which is true; but not the whole truth, because it confuses desire with duty. We all know that it is possible to follow duty rather than desire, and Mr. Mallock's elaborate attempt to get rid of the distinction proposed by Dr. W. G. Ward between 'spontaneous impulse' and 'resolve,' by no means succeeds in obliterating the distinction. Nothing is, of course, easier than to say that when a man does a duty which is painful, instead of following a desire which is pleasurable—as in Dr. Ward's illustration of a public man preparing for a day's sport and stopped by a sudden call to important business—he does it because he desires, in the ultimate, to do what is right. But this is a superficial and one-eyed analysis, unwarranted either by clear thought or intelligible speech. Duty is not desire, and no sophistry of language can make it such. The sense of oughtness is *not* a mere particular case of desiring, but is a unique conviction entirely confined to a moral being. Our dogs and horses have manifest desires, but no appreciation of duty can be translated to them. Every alleged instance is a mere case of association.

But with man it is only a verbal shuffle to call a strong sense of duty a case of mere desire. That which we feel ought to be, is often enough that which we do *not* desire to be. That which I ought to do, is what I ought to do ; it admits of no further analysis. It is not only true that—

> Because right is right, to follow right
> Were wisdom in the scorn of consequence.

But to follow right, so far as I know it, is wisdom in the scorn of desire. A good resolve does, therefore, differ from an impulse just in this very respect, that the former involves a perception of and a deliberate self-acting response to the call of the 'ought,' whereas the latter is the mere undeliberated result of suggestion. When Mr. Mallock asserts that 'in reality, so far as reason and observation can guide us, the one is the result of circumstances no less than the other, both are equally mechanical,' the only reply that seems possible is a kategorical denial. At the outset, mechanical resolve is a contradiction in terms. But when he goes on to say that 'if resolve differs from spontaneous impulse at all, it differs only as a donkey-engine from the main machinery of a locomotive, with parts of which now and then it puts itself into gear '—the wit of a child can see that these last four words give away his entire case. Apart from the unsuitable and untrue analogy suggested—between an engine and a resolve—assuredly this supposed action is what a donkey-engine never did and never will do. If it comes into gear with any part of the locomotive, it is always and only, because some mind outside itself decides that it shall do so. But a resolve decided by some one outside the resolver, is again a contradiction in terms, and unthinkable.

Dr. Momerie is right in affirming that 'when a number of motives are presented to an ego, he need not, and in fact he generally does not, yield at once to any of them. He can pause, he can reflect, he can call up new and more powerful motives.' Desire may come in like a flood; but he can call up the sense of duty, and by attention to it make it stronger than desire. Or having called it up, he can again dismiss it and let desire prevail. This is everyday experience on the part of almost every one. And Mr. J. S. Mill's summary does not alter the case in the least, when he says that even after duty has been done, 'I am convinced that I could have chosen the other course had I preferred it; but not that I could have chosen one while I preferred the other.' Such a tautologous shuffle was unworthy of a logician. For what is a choice but a preference? And what is this collection of words, but an avowal that I could have chosen had I wished to choose, but not have chosen if I did not choose. Which is meaningless verbosity. If choice is choice, three things are always necessarily assumed. First, that there is a chooser; secondly, that there is an alternative from which to choose; and, thirdly, that neither one side of the alternative nor the other need be chosen. If one is chosen, it was equally open to the chooser to choose the other. Express it in what terms we please, such a psychological process alone is choice. Hedge it with what metaphysical difficulties we may, it is also fact, *solvitur ambulando*, a myriad times a day.

(6) Thus we are bound to see, once more, that moral responsibility necessarily involves the free choice upon which true Determinism insists. Lotze shaped his philosophy, says Prof. Upton, according to the clear conviction that 'the terms " sin " and "moral responsibility," without the possibility of real choice, without the presence of any alternative, are *voces et praeterea nihil*, a delusion and a sham.'[1]

True Determinism never suggests such an unthinkable conception as a will without a motive; but it does protest, alike in the name of philosophy and of fact, against the yet more unthinkable notion of a will so dominated by motive that there is no room for real choice. The motive is indeed to the volition just what the causal self permits it to be; neither less nor more. As Dr. Otto puts it, ' the free spirit in the uniqueness of its moral laws, reveals itself as lord over all the motives, the lower feelings of pleasure and of pain that have their play within us.'[2]

---

[1] *Hibbert Lectures*, p. 290. In a note a little further on (p. 294) attention is rightly called to the lucid statement of Mr. A. J. Balfour, in regard to the attitude of Absolute Idealism hereupon, i.e. that a man is free if what he does is the expression of his character. 'If it be, and yet his character itself is represented as the outcome of pre-natal conditions and circumstances over which he has had no control, such a theory destroys responsibility and leaves our actions the inevitable outcome of external conditions not less completely than any doctrine of controlling fate, whether materialistic or theological.'

[2] *Naturalism and Religion*, p. 324, to which may well be added, for sake of the emphasis which comes by reiteration, the following unequivocal statement by Prof. Romanes, ' However strong the determining influence of a motive may be, if the will is a first cause the motive must belong to a different order of causation from a (physical) motor. For, no matter how strong the determining influence may be, *ex hypothesi*, it can never attain

(7) How real and deep-seated is the conviction of the genuine nature of choice as the basis of moral responsibility, is witnessed not merely in the sense of power to do the right which ought to be done, but in the bitter feeling of remorse which follows when the wrong has been done, and cannot be undone. It is utterly useless for philosophers such as Spinoza and Hume, or the popular advocates of Determinedism above mentioned, to assure us that remorse is a mistake, and that self-reproach only makes two evils out of one. The knowledge which the evil-doer possesses that he might have done the opposite, is too deeply interwoven with his whole self-consciousness to be torn out by a hasty appeal from a superficial theory. Macbeth's hell will appeal to all that is deepest in us, as long as humanity lasts, and the essence of the appeal is not the actuality but the justness of the remorse. The sting of conscience for evil-doing is, as Dr. Momerie says, certainly not 'the peculiar idiosyncrasy of fools.' On the contrary, it is ever to be found in the purest, wisest, noblest of the race, and is only altogether absent from those who have become irretrievably degraded. Freely may we grant that all thought of remorse, as of moral responsibility, is absent from Prof. Hamon's 'tiger,' or Mr. Blatchford's 'steam-engine,' or Mark Twain's 'machine'; but the degradation involved in such a natural and necessary consequence from a man's being completely determined, is too manifest to need emphasis. Certainly Coleridge, in his *Aids to Reflection*, has not

to the strength of necessity. The will must ever remain free to overcome such influences by the adequate exercise of its own power of spontaneous action, or by supplying, *de novo*, an additional access of strength to some other motive.'—*Mind and Motion and Monism*, p. 159.

spoken too strongly in affirming that 'with a Deterministic system of human nature, not all the wit of man, nor all the theodicies ever framed by human ingenuity before and since the attempt of the celebrated Leibnitz, can reconcile the sense of responsibility, nor the fact of the difference in kind between regret and remorse.'

(8) The real reason of the bitterness of remorse, moreover, is always not merely in the conviction that the evil might have been good, and that the wrong need not have been done, but that in every such case the determiner of the tragic fact that the wrong was done, and the evil did come to pass, was unmistakably the man himself. The very core of a man's remorse in regard to an irrevocable wrong, is not found simply in the conviction that it need not have been, but in the further assurance that it would not have been but for him. The true Determinism which lies at the base of all sane human action is too actual, too clear, too strong, too ineradicable, to be driven or bribed or juggled away, by the customary play of words concerning motives, and desires, and circumstances, and character. The man himself knows well that his motives were not forces which carried him away willy-nilly. He recognizes as true the description that motives are 'reasons by reflection upon which an ego may have recourse to self-adjustment, but not forces by which he is involuntarily adjusted.' He knows in himself that his desires are ultimately what he makes them, either floating mists weighing next to nothing through his own refusal and dismissal, or mountain torrents sweeping all before them through his passionate encouragement or intense attention. He knows that he is not the slave of circumstances. If he does not know that, he knows

nothing. There is that in him which, as J. S. Mill so candidly said, even in his yielding to pressure makes him know both that he is yielding, and that he need not yield.[1]

The man himself is more than his motives, or his desires, or his heredity and environment. And it is the action of this self which is for ever necessary to confer moral equality upon any action. For the moral must in every case be the personal—but personal action can only spring from a free, i.e. a real personality. Mr. Mallock's supposed dilemma is no dilemma at all. 'An act wholly the result of causation is an act morally meaningless. An act wholly uncaused is both morally meaningless and impossible.' In reply to which we may well ask, What then? If the former clause sounds the death-knell of false Determinism, assuredly the true Determinism is unaffected by the sonorous deliverance of the latter clause. For, as we have abundantly shown above, nothing is further from its significance than 'an act wholly uncaused.' I am the cause of my acts. If I were not, they could not be my acts at all.

---

[1] How hasty and superficial a writer can be when his mind is completely resolved to support some theory, is illustrated once again in Mr. Mallock's attempt to make out that 'in every spiritual conversion and in every moral struggle, we shall find some external circumstance presented to us as the determining factor. To Paul the voice of Jesus comes crying direct from heaven.' But it is an utter misrepresentation to say that the voice which comes, no matter how directly, from heaven, is necessarily the determining factor. Christ Himself contradicted that as emphatically as language permits. Whilst as for Paul, his own description of his own case is put once and for all in his reply to Agrippa (Acts xxvi. 19)—'Whereupon, O King, *I was not disobedient* to the heavenly vision'—which flatly contradicts Mr. Mallock's suggestion, and summarizes in one vivid focus the whole New Testament teaching of true Determinism, in calling upon every man to determine for himself to turn from evil and pursue the good. Completely determined obedience is nonsense.

In that they would not be at all but for my personal determination that they shall be, there is both an exhibition of direct causality and the demonstration of the true Determinism which in all human action recognizes the effect of a causal self.

(9) This plain and sufficient statement of the only valid foundation of morals is unaffected by a common assault made upon it, which may be illustrated once again by Mr. Mallock's statement. What is finally meant by his phrase ' an act wholly uncaused ' we know very well. It has been already acknowledged above as a mystery beyond penetration. But it will do us no harm to face it yet again. Buridan's ass which died of starvation between two equally attractive trusses of hay, is still in view. The rejoinder to the above reply that I am myself the cause of my actions, would undoubtedly be, that I cannot act without a motive, a motiveless volition being as we have agreed, unthinkable. If, then, I cannot cause an action, i.e. make a motive strong enough to issue in a volition, without a motive, is not some motive the cause of such attention on my part, and does not that motive determine me? To this, which is confessedly the crux of the whole question, as above intimated, only a partial answer can be given. Perhaps Mr. Taylor's summary comes as near as any words can ever do, to a fair solution.

' I am most free when acting for the realization of a coherent rational purpose, not because my conduct is undetermined, in other words, not because there is no telling what I shall do next, but because it is at such times most fully determined teleologically by the character of my inner purposes and interests —in a word by the constitution of my self.' [1]

It is the self which acts, which causes actions.

---

[1] *Elements of Metaphysics*, p. 367.

Not a self as neutral as Buridan's ass, nor an alternative so mathematically equal as those two trusses of hay must have been; but a self which has a constitution, i.e. a character, and acts according to the character without being confused with or determined by the character. Beyond this we cannot go. Nor, indeed, is it necessary that we should try. Lotze's dismissal of this crux might well suffice for lesser minds than his. 'Of course it is incomprehensible and inexplicable; for if it were comprehensible and explicable by the human intellect, if, that is, it could be seen to follow necessarily from the pre-existing conditions, then such a choice from the very end of the case would not be free at all.'[1] But when it comes to a matter of simple incomprehensibility, we may well be content to leave it in such a case as this, seeing that there is no one single thing[2] even in the simplest instance, which we do actually comprehend. Prof. Upton is well warranted in his above-quoted conclusion that 'it is, therefore, wholly futile to seek to invalidate man's consciousness of freedom of choice in moments of temptation, on the ground of its inconceivability.'

(10) This certainty remains, and may be added as a finally decisive weight in the whole balance, that whether conceivable or not, upon this basis of true

---

[1] See Prof. Upton's valuable *Hibbert Lectures* for 1893, p. 290.

[2] When a man waves his walking-stick, Sir Oliver Lodge has recently assured us, all science cannot tell him how and why it is that the end of the stick which he does not hold in his hand, should move at the same time and in the same way as the end which he does hold. Whilst in his book upon the recent development of physical science, Mr. Whetham states unequivocally that 'the ultimate explanation of the simplest fact remains, apparently for ever, unattainable.' If the simplest is thus beyond our analysis, is it rational to refuse to accept the most complex fact, which yet is a fact, because it too is beyond us?

Determinism, men in general construct their moral systems and put them into practice day by day. Prof. Poynting well says hereupon, that 'whatever conclusion we may come to in the quiet of our studies, we are certain, all of us, in everyday life, that this power of choice exists.' As we have pointed out above that there is no place in decent society where the false Determinism is acted on, so may the positive converse be here asserted, that in every realm of normal human life the true Determinism is accepted and practised. In all our relations with our fellow creatures, domestic, social, civil, commercial, political, national, international, the only code of morals which works, is that which regards man as possessed of power of choice sufficiently free to lead us to hold him responsible for all his words and deeds—on the sole but sufficient ground that he was not compelled, either by internal or external constraint, to utter the one or do the other. Whether his moral standard was high or low, he ought to have done the best he knew. He could have done it had he so willed. What he did do, therefore, was his own act and not the mechanical result of temperament or circumstances. For which reason he is rightly and always held guilty for the wrong, and worthy—not of praise, which is so often stupidly asserted, but—of approbation, as having done what he ought to have done. Liberty, duty, responsibility, these constitute the only foundation upon which any valid system of morals can ever be constructed. They are as inseparable as the three sides of a triangle, and the sum of the angles which those sides contain is not more surely two right angles, than is the total influence of these three principles the most effective moral philosophy known to mankind.

(ii) *The Only Possibility of Character*

Men may be moral beings, and yet poor specimens of morality; even as an invalid is human, but a poor type of human physiology. Personal character is more than morals, even as good music is more than theoretic harmony. In philosophy morality is implicit, it is explicit only in character. Yet once the grade of animalism and the realm of sense have been left behind, it is acknowledged as beyond controversy that character is the supreme possession and highest dignity of a human being. The burning interest in what is known as the ' free-will controversy,' which has lasted for ages, and is keener now than ever, is ultimately due beyond all doubt to universal acknowledgement of the importance of human character. Without character, human nature—to repeat Prof. Haeckel's phrase—' sinks to the level of a placental mammal.' But as character is the incarnation of morality, so is morality, as we have seen, the expression of human freedom. Whereas morality is a philosophical conception, character is a practical exhibition. But for both alike, the necessary and eternal postulate is freedom. Upon its actuality turns, as on a pivot, every valid estimate of individual worth and conduct in actual life. All our thoughts about the great men of history and their doings would be, as Mr. Mallock has truly said, ' absolutely meaningless, if it were not for the inveterate belief that a man's significance for men resides primarily in what he makes of himself, not in what he has been made by an organism derived from his parents and the various external stimuli to which it has automatically responded.'[1] It would be the easiest of

---
[1] *Reconstruction of Belief*, pp. 86, 92.

tasks to show that if this 'inveterate belief' could be taken away, all that makes human life most real in its interests and precious in its possibilities, would be gone at one stroke. It is therefore not in the least too strong to avow, with the writer just quoted, that 'the belief in human freedom is as essential to our moral and aesthetic life, as, within its own limits, is the counter-belief in the general uniformity of nature; and those even who reject it theoretically are compelled unconsciously to assume it.'

Yet we are told, and with no small measure of truth, that 'Determinism is spreading on all hands,' and that 'this great theoretical revolution has had no practical consequences whatever. Most assuredly it has led to no deterioration of character. Character has improved gradually and considerably during the last hundred years.'[1] The writer of this estimate exhibits, however, the saving grace of honesty in the further statement that 'it is by no means a clear result of the triumph of Determinism.' In very deed it is not. For not only is the apparent harmlessness of Determinedism explained on the principle intimated above, viz. that all poisons are harmless so long as they are not taken, but there have been, and are, many and great influences at work tending in the right direction, and that is certainly not in the direction of the 'complete determination' of human nature asserted. Not only is there no one realm of human life in which such a doctrine has been acted on, but the recent popular crusade in which 'leaders like Mr. Blatchford have contended with sincerity and plausibility, that the full acceptance of the truth of Determinism would lead to a great moral uplifting,' has answered itself in the eyes of the vast mass of

---

[1] Mr. Jos. McCabe, *R.P.A. Annual for* 1910, p. 60.

those to whom it was addressed, by its own inherent absurdity. A doctrine which promises 'moral uplifting,' through the belief that no man can help anything he does, and is, therefore, never responsible for his words or actions, is so grotesque in its impracticability, to say nothing of false philosophy, that no 'plausibility' could save it from becoming what it is already, a mere spent wave of verbal froth. The rushing tide of foaming words has ebbed out, and left nothing but a tangle of weeds behind it. But the doctrine which cannot be practised, ought not to be preached. And, *per contra*, all the more earnestly should that philosophy be maintained which not only can be practised, but upon which, practically, human society is obliged to act from day to day, on pain of becoming a chaos or a Bedlam. The essence and extent of the dependence of human character, both in the individual and throughout society, upon true Determinism, as distinct from false, may be clearly seen in the following particulars.

(1) The first necessity for valid thought is to differentiate the true significance of the term, as we have already partly seen above. Prof. Rudolf Eucken has truly said recently that 'we speak without misgiving of an inherited character, of a character acquired by adaptation, habit, and the like. The uncritical use of the word in such divergent senses is a fruitful source of ambiguity and confusion.'[1] When nothing more is really meant, or can be signified, than temperament or constitution received by heredity, to call it 'character' is but the abuse of a great word. It is true that the term may be applied, in a well-understood and modified sense, to animals and things. We may

---

[1] *Encyclopaedia of Religion and Ethics*, Vol. III, p. 365.

speak of the character of a dog, or the character of a district, but in all such cases the limitation is so manifest as scarcely to suggest confusion. But with a human subject it is different. A man's character is something of an entirely different order from the character of a building, or of a tree. The significance of the term is measured by the subject to which it is applied. It covers and comprehends the whole capacity; but this, in man's case, is so unique, that its connotation is only satisfied by the one greatest significance of all, which we know as 'moral character.' Even in ordinary parlance, by a man's 'character' is always understood, not his bodily form or mental disposition, but that personal use of all those powers which gives them a moral value and imparts a moral quality to his whole personality. His manhood is high or low, coarse or refined, good or bad, according to his character.

(2) Using the word, then, henceforth, in this sense, the very first duty of moral philosophy is to lay all possible stress upon the distinction between character and heredity. This distinction is expressed by Prof. Taylor in his *Elements of Metaphysics*, with a clearness which merits special attention.

'Though it may be true that a man's behaviour in a given situation is an expression of his "character," yet the character is not the same thing as congenital disposition. The disposition is the mere raw material of the character which is formed out of it by the influence of circumstance, the educational activity of our social circle, and deliberate self-discipline on our own part. And the character thus formed is not a fixed and unvarying quantity given once and for all at some period in an individual's development and thenceforward constant; it is itself, theoretically at least, in the making throughout life; and though you may from personal intimate acquaintance with an individual man feel strongly convinced that his character is not likely to undergo serious changes after a certain time of life, this conviction can never amount to more than what we properly call moral certainty, and is never justified except on the strength of individual familiarity.'[1]

Upon the distinction thus forcefully outlined, too much emphasis cannot be laid, as already intimated, for it is the key to the whole situation and the first item in the whole philosophical denial that a man is a mere creature of heredity and environment.

(3) We are, however, continually assured that all idiosyncrasies manifestly attaching to an individual which cannot be accounted for by heredity, may be ascribed to environment. Having noticed this also already, it only remains to lay additional stress upon the manifest fact that 'character' is distinctly more than heredity and environment put together. These alone can never any more constitute moral character, than hydrogen and oxygen would become water without the fusing electric spark. We shall see more fully, presently, how meaninglessly superficial and false is Sir Leslie Stephen's declaration that 'action proceeds from character, and character is not made by us, but determined by the Creator.' Even Mr. McCabe acknowledges that in the 'residual power of self-determination and choice we have something that ought to be emphasized by Determinists.' Most wisely does he add that in face of all the reiterations about man's being a creature of heredity and environment—' many of us have a feeling that the conviction of human power has been in some danger of being washed away in the flood of Determinist argument.' But until it is definitely understood that character involves just such real 'human' power as cannot be attributed to heredity and environment, the danger referred to will remain,

[1] p. 374.

even if it does not grow. This writer, however, deserves all credit for the candour which prompts him to say plainly, from such a standpoint, that—

'The most valuable power you can give a man is the assurance that he can dominate hereditary tendencies—it has been done repeatedly—and transform the environment about him. We have paid our tribute to the truth of Determinism. Can psychology help us to recover our manhood?'[1]

No more pertinent or potent truth can be put into speech, than that which this question implies. Assuredly, without such capacity for character, manhood is gone. But if Determinedism were true, character would be no more possible for a man than for a marionette.

(4) It is of the utmost importance that there should be no misunderstanding here. The character without which manhood is lost, cannot be given or received, under any conditions whatever, any more than it can be bought or sold, borrowed or stolen. The utmost that the best hereditary tendencies and environmental influences can confer upon a man is the 'raw material,' out of which character may be made. The making is neither more nor less than the use of this material by the self-conscious personality. When the fact is borne in mind that there may be bad heredity as well as good, and that environment may hinder quite as really as help moral progress, there emerges at once the difficulty no less than opportunity of making the character which can come in no other way. Sir Oliver Lodge has truly and tersely summed up the situation in saying that—

'We are not machines or automata, but free and conscious and active agents, and so must contend with evil as well as rejoice in good. Conflict and difficulty are essential for our training and development, even for our existence at this grade.

---

[1] *R.P.A. Annual*, 1910, p. 65.

With their aid we have become what we are, without them we should vegetate and degenerate.'¹

(5) The stress of philosophy, as well as of experience, here falls upon the fact that we are active and conscious agents. In other words, the character that cannot be given or received, if it is to exist must be made by the self. Any other statement concerning the origin of character would involve a contradiction in terms. Be the love of parents what it may, the utmost that it can do towards a child's character, is to appeal to it to make its own. If, according to Novalis, ' a character is a completely fashioned will,' the only possible fashioner is the man himself. Prof. Rudolf Eucken remarks with too good reason that ' in our own age the dearth of character is manifest,' and he suggests that the activities, doubts, fast living of the age are sufficient explanation, seeing that ' character can be formed only in virtue of personal decision and action.'² No metaphysical difficulties in regard to our understanding the nature or the action of a transcendental ego, can lessen the certainty or the importance of this demand for the definite operation of the conscious self. It is not enough to say with Dr. Illingworth that this ' self-assertion in the strict sense of the term, or self-affirmation, is the fundamental instinct of our personality.' It is more. It is the absolutely indispensable condition of the recognition of our personality, and of our character, by others. One is disposed to forgive Mr. Mallock many of his rash assertions for sake of the clearness and emphasis with which he finally puts this cardinal truth. ' Three-fourths of life as enjoyed by us and as stimulating our interests, depend on the

---

[1] *Substance of Faith allied with Science*, p. 51.
[2] *Encyclopaedia of Religion and Ethics*, Vol. III, p. 365.

personal judgements which we form of ourselves and of one another. But if we did not suppose them free, our judgements would have no meaning.' If we call up all the noblest characters of history, or, for that matter, all the vilest, 'once let us suppose these characters to be mere puppets of heredity and circumstance, and they and the works that deal with them lose all intelligible content, and we find ourselves confused and wearied with the fury of an idiot's tale.'[1] All that makes real life most real, most precious, most stimulating, most potent, is not merely derived from the interplay of varying characters, but from the universal postulate that these characters are each and all self-made. Pride, envy, lust, greed, cruelty, and the like, are hateful not so much on Utilitarian and Hedonistic grounds, as because they are manufactures of the free activity of a self-determining personality. All talk about separating the agent from the act, is as absurd as a suggested separation of the sun from its heat and light. That which makes heroism to be heroic, is the fact, never doubted in actual life whatever philosophers may say, that the hero put himself into his act. A mechanical hero is unthinkable. A heroic automaton is an absurdity. The heroic character was earned by action which was not only actually done by the man himself, but need not have been done. It is the incarnation of a definite choice of the higher in presence of a lower possibility, which constitutes the character we admire. As for love, who but an idiot would submit to the embrace of a marionette? Even the kiss of a Judas would be better than that of a clock-work model. If, as one may well believe, the deepest, cruellest, direst tragedies on earth are love tragedies,

---

[1] *Reconstruction of Belief*, p. 83.

what is the essence of them all? This; that the coldness, or the unfaithfulness, or the desertion, is in every case the unmistakable expression of a real self. Mystery or no mystery, it requires a self to move a self. The lover's intensity is the fire in which his very soul is burning, and to offer him in return a fireless, soul-less brazier, no matter whence or how it came, would be but mockery to the uttermost. No further words are needed to describe the innumerable illustrations of the same principle in all the ways of human life. Whether man's relations with each other be domestic, social, civic, commercial, or political, they are all and always, without any exception, carried on under the definite understanding that every man is to be credited with his own character. On no other terms would life be either desirable or possible.

(6) The next step here towards the establishment of true Determinism, is the appreciation of a truth more philosophic than practical, yet emphatically essential, viz. that in no case is character to be regarded as the man himself. It is vain, confessedly, to shrink from the metaphysical difficulty which herein confronts us. Yet it need neither be minimized nor magnified, for its necessary treatment is as plain as unsatisfactory. We have no powers either of analysis or of description which can do justice to the reality. Affirmation, indeed, is easy enough, as when Mr. Pearson quite comfortably declares that—

'The self which we do know in experience, whatever its hidden nature or constituents may be, the self to which all conduct must be referred, is the self which is manifested as character. Character, in short, in relation to conduct, *is* the man; and though for the sake of convenience we may speak of a man's character, it is not to be supposed that a man is something distinct from character.'[1]

Now this, at the utmost, is mere assertion; and no valid support is given to it by insisting that 'even if such an uncaused self exists, it must be a metaphysical unit of which we can have no positive knowledge.' Knowledge more positive than my own consciousness that I am, and that 'I am I,' it is impossible to conceive. That my powers of analysis cannot draw a clear line of differentiation between me and my character is altogether another thing. The metaphysical unit in this case at least stands for an unshakable reality, whatever be the limitations of our analytical powers.

It is easy to say that we speak of a man's character 'for the sake of convenience.' This simply begs the question at issue; as also does the further assertion that it 'is not to be supposed' that a man is something distinct from his character. Why is it not to be supposed? Because we cannot conceive of a naked characterless ego? But no more can we conceive of life apart from organism. Is it then demonstrated that life *is* organism? We cannot conceive of good music apart from a player. Must we then say that in relation to music, the music *is* the player? Whether he plays from memory, or by nature, or by inspiration, we can no more identify that which is played with the player, than we can separate them. Indeed the inseparableness in fact is the very condition of the separableness in thought. That is why we speak as truly of a man's character as, necessarily, of a player's music. It is *his* certainly; therefore it is not *he*. Nor can any subtlety of thought or sophistry of speech ever obliterate the

---

[1] *Some Problems of Existence*, p. 92.

unmistakable distinction. So long as the phrases 'my character,' 'your character,' 'his character,' bear any intelligible significance or convey any reality, the very fact of possession which is asserted, connotes also that of distinction. That which I possess, is certainly not I. That the possessed should also be the possessor, would be a manifest contradiction in terms.

It is not surprising, therefore, that we should find even Prof. Green virtually contradicting himself herein, for all his confessedly careful and skilful dissection of man's mental powers in the *Prolegomena*. Thus he writes on one page, plainly enough, that ' the character is the man, who is thus not determined except as he determines himself.'[1] Yet almost immediately after, in replying to an objection, he says—' But the question itself implies that the questioner is not an instrument of natural forces, but a self-distinguishing and self-seeking consciousness.' Whereupon we must be permitted to ask, *is* then a self-seeking, self-distinguishing consciousness a character ? Surely language is useless if consciousness and character are synonyms. Further on[2] we read that ' the will, then, is not some distinctive part of a man separable from intellect and desire, nor a combination of them. It is simply the man himself, and only so the source of action.' Here, again, we cannot but point out that if the character *is* the man, and if the will *is* the man, then the character *is* the will. Which is assuredly not true, if any emphasis at all is put upon the ' is.' Why, then, we may well ask, is it ' not to be supposed ' that the true account in each of these cases, is that the man himself possesses both character and will, possesses them so

---
[1] p. xviii. [2] p. xxii.

really that to speak of 'a man's character,' or 'a man's will,' becomes the only accurate description of reality?[1]

If, as Prof. Green affirms, ' the whole question is one of consciousness, a question of the relation in which a man consciously stands to objects which exist only in and for consciousness,' then even Prof. Sidgwick's latest softened verdict gives a clearly sufficient answer—

'I find it impossible not to think that I can now choose to do what I conceive to be right and reasonable, however strong may be my inclination to act unreasonably, and however uniformly I may have yielded to such inclination in the past.'[2]

And one is bound to add, without desiring to foreclose all discussion, that an unequivocal affirmative seems thus to be the only and the final answer to Dr. Martineau's crucial question—' is there not a causal self, over and above the caused self, or rather the caused state and contents of the self, left as a deposit from previous behaviour?'[3]

(7) When the significance of words is kept steadily in view, the language even of those who would identify character with self, gives away their case. Thus Prof. Green, besides laying stress upon the

---

[1] Prof. Upton, in his valuable account of Dr. Martineau's philosophy, gives a useful summary. ' It is very common now, both among empirical psychologists and idealists, to say that in an act of choice, the selection is determined by the character at the time, that, in fact, the character is identical with the self. This is, as Dr. Martineau clearly shows, the $\pi\rho\hat{\omega}\tau o\nu$ $\psi\hat{\epsilon}\hat{\upsilon}\delta o\varsigma$ which vitiates the modern Deterministic reading of man's moral consciousness. If we examine our actual experience in the moral crises of our lives, we cannot, I think, fail to perceive that while it is the state of our character which determines the nature of our temptations, it is not to the character, but to the self which has the character, that the ultimate moral decision is due.'—p. 208.

[2] *Methods of Ethics*, Vol. II, pp. 264–293.

[3] *Study of Religion*, Vol. II, p. 227.

'action of the self-presenting ego,' says that 'a character is only formed through a man's conscious presentation to himself of objects as his good, as that in which his self-satisfaction is to be found.'[1] It would be difficult to express more definitely the fact that a man 'is something distinct from his character.' If for the term 'man' we substitute the true philosophical synonym, 'personality,' then, however freely we concede that personality ' must for ever remain an enigma—so far as its innermost nature is concerned it is the undeterminable *ding-an-sich* of Kant '—the difference between it and character is plainly expressible when we say that it is an entity, whilst character is a quality. An entity may have quality, but it is a case of possession, not identification. The reality of the possession is the pledge of the non-identification. Even as it ever is and must be true, that that which I possess is not and cannot be myself. Etymology, indeed, in this case would be a safe guide. For well we know that the ancient χαρακτήρ was ' a mark or token impressed on a person or thing, by which it is known from others.' It is not enough to say that by how much such a mark is to be distinguished from that on which it was impressed, by so much is character distinct from personality. For the truth which finds no parallel in things material, or in other creatures, is, that the personality puts its own mark upon itself, and that mark is its character. So that whenever we speak of a certain individual as being a noble character, we know that strictly speaking there is no such thing. What we really mean is that a personality has ennobled himself by creating in and for himself a certain quality of character. He has put a good mark upon himself.

---

[1] *Prolegomena*, p. 125.

(8) If this much be received as true, on the witness of experience, no less than of clear thought, only one inference is possible, i.e. that the self is free. What this inferred freedom does not mean, has been sufficiently explained above. What it does mean seems unmistakable. The self is free in that it can act, or not act, upon appeal. The sources of influence by appeal are confessedly varied and innumerable. But no one of them, no group of them, is of such force as to compel the 'self-distinguishing consciousness' to take the line of action suggested. Nor can we be frightened from this conclusion by the raising once again of the ghostly crux which refuses to lie still in any grave. On every appeal the self must take some line of action. That means choice, and choice means endorsed motive. Then why endorsed? Because of previous character? But that character, to be character, must have been self-made through a series of choices—and so on *ad infinitum*. True. But as surely as every step in such a regress involves a real reason for choice, so does it involve a real choice. And a real choice can never be determined by anything. The question comes to be thus of the same order as the query whether the hen or the egg came first; and must be left in the same category of unanswerables. We can get no farther than the whole sentence of Prof. Green takes us—

'When we say that the character of a man and his consequent action, as it at any time stands, is the result of what his character has previously been, as gradually modified through the varying response of the character to varying circumstances, and the registration in the character of residua from these responses, we must assume as the basis of character throughout, a self-distinguishing and self-seeking consciousness.'[1]

---

[1] *Prolegomena*, p. 133.

But when our analysis of the method of this self-distinguishing consciousness fails us, two truths which cannot and must not be missed, emerge. The first, in accordance with the attitude of the writer just quoted, and in his own words, is that—

'If a man's action is not the result of character or circumstances, if it is not the expression of a character in contact with certain circumstances, there must be some further element that contributes to its determination. What is that further element? Free will, some one may say. Very well; but free will is either a name for you know not what, or it is the essential factor in character.'[1]

The second, keeping these words in view, is that the 'know not what,' which is the 'essential factor in character,' is, we know, not mere 'free will,' because will, to be will, must be the will of some one. A will apart from a self is unthinkable. No one's will, is a non-entity. But will is the expressed energy of the real self which is, in very deed, the 'know not what,' though of it we know more surely than of anything else whatever, that it *is*. Whatever else I know not, I know that I am I; and that I choose; and that therefore I am free. The proof of my freedom is that besides knowing that I am, I know that I am somewhat endowed with moral capacity. Furthermore, that moral quality which now constitutes my character, I know to be my very own creation, out of the material supplied first in constitution and afterwards by circumstances. The experience of each hour yields also the indubitable conviction that I am truly and freely creating still; in other words, making my character better or worse, every day I live. Whether this be Pragmatism or not, it is an equally true and sufficient philosophy.

---

[1] p. 127.

(9) It carries with it, one must own, a tremendous consequence, viz. that character which has been, can be, and is being, completely self-made, can be at any time self-altered. Freedom, of course, is timeless and faces all directions. But in accordance with the limitations of our nature, we distinguish between past, present, and future. That each man has a character means that he, as a creature bound to go on living, is, in facing the future, either fortified for good or handicapped for evil by the character which up to the present he has himself made. The influence of such a contribution to the future is as immeasurable as real. But it is inevitable. The present is beyond controversy. That which is, is. But the irreconcilable difference between Determinism and Determinedism looms out more largely here than anywhere. For the past, that which was either had to be, or need not have been. In the former case there are many things we regret as objectionable and painful, though they could not under the circumstances be evil. In the latter case, they may have been so evil that their unalterableness yields now only remorse. But regret and remorse belong to different worlds.

As to the future, there is before us either a 'may be' which is not yet settled, or a 'must be' which we can only face in helplessness. The former yields hope, with corresponding stimulus. The latter means despair in expectation of evil, indifference in view of good. I either am, or am not, a 'link in an immense chain of causation in which the slightest element of uncertainty is impossible.' But if that which I do I must do, all thought of freedom is at an end. Whether I know that I am a slave, or think myself free, is quite irrelevant. 'Man is the inevitable product of his heredity and environment.'

Whilst as for his actions—'he could not help wishing them, the conditions once given.' So declares the Determinedist oracle. But the certainty of free self-consciousness scatters these murmurings of helplessness as the sun dispels a morning fog. Daily experience emphatically repudiates these ascriptions of guiltless and worthless automatic helplessness to what Prof. Ferrier rightly styled 'that free and self-sustained centre of underived activity which we call man.' Whether we think of the future of our nearest and dearest and best, or the past of humanity's cruellest and worst, that which we really fear in the former case, is what may be; that which is most deplored in the latter, is what need not have been.

For the freedom which enables the self to continue the making of character now, does so by making possible not only confirmation of but resistance to character thus far acquired, and, if necessary, transformation of that character into something other. The appeal to facts here is beyond cavil. In Mr. McCabe's words, 'Man can dominate hereditary tendencies — it has been done repeatedly.' Records altogether reliable of such indubitable transformations are not only to be found on the pages of Prof. James's Gifford Lectures, or Mr. Begbie's *Broken Earthenware*, as intimated above, but in every city of every civilized country. The relation of such transformations to religion, we have for the moment postponed. The point of concern here is to mark that these are cases which can be truly described in no other way than as self-altered characters, i.e. characters resisted, or changed, by the action of the self, in response to stimulus or appeal. To say this, it must be confessed, will bring us face to face with a plain yet critical question to which direct answer must be given, without evasion or hesitation—'Can the self act apart from its character?' And the answer must be—'Yes; it can.' For it does. Once again, *solvitur ambulando*. I am aware, in some respects maybe, too well aware, of the reality and nature of that character which now inseparably attaches to my personality. But I am equally aware that it is my character, and is neither my master nor myself. I am alike free and constrained to echo J. S. Mill's remarkable words, ' My habits are not my masters but I am theirs ; even in yielding I know I could resist ; if I were desirous of altogether throwing them off, there would not be required for that purpose a stronger desire than I know myself capable of feeling.' That which corresponds to actual experience herein, is well expressed, as Dr. Martineau points out,[1] by Prof. Sidgwick's avowal in the first edition of his *Methods of Ethics*. 'It is impossible for me to think at each moment, that my volition is completely determined by my character and the motives acting upon it.'[2] In such case, plainly, I am distinct from my character. That is an indubitable fact of experience. But experience must stand, whatever falls. From fact, however, rational inference may be drawn. The fact that character is altered, shows that it can be altered. That it can be altered now, is sufficient pledge that it need not have been what it was before. There neither is now, therefore, nor ever was, any

---

[1] See *Dr. Martineau's Philosophy*, by Prof. Upton, p. 210.

[2] It was doubtless the perception that such a sentence gave an irretrievable *coup de grâce* to Determinedism, which led the erudite author to attempt its modification in later editions. Whether anything was gained by such attempt, the student may be left to judge.

'impossibility' in the formation of character. Character that had to be, would be a contradiction in terms. Character is always the result of true Determinism. For it is what it is, and is going on to be what it will be, because I, and no other in the universe determine it.

(10) However contrary to some of the strongly expressed opinions of avowed Determinedists, may be this freedom of self which is involved in the making and changing of character, nothing would be easier than to multiply instances in which it is, to all intents and purposes, acknowledged by those who deny it. The following specimens, taken in connexion with the foregoing, should be both interesting and impressive.

The most popular exponent of Determinedism, who does not shrink from declaring himself also a fatalist, yet commits himself, as we have seen, to the statement 'I believe I am what heredity and environment have made me, but I know that I can make myself better or worse, *if I try*'—and actually refuses to see any contradiction between the avowal which we here italicize, and the alleged mathematic fixation of his will before he was born!

Again, Mr. Pearson, whose strong pleas for the complete determination of every human volition we have sufficiently noted, also declares that 'if personal continuity is to be preserved at all, in any future stage of existence, the man must pass into this with the character *acquired* during the preceding stage.'[1] But if language is to have any meaning at all, it is sheer mockery to talk of a man's having 'acquired' a character which was completely determined for him by temperament and circumstances. To say

---

[1] p. 98.

that a piece of iron in water acquires rust, or a stone acquires moss, or a ship's keel acquires barnacles, is in each case pure metaphor. Real acquiring, as applied to moral character, necessarily demands effort, and effort means freedom, if it means anything at all.

Or consider again the following remarkable words of one of the most able and acute of avowed 'Determinists.' Says Mr. McCabe—

'In the trivial acts of daily life, no less than in the graver dilemmas that confront every man at times, we have an extraordinary sense of choice and self-direction. Further, it is not too much to say that the efforts of Determinist moralists to expound a new philosophy of guilt, remorse, censure, and punishment, have not been wholly successful. Our criminology is confused and halting; our moral phraseology of praise and blame somewhat hollow. Stephen, the acutest of all, turns from the point with an expression of disdain but a very plain uneasiness. Sidgwick is so far intimidated that he prefers to believe in free will. The plain question remains, can we praise a Darwin for braving a flood of obloquy rather than conceal the truth, or must we merely admire the excellence of his moral machinery? Can we blame the friend who lays his life and home in desolation through drink, or must we merely deplore the ineffectiveness of the moral department of his cerebral cortex?'[1]

From the writer's standpoint, it is a brave confession, which certainly seems to merit praise on the score of candour, whatever becomes of his 'cerebral cortex.' Yet one wonders greatly that a mind thus plainly candid and acute, should present us with such monstrosities as 'moral machinery' and a 'moral cerebral cortex.' If these phrases are to stand, then we may with equal truth and right settle the questions he asks by appeal to a moral gramophone, or by reference to a moral biceps.

---

[1] *R.P.A. Annual*, 1910, p. 61.

It can, however, occasion no surprise that lesser lights should appear befogged, when such an authority as Mr. J. S. Mill answers himself in precisely similar fashion. Thus in the very midst of his protest against liberty, he not only, as already intimated, rejects with scorn the term necessity, but expresses himself thus—

'We shall find that this feeling of our being able to modify our own character, if we wish, is itself the feeling of moral freedom which we are conscious of. We must feel that our wish, if not strong enough to alter our character, is strong enough to conquer our character when the two are brought into conflict in any particular case of conduct.'[1]

But if our 'wish,' to employ his terms, is strong enough to conquer our character in the conflict, what is that but alteration, and alteration brought about by freedom? If any doubt remains, it ought to be dispelled by his further avowal—

'The free-will doctrine, by keeping in view precisely that portion of the truth which the word necessity puts out of sight, i.e. the power of the mind to co-operate in the formation of its own character, has given to its adherents a practical feeling much nearer to the truth than has generally, I believe, existed in the minds of Necessitarians.'[2]

(11) Such acknowledgements as these may well serve as an answer beforehand, to the attempts still made to drive home Determinedism by reference to the relations between mind and brain, more particularly as regards the dependence of mind to so large an extent upon brain. The folly of the jaunty assertion of popular philosophy, that 'the brain is the mind,' has been sufficiently exposed above; but the well-deserved dismissal of such a superficial oracle by no means settles the whole case. If we turn once more to Mr. Mallock, for a vivid and ruthless exposition

---

[1] *Logic*, Book VI, ch. ii. [2] *Logic*, Book VI, ch. ii, § 3.

of the Naturalistic attitude, we find him almost jubilantly declaring that through the study of modern physiology 'we arrive by yet another and a final route at one demonstration more that free will is impossible. It has thus stopped the last earth in which the phantom of freedom could hide itself.' And the natural result of all is that man 'is nothing but a mere machine, who, whatever he does, deserves neither praise nor blame, since whatever he does he could not have done otherwise.'[1] We need not dwell upon the curious attitudes always discoverable in such attempts to settle the whole question by a wave of the hand. One might remark in passing that a phantom which requires earth in which to hide itself, is well matched by a mere machine of which we may speak as 'who' and 'he,' and keeps good company with the notion that an automaton ever 'does' anything. When the vigorous and sweeping assertions of Mr. Mallock hereupon are taken calmly, they come only to the surely grotesque suggestion that accidents, diseases, and surgical operations, with their results, supply us with 'what previous philosophers had not, a Determinism from which there is no escaping,' as regards all human actions and human character. To do justice to his position—

'Since in a word, the brain is shown to control the will in those very domains of conduct in which freedom is most vehemently claimed for it, to suppose that the will is a separate and independent force which imposes its orders on an organism of which it shows itself so frequently to be the slave, is to indulge in a supposition for which science not only offers no evidence but which all the evidence collected by science contradicts.'[2]

---

[1] *Religion as a Credible Doctrine*, p. 149.   [2] p. 142.

Hereupon, one may say, first, that a careful perusal of Dr. W. H. Thomson's recent volume on *Brain and Personality*[1] will suffice to show how utterly this deliverance begs the whole question at issue, and is contradicted by the very science which it professes to revere. One sentence from this thoroughly trained witness shall stand for the rest—[2]

'In the order of development, physiology emphatically states, and the whole world proves it to be true, that the mind is not only the subordinate, but well nigh invariably, the merest servant, in man of the will, and by it often as despotically ruled as the mind in turn often despotically rules the body.'

Mr. Mallock makes a great point of the case of Phinehas Gage, well known to students as the 'American crow-bar case,' which happened some forty years ago, when the young man named was so strangely the victim of an explosion that a pointed iron bar, more than a yard in length, was blown straight through the upper portion of his skull. Full details will be found in Dr. Calderwood's careful analysis of the whole matter in his volume on *The Relations of Mind and Brain*.[3] It was certainly remarkable that he not only survived the accident but lived some thirteen years longer, showing, however, very different mental and moral characteristics from those displayed before it occurred, so that his acquaintances said he was 'no longer Gage.' Yet

---

[1] Hodder & Stoughton, 1907.

[2] That Dr. Thomson is well qualified to speak, is manifest from his position as Physician to the Roosevelt Hospital; consulting Physician to the New York State Manhattan Hospital for the Insane; Consulting Physician to the New York Red Cross Hospital; formerly Professor of the Practice of Medicine and of Diseases of the Nervous System, New York University Medical College; Ex-President of New York Academy of Medicine, &c.

[3] pp. 395-400.

it was, after all, only an extreme case of what has happened, times without number, to a smaller extent. The point which advocates of Determinedism seek to make is that such incidents, or accidents, show that mind and morals are after all nothing but functions of the brain. Mr. Mallock derides Schopenhauer, as a thoughtless ignoramus, for saying that 'we never read that after an accident of this kind character has undergone a change, that a man has become better or worse, that he has lost or gained any particular propensities or passions; no, never.' But the contempt is scarcely called for. Schopenhauer could not be expected to know facts which have been only carefully watched or recorded since his day, and there is much to be said in the light of our fullest and latest knowledge, for the opinion that a man does not become morally better or worse through any accident. Moral character is always and only possible in the degree in which responsibility obtains, and in the case of Gage Dr. Calderwood rightly remarks that 'if anything be obvious it is this, that as Gage was not responsible for the accident which befell him, so neither was he responsible for the difficulty in controlling himself which he afterwards experienced.' Indeed, speaking generally, in so far as an accident deprives a man of his usual powers of self-control, he becomes more or less insane. Whilst as regards every type of 'moral perversion' found amongst the insane, it can 'with no show of reason be described as immorality, but only as insanity, a disordered brain and an excited physical condition.' Moral character, to be such, assumes normal possession of human faculties and powers. There is no moral argument from the abnormal to the normal. There is only a call for pity and help, as in the case of any other disease.¹ But the psychological straits to which special pleaders for Determinedism are reduced, plainly appear in the following remarkable utterance of Mr. Mallock—

'To present the matter in its most general aspect, the various faculties and states of mind are now shown to be located in distinct cerebral areas; and thus the mind or cell, which in pre-scientific days men were able to look upon as a singular and indissoluble entity, is now revealed to us as a something made out of many bits, which is susceptible in theory of being taken to pieces altogether, and is often, in reality, taken partly to pieces by accident or by experiment.' ²

It is difficult to speak respectfully of any writer who sets forth such a hash as this under the guise of science. Any writer who in these days can deliberately print such a phrase as 'the mind *or* cell' really merits no further regard. If 'mind' and 'cell' are synonyms, philosophy is a delusion. But further, to avow that because certain faculties of the mind are expressed through located areas of matter, therefore the mind itself is 'made up of many bits (!)' is as absurd as to to say that because an organ has many notes and stops whereby its different sounds are produced, therefore the player is made up of as many bits as there are sounds. It is on the same scientific level as the ancient but effete suggestion of

---

¹ The easy confidence with which misleading statements under this head are issued to the people, may be illustrated once more from the book *Not Guilty*, where the writer says that—'Many of our wrongdoers are ignorant, or diseased, or insane, or mentally deformed.'—p. 19. Every item of which is false. As to the ignorant, no man is a wrongdoer unless he knows what he is doing. Hence, the insane can never be wrongdoers because they never know. Whilst as to the diseased and mentally deformed, in the degree to which these descriptive terms are true, any human being is relieved of responsibility and becomes a sufferer, not a wrongdoer.

² *Religion as a Credible Doctrine*, p. 134.

materialism, that the brain secretes thought as the liver secretes bile. And there is no more truth in it than in the affirmation that when an organ 'ciphers,' or a stop goes wrong, there is something the matter with the player. Everyone knows that the best organist in the world cannot produce diapason tones from the oboe pipes, any more than he can produce the sounds of a flute from the pedal stops. But if any one, or all, of these should refuse to work properly, what does it show in regard to the player? Nothing but this, that he is handling a disordered instrument. Nor need there be any shrinking from the employment of such an analogy. For it is a perfectly competent witness who has assured us, in the words already quoted above, that 'the facts both of brain anatomy and of brain physiology indicate that this organ of the personality is never other than its instrument, while the personality itself is as different and as separate from it as the violinist is separate from and not the product of his violin.'[1] But in face of the boldness with which such statements as Mr. Mallock's are now noised abroad, it may be useful to record here the avowal to the contrary of Dr. Rudolf Otto—

'The simile of an instrument and the master who plays upon it, which is often used of the relation between body and mind, is in many respects a very imperfect one, for the master does not develop with and in his instrument. But in regard to the most oppressive arguments of naturalism, the influence of disease, of old age, of mental disturbance due to brain changes, the comparison serves our turn well enough. For undoubtedly the master is dependent upon his instrument; upon an organ which is going more and more out of tune, rusting, losing its pipes, his harmonies will become poorer and more imperfect.'[2]

When, again, Mr. Mallock singles out the practice

---
[1] Dr. W. H. Thomson, *Brain and Personality*, p. 234.
[2] *Naturalism and Religion*, p. 355.

of chastity as 'showing how sexual virtue is empirically at the mercy of the brain,' he seems strangely unable once more to distinguish between that which is physical and that which is moral. If there be actual brain disease, its consequences can never be sexual 'vice'; for vice, by the very nature of the case, presupposes a normal body. To say that any virtue is at the mercy of the brain, is to identify the physical with the moral, which assuredly puts an end to the latter altogether.[1]

The confusion referred to above by Prof. Eucken, which not seldom arises from the loose employment of the term 'character,' is illustrated yet again when Mr. Mallock asserts that heredity 'gives us our various characters, as it gives us our various faces.' For here, once more, if the term 'characters' is intended to convey anything more than mere physical constitution—the receipt of which by heredity no one disputes—we have the moral put on the same level with the physical. Whereas heredity, including atavism, never yet did, or could, confer moral character upon any one. Its very utmost function is, one must repeat, to supply the 'raw material' out of which character may be made. The same principle applies exactly, in regard to that normal condition of brain which we know as health. True morality assumes the normal healthy brain, just as

---

[1] The further illustration employed is as false as it is flippant. 'When the operation of castration is performed on a boy under a certain age, the formation of such thoughts never takes place again. The surgeon's knife succeeds where the spiritual struggle may fail, and whatever may be the boy's subsequent character otherwise, he at least merits the blessing pronounced on the pure of heart.' Unless the writer's brain was so completely determined beforehand that he 'could not help' writing this last ribald sentence, he ought to be ashamed of its amazing and repulsive superficiality.

the rendering of good music assumes and requires a properly tuned instrument. The harmonies then result from the use of the instrument, even as character results from the use of normal human powers. It would be interesting to know how many or how few notes of the piano must be out of tune, to make impossible the rendering of Beethoven. Could Mendelssohn's famous Concerto, or one of Paganini's masterpieces, be performed on a violin with only three strings? Such an instrument would at least require to be in the hands of a Mischa Elman. It would be no disgrace, even to a good player, to decline such a task.

The summing up, therefore, of all attempts to prove Determinedism by means of brain lesions, comes to nothing more than this, that given an imperfect instrument, only imperfect music can be produced. That the human self manifests its free causal activity through brain and nerve in the human body, is acknowledged on all hands. But no more. The assumptions which lie at the base of these would-be demonstrations of cerebral Determinedism, cannot be for a moment conceded. They are without any significance for their purpose, until and unless it be demonstrated that there is no self distinct from the cerebral organisation; that there is no mind apart from the brains; that there is no soul distinct from sensation; that there is, in a word, no entity in human personality distinct from the 'function of the phronema.' But these are, as we have seen, the realities with which we must start, not the suppositions with which we may possibly close, our investigations. Indeed, and as a matter of fact, every investigator, be he naturalist or theist, does so start, and it is a poor philosophy which compels the philosopher both to doubt his own existence and deny the worth of his philosophizing. When we start with the experience which affirms the reality and activity of the ego because it can do no other, we can appreciate the tragedy of brain injury or failure deeply enough without adding to it the immeasurably greater tragedy of the nemesis of all morality. Dr. Calderwood might well ask in such case—

'Shall we say that moral character can melt away like snow before the breath of spring? Has the law of continuity so slight application in human life as to admit of a complete reversal with change of health? Or shall we say that the change in physical condition which has induced the brain disorder has imposed a physical barrier to the action of mind, and yet has left in operation all the functions of merely animal life? The more carefully we classify, distinguishing in detail the several phases of restraint as they appear, and the intellectual activity of the patient's suffering under these, the more obvious does it become that the facts are such as cannot be explained on the hypothesis that brain is the governing power in life.'[1]

Moreover, the reader of such picked instances as Mr. Mallock and others allege, must never forget that, as Dr. Otto so vividly points out, 'there are luminous facts on the other side which are much more true.' Prof. Schäfer might well remark, in his text-book of Physiology, that—

'So much has been made of certain clinical cases in which an extensive lesion of the frontal lobes was followed by diminution of the intellectual faculties, and by a change for the worse in the general disposition of the individual, that it is important to ascertain what the clinical evidence on this point really amounts to. Welt collected 59 cases of lesions confined to the frontal region in man; of these 47, or about 80 per cent, showed no change in intellectual capacity or character; and only 12 out of the total number, or 20 per cent, had such changes recorded

---

[1] *The Relations of Mind and Brain*, pp. 392, 378.

against them. It is clear, therefore, that the doctrine of special localization of the intellectual faculties in this portion of the frontal lobes rests on no sufficient basis.'[1]

It is well known by physiologists that brain disease may exist, even to a great extent, without any experience of mental uneasiness, or any indications of mental restraint or disorder. Dr. Ferrier showed that even a whole cerebral hemisphere might be disorganized without any mental symptoms. Whilst Dr. Rudolf Otto goes so far as to make the weighty affirmation that—

'The melancholy field of mental diseases yields proofs against naturalism to an even greater degree than for it. It is by no means the case that all mental diseases are invariably diseases of the brain; for even more frequently they are real sicknesses of the mind which yield not to physical but to psychical remedies. And the fact that the mind can be ill, is a sad but emphatic proof that it goes its own way.'[2]

On Mr. Mallock's principles, every man past his prime must proceed on to ever-increasing feebleness of mind, ending invariably in dotage. But Goethe, Schleiermacher, Gladstone, Martineau, Lord Kelvin, Wallace, General Booth, and hosts of others, have vividly contradicted such a principle. That their bodily powers waned was manifest enough; and that the brain shares in such general decay will not be questioned. But that there was any corresponding decay of mind, or enfeeblement of personality, let alone decline of morality, is altogether untrue. It is for those who talk about a blow on the head altering moral character, to say how with wasting brain, intellectual power can be maintained, and moral excellence grow ever greater until the end.

---

[1] Dr. W. H. Thomson, *Brain and Personality*, p. 221.
[2] *Naturalism and Religion*, p. 356.

The innumerable instances in which such maintenance of mind and morals does take place, cannot and need not be particularized here. They are intelligible enough in the light of the existence and activity of a causal self which is necessarily conditioned, though never created, by the instrument it has to employ. But they are quite inexplicable on the theory of a mere mass of matter simply functioning according to a physical vitality which absolutely determines all its motions. When the coal supply is exhausted and the fires die down, the best engine-driver on earth cannot get full speed out of his engine. But if any engine in such a condition did continue to do its accustomed work, it would mean that in some way or other, whether unscientific or uncanny or otherwise, there must be a power at work beyond the mechanism of the engine. We should be no more able to deny it than to trace it.

The scientific tendency of the last century undoubtedly was to make more and more of brain, and proportionately less of the something which is beyond brain in the experience of life. The triumph of the physical element became assured enough to permit it to laugh the metaphysical to scorn. But as the last laugh is said to be the best, the latter is now passing out of the region of scorn into the promise of full recognition. It has been said long enough that the brain makes the man; it is now coming to be seen that it is much more true to affirm that the man makes the brain. That high intelligence goes along with a much convoluted cerebral cortex may be considered as established. But, in the words of an expert, 'This does not prove at all that such men become eminent because they were born with such convoluted brains.' However much men may differ through heredity, as to brain, ' the fact remains that the special mental capacities for which certain men have become eminent, were all acquired and were not congenital. In other words, a great personality may possibly make a great brain, but no brain can make a great personality.'[1] If this last sentence is true, it is more than enough to give us furiously to think. It points unmistakably in the direction of a true Determinism which applies in some real degree even to the injured and the insane,[2] but finds its supreme and normal sphere in those who are endowed with ordinary human powers and average health.

So far, then, from accidents, diseases, or surgical operations, being the final proof of Determinedism, after the drastic fashion suggested by Naturalism, they do but testify to the reality and potency of the something-more-than-brain which works in every hour's experience. It stands to reason that so indescribably complex an organ as the human brain

---

[1] Thomson, *Brain and Personality*, pp. 227, 228.

[2] Thus as to the famous Gage case, Dr. Calderwood points out that whilst he was not responsible for the increased difficulty in self-control which came about through his accident, ' it does not, therefore, follow that it was not his duty to begin an entirely new effort at self-control required in his altered circumstances. His greater difficulties entitled him to greater consideration, but did not put an end to his obligations.' So again, even as to the insane, Dr. Maudsley, who will not be deemed either lacking in experience or disposed to favour metaphysics, suggests that the main thing to be done is to get the patient's ' thoughts engaged—to make him step out of himself.' Whilst as to insanity itself—' However it be brought about, it is the dethronement of will, the loss of the power of co-ordinating the ideas and feelings ; and in the wise development of the control of the will over the thoughts and feelings, there is a power in ourselves which makes strongly for sanity.'—Calderwood's *Relations of Mind and Brain*, pp. 391, 409.

should be correspondingly liable to disorder, and the way no less than the degree in which such disorder may affect the mind, may well be as marked as mysterious. But no allocation of areas in the brain cortex affords the least reason for identifying thought with molecular motion, or personality with cerebral function. When we say that brain is the organ of mind, we affirm, in the sober light of latest science, that which is at once the most rational explanation of experience, and the mystery which no human knowledge even promises to fathom. But we have therefrom no right whatever to assert that a disordered brain means a disordered mind; or that the condition of mind, let alone the moral character, is determined by the condition of brain. It is much more in consonance with all the facts to regard mind as the moulder of brain, so that the Determinism which alone is true, regards the man as the creator, to an unmeasured extent, of the organ he uses; however much, through influences beyond his control, he may be hindered by its defects or hedged in by its limitations. Anything beyond this comes under the head of insanity, where, of course, moral character is out of the question.

(12) It becomes necessary in this connexion to emphasize the unparalleled uniqueness of human character. All the more so because of the manifest tendency in Naturalistic quarters not merely to jettison manhood altogether by reduction to thinghood, but, by way of lessening the shock which such an estimate must give to sober minds, to elevate the animal world whilst lowering the human, so as to bring about the closest possible approximation. Thus Prof. Haeckel does not hesitate, as we have seen, to affirm that 'our own human nature, which exalted

itself into an image of God in its anthropistic illusion, sinks to the level of a placental mammal, which has no more value for the universe at large than the gnat, the fly of a summer's day, the microscopic infusorium or the smallest bacillus.'[1] We need not here descend any lower in this scale than the 'placental mammal,' because the most determined opponent of human freedom has never suggested that gnats, or flies, or bacilli, should be credited with the possibility of moral character. The point to be emphasized is that the attempt to elevate even the higher animal to human moral fellowship, is no more justified than the philosophy which would degrade the human being to an automaton. The candid words of Mr. McCabe quoted above, ought indeed to save us the trouble of discussing the matter further.[2] But it seems necessary to repeat that the 'residual power,' which is thus frankly acknowledged, can only logically be emphasized by true Determinists, not by those who falsely call themselves by that name, whether their interpretation of its significance be 'hard' or 'soft.' It is an excellent suggestion that the basis of our moral terminology should be the conscious possession of a power of self-determination, for this, besides putting an end to all theories about man's being completely determined in all his volitions, sufficiently removes him also out of all comparison with any other creature

---

[1] *Riddle of the Universe*, cheap edition, p. 87.

[2] To obviate the necessity of turning back—'Most psychologists would, I think, agree with Stout that man differs from other animals in having the power of self-determination and choice, and it seems to me that in this residual power we have something that ought to be emphasized by Determinists whose language is often quite inconsistent with it, and a possible basis for the reconstruction of our moral terminology.'

on earth. The very most, indeed, that can be said concerning even the highest animals, whether dog, or horse, or elephant, or chimpanzee, is that they possess highly-organized nervous systems, which bespeak complex faculties of sensation; that they are endowed with instincts which sometimes merge into elementary reasoning powers; and that they have some rudimentary self-consciousness. More than this cannot truthfully be affirmed.

But what they lack, as compared with human nature, is decidedly more manifest and more significant. (i) The very wonderfulness of their instincts puts emphasis upon their limitations, for their mental activities are not purposeful. Now purposeful activities are, as Kant has said, not merely adjusted to an end but directed by the idea of an end; and Prof. Mackenzie well points out that 'even the higher animals, in so far as they are guided by mere instinct, cannot be supposed to have any such idea. They move towards certain ends, but they do not will these ends. They have an end, but no purpose.'[1] (ii) They have no power of abstract thought or generalization, and so are incapable of the attention and deliberation which form indispensable parts of conscious volition.[2] If the photograph of the most intelligent dog be shown to him he will smell it, and possibly lick it, but certainly not see it. (iii) The difference between the animal self and the human self is thus immeasurable. That the animal is conscious we cannot

---

[1] *Manual of Ethics*, p. 85.
[2] Thus Schopenhauer says that 'Reason has always been understood to mean the possession of general, abstract, non-intuitive ideas named concepts, which are denoted and fixed by means of words. This faculty alone it is which, in reality, gives to men their advantage over animals.'

doubt. But that it is conscious of itself we cannot believe. In Prof. Mackenzie's words—' a mere animal has not a self in the full sense of the term. Its self is simply the feeling of the moment.' It remains always in the condition of the human infant, who, as pictured above—

> Has never thought that 'this is I.'

There being thus no real self, there can be no genuine volition following upon attention, deliberation, and selection of motives. Morality, therefore, is out of the question. (iv) Being thus non-moral, it follows that animals are incapable of sin, having no sense of right or wrong. All the approaches to such a sense which are sometimes specified, are almost certainly nothing more than results of association—as when a dog is whipped out of a butcher's shop, or a cat aiming at fish is kicked out of the larder. (v) Moreover, there is no apparent possibility of creating such a moral sense, for animals show no capacity for such development.[1] The task of educating an animal, in any sense approaching the education of a child, is so hopeless that no one undertakes it. The most exceptional cases ever

---

[1] Dr. Otto well remarks hereupon that ' The very example that naturalism loves to cite in its own favour, makes its error clear. It asks whether the difference, let us say between a Fuegian and one of the highest mammals such as an ape, is not much less than that between a Fuegian and a European. This sounds obvious if we measure simply by habits, morals, and probably also the content of feeling and imagination in a savage as we find him. And yet it is obviously false. I can train a young ape or an elephant and can teach it to open wine bottles and perform tricks. But I can educate the child of the savage, can develop in him a mental life equal in fineness, depth and energy, frequently more than equal to that of the average European, as the mission to the Eskimos and to the Fuegians proves, and as Darwin frequently admitted.—*Naturalism and Religion*, p. 333.

known have never even come within sight of anything that could be called moral education. (vi) There is thus no possibility of character in animals. 'Character,' says Prof. Stout, 'only exists in so far as unity and continuity of conscious life exists and manifests itself in systematic consistency of conduct. Animals can scarcely be said to have a character, because their actions flow from disconnected impulse.'[1] Animals may safely be described as conscious automata. But when the automatism is real, the consciousness is irrelevant, so far as moral character is concerned.

The contrast between all this and the human mind is alike immeasurable and inexpressible. 'The human spirit is more than all creatures, and is in quite a different order from stars, planets, and animals.' And the difference in the order consists in this that 'man can will good, and can pray; and no other creature can do this.'[2] If it be true that 'a man's acts are his own only when he is himself in doing them,'[3] then either he never acts at all or he is the creator of his own character, the ruler of his conduct, and the arbitrator of his own destiny, as no other creature known to us can be. He determines, and therefore is not determined.

(13) When all other creatures are left out of account, it still remains to point out that character is the highest pinacle of even human development, and is, as such, only conceivable along the lines of true

---

[1] *Manual of Psychology*, p. 633.

[2] Otto, p. 331. And further—'What is implicit in him as *homo sapiens*, a member of a zoological order, is nothing more than the natural basis upon which in human and individual history he may build up an entirely unique and new creation, an upper storey, the world of life and of spirit.'—p. 335.

[3] Mackenzie, *Ethics*, p. 96.

Determinism. Just in the degree in which any human character is acknowledged to be pure and lofty and noble, it is unthinkable as the completely determined result of heredity and environment. Such a character could not be so made, any more than sheer force can make love. Even if, by a strain of the imagination, we could think of a beautiful character as being a result of such compulsion, it would altogether lose its charm. It would cease to be beautiful, through our very knowledge of its source.[1] Let any one with an open mind think of the character which by tender faithfulness or noble unselfishness or purity of purpose, has most of all impressed him, and then ask whether an adequate account of such a moral and spiritual reality is supplied in the shibboleths of Naturalism of which the following is a fair specimen. 'Possessing a certain deliberation in our movement through the cultivation of our senses, and our experience or knowledge given through them, we yet are at bottom, living marionettes completely at the mercy of our environment.'[2]

---

[1] As these lines are being written, the papers announce the prospective removal of Rev. Dr. Jowett to New York, with the following comment, as a fair summary of the general feeling. 'Dr. Jowett's influence is as widespread as it is profound. It owes nothing to sensationalism or extravagance. It is the slow but sure growth of a character of rare temper, of a mind of finely balanced parts, and of a spirituality that is unfailing in its gracious appeal.' Can any person of ordinary intelligence think of such a character and such influence as but the completely determined result of the accidents of the preacher's temperament and circumstances? If he can, it is at least certain that the words which are added would be absolutely meaningless. 'Few men of our time have won a more secure place in the hearts of men of all creeds and parties.' It requires a heart to win a place in hearts, and however little of the process language can express, the two elements which are absolutely and for ever excluded, are mechanism and compulsion, and these constitute the very *sine quâ non* of Determinedism.

[2] *From Matter to Man*, A. R. Dewar, p. 262.

It would be just as reasonable, and as scientific, to attribute a gorgeous rainbow to the fortuitous jostling of a child's box of paints.

(14) It is not too much to say, speaking generally, that the reality of character as a human self-creation, whether for weal or woe, is tenaciously held by the average man as a standing protest against the alleged tyranny of fate, or inexorableness of destiny. It is an easy thing to form an 'Omar Khayyám Society' in appreciation of the genius of FitzGerald's translation of the ancient Pessimist's legacy; but do these accents of Determinedism express the mind of humanity in general, let alone of its nobler specimens?

> Into this Universe, and why not knowing,
> Nor *whence*, like Water willy-nilly flowing:
> And out of it, as Wind along the Waste,
> I know not *whither*, willy-nilly blowing.
>
> What, without asking, hither hurried *whence?*
> And, without asking, *whither* hurried hence!
> Another and another Cup to drown
> The Memory of this Impertinence.[1]

We know that they do not. The verdict of history, no less than the persistent voice of the individual conscience, pronounce such a gloomy vision nothing better than a nightmare. There is that within the breast of every man who has not fouled his nature or wrecked his manhood, which makes him refuse such a notion with fearless scorn.

'Blame not Heaven for your tyrants, blame yourselves,' said Solon of old; and the ages have echoed the conviction down to this hour. The voice of Cassius rings on throughout every generation—

> The fault, dear Brutus, is not in our stars,
> But in ourselves, that we are underlings.

---

[1] xxix, xxx.

Macbeth's misery and Othello's remorse are no mere dreams of a dramatist. They are the equally unmistakable, unquenchable, irrepressible protest of the human soul that man is man, and so not merely master of his fate, but himself the actual doer of his deeds of ill, no less than the actual creator of his character for good.

(15) In one final word, nothing short of the true Determinism which recognizes in man a free, active, causal self, as the determinant of volitions, can give any account of the real essence of character; or explain the unmeasured appreciation of character which obtains amongst all grades of respectable human society; or satisfy the growing need for more and higher character as civilization advances.

(i) Certainly Determinedism can give no such explanation or satisfaction; for upon its principles as we have seen, character is no more possible under modern ' soft Determinism ' than under the iron heel of ancient Necessitarism. Whatever else be true of it, character is a personal quality which cannot, under any circumstances, be either given or received. Compelled character is unthinkable, no matter whence the compulsion. Wherever character exists, it is made—created—by the personality to whom it belongs. In other words, all real character is the sign of a real maker, i.e. one who really acts, and who, in order to act, must be so far free. The character of every person is, and can only be, what he or she determines it to be. When it is asked—in Prof. Mackenzie's words—' How can any one be regarded as responsible for the formation of his own character, seeing that he is born with particular inherited aptitudes and tendencies, and that the whole development of his life is determined by the moral atmosphere in which he is placed?"[1]—the answer is that such a statement is not true. The 'whole development of his life' is *not* determined by any environment, any more than it is by any heredity. This could only be the case with a selfless automaton, and there is no need to reiterate that that is precisely what a man *is not*. ' In a sense we choose our own universes, but the " we," the self that chooses, is not an undetermined existence.' May be. No more is it a determined existence; for that, if the self does choose, would be a contradiction in terms. Call it mystery, or antinomy, or what you will, the self is that without which there can be no true choice, no real action, and, therefore, no formation of character. The part played by the self is undoubtedly, at the maximum, a co-operation. It may be reduced to a minimum. But the minimum is as absolutely essential, as was the touch of the child's finger on the electric button, which touch, however gentle, caused the blowing up of Hell Gate at New York Harbour.

(ii) Only the knowledge and acknowledgement of this absolute necessity for real action on the part of self, can make rational the appreciation of character which obtains the wide world over. We have noted above that all men admire heroism. But what would there be to admire in the noble discipline of the men of the *Birkenhead*, or the heroic defence of Rorke's Drift, or the brave attempt of Capt. Sperling to save the drowning passengers of the *Berlin*, or a thousand other deeds of gallantry, if it were settled that in every such case the deed was completely determined beforehand, so that each man could no more help what he did, than the soldier's

---
[1] *Ethics*, p. 101.

rifle could help firing when the trigger was pulled, or the boat could help facing the raging billows when propelled by the oars? Did any sane man ever admire an heroic boat, or an heroic gun? Here Mr. Mallock is right, beyond all controversy, in his affirmation that the 'essential element in our admiration is recognition of conduct which originates in a man's conscious self; which he has deliberately chosen when he might just as well have chosen the opposite; and which is not imposed upon him by conditions either within his organism or outside it.'[1] It is equally true on the dark side of human life and history, that the real and only reason for reproaching a thief, or scorning a traitor, or condemning a murderer, or deploring the fall of a woman, is the 'passionate belief in the tragic freedom of personality.' Reasonable men will always condemn bad character, and revere good character—let philosophers say what they will—because the good and the bad alike are the result of such personal determination as never was, and never could be, completely determined without the consent, i.e. the co-operation, i.e. the real action, of the uncompelled self.

(iii) It is, moreover, only this recognition of true Determinism in the appreciation of character, which can yield any hope in response to the crying need for character which increases with every decade of advancing civilization. Be the mystery of individual life and the growing intensity of the social struggle what they may, there is no promise of the future save in human character, and no possibility of character save in genuine personal Determinism. 'The formidable array of cumulative evidence' offered for Determinedism—to use the language of Prof. Sidgwick's

---
[1] See also *Religion as a Credible Doctrine*, p. 248.

well-known *Methods of Ethics*—may be as apparently overwhelming as language can express, but there is always to be reckoned with ' the immediate affirmation of consciousness in the moment of deliberate action.' Whether this be a Pragmatic antinomy or not, it is sufficient. And it is because men know it to be both true in themselves, and reliable in their relations with others, that the world of mankind is acting now, and will go on to act, upon the philosophy which denies the omnipotence of heredity and environment, and which calls upon every man to play the man in becoming ' soldiers of the ideal,' as Prof. Mackenzie has it, such that ' those who fail to struggle for it must be treated as deserters, and those who deny its authority as guilty of *lèse majesté* against the dignity of human nature.'[1] That is at once a potent plea for character, and an unmistakable pointer to the measureless gulf which lies between the false and the true Determinism.

(iii) *The Only Way of Upward Evolution.*

Patient and careful scrutiny of the writings of modern Determinedists produces a growing perception that they seem to be ' determined ' to contradict themselves, and so give away completely the cause for which they so strenuously labour. This has been manifest enough in the statements already given which relate to the experience of any present moment. But it is even more markedly so when, in accordance with the constitution of our nature, the future is contemplated. The plain fact is that

---

[1] *Ethics*, p. 102.

no man has ever yet attempted to state Determinedism without contradicting himself; and there is no risk whatever in the prophecy that such a task never will be accomplished; any more than there is in pointing out that no man will ever deny his own existence without self-contradiction. As the matter is even more important than interesting, it may be well, before definitely facing the relations of Determinedism to the future, to pass before the mind in brief yet clear panoramic procession, its self-contradictions relating to the present.

Mr. Mill, as we have seen, tells us one moment that the doctrine of philosophical necessity is a 'mere interpretation of universal experience, a statement in words of what every one is internally convinced of,' and immediately proceeds to denounce the use of 'so extremely inappropriate a term as necessity for the simple fact of causation.' Then further, whilst insisting that 'the causation of our volitions by motives, and of motives by the desirable objects offered to us, combined with our susceptibilities of desire' is sufficiently established—here plainly enough, 'causation' = complete determination, i.e. compulsion—he at the same time acknowledges that we have a consciousness of moral freedom which means that a man 'feels that his habits or his temptations are not his masters, but he is theirs, that even in yielding to them he knows that he could resist.'[1]

Prof. Huxley, we know, also avowed that there was no harm in saying 'that man is nothing but a machine,' so long as we admit that which is a matter of experimental fact, i.e. that it is a machine 'capable of adjusting itself within certain limits.' But no man

---

[1] *System of Logic*, Book VI, ch. ii.

has ever seen such a machine or ever will. Automata and calculating machines never were, or will be, 'self'-adjusting. They are pure mechanism throughout. In addition, moreover, to the famous expression of willingness to be ' into a sort of clock ' which should ' do what is right,' as if that were not self-contradiction enough, we have the further avowal that ' the only freedom I care about is the freedom to do right, the freedom to do wrong I am ready to part with on the cheapest terms to any one who will take it of me.'[1] Which is tantamount to the offer to part with one side of the sheet of paper on which he wrote it, in order to make more sure of the other.

Prof. H. Sidgwick, whose treatise on the *Methods of Ethics* is regarded as the finest and strongest demonstration of Determinedism, in Mr. McCabe's phrase ' prefers to believe in free will.' And we cannot but recall the words of his last edition—' I find it impossible not to think that I can now choose to do what I conceive to be reasonable, *however strong* may be my inclination to act unreasonably.'

Prof. Haeckel, whose iconoclasm leads him to declare that ' the freedom of the will is not an object for critical inquiry at all, for it is pure dogma, based on an illusion,'[2] confesses elsewhere that ' Beyond all doubt the present degree of human culture owes, in great part, its perfection to the propagation of the Christian system of morals, and its ennobling influence.'[3] But surely every one knows that personal freedom is the very essence of the Christian system of morals, and the mainspring of its ' ennobling influence.'

---

[1] *Lay Sermons*, p. 296.
[2] *Riddle of the Universe*, cheap edition, p. 6.
[3] *Confession of Faith*, p. 66.

Dr. Callaway, who writes with such ineffable scorn against the 'loose-thinking free will hypothesis,' avows that 'our wills are not forced by an external power[1] but are regulated by our own consciences.' As if a 'completely determined' automaton could possess a 'conscience.' Yet again: 'Woe to the man who defies the laws which hem us in.' How a 'completely determined' will can 'defy' the laws which determine it, remains to be shown.

Mr. Bertrand Russell, again, in the very midst of his avowal that the grounds in favour of 'Determinism,' i.e. Determinedism, are overwhelmingly strong, declares, 'We apply praise or blame, then,'[2] and we attribute responsibility where a man having to exercise choice, has chosen wrongly.' Whereas the least educated man in the street must see that a completely determined 'choice' is an absolute contradiction in terms. There never was such a thing and never will be, until round squares abound along with white blackbirds. As if it were any rational reply to say that 'what Determinism maintains is, that our will to choose this or that alternative is the effect of antecedents'! If it be the mere effect of antecedents, it is an absolutely hopeless result of those antecedents; in which there is no more room for choice than there is for a cartridge

---

[1] In this, as an interesting specimen of the harmony existing between Determinedists, he is flatly contradicted by Mr. Blatchford, who declares that—'Heredity makes and environment modifies a man's nature, and both these forces are *outside* the man.'—*Not Guilty*, p. 23. (Italics his.)

[2] Once more flatly contradicting other most confident Determinedists, such as Messrs. Hamon, Cotter Morison, Blatchford, &c., whose dogma is unmistakable—'No man can under any circumstances be praised or blamed for anything he may say or do. That is one of my deepest convictions.'—*God and My Neighbour*, p. 137.

in a rifle to explode, when struck by the hammer after the pulling of the trigger.

Mr. N. Pearson, whose trenchant words have been fully given above, we have found actually telling us on the same page, that 'every man is born with a certain character, and whatever the history of its origin may be he did not make it for himself;' and then that 'every man must pass into any future state of existence with the character *acquired* during the preceding stage.' Will any microscope avail to discover for us the difference between making a character for oneself and acquiring it?[1]

Prof. McTaggart, from whom naturally great things might be expected, reiterates the same self-contradiction as Mr. Russell—'the ordinary Determinist believes that while the event may well be determined by his choice, his choice is in its turn completely determined.' From which, beyond all question must be inferred, that there is no philosophical difference between an event and a choice. But, with all respect, it must be persistently submitted that a choice which is a mere 'event,' is no choice at all. For a genuine choice is a new creation. It is an act, not only an event. And the difference between the two is as unmistakable and as undeniable, as the difference between the actions of a child and the performance of an automaton. An event may be determined, but a choice cannot be.

Mr. Blatchford thinks nothing of self-contradictions, but even amidst the host of such with which his pages are garnished, some stand out as lofty peaks in a mountain chain. As if it were not enough to avow that 'I believe I am what heredity and environment made me, but I know that I can make

---

[1] *Not Guilty*, p. 249.

myself better or worse, if I try,' we find the refreshing avowal that 'the greatness of a nation does not lie in its wealth and power, but in the character of its men and women,'[1] side by side with the dogma that 'whatever a man does, is the only thing he can do.' So that if he should cruelly murder a little child, he is not to be blamed, because 'he could not help doing it.'[2] Similarly, if he should lay down his life to save a child, it is nothing ; for he could not help it. May one not well ask, then, where character comes in ? If it be, as we fervently trust it is, ' the glory of manhood and womanhood not to have something but to be something,' is it not beyond mortal vision to see how any man can ever ' be ' anything, if he can no more help himself, and is no more to be accounted responsible,[3] than a draper's dummy ?

Mark Twain's exemplification of the same lofty indifference to self-contradiction, is not only the latest, but the most curious. Out of many instances, one shall suffice. Here, with many thuds of verbal reiteration we are assured that man is ' merely a machine, nothing more. You have no command over your mind, it has no command over itself. It is worked solely from the outside, that is the law of its make: it is the law of all machines.'[4] Forthwith, in a page or two, we are informed, with equal assurance, that the ' only impulse that ever moves a person to do a thing is the impulse to content his own spirit, the necessity of contenting his own spirit and winning its approval.' How much humour is required to conjure up a machine moved with the impulse to win its own approval, we will leave to posterity to decide. One other feat, we

---

[1] *Not Guilty*, p. 249. [2] *Not Guilty*, p. 203.
[3] *Not Guilty*, p. 10. [4] *What is Man?* p. 10.

remember, it will also have to perform, which will be a decided novelty. It will have to blush. For it is the same humorist-would-be-philosopher who declares that 'Man is the only animal that can blush, or needs to.' A row of blushing machines would be admirably suited for a Determinedist museum.

These instances should suffice to throw up into lurid relief what Prof. James characterized as the 'dilemma of Determinism.' They all look backwards rather than forwards, and contemplate only the effects which follow from the action of the past upon the present. Now, however, it is our duty to go further, and ask not merely how the present has come about, but what is going to be that result of the present which we call the future. Is that also a hopeless 'must be,' which nothing can avail to alter, seeing that what is is only what has been, and what will be can only be what is? Or is there a 'may be' which admits of contingencies, and so gives us at once a wider and a more hopeful vision? No question can be more full of interest or fraught with such unmeasured consequences. The instinctive repugnance felt by all ordinary minds to the notion of a complete determination which plainly robs them of their manhood,[1] becomes a genuine apprehension when the future is contemplated. The question naturally arises as to what would be the

---

[1] Mr. W. F. Cooley of Columbia University writes truly in *The International Journal of Ethics* for January, 1911, 'There is evidently some principle of self-maintenance about every real individual, organic or inorganic, a principle which, not improbably as it seems to me, is the root of the instinctive repugnance of men's minds to the Necessitarian theory on its first presentation. I confess my inability to discover why an instinctive repugnance of this sort is not as genuine a natural phenomenon and as significant as the repulsions of a magnet or the affinities of a chemical element.'—p. 208.

effect hereafter upon morals and upon human well-being in general, if the principles so loudly proclaimed under the name of 'Determinism,' obtained wide acceptance, and became the actual basis of social intercourse, civic life, national and international relationship. In a word, how would character be practically affected if it were taken as demonstrated that all human volitions are completely determined, as stated so frequently above?

That weakening, if not destruction, of character must follow, and be accompanied with disastrous influences upon the future of the race, is a suggestion so natural, and indeed inevitable, that the most vigorous protests have been made, and the most subtle reasonings employed, by avowed 'Determinists,' to meet and if possible dispel it. Those who appeal simply to the people, treat it in a very jaunty fashion. 'If you wish to realize the immense superiority of Determinist principles over the Christian religion, you have only to imagine what would happen if the Determinists had a majority as overwhelming as the majority the Christians now hold.'[1] But any sensible imagination declines the task. Civilisation has faults enough, God wot; but the change for the worse which would ensue if no man were held responsible for anything he said or did,[2] would be like passing from a vigorous election struggle into a lunatic asylum; or from a street brawl, which has its limits, into the blood feuds of savages, which have none. Mark Twain would comfort those who are appalled at the prospect of such a coming Armageddon of remorseless machines, by the assurance that ' the whole human race is always content, thoughtful, and proud, no matter what its

---
[1] *God and My Neighbour*, p. 143.   [2] *Not Guilty*, pp. 10, 203.

religion is, nor whether its master be tiger or house-cat.' Grim humour, in very deed!

No less confidently Mr. McCabe declares, as quoted above, that there are no practical consequences at all. But he does well to add that it is ' by no means clear that the improvement of character during the last century is a clear triumph of Determinism.' To assert that, would be self-contradiction indeed. Dr. Callaway strongly protests that men ' will not be such fools' as to act upon their irresponsibility. ' For a time the effect of the old mistaken teaching may be seen here and there in moral wavering,' but in the end, ' character will be built upon a more solid basis.'[1] Mr. Bertrand Russell affirms that ' it is not Determinism but free will that has subversive consequences.' But his conception of Determinism is ' soft,' in that it applies praise or blame to conduct, as seen above, so that his attitude is modified. Mr. N. Pearson is very bold, and roundly declares that ' Determinism is only unconvincing to those who refuse to be convinced '—which, of course, would settle the whole matter in very oracular style— ' and those who shrink from the conclusion out of fear of its supposed consequences.'[2] The present belief in free will, we are told, is ' propped up rather by groundless fears of the dangers of discarding it than by any solid evidence in its favour.'

Prof. McTaggart thinks that he has shown that ' there is nothing in Determinism which makes judgement of obligation absurd, or which renders it absurd to be moved by the regard for duty.' More fully he asserts, with the future in view, that ' it is also clear that if the question whether virtue or wickedness

---

[1] *Agnostic Annual*, 1905, p. 29.
[2] *Problems of Existence*, pp. 160, 115.

will finally prevail is to be settled at all by metaphysics, it can only be settled on the basis of Determinism. For virtue and wickedness are dependent on the will, and if Indeterminism be true, it is impossible to predict the future state of the will of any being, or of all beings.'[1] To which, with all respect, one must plainly reply that to talk about 'wickedness' being dependent on the will, when the will, *ex hypothesi*, is completely determined, is no more valid moral philosophy, than to lament the wickedness of a tramcar whose motions are similarly determined.

These protests are given as fair specimens of the way in which the advocates of Determinedism seek to allay the fears which are not unnaturally aroused by their alleged scientific theories. One might be forgiven for saying in regard to them all, in the language of Hamlet's mother—'Methinks the lady doth protest too much.' For even if these assurances are on their part sincere, they point none the less to a very real misgiving on the part of ordinary men, whose estimate of human nature after all is that of the Poet—

> Not only cunning casts in clay;
> Let Science prove we are, and then,
> What matters Science unto men?
> At least to me? I would not stay.[2]

Certainly no question can be greater, or graver, than whether the human future is, or is not, to be better than the present. For whilst no man would deny that the condition of things around us is vastly better in 1911 than in 1811, it is equally beyond all controversy that in a myriad respects the present is very far from being satisfactory. The air is thick with problems involving the physical, intellectual, moral,

---

[1] *Some Dogmas*, pp. 172, 175.   [2] *In Memoriam*, CXX.

and social well-being of a greater number of our fellow creatures than ever before. If Mr. Kidd's estimate be warranted, that 'the fact of our time which overshadows all others is the arrival of democracy,' that fact in itself promises no millennium unless there be some real guarantee that it will be of a nobler character than both the democracies and aristocracies of the past.

Prof. James said well, amongst his last words, that—

'Surely the only *possibility* that one can rationally claim is the possibility that things may be *better*. That possibility, I need hardly say is one that, as the actual world goes, we have ample grounds for desiderating. Free will, thus, has no meaning unless it be a doctrine of *relief*. As such it takes its place with other religious doctrines. Between them they build up the old wastes and repair the former desolations.'[1]

Unless we are to declare with Schopenhauer that all moral progress is an illusion, or with Spinoza that regrets for past failures only make two wrongs out of one, a doctrine of relief is precisely what is wanted in every realm of modern life, nationally no less than individually. Physical evolution is said to have found its terminus in the *genus homo*; but whilst the limits to mental evolution are certainly not in sight, still more must every man deserving the name desire that there may be most real further development in moral character, as also in the fuller application of higher ethics to all our civic, social, commercial, national, and international affairs. Without such a hope, the life of the race is not worth maintaining. It is unmeasured relief and inspiration for every individual, to be assured, in the words of Prof. Mackenzie, that 'there is no stone wall in the way

---

[1] *Pragmatism*, p. 120.

of a man's progress'—but there lurks a corresponding possibility of tragedy in the true reminder—'there is only himself.'[1] Both possibilities, the dark and the bright, become enormous on the scale of the nations. It is, therefore, no light matter to endeavour to show in brief space, how and why, in spite of all the protests just adverted to, and all the strong language as well as subtle thought expended on its advocacy, Determinedism is a downgrade doctrine which would, if heeded, transform the dark possibilities of the future into darker actualities, and shut out the bright as surely as a thunder-cloud blots out the sunshine. This is here definitely affirmed on both negative and positive grounds. Negatively, the false Determinism yields no relief, no inspiration, no hope, when the future is calmly surveyed from the standpoint of the present. Positively, the true Determinism offers all these three, relief, inspiration, hope, as unmistakable realities and to an unmeasured extent.

Dealing first with the negative, it is not too much to say that Determinedism is a doctrine of despair. It 'makes of the whole world of erring men a hospital, and pronounces every patient an incurable; it is ready to grant kindly, considerate treatment to each, but holds out hope of recovery to none.'[2] Dr. Warschauer's words are well weighed, and all who desire genuine upward evolution will accept his consequent query as rational—'Who would not rather submit to the sterner physician whose ministrations promise to medicine him back to health again?' For what does Determinedism offer us when, driven by the very make of our nature, we ask

---
[1] *Ethics*, p. 102.
[2] *Problems of Immanence*, Dr. Warschauer, p. 147.

ourselves and each other what is before us, and whither we are tending? Its necessary reply is cold enough to chill every soul to its marrow. We are tending nowhere; and that which is before us is just that which has been behind us! That such is the prospect presented by the false Determinism there is no room to doubt, whether we listen again to the ancient poet or allow a modern psychological expert to voice it for us.

When, for instance, we are told, as above,[1] that—

> With Earth's first Clay They did the last Man's knead,
> And then of the Last Harvest sowed the Seed:
>   Yea, the first Morning of Creation wrote
>   What the Last Dawn of Reckoning shall read—

such words must not be admired for their vividness, unless for similar reason the massacre of Cawnpore was admirable. For they bespeak the wholesale murder of all the highest aspirations that can throb in a human breast, and the ghastly interment of every noble hope. That which was, is; that which is, shall be. So that as regards any hope that 'men may rise, on stepping-stones of their dead selves to higher things '—it is but a mocking mirage, an 'inveterate illusion,' to be classed with the delusion which leads a man to believe that he is free when he is in reality a slave.

But let the modern man of science phrase it—

'What does Determinism profess? It professes that those parts of the universe already laid down absolutely appoint and decree what the other parts shall be. The future has no ambiguous possibilities hidden in its womb. The part we call the present is compatible with only one totality. Any other future complement than the one fixed from eternity, is impossible.'[2]

This witness is true, and the truth to which he testifies is serious indeed. For evolution which we

---

[1] See p. 33. [2] James, *The Will to Believe*, p. 150.

now regard as proven and believe to be so potent, is hereby reduced to a succession of mere meaningless changes, and, as Mr. W. F. Cooley points out,[1] the only possible inference is that the world has ceased to develop, so that any promise of new and higher types of being is for ever impossible. There would really seem to be no necessity for the ocean of words poured out upon the situation. It is but adding tantalization to tyranny, to tell a man that he is free to act in accordance with his character, when his character has been completely determined for him before he is born. Such freedom is a mockery. It regards a man as merely and purely an effect. As such, he never is nor ever can be the true cause of anything. That which he seems to himself to have caused is merely a result of something that preceded, transmitted through his own delusion. He can never really act. That which he seems to do was merely done through him by resistless antecedents, as the pen which writes these words, after all, never does anything, but is simply acted on from beginning to end. So that there is as much hope of a pen's becoming a hand, as there is of a bad man's becoming a good man, or a corrupt nation developing into a righteous one, through a new beginning.

That which we have been accustomed to call moral evil, then, of course, ceases to be such, for whatever its nature or consequences, it could not be helped; and that which cannot be helped can never under any circumstances possess moral quality, however much it be useful or useless, painful or pleasant. But for such happenings and consequences, there is no prospect of alteration. As they come

---

[1] Of Columbia University, in *The International Journal of Ethics* for January, 1911.

helplessly out of the past, so will the future come helplessly out of them. That which we call 'evil,' be it what it may, in a man or in the race, has no option but to repeat itself. As for the seeming advance of civilization over savagery, the statesman has added nothing to the good that was in the savage, nor subtracted anything from the evil. Changing environment has merely made patent that which previously was latent. So that civilization comes to be merely a revelation of evil mixed with good, rather than a gradual defeat of evil by good. This latter would be a real change, which is against the principles of Determinedism. But it is just such change as is needed, if the future is to be better than the past It is no wonder, therefore, that our psychological expert, after many years of careful survey, both practical and scientific, should be constrained at last to declare aloud that in hopeful contrast with this doctrine of despair—

'Free will pragmatically means *novelties in the world*, the right to expect that in its deepest elements as well as in its surface phenomena, the future may not identically repeat and imitate the past. Persons in whom knowledge of the world's past has bred pessimism, may naturally welcome free will as a *melioristic* doctrine. It holds up improvement as at least possible; whereas Determinism assures us that our whole notion of possibility is born of human ignorance, and that necessity and impossibility between them rule the destinies of the world.'[1]

From the arctic barrenness of the false Determinism, let us turn to the promise of spring which is associated inseparably with the true. If there is to be any upward evolution of humanity, if the future is to do anything more than change the forms of the evils which have hitherto cursed the race and beyond all physical calamities have blighted and blasted

---
[1] W. James, *Pragmatism*, p. 119.

human lives, the real betterment will have to come through one channel and one only, viz. moral character. We have seen that heredity and environment do not and cannot give this; happily also they cannot prevent it. Be the philosophical mystery of character's formation what it may, pragmatically the case of the future's weal or woe is truly stated by one of our ardent social reformers—

'I candidly confess to you that I can see no hope for the people for the future, unless we can appeal to the *character* of the people, unless first of all *character* is established like a bulwark in our midst. You cannot have things done for you and be a man of character. The man of character is the man who believes in self-help and self-respect. He insists upon taking the responsibilities upon his own shoulders, insists upon being enfranchised so that he shall not be the recipient of good things, but the doer of good things. The man of character has a power in him which makes him an active and not merely a passive man.'[1]

This ideal should recommend itself to every thoughtful man whether he be Idealist or Pragmatist. Probably no one will be found to deny it, even amongst those who avow themselves 'scientific Determinists.' But this creation and development of character is utterly and for ever impossible in a world of puppets, such as men cannot but be if all their volitions are completely determined at their birth. Such a creature never really acts at all, never creates, never makes anything. Seeing then, that character, i.e. moral character, as pointed out above, never exists save by a new creation, to a completely determined will the character which Mr. J. R. Macdonald reveres, is for ever impossible.

The helplessness of the popular advocacy of Determinedism is only equalled herein by its superficiality. 'We are all creatures of heredity and environment.

---

[1] Mr. J. Ramsay Macdonald, *see* p. 74 above.

No man can select his ancestors; no man can select his environment.' Were such a summary the whole truth, moral character and all it involves would be as impossible to humanity as flight to a hippopotamus. But it is a compound of fallacies. If a man cannot select his ancestors, he can select the degree of influence which they shall have upon him, and a large part of genuine character resides in personal conflict with hereditary tendencies. That which Huxley, in his famous Romanes lecture, so strongly asserted in regard to the macrocosm is every whit as true for the microcosm. 'Let us understand once for all, that the ethical progress of Society depends not on imitating the cosmic process, still less in running away from it, but in combating it.' Assuredly ethical progress in character depends not upon yielding to that which heredity confers, but rather upon definitely contending against it. And even if the legacy of heredity be good, the scope for character appears in the need and the opportunity to make it better. It is quite as necessary for the upward evolution of the race that the man with five talents should make of them other five, as that the man with one talent should learn not to contemn or neglect his inferior powers.

On the other hand, we must repeat that no statement can be more false than that 'no man can select his environment.' For it is precisely what every man is doing, to some extent, every hour of the day. As the little ones do it in their play, so with added emphasis do they when love's after-dream fascinates their vision. And in the greyer days which often fill up middle life, there is yet greater scope for that ceaseless selection of environment upon which so much relating to character depends. The philosophy which openly declares that a man cannot choose the company he keeps, condemns itself as a pragmatic no less than metaphysical delusion.

When the advocate of true Determinism is pressed for definite answer as to what is in the adult and normal man more than heredity and environment, he is not troubled to answer. One might as well ask—were not all physical analogies imperfect—what is there in the full-blown flower more than in the stem and in the soil ? The reality of personality, and its development into moral personality, are factors in every human life which heredity does not confer, nor environment create. The whole case has been so admirably expressed by Willoughby in his *Political Theories of the Ancient World* that it is worthy of special attention here.

'The central concept of modern ethics is the moral personality of man. This implies that each individual is able and is impelled to formulate for himself an ideal of perfection towards the attainment of which he is conscious of an obligation to strive. This consciousness of obligation, which takes the form of a kategorical imperative posited by his own reason, carries with it the logical assumption first of a freedom of the will, for without this there would not be even the capacity to obey the obligation which is felt, and secondly, of an inherent right to be allowed to realize in fact, so far as is compatible with the reciprocal right of others, those conditions of life which are employed in the ordeal of personal development which each forms for himself.'[1]

In the development of such personality by the undetermined self-Determinism of each individual, lies the only possibility of creating the necessary conditions for the future moral progress of society. We have already noted Mr. Wells' phrase—' I regard myself as a free responsible person among free responsible persons. On that theory I find my life

---

[1] See *Democracy and Character*, by Canon R. Stephen, p. 77.

will work, and on the theory of mechanical predestination nothing works."[1] The truthfulness of such an attitude becomes clear in the degree to which it is thoroughly scrutinized.

(1) It is certain that there can be no vision of betterness for the future which does not include the possibility and actuality of repentance for the past. If everything that has been had to be, through being completely determined from the beginning, not only has nothing bad ever happened, but if it be permitted to call a thing bad because it is a case of suffering, nothing better can ever be. That which cannot be consistently bemoaned cannot be possibly improved. As Prof. James reminded us, to call a thing bad means that that thing ought not to be. When it belongs to the past, it ought not to have been. But if it was completely determined, then there is no room for an 'ought' of any kind. 'When murders and treacheries cease to be sins, regrets are theoretical absurdities and errors,' says the same high authority. But we require no one to tell us that when repentance is absurd, resolution is ridiculous. If some erudite philosopher is prepared to support to the uttermost the village dame whose explanation of every tragedy is simply that 'it was to be,' then it is he who rings down the curtain upon the possibility of any amelioration in a future which similarly has to be. Man can only—

> Move upward, working out the beast,
> And let the ape and tiger die—

by actions proceeding from resolutions which have their roots deeply struck down into what *ought not to have been*, whilst their resulting foliage waves its arms in the light of what *ought to be*. To call upon

---

[1] *First and Last Things*, p. 52.

a man to repent, when all his so-called 'volitions' were 'mathematically fixed' at his birth, is but the babble of imbecility. And where repentance is but foolishness, regeneration is unthinkable.

(2) Granted the possibility and rationality of repentance for wrong, conflict for the right becomes at once privilege and duty. Prof. James' definition of moral action as 'action in the line of greatest resistance,'[1] comes as an admirable comment from a genuine philosopher, upon the candid and emphatic acknowledgement by a scientist, in Huxley's famous Romanes Lecture. If some things that are, ought not to be, and if some things that have been, ought not to have been, then somewhere and somehow the effects which would naturally follow from such causes must be obviated, if the future is to approximate more clearly to what ought to be. But as it is impossible to intervene between a cause and its natural effect, the only way in which the evil that has been can be prevented from repeating itself for ever, is by the creation of new counteracting causes with their corresponding effects. This is what Prof. James has plainly in view when he asserts that free will 'pragmatically means novelties in the world,' and that it is a melioristic doctrine. But we look in vain for the introduction of any such new causes in the closed circle of Determinedism. Mr. Fiske has said only too truly that 'evolution and progress are not synonymous terms. The survival of the fittest is not always a survival of the best, or of the most highly organized. The environment is sometimes such that increase of fitness means degeneration of type.'[2] What is needed is a power to prevent evil effects from becoming further causes; a power to

---

[1] *Psychology*, Vol. II, 548. [2] *Through Nature to God*, p. 66.

bring about alteration in heredity and environment; a power that shall so contend against that which is but ought not to be, as to transform it into that which both ought to be, and is. No settling down into the belief that man is a creature of circumstances whose every volition is completely determined at his birth, will ever result in such dynamic influences. Nothing in the whole realm of possibility is equal to such a task—

> But this main miracle, that thou art Thou,
> With power on thine own act, and on the world.

That, however, is the true Determinism, which in its connotation of a real, free, active, causal self, as the determinant, differs from the false as a man differs from the tools with which he works.

(3) Real ethical progress, however, demands not merely that there should be a process of elimination going on by which evil, with all its associations, shall be weeded out; but at the same time, and in order to that very end, that there should be a corresponding development of good from more to more. It is, of course, always true that evil can only be overcome by good; but for the required increase of good there must be a ceaseless occurrence of new creations. If one may employ once more a physical analogy as a pointer, at least, to metaphysical truth, the reason why the grain of wheat sown in the soil yields thirty-fold increase, whilst the pebble under the same conditions becomes nothing but itself, lies, we know, in that mysterious something that we call life, possessed by one and not by the other. Certainly no less difference, as a source of purposive energy, lies in the conviction of the true Determinist as compared with that of the man—if such there be—who seriously believes that all his volitions are

completely determined before he is conscious of them.

The truly deterministic conviction in this case is, indeed, three-fold. (i) It is an inspiring conviction of actuality, not—in Prof. James's phrase—'the dull rattling off of a chain that was forged innumerable ages ago.'[1] Life would not be worth living if once the notion gripped us that we were mere pawns in a game, moved thither and hither by resistless powers for purposes which could never be really our own. It is the conviction that I, and none other in heaven or earth, am determining my acts, and, therefore, my habits, character, influence, destiny, that makes life to be so suffused with reality and spiced with interest that mankind is manifestly content to live for the sake of living, whilst the suicide is an exception and a monstrosity.

(ii) It is also a conviction of possibility, which gives zest to every day's conscious effort, because of the distinct and inalienable hope that it is telling upon the future, i.e. that the future may become through it what that future would never be without it. Most

---

[1] W. James, *Psychology*, Vol. I, p. 453. In his important work, *The Will to Believe*, the same writer well says that 'this life *is* worth living, *since it is what we make it from the moral point of view*, and we are determined to make it from that point of view so far as we have anything to do with it, a success.' The italics are his, but the phrase 'we are determined' is somewhat unfortunate, for although it is a very common expression, its true significance is exactly the opposite of its form. We make life a success, if at all, not because we are determined but because we determine so to do. In ordinary speech, 'I am determined' is an innocent phrase, because every hearer knows that the speaker means either 'I have determined' or 'I do hereby determine.' But in writing on the subject, the modern confusion demands that there should always be exactitude in every term employed.

truly does Prof. J. Ward assert that 'for us, experience as a whole consists from end to end of contingent truths.'[1] It is the contingency which makes the present to tingle with reality, and supplies the inspiration without which life would be either what Prof. James calls a 'lubberland' of insipidity at best, or a Stygian morass of despair at worst. As in economics the magic of personal property is shown to be absolutely indispensable to any social stability or progress, so in morals is the conviction that with each moment's volition we are really doing something that will tell in the hereafter, and are not merely being pushed about as the playthings of the past, equally essential to development and progress.[2] The sense of property is the sense of power; and the sense of the possession of power is ever the strongest dynamic towards its use, whether for good or ill. If the notion should once really grip a man that his actions have been so completely determined beforehand, that no responsibility for them rests upon him, the conviction that he has therefore no power to act for himself, would either paralyse his manhood into the listlessness of mechanical monotony, or let him loose in human society as a tiger from a jungle. Nothing is so paralysing, both physically and morally, as the sense of helplessness; nothing is

---

[1] *Naturalism and Agnosticism*, Vol. II, p. 282.

[2] Here again, Prof. James has expressed the truth with such clear force that his words cannot be improved upon. 'The great point is that the possibilities are really here. Whether it be we who solve them or He working with us, is of small account, so long as we admit that the issue is decided nowhere else than here and now. This reality, this excitement, are what the Determinisms, hard and soft alike, suppress by their denial that nothing is decided here and now, and their dogma that all things were overdue and settled long ago.'—*Will to Believe*, p. 183.

so stimulating as the sense of power.[1] Mr. McCabe does well to lay stress on the 'human power' as the hope of the future. But to be such, it must be real power, and not the self-deceiving illusion which is all that Determinedism will allow to humanity.[2]

(iii) Whatever else may be dim or uncertain as to the future of human society, there can be no doubt that the way of hope *is* the way of power. Be the ultimate source of the evils that afflict humanity what it may, their actual hold upon society is as the clutch of an octopus. The resistance of the forces of heredity and environment to upward evolution, can only be compared for might to hydraulic pressure. On the social as well as on the individual scale, the moral development has to take place in the line of greatest resistance. Correspondingly great is the need of genuine human power, and the inspiration which is inseparable from its conscious possession. Mr. Benjamin Kidd's weighty words merit special attention in this regard.

'All anticipations and forebodings as to the future of the incoming democracy, founded upon comparisons with the past, are unreliable or worthless. Neither in form nor in spirit have we anything in common with the democracies of the past. The gradual emancipation of the people and their rise to supreme power has been, in our case, the product of a slow ethical development in which character has been profoundly influenced, and in which conceptions of equality and of responsibility to

---

[1] In this connexion, Prof. James quotes Carlyle's vivid protest. 'The everlasting No had said, "Behold thou art fatherless, outcast, and the universe is mine"; to which my whole Me now made answer, "I am not thine, but free, and for ever hate thee." From that hour, Teufelsdröckh-Carlyle adds, "I began to be a man."'—*Will to Believe*, p. 45.

[2] Dr. Warschauer points out hereupon that Nietzsche acutely substitutes the phrase 'will to exert power' for Schopenhauer's 'will to live.' One might add that Prof. James's 'will to believe' involves both.

each other have obtained a hold on the general mind hitherto unparalleled. . . . The fact of our time which overshadows all others is the arrival of democracy. But the perception of the fact is of relatively little importance if we do not also realize that it is a new democracy. . . . Its revival is the crowning result of an ethical movement in which qualities and attributes, which we have been all taught to regard as the very highest of which human nature is capable, find the completest expression they have ever reached in the history of the race.'

There are probably few who would wish to dispute the accuracy of this statement viewed historically. But its moral significance, as we have seen, unfortunately opens a wide door for discussion. The meaning, the origin, the power, the promise, of this 'ethical movement,' are all involved in the crucial question whether man is but a powerless automaton, deceiving himself into a dream that he is freely acting whereas he is only carrying out the irresistible behests of the past; or whether he is genuinely free to act, according as his knowledge of the past and present, together with unbounded possibilities in the future, call upon him to act. For the 'new democracy' with all its undeniable potentialities, there can be no interest at once so great, so grave, so pressing, as the question whether each man composing it determines his own act, character, conduct, influence; or whether he is but one amidst a numberless host of shuttles in the complicated machine of human society, flying willy-nilly, to and fro, according to a completely determined scheme, which neither he nor his fellows can in the least degree affect by any of their self-deluding imaginations of free action. This much is certain, beyond all controversy, that human society, taken at the very best we know of it thus far, is organized upon the former supposition and not

---

[1] *Social Evolution*, pp. 328, 329.

upon the latter. 'All rational practical action,' as Miss Benson truly says, 'rests on the assumption that there are laws of character and thought, combined with an originating and self-controlling power.'[1]

An 'ethical movement' has indeed been the reason of all genuine improvements in the social ideals and practices of this century, as compared with preceding centuries. A still more pronounced and farther-reaching ethical movement, is the only ground of rational hope in regard to the greatly desired advance in human well-being before the twenty-first century shall dawn. But there never was, is, or will be, an 'ethical movement' upon Determinedist lines. The false Determinism which insists that all a man is, or ever will be, has been completely determined by what he was as a foetus in embryo, together with subsequent resistless environmental pressures, affords no room whatever either for moral movement or for ethics. If, as we are assured, a man can no more sin than a steam-engine, and is no more free really than a machine, ethics become unthinkable. An ethical movement amongst steam-engines is, verily, an absurd

---

[1] *The Venture of Rational Faith*, p. 73. Dr. Amory H. Bradford writes also what is surely incontrovertible hereupon—'Society is organized upon the presumption of freedom. Every law on the Statute Book presumes that it may be both obeyed and violated, and equally that each individual in a normal condition may choose for himself either to obey or disobey. And Society in general has virtually unquestionable faith in the principle. When wrong has been done, the common judgement of men, after all due allowance has been made for palliating circumstances, holds transgressors responsible for their choices. Human institutions are no doubt imperfect, but they do not in their inmost and essential nature bear witness to falsehood. Consciousness, in spite of all the voices that attempt to smother it, utters its unceasing assertion of freedom.—*Heredity and Christian Problems* (Macmillan), p. 95.

way to a Millennium. The truth of Mr. Kidd's estimate becomes vivid indeed by comparison. 'Qualities and attributes, the very highest of which human nature is capable' are absolutely necessary if moral development, rather than reversion to the animal type, is to be the promise of the future. If it be true that these have found in present-day democracy the completest expression they have hitherto reached, facts certainly point with tragic insistence to the growing need for a much more complete expression than we see as yet. But that truth is a stimulant, not a deterrent.

The counsel, on the other hand, that in the midst of the conflict with potent influences for ill, men are to fling aside these highest qualities and attributes as so much *impedimenta*, and regard themselves as but 'dumb, driven cattle,' to whom only a few skittish freaks of self-delusion are permitted by the inexorable forces behind them, is a counsel of despair, which, one may hope, will be as definitely rejected by all the noblest of our race to-day as it has been by all chief leaders in the ethical movements of the past. Prof. Eucken has well said, in his most recent utterance that 'no one who truly cares for the development of individual character will attempt to direct the course of a man's life by mere mechanical rules and methods. The reformer in this sphere must have faith in freedom, and must not shrink even before the dangers which freedom undoubtedly carries with it.'[1] The risks of freedom are undoubtedly part of its price. But as Mr. J. S. Mill said well that it was 'better to be a man dissatisfied than a pig satisfied,' one may surely add for these later days that it is better to be a man free to fall as well as to rise, than

---

[1] *Encyclopaedia of Religion and Ethics*, Vol. III, p. 365.

to be Haeckel's 'placental mammal,' or Mark Twain's 'machine,' which could never do either.

The hope of the future is indeed twofold, in that it faces the dark past no less than the favourable present, with helpful inspiration. The true Determinism is a voice from above, as well as from within, which assures us all that not only may men break away from the paralysing grip of a dead past, but that on the ladder of a living present they may climb to heights of personal, moral, social, national, international nobility, as yet undreamed of in humanity's history. There is no granite wall of fate before men, but an open door. There is no need to fall back into the old quagmire of pessimism and wail out—

> Ah Love! could thou and I with Fate conspire
> To grasp this sorry Scheme of Things entire,
>   Would we not shatter it to bits—and then
> Re-mould it nearer to the Heart's Desire![1]

There is a better hope, and a nobler inspiration. If science cannot give it, assuredly science cannot take it away. It is the human cry, whenever the human is not dragged down to the animal, or crushed beneath the mechanical. Whether metaphysics can define and outline it for us in clear shape or not, ten thousand times ten thousand hearts and lives have proved in the past, and are proving now, with the future in full view, that Enid's song[2] was no hysterical outburst of weakly sentiment, but the worthy and inspiring battle-cry of true Determinism for all genuine manhood and womanhood—

> Turn, Fortune, turn thy wheel and lower the proud;
> Turn thy wild wheel thro' sunshine, storm, and cloud;
> Thy wheel and thee we neither love nor hate.

---

[1] *Omar Khayyám*, LXXIII.
[2] In Tennyson's *Marriage of Geraint*.

> Turn, Fortune, turn thy wheel with smile or frown;
> With that wild wheel we go not up nor down;
> Our hoard is little, but our hearts are great.
>
> Smile and we smile, the lords of many lands;
> Frown and we smile, the lords of our own Lands;
> For man is man, and Master of his fate.

The real freedom which that implies, is the hope of the future. Other than that there is none, for the individual, or for the race.

(iv) *The Only Basis of Religion*

By religion is here intended Christian Theism. Reasons for assuming the rationality of such Theism, have been given elsewhere.[1] The matter for consideration here is the relation of human nature to Theism, regarded as rational religion. To all real religion, three factors are essential:[2]—(i) An object of worship; (ii) A bond of obligation; (iii) An ideal of service. These may vary endlessly in kind and in degree, but the main principles remain the same. Whence it is manifest at once, that Pantheism can no more be a religion than Atheism, for in neither case is there anything to worship, or any obligation to serve. But religion may be ruled out of thought not only by making God such as cannot be worshipped, but by making man a creature neither capable of worship nor of obedience to lofty ideal.

---

[1] See *Theomonism True* and *The True God* (Charles H. Kelly), by the present writer.

[2] Much common talk of to-day is represented in the phrases—'to do good is my religion,' or, as put in *God and My Neighbour* (p. 189), 'my religion is to do the best I can for humanity.' But plainly this is no religion at all; it is simple philanthropy. However good any man's intentions are in this respect, they constitute no warrant for attributing false meanings to well-known and well-understood words.

374 DETERMINISM: FALSE AND TRUE

If there be in a man no genuine individuality, if his personality is so nebulous that it can never be separate enough from the source of all being to be definitely antithetic, worship is impossible. Taking worship as reverent love, it is as true on the transcendent scale as on the lowliest, that love involves just as real distinction of personalities as desire for communion. It is the very reality of the separateness which creates the possibility, and stimulates the yearning, for fusion. Even the absolute dependence of the new-born babe upon a mother's love, puts emphasis upon the actual separateness of its being from the source whence it has sprung.

Again, as we have shown, if there be no real freedom, there can be no real responsibility. If the freedom were a dream, so, too, must be the responsibility. And upon the flimsiness of an imaginary responsibility no genuine bond of obligation can be framed. Unless the etymology of the term 'religion' be wholly misleading, the very root notion of its significance is a bond. But its inseparable connexion with worship shows that it must be a willing bondage. The true worshipper binds himself, he cannot be bound *ab extra*. Compulsory reverence and compelled love are alike unthinkable. Man must be free if he is to acknowledge the bondage of the kategorical imperative of duty. It is no less certain that if religion, as represented in Christian Theism, sets before men a high ideal of character, and an inspiring hope of the future, both these assume him to be so far a free and causal agent, that he can to an immeasurable extent make the future out of the present, as surely as in his character he has made the present out of the past.

The false Determinism, therefore, which makes a

man to be merely a transition-point for forces completely determined beforehand, in reducing personality to a mental fiction, makes religion for ever impossible. It is thus quite natural, on the part of Prof. McTaggart, that he should, as a pronounced Determinedist, issue a volume upon *Some Dogmas of Religion* with the express purpose of destroying two at all events of the three basal conceptions of Christian Theism, viz. God and Freedom, whatever be his doctrine of Immortality. But when the premiss is shown to be invalid, the conclusion need not trouble us. If God could be shown to be an inaccessible though all-absorbing Absolute, man would be truly a moral cipher. Or if man could be shown, on true principles of psychology and metaphysics, to be nothing more than a focus of converging forces, there would be certainly no capacity for such religion as Theism postulates. But, in view of the abundant reasons for denying both these suppositions, it is open to us to consider how Theism and the freedom of the human self stand correlated, as the basis of rational and inspiring religion.

Assuming, therefore, the being and government of God, as given in Theism, there are four essentials to all real religion on the human side: (i) The recognition of a bond of obligation, in responsibility for doing right, so far as known, according to the Divine will. (ii) The power to respond to that obligation, or to reject it. (iii) The possibility of definite co-operation with the Divine will or antagonism thereto. (iv) The recognition that such co-operation is the only way to the attainment of the ideal, both individually and collectively.

Now all these are alike impossible on the theory of Determinedism. If man is completely determined, religion is no more possible to him than to the clothes he wears. If, indeed, we are to take the words of our learned Professor as representative, the false Determinedism for which he pleads fails here to justify itself, as egregiously as ever.

'God's judgement—on the hypothesis that there is a God to judge—about the moral state of any man, could not be affected by Determinism. If a man is bad, he is bad, even if he is so necessarily, and the Omniscient Being would recognize this badness.'[1]

It would be difficult to find a statement more remarkable for self-contradiction. It is staggering enough to the ordinary man to be told that, for the purpose of righteous judgement, it does not matter whether in all a man's actions he can help himself or not. It is still more so when such an authority talks about a man's being bad ' necessarily ' ! Surely it is one of the most elementary lessons in philosophy that moral quality can never, under any circumstances, attach to compulsory actions. One might otherwise just as well blame a revolver for a murder as the man who fired it. There ought to be no need for the reminder that necessary badness is as real a contradiction in terms as a living corpse. Last, though not least, it is important to notice that, although God's judgement cannot be 'affected by Determinism,' yet on its very principles, He will 'recognize' what cannot be helped. Surely the degree of such recognition is the measured extent to which Divine judgement *is* affected on 'Deterministic' principles. However, we are indebted to the writer for a frank statement of the plain issue which has to be faced, and that is most important.

---

[1] *Some Dogmas*, p. 164.

'It is argued by the Indeterminists that it could not be right for God to punish men, if their actions were inevitably determined by the natures which He had given them, and the circumstances in which He had placed them.'[1]

This is most true; and by every word of it those who deny that man is completely determined will be prepared to stand. We have seen how, in the light of philosophy, all experience as well as practical life, protests against such complete determination; we have now to see whether, on the assumption of Divine government, there is any necessity for dismissing such protests as unwarranted. Now it must be plainly pointed out that the case is precisely the same whether it be presented in the form of Hegelianism, or the Absolute Idealism of Caird and others, or the Calvinism of the religious schools. The assumption, or assertion, or supposition from all these quarters, really amounts to this, that if there be Divine government it must be that of Divine omnipotence, and Divine omnipotence connotes human impotence. But let us take the academic statement. In view of the Indeterminist opposition, as above stated, we are told—

'It seems to me that the answer is this. If there is an omnipotent God, we are not responsible to Him for our sins, either on the Determinist view or the Indeterminist. If there is a God who is not omnipotent, then we can be as well responsible to Him for our sins on the Determinist view as we can on the Indeterminist—or indeed better, as we shall see later on.'[2]

The last clause here will not, certainly, trouble us, when it is borne in mind that on the principles of this false Determinism, we can be responsible for nothing, either to God or to man. But as the matter is of such vast importance, it is desirable to proceed by distinct steps to a clear issue.

---

[1] *Some Dogmas*, p. 164.   [2] p. 164.

378 DETERMINISM: FALSE AND TRUE

(1) It is strange that in these days it should still be necessary to clear away confusion as to the true significance of omnipotence. It is stranger still that from such high quarters as an academic chair, crass notions should be propounded which can only be met by direct contradiction. We cannot be greatly surprised when a popular journalist, undertaking to teach philosophy, commits himself to the superficial statement that 'if God is all-powerful, he could have made a man who was incapable of evil.'[1] He is apparently incapable of seeing a contradiction in terms, even when he employs it. But that a Professor of philosophy should deliberately print that 'there is nothing that an omnipotent being cannot do,'[2] is simply astounding. 'Even if the two ideas were logically contradictory, a really omnipotent being cannot be bound by the law of contradiction.' This, from an avowed philosopher, seems incredible. According to it, omnipotence can be called upon to make a round square, and can be denied in the event of failure! By the side of such utterly unphilosophical assertions it may be well to put sober words like those of Dr. Thompson, which truly represent rational thought hereupon.

'Omnipotence is not, as commonly thought, the power to do anything anyhow; it is rather the capacity to accomplish anything dictated or prompted by reason and righteousness. To Theist and Christian alike, there is no such thing as an absolute Almighty power, that is a power unfettered by any principle and free to effect any imaginable thing.'[3]

---

[1] *God and My Neighbour*, p. 135. [2] *Some Dogmas*, p. 166.
[3] *Huxley and Religion*, pp. 82, 83. Even the virulently Anti-Christian journal known as the *Free-Thinker*, here speaks the truth, as against the academic Professor, when, in answer to a correspondent, the Editor writes (October 14, 1906)—' God not being able to make a round square is no argument against His omnipotence, for a round square is a meaningless term, a contradiction in terms, nonsense.'

The suggestion that omnipotence means simply and absolutely the power to do anything, anyhow, is on the level of a village school. The only rational statement is that it signifies the power to do anything that can be done, i.e. anything which does not involve a contradiction in terms. If, however, a black white be such a contradiction in terms that it is absurd to call upon Omnipotence to make it, it is not more so than the following—

'If God had to choose between making our wills undetermined and making them good, I should have thought He would have done well to make them good. But we need not decide this point.'[1]

With all respect, this is precisely the point that we do most emphatically need to decide. Apart from the quite unnecessary flippancy of the phrase, a philosopher ought to know that 'to make wills good' involves a contradiction in terms every whit as real as a white black or a square round. 'If,' says this writer, 'the word omnipotent is taken seriously.' The difficulty is to take such criticisms seriously. Assuredly the suggestion that wills can be made good, rules serious argument out of the question altogether. 'Made' goodness is simply unthinkable, self-contradictory, meaningless verbiage—nonsense. Nor is there the least difficulty in replying to the assertion that 'the defence says that God could not secure the benefits, whatever they are, of undetermined volition without also permitting the evil of sin.'[2] For it is a perfectly sound defence. 'The benefits of undetermined volition' are plain enough, viz. the possibility of the real action of a causal self, without which humanity is a living lie, and morality is as impossible for men

---

[1] *Some Dogmas*, p. 165.   [2] p. 166.

as for steam-engines. It is, moreover, too manifest to call for argument, that a man cannot be free to do good without being at the same time also free to do evil. The implication that a man could be made who shall be able, i.e. free, to do good, without any possibility of doing evil, is unworthy of the name of philosophy. Even common sense disowns it. Nor is it helped in the least by the accompanying plea—

'Thus even on the Indeterminist hypothesis we are not responsible for our sins to an omnipotent God. For He could have prevented the sins without introducing any counterbalancing evil into the universe. And secondly, He would not be justified in checking sin by pain, since pain is intrinsically evil.'[1]

This last clause is on a moral level with the rest,[2] for no more irrational confusion can be made than to identify pain, which at the utmost is physical, with evil, which at the least is moral. If the physical and the moral are one, then *cadit quaestio*, we need discuss no more. Whilst also loose rhetoric may be pardoned in popular journalism, it is a capital offence in a treatise which claims to be the exposition of dialectically superior philosophy. Wherefore, speaking carefully, it is altogether untrue that 'on the Indeterminist hypothesis' God introduced counterbalancing evil into the universe. Hegelian dialecticism should surely be able to appreciate the distinction between the potentiality and actuality of evil.[3] That which alone can be attributed to

---

[1] p. 166.

[2] It corroborates the remark of Mr. J. H. F. Peile in his most valuable *Bampton Lectures* for 1907, that 'The belief that pain is the one real evil infects much of our social and philanthropic effort of to-day, and is the chief obstacle to the acceptance of real Christianity. But short of Christianity, reason and experience teach us better things.'—p. 65.

[3] As a matter of simple fact there is more real philosophy in one sentence of Dr. F. R. Tennant's *Origin and Propagation of Sin* than in many pages of such writings as are here quoted.

Omnipotence, is the introduction of the potentiality of evil, that is, the creation of beings capable of moral evil, and so of sin. To suggest that Omnipotence could have 'prevented sins' without making men capable of sin, is sheer self-contradiction. For unless there were creatures capable of sin, manifestly there would be no sins to prevent. To talk about 'preventing the sins' of completely determined automata, is mere babble of senseless sounds.[1] It seems, therefore, still necessary to endeavour to make clear what can, and what cannot, be expected from Omnipotence.

(2) It is undoubtedly possible to Omnipotence to create free beings, i.e. creatures not only endowed with the powers of volition, but by reason of that very endowment not completely determined beforehand as to the use of such powers, and so able to make real choice between alternatives. There is no contradiction, no self-contradiction, in such a supposition, and, assuming God to be such as Christian Theism affirms, there are sufficient reasons why He should do so.

(3) Such creation of autonomous beings necessarily implies the limitation of Omnipotence, because so

---

'It follows, then, that responsibility for the possibility of moral evil, and for the opportunities for its realization, lies with God; that responsibility for the actuality of moral evil lies with man.'—p. 122.

[1] In this connexion it is worth while to quote another well-expressed sentence from Dr. W. H. Thompson's monograph on *Huxley and Religion*. 'J. S. Mill's dilemma "either God is not omnipotent or He is not perfectly good," is no dilemma at all. It is open to every one to believe in God and yet believe that the evolutionary process was set going by a benevolent Being with fore-knowledge of the results. Power in any moral being is necessarily subject to the direction of moral principles, and in a perfect being it must be wholly under the control of reason, love, and righteousness.'—p. 84.

long as a free being exists, even Omnipotence cannot coerce him, and cannot be called upon to do so. A being at once free and compelled is altogether unthinkable. The Divine will, in this case, meets its limitations in the human will. But it is no self-contradiction, because this very antithetic capacity of the human will, is itself the creation of Omnipotence. It is thus as necessary as sufficient to speak of the creation of free moral beings, not as the limitation but the self-limitation of Omnipotence.[1] This is at once possible and rational, as well as ratified in the true philosophy of human consciousness.

(4) To assert the absoluteness of Omnipotence, whether in the form of complete transcendence, or of universal Immanence, so as to involve, in regard to human beings, an altogether overwhelming influence upon their volitions, is wholly unphilosophical. For it necessarily connotes either (i) a self-contradiction, in denying that Omnipotence can create free beings; or (ii) a begging of the whole question, in assuming that human beings are utterly helpless and therefore not free. This, as above shown, is distinctly denied by human consciousness; and it can never avail to dismiss that as an illusion, because if there be any grounds for taking consciousness as an illusion, there are equal grounds for taking the illusion itself as an illusion, and so on *ad infinitum*.

---

[1] It is just this one adjunct which is required to make Mr. J. S. Mill's remarkable avowal in his *Three Essays on Religion* (cheap edition, p. 106), a wise and worthy statement of the Theistic position. 'The power of the Creator once recognized as limited'—i.e. self-limited—'there is nothing to disprove the supposition that His goodness is complete, and that the ideally perfect character in whose likeness we should wish to form ourselves, and to whose supposed approbation we refer our actions, may have a real existence in a Being to whom we owe all such good as we enjoy.'

(5) As there is nothing contrary to Omnipotence in the creation of free beings, so is there no contradiction, further, to Omnipotence, in asserting that, having been once endowed with freedom, through the evolutionary processes which have culminated in human volition, such beings cannot be divinely coerced. Here it seems advisable to turn to another specimen of the modern special pleading for false Determinism, in order to elucidate the truth. Thus Mr. N. Pearson writes—

'As between the man and God, the question is, not who is responsible for the act, but who is responsible for the character from which the act proceeded. Now it is obvious that every man is born with a certain character, and whatever the history of its origin may be, he did not make it for himself and it cannot be imputed to him. Secondly, as between man and God, the responsibility for conduct which springs from character, lies on the author, not on the possessor of character; and it is impossible to believe that a righteous God will hold a man morally responsible for such conduct.'[1]

The loose way in which the term character is employed in such sentences as these, has been sufficiently exposed above. But the only plausibility which for a moment they exhibit, depends altogether upon that looseness. Let the word character be properly stated as moral character, and the irrationality of such pleading becomes evident at once. For the truth is exactly contrary to what is here represented; in that no man is ever born, or ever could be born, with a character, whilst every man who has a character *did* make it for himself, and is not merely the possessor, but the author of that character. Hence, the Determinedist attitude here assumed, is alike impossible and unthinkable. God cannot give any man character, for that would imply Divine coercion

---
[1] *Some Problems of Existence*, p. 97.

to goodness or badness, which would be a contradiction in terms, and therefore utterly meaningless. The ignoring of this most elementary fact in moral philosophy by a recognized teacher, is indeed amazing. One more specimen must suffice.

'We may say, therefore, that an Omnipotent God could have prevented all the evil in the universe if He had willed to do so. It is impossible to deny this, if omnipotence is to have any meaning, for to deny it would be to assert that there was something that God could not do if He willed to do it.'[2]

The importance of the matter is sufficient excuse for repetition here of what has been sufficiently shown above. In the interest of truth, it is well to have an opportunity of giving kategorical and emphatic denial to a plain statement. So we say in direct reply to this assertion, and with all distinctness, that, assuming the God of Theism, He could *not* have prevented all the evil in the universe by simple exercise of will. Moreover, it is *not* impossible to deny the opposite; for if 'Omnipotence is to have any'—rational—'meaning,' there *is* something which God 'could not do if He willed to do it.' If rationality is to be set aside, then indeed Omnipotence can be called upon to make round squares, black whites, hot colds, and creatures at once free and coerced—men who are also marionettes. But so long as we are rational

---

[1] So when Sir Leslie Stephen wrote, as already noted above (p. 307), 'Action proceeds from character, and character is not made by us but determined by the Creator,' Mr. Gladstone administered at once a rebuke and a reply in the true avowal that 'In man character is a growth, the result of acts performed in series. For the choices of these acts and the shaping of his character through them, he is provided with governing faculties, with conscience to sever right from wrong by internal action, and with the self-determining power of will to accept or repudiate the authority of conscience, and to place action in harmony or conflict with it.'

[2] *Some Dogmas, &c.*, p. 210.

beings—and if we are not, assuredly there is an end of philosophy[1]—to represent Omnipotence as the power which could work self-contradictions *ad libitum* is but pitiful absurdity.[2]

(6) Furthermore, this is certain, that if human beings could be divinely coerced, just as surely as if they could be completely determined by heredity and environment, there would be an end for ever to personality, morality, and religion. Let us listen again for a moment to Mr. Pearson—

'But, say the Libertarians, it is idle to hold up to man any moral ideal if he has no free power to choose either the right or the wrong. If his conduct is determined inexorably by circumstances beyond his control, praise and blame become futile and moral judgement impossible. The answer is simple. Praise and blame are but shifted from the agent to the act. An honest man is the noblest work of God. Though his honesty be of God's fashioning rather than his own, we can recognize the worth and nobility of the Divine work manifested in him.'[3]

How writers otherwise intelligent and apparently

---

[1] 'We are nothing, if not logical.'—The late Prof. Stanley Jevons.

[2] It would be as profitless as wearisome to take *seriatim* all the strange assertions found in the volume referred to. One more may, perhaps, be quoted, as typical of the rest. 'If God is omnipotent it is impossible to account for the evil of the universe in this way,' i.e. by moral free agency. 'Indeed, if God is omnipotent, it is impossible that He can be good at all. This would not be affected by the freedom of the human will, since gratuitous permission of evil would be as fatal to the Divine goodness as the gratuitous creation of evil.'—p. 167. 'Gratuitous permission.' Such a phrase may suit a sentimentalist but is unworthy of a philosopher. It is simply meaningless and unthinkable. As Sir Oliver Lodge has truly said recently—*Substance of Faith allied with Science*, p. 51— 'Goodness would have no meaning, if badness were impossible or non-existent.' If, consistently with a good and omnipotent Creator there is to be good in the universe, there must be at least the permission of evil. There is no possibility of anything 'gratuitous' about it.

[3] *Some Problems of Existence*, p. 100.

sincere can hoodwink themselves with such phrases as these, does indeed pass comprehension. The verbal glamour disappears upon a moment's steady gaze. The answer to the Indeterminist's valid assertion is indeed very 'simple.' Blame is 'shifted to the act.' But it is a pitifully irrational shifting, as has been sufficiently shown above. An act, apart from an agent is absolutely nothing; it is not even conceivable. To blame an act apart from an agent, is more foolish than to blame a pen for writing wicked words, apart from the writer. We are told that it is 'under the slightly different forms of approval and disapproval.' But this is still merely a verbal shuffle. The plain question to be fairly faced is, Can an act be approved whilst the doer remains characterless? And the unhesitating answer is— No; it cannot. The moral worth of actions depends not upon physical motion, but upon moral motive. Determinedists ought to be the last in the world to ask us to think of actions apart from motives. As to an honest man being 'the noblest work of God,' certainly Pope never intended his well-known line to be used as a tool of Determinedists. The fallacy of the above writer's comment upon it may be well exposed even by another of the same school. For this is what we find in Mark Twain's latest issue—

Young Man: 'A wiser observer than you has recorded the fact that an honest man is the noblest work of God.'

Old Man: 'He did not record a fact; he recorded a falsity. It is windy and sounds well, but it is not true. God makes a man with honest and dishonest possibilities in him, and stops there. The man's associations develop the possibilities the one side or the other. The result is accordingly an honest man or a dishonest.'[1]

---

[1] *What is Man?* p. 72.

Here the word 'falsity' is justified, if the words are to be pressed as the poet would never have pressed them. Surely the question is a straightforward one and calls for an unevasive answer — if a man's honesty ' be of God's fashioning rather than his own,' how can he be truly called an honest man at all? He may be the tool of an honest God; he cannot be more. To represent honesty as made for a man, and in a man, apart from 'his own' decision, is again mere verbal mockery. It will be seen also that Mark Twain's suggestion is little better. How can a man's 'associations' develop an honest man, apart from the moral decisions of the man himself? They never did; they never can; they never will. As usual, however, the Determinedist special pleader gives away his whole case when he proceeds to expound it. Says Mr. Pearson—

'With the gentler charity which Determinism makes possible, we shall see in the *wrong-doer*, not a stubborn enemy to the right, but a *struggling soul* whose lesson is not yet learnt. Though moving indeed along a distinct course, man is not moved puppet-wise as the Libertarians vainly talk, but as an intelligent and *sympathetic* minister, whose whole nature *aspires* to the goal whereto the Divine Power is *leading* him.'[1]

The italics we add speak for themselves. Any fair-minded reader can judge whether there is left any meaning in words if struggling, aspiring, sympathetic ministers, who are being led, not driven, in any direction, are completely determined. Only in that they are not so, can personality, morality, religion, remain possible for human beings.

(7) Christian Theism, again, as the highest type of religion, assumes the Divine need of man, no less than the human need of God. Whether men have

---

[1] p. 102.

valid reasons for believing that God is love, may be reserved for discussion elsewhere. But if God be love, as Christian Theism postulates, love must desire love, i.e. the Divine nature must desire communion with a creature capable of loving. However imperfect all our anthropomorphic terms may be to express relations between man and God, at least they are real enough and clear enough to make plain the main point here, viz. that such communion with God as the Divine nature calls for, and religion desiderates, would be utterly impossible on the lines of a false Determinism. For this would make man either a mere creature of heredity and environment, or a tool in the Divine hands, no more capable of reciprocating love than a walking-stick.

'If the final cause of the eternal creation of the cosmos is not primarily the present satisfaction of the full demands of man's questioning intellect, but rather the institution of the highest personal relations between the Absolute and his rational offspring, then it is indeed inconceivable how this end could have been gained save by imparting to man a measure of moral freedom. The conferring upon man the faculty of moral freedom is, I apprehend, an indispensable feature in that supremely rational scheme of creation through which the eternal love of God seeks to confer the highest possible blessedness on creatures who are fashioned out of His own substance and made after His own image.'

So writes Prof. Upton in his Hibbert Lectures.[1] A few pages further on the lecturer quotes, with most effective aptness, Goethe's lines—

> Freundlos war der grosse Weltenmeister,
> Fühlte Mangel, darum schuf er Geister.[2]

---

[1] pp. 292, 293.
[2] p. 303.
> Lonely was the mighty Lord of all
> Nor felt His real need supplied—
> Till spirits answered to His call.

And it would be difficult to find words expressing the truth more fully in few words.

(8) This real self-limitation of the Divine nature in the creation of free beings capable of moral action, makes possible and calls for the co-operation of such beings with God, in whatever conflict there may be between good and evil. We have seen that God, being both good and (rationally) omnipotent, could not prevent evil without at the same time preventing good, and so permitting the universe to remain in a condition of moral vacuity which would amount to self-contradiction. When the possibility of evil becomes actual evil, then also arises with it the opportunity on the part of the good, as free beings, to co-operate with the source of their freedom, in doing the utmost that can be done with evil moral beings, i.e. by appeal, to overcome the evil with good. One of the most remarkable testimonies in the whole history of religious philosophy, is that of Mr. J. S. Mill to this very effect. When the limitation of Omnipotence which he contemplates is understood as the self-limitation which Christian Theism postulates, it would be difficult to find a truer or more noteworthy conception than the following. He is speaking of what he terms the 'religion of humanity'—

'To the other inducements for cultivating a religious devotion to the welfare of our fellow creatures as an obligatory limit to every selfish aim, and an end for a direct promotion of which no sacrifice can be too great, it superadds the feeling that in making this the rule of our life we may be co-operating with the Unseen Being to whom we owe all that is enjoyable in life. One elevated feeling this form of religious idea admits of, is the feeling of helping God, of requiting the good He has given us by a voluntary co-operation which He, not being omnipotent, really needs, and by which a somewhat nearer approach may be made to the fulfilment of His purposes.'[1]

---

[1] *Three Essays on Religion*, cheap edition, p. 108.

(9) Such an appeal to human nature, together with the response to it, constitutes the very essence of real religion. For it embodies two distinct impulses which lie at the very heart of a religious life, viz. (i) The sense of value as a living personality, in being a real object of Divine solicitude,[1] and (ii) the sense of power in being able to initiate real and helpful good, as an unfailing inspiration towards the highest and noblest service. This sense of worth and of power to make character, as well as to influence others in doing the same, constitutes the very heart of religion. To assert that 'there cannot be two supreme rulers of man's career; if it is really in God's hands, it cannot also be left entirely to man's discretion' is altogether wide of the mark. For it ignores that very possibility of co-operation which is at once the condition and the explanation of all moral action. Christian Theism never contemplates any 'supreme ruler of man's career.' For that would mean either a tyrannic Absolute, crushing the manhood out of him, or a self-created, self-sufficient man, ignoring his derivation from and dependence upon God. Human character is no more by any possibility 'really,' i.e. wholly, in God's hands, than it is 'left entirely' to man's discretion. As to the difficulty of distinguishing between the human and the divine share in such co-operation, the words of Mr. Pearson himself may suffice to illustrate it with

---

[1] 'Mr. C. W. Oman, in his *Byzantine Empire*, asserts that the improvement of the condition of women, infants, slaves, at the time of which he writes, could be "directly traced back to a single fundamental truth. It was the belief in the importance of the individual soul in the eyes of God, that led the converted Roman to realize his responsibility, and change his attitude towards the helpless beings whom he had before despised and neglected.'—See 'B.C.—A.D., or the Difference Christ has made,' by G. Jackson, in *What is Christianity*, Vol. II, p. 94 (C. H. Kelly).

TRUE DETERMINISM

quite sufficient clearness for our purposes here, as pleading for moral responsibility—

'Though man could not be gifted with wisdom and goodness as a birthright, he could be set to *win them for himself* under the schooling of experience, and for aught we can tell he may prize them as *an achievement* more than he would have prized them as a boon.'[1]

The words italicized serve to show how, as ever, the attempt to state Determinedism with anything like frankness, issues in contradicting it. For the man who wins goodness for himself as a real 'achievement,' cannot assuredly have been completely determined before he was born. On the other hand, the representation of man as a moral being using the power with which God has endowed him, in accordance with what to him appears right, is an ideal of co-operation which satisfies all the conditions of a valid religious philosophy. For, in Prof. Upton's words, it 'sacrifices nothing really valuable in man's individuality, and at the same time does full justice to the universal immanence of God in nature and in humanity.'[2]

(10) On the opposite principles of alleged Determinedism, religion would be, for definite reasons, altogether impossible. (i) There could be no possibility of worship, because there would be no personal antithesis. Where there is no separateness there can be no devotion. As Hegelian Idealism, equally with Spinozistic Pantheism, 'cannot allow to the individual man the possession of a real and permanent self,' but is obliged to think of man as 'merely a transient phase in an eternal process of thought-evolution,' so does complete determination of character under the guise of Divine control, reduce man

---

[1] *Some Problems of Existence*, pp. 110, 111.
[2] *Hibbert Lectures*, p. 289.

to a non-moral mummy, in whom worship is inconceivable. 'This denial of any real and permanent individuality and causality to man as distinct from God, has for its necessary counterpart the effacement of any effective distinction between God and the world of matter and mind.'[1] With such effacement, the possibility of worship and of religion passes away for ever.

(11) But even if worship were mentally possible under Determinedism, in any form, it would be morally impossible, because under its auspices God would be absolutely responsible for all the suffering in the world—by far the greater part of which arises from what we now know as moral evil—and as such would be quite unadorable. Mill's supposed dilemma has been sufficiently disposed of above. But it is still presented by modern writers as if it were new and had never been answered. Mr. Pearson still asks, 'How can evil find place in the scheme of the Deity who is at once benevolent and omnipotent?' He himself supplies the answer—

'When we recognize frankly what all the facts point to, i.e. that the Deity in His relation to man works under conditions, self-imposed it may be, but still conditions which preclude the exercise of omnipotence, then and not till then can we dispel the doubts which cluster round the conception of a Divine author of evil.'[2]

The self-imposed conditions under which Deity works in the case of human nature, are manifestly and sufficiently those which false Determinism denies, viz. the endowment of man with moral free agency which has confessedly made possible all the good there is on earth, but has also necessarily permitted all the evil. There is in this neither the

---

[1] Upton's *Hibbert Lectures*, p. 322. [2] *Problems of Existence*, p. 143.

giving up of omnipotence, nor the denial of goodness. For, as we have seen, Omnipotence cannot rationally be called upon to compel a free being, nor can Divine goodness be impeached when by a free being the ability to do either good or evil is used in the latter direction. The badness, if badness there be, is not in the bestowment of the power, but in the misuse of it. According to false Determinism, man has no power to misuse; he is completely determined by the author of his being. In which case, certainly, whatever evil may be brought about through him, he is but the occasion of it, not the cause. The cause is in the Divine power which works through him, and which becomes thereby, as Mill declared, so much more hideous than attractive as to be utterly beyond worship. Then is not the Author of the power to do evil responsible for the evil that is done? Certainly not, so long as there is a real agent; any more than George Washington's father was responsible for the havoc which the boy wrought with his new hatchet. But had the boy not been a boy, had he been instead a chisel in his father's hand, then assuredly for the mischief which was chisel-wrought, the father would have been responsible.

It is not often that avowed Christian advocates commit themselves to this false Determinism on religious grounds. Nor is the case improved when they do. When, for instance, we are told[1] that 'all our actions are caused by laws; that the laws are caused by God, and that a mighty and good God is responsible ultimately for all events'—the theology is as bad as the metaphysics. No human action was ever yet caused by law; but if God is responsible

---

[1] In the report in *The Clarion* for June, 1909, of a sermon by Rev. G. T. Sadler. See also pp. 7, 23, 56, 107-113.

for all the wrongs and cruelties of civilization, to say nothing more, then God would be only the 'almighty devil' that Mill contemplated. It is a mere Determinedist shuffle of words to say that 'Liberty is by law; by obeying the deepest law. Necessity is not opposed to freedom. Freedom is through necessity.' For in order to 'obey' any law, a man must be also free to disobey. If necessity means anything, it means compelled action; and compelled action never yet gave rise to freedom, nor ever will. 'As we do God's will more and more we are free,' may be true in a real Christian experience; but it is equally true on plain moral principles that in order to 'do God's will' at all, we must be free. If we are not free before we do it, we shall assuredly never be free after doing it, for it will never be done at all.

Meanwhile, the fact remains, alas! that evil, with unutterable consequences of degradation and misery, is, as it has so long been, tragically part of the sum of human existence. And by the Determinedist—whether Hegelian, Absolute Idealist, or Calvinist matters not—' no portion of this moral evil can be ascribed to the antagonistic causality of man. In his view every feature in the process, the basest and cruellest, as well as the noblest and most beneficent, are equally indispensable features in that process of self-evolving thought which constitutes the universe.'[1] But that is to make God a monster, and His worship in religion impossible. On the contrary, whatever painful problems may lie beyond our present solution, the hope of the Christian Theist is as much more noble as more rational than the foregoing.

'In his view this sin and wickedness is an absolute evil, but it is an evil which is permitted to exist by the eternal Cause;.

---

[1] Upton's *Hibbert Lectures*, p. 325.

the effacement of it would mean, at the same time, the effacement both for God and man of the possibility of reaching the highest spiritual good, and though it is permitted to exist, the limitation of it is ensured by the reserve of possibilities which are still open before the Divine causality.'[1]

In this case the contradiction between Divine goodness and rational Omnipotence vanishes, worship becomes possible, and religion rational.

(iii) It cannot be questioned, moreover, that repentance, as distinct alike from the shallowness of mere regret and the despair of remorse, forms an integral part of religion. Repentance carries with it the felt need of a forgiveness which may be hoped for. But all these concepts are pure illusion according to Determinedism. If man is completely determined, sin is unthinkable. The 'hard Determinism' of the popular journalist that 'man can no more sin than a steam-engine,' is more logical than the soft Determinism which talks about pain 'slowly building up in a man a body of wholesome aversions from the wrong.' Right and wrong, for a man completely determined, are truly as absurd as for the crank and piston of an engine. The sense of sin becomes as unthinkable in the man who murders his brother, as in the tiger who mauls and eats the murderer. To put all into a word—'were it not for the reality of our individuality, there could be no sin, no heroism, no sense of estrangement from God, no joy of reconciliation with Him.'[2] In such case there is an end of religion in its highest reach, no less than in its simplest elements. If religion in its purest heights signifies communion with God as the source of all good, there can be no more such communion on the lines of false Determinism than between a man and

---

[1] Upton's *Hibbert Lectures*, p. 324.   [2] p. 287.

the tools he uses or the house he builds. The love and trust between father and child are for ever unthinkable.

(iv) In taking Christian Theism for granted as the highest type of religion, it is included also that we may take the Christ of the Gospels as the fullest exponent and example of that religion. As it is always alike fair and necessary to test any theory by applying it to the most difficult example, so is it equally necessary and reasonable, in regard to the relations between false Determinism and religion, to test the former by applying it to the most conspicuous example of the latter. As applied to Christ, then, it would involve first the assumption that He was in His whole character completely determined; every act of His will mathematically fixed before He was born; so that He could not possibly do other than He did. And secondly, that in all those relations to God and good which religion contemplates, He was under Divine necessity to be and to do all things. Does such a theory harmonize with and explain the facts of His life, character, and influence? One might as well ask if the mechanism of an organ accounts for the music when a master of the art is playing. The notion of Divine coercion is not only in His case morally unthinkable, but is flatly contradicted by the plainest and strongest utterances in the Gospels.[1] The suggestion of complete determination becomes really absurd, and positively repellent, in view of the whole truth concerning that marvellous and unique career.

True, Prof. McTaggart's words here recur,[2] that 'the

---

[1] No results of the Higher Criticism would affect this estimate, as Prof. Schmiedel himself has shown in his little monograph, *Jesus in Modern Criticism*.   [2] See p. 126 above.

little we know about the life of Jesus suggests that He combined an invariable intolerance of sin, with an almost invariable compassion for the sinner.'[1]

Even if we take this statement as it stands, its main elements are utterly subversive of false Determinism. For (i) It postulates sin as a reality, which it can never be if the character from which volitions proceed is helplessly determined. (ii) It acknowledges the reality of the agent, i.e. the sinner, as against the inane suggestion sufficiently considered above, that the wrong act is blameworthy, but the wrong actor is nothing to be accounted of. (iii) Compassion for a sinner not only makes no excuse for the reality of the sin, but identifies the sinner with the sin, and as such pities him and so holds him responsible. The notion that a sinner is to be pitied because he could not help sinning, besides being a self-contradiction, is not discoverable by the most microscopic analysis in the whole doctrine of Jesus.

---

[1] p. 173. The writer also remarks that—' There is no logical incompatibility between pity for sinners and the resolve to extirpate sin.' Which strikes one as a strange assertion from such a source. (i) How there can be ' sin ' when every volition is completely determined, is a problem well left unsolved. When it is solved on Determinedist lines, it will be necessary to inquire what to do with sinful gramophones. (ii) The ' resolve' to do anything is no less difficult to explain when it is remembered that ' Every act of a man is the latest link in an immense chain of causation in which the slightest element of uncertainty would be impossible.' For if a resolve does not connote genuine initiation, a new start, it is meaningless. (iii) The resolve to ' extirpate sin ' is, from the Determinedist standpoint, the greatest curiosity and contradiction of all. For as sin without volition is impossible, not only does sin itself become impossible under Determinedism, seeing that a compelled volition is unthinkable, but the ' extirpation' of volitions is a task before which psychology may well stand appalled. So far as we can see, there is no prevention of volitions save by volition. But if, *ex hypothesi*, the former have all been mathematically fixed long ages ago, how is the latter to work ?

As to the hint that we only know a 'little' about the life of Jesus, this is not the place to show how much that amounts to, in the light of modern criticism, but even if we leave out of account all 'orthodox' estimates, some of the greatest and keenest unbelievers in history will supply us with material enough to discover whether the life and doctrine and character of the Christ of the Gospels, are amenable to the conditions prescribed by the false Determinism we are examining. Dr. D. F. Strauss, for instance, declares that—

'Amongst the personages to whom mankind is indebted for the perfecting of its moral consciousness, Jesus occupies, at any rate, the highest place. With reference to all that bears upon the love of God and of our neighbour, upon purity of heart, and upon the individual life, nothing can be added to the moral intuition which Jesus Christ has left us.'[1]

Mr. J. S. Mill asks—

'Who among His disciples or among their proselytes was capable of inventing the sayings ascribed to Jesus, or of imagining the life and character revealed in the Gospels? Certainly not the fishermen of Galilee, still less the early Christian writers. About the life and sayings of Jesus there is a stamp of personal originality combined with profundity of insight which must place the prophet of Nazareth, even in the estimation of those who have no belief in His inspiration, in the very first rank of the men of sublime genius of whom our species can boast.'[2]

Mr. W. E. H. Lecky's estimate in his *History of European Morals*, is scarcely in need of repetition—

'An ideal character which, through all the changes of eighteen centuries, has inspired the hearts of man with an impassioned love, has been not only the highest pattern of virtue, but the strongest incentive to its practice, and has exercised so deep an influence that it may be truly said that the simple record of three short years of active life has done more to regenerate and

---

[1] *New Life of Jesus*, ed. 1864, p. 625.
[2] *Three Essays on Religion*, cheap edition, p. 107.

soften mankind than all the disquisitions of philosophers and all the exhortations of moralists.'[1]

Whilst the erudite author of *Ecce Homo* sums up a glowing passage, which would only be spoiled by incomplete quotation, in one pregnant sentence—

'It was the combination of greatness and self-sacrifice which won their hearts, the mighty powers held under mighty control, the unspeakable condescension, the cross of Christ.'[2]

These will suffice. They represent a minimum upon which we may rest as reliable. Whether they do amount to a 'little' or not, is irrelevant for our present purpose. They amount at least to enough to shatter any attempt to apply to Him the false Determinism which would make men mere tools of Omnipotence, marionettes of heredity and environment, clock-dials mechanically indicating the works of a character over which they had no control. Keshub Chunder Sen, the Indian reformer, gives us a vivid glimpse of the 'greatness that dwelt in Jesus'—

'Poor and illiterate, brought up in Nazareth—a village notorious for corruption—under demoralizing influence, His associates the lowest mechanics and fishermen, from whom He could receive not a single ray of enlightenment, He rose superior to all outward circumstances by the force of His innate greatness, and grew in wisdom, faith, and piety, by meditation and prayer, and with the inspiration of the Divine spirit working within Him.'[3]

To account for this on the principles of Determinedism would involve a sinister miracle of self-contradiction and self-delusion. The great bulk of Determinedists may well be anti-Christian, for so long as the historicity of the Jesus of the Gospels

---

[1] Vol. II, p. 9.   [2] Cheap edition, p. 17.
[3] *Lectures and Tracts*, p. 9.

remains an object of rational acceptance, so long will it be as impossible to account for Him or explain Him on their principles as to reverse the motion of our planet in its orbit.

(v) We are driven, however, by the attitude of some who style themselves 'religious Determinists' to make a final note in reference to the Bible. This may be taken, as a whole, when reasonably interpreted, as the manual of Christian Theism. Influences many and varied, both in the past and present, combine to compel the question as to whether the Bible lends any real support to modern Determinedism. And the answer is, that its whole verdict is emphatically to the contrary. But in full view of the prolonged controversy hereupon, a few main principles may and must be clearly laid down.

(1) The age-long religious conflict referred to, has not been really scriptural but theological. It has not resulted from the possession or use of the Bible, but from the application of special methods of interpretation, Augustinian, Calvinistic, Puritan. These interpretations, again, have rested on a false theory of inspiration—partly necessitated by the Reformation—which has been for the last three centuries fastened upon the minds of English readers by the unquestionably Calvinistic bias of the otherwise remarkable translation of 1611.[1] Mr. Pearson

---

[1] Even in the Revised Version, although such unpardonable mistakes as Acts ii. 47—'such as should be saved' to represent a present participle—have been corrected, the ancient confusion of 'shall' and 'will' is retained, with a significance always misleading to the average modern reader of English. 'Lord, and what *shall* this man do?'——'Thus He spake signifying by what manner of death He *should* glorify God,'—must here suffice as typical instances of numberless cases in which the simple future in Greek is represented by the imperative or conditional in English, thereby conveying the unwarranted notion of force and lending colour to predestination.

doubtless voices the feeling of many when he asserts that 'free-will theologians in dealing with this question have to encounter a special difficulty in the strong Deterministic tendencies of Bible teaching.'[1] Without entering here into theological discussion, it is sufficient to affirm that these 'Deterministic' tendencies have been greatly exaggerated under the two influences mentioned, viz. Calvinistic bias and inadequate translation. Both these influences are in course of correction, and truer views are emerging. From the standpoint of the true Determinism there are no real difficulties whatever in the Bible, when allowance is made for Eastern forms of thought, and accurate knowledge together with rational principles are assumed and applied.

(2) Predestination, for instance, in the commonly accepted sense of Calvinistic theology, is not to be found in the Bible anywhere. It need not be denied that, as Mr. C. A. Row pointed out, predestination in this very sense 'underlies the confessions of faith of nearly all the churches which sprang out of the Reformation.' This is sufficiently explained by the need felt for an 'infallible' book, when parting from an 'infallible' church which bound men to a false theory of scripture and saddled upon them the ignorances and theological prejudices of preceding authorities. But that has no more to do with the true interpretation of the Bible, than the acceptance of Ptolemaic astronomy in pre-Copernican times has to do with the science of to-day. The modern 'religious Determinist' gives us this definition—

'In speaking therefore of an act as predestined, we mean that it is to be brought about by the power of God; and secondly, that the predestination of the act necessarily involves the predestination of the agent's volition which produces the act.'[2]

---

[1] Pearson's *Problems of Existence*, p. 105.   [2] Ib., p. 104.

Such may well suffice as a true statement, and as being therefore of service in giving opportunity to affirm that, so far as regards moral character, which is the one and only point of consideration here, of such predestination the Bible knows absolutely nothing. We must indeed go farther, and affirm that of such predestination the Bible, as a collection of sacred writings, never could know anything, without becoming as philosophically false, morally useless, and socially mischievous, as the ancient rhapsody which declared—

> The Ball no Question makes of Ayes or Noes,
> But Right or Left, as strikes the Player, goes;
> And He that tossed thee down into the Field,
> *He* knows about it all,—HE knows,—HE knows.

> The Moving Finger writes; and having writ
> Moves on: nor all thy Piety nor Wit
> Shall lure it back to cancel half a Line,
> Nor all thy Tears wash out a Word of it.[1]

The ancient pessimist, however, had the sense to see what some of his modern successors strangely miss, i.e. that predestination and sin were absolute incompatibilities—

> O Thou, who didst with Pitfall and with Gin
> Beset the Road I was to wander in,
> Thou wilt not with Predestination round
> Enmesh me, and impute my Fall to sin.[2]

That the Bible has something serious to say about sin, may be taken as beyond dispute. But to that very extent, it is a standing rebuke to all who have ever credited it with the philosophical as well as theological monstrosity of predestination.[3]

---

[1] *Omar Khayyám*, L, LI.   [2] LVII.

[3] Hereupon, therefore, Mr. Aubrey L. Moore did not speak too strongly when he wrote that—' If Calvinism is Christianity, *cadit quaestio;* it is madness to attempt any longer to defend the morals of Christianity. Calvinism is not accidentally but

(3) Again. The principles of Determinedism which are assumed by 'religious Determinists,' are not in any way necessitated by the Bible doctrine of Divine government. As this is a matter of vast importance, it will be well to examine what is advanced from the standpoint of false Determinism. Thus Mr. Pearson writes—

'The recognition of a Divine purpose in nature which so easily accords with Determinism, is hopelessly incompatible with any philosophy or any religion which insists on the freedom of the will. If we regard the world and its order as the scheme of a Deity who has knowledge enough to foresee the end which He wills, and power enough to realize it, we cannot but suppose that every detail of the scheme, including human acts and the volition which bring them about, is under His control. If He decrees the ends He must also decree the means; and consequently human acts which form part of the means must be the direct result of His will; in other words, must be inevitably foreordained. In such a scheme there is obviously no room for human freedom, which would imperil or wreck it millions of times a day. If it is part of God's scheme that a man should do a particular act, he cannot be left with any free power of choice in the matter; and if the act is foreordained, the agent's volition to do it must also be foreordained. The objection is an old one, but it is usually kept in the background by Libertarians as much as possible, and it has never been effectually answered.'[1]

The last sentence is doubly false. For, first, those who maintain man's moral free agency have no reason whatever to shrink from such a statement; and, secondly, as a matter of fact, it has been answered times without number. Whether 'effectually,' or not, depends upon the question whether certain minds are open to reason herein.

---

essentially immoral, since it makes the distinction between right and wrong a matter of positive enactment, and thereby makes it possible to assert that what is immoral for man is moral for God, because He is above morality.'—*Science and the Faith*, p. 119.

[1] p. 108.

But the above summary is valuable, in that it enables us to answer an old objection once more and quite plainly. There are five sentences, then, in this statement, of which the first may be neglected, seeing that it is mere assertion, typical alike in its confidence and in its lack of rational warrant.

The second sentence calmly begs the whole question at issue by a supposition. 'We cannot but suppose that . . . human acts and volitions' are under His control.' Here it is assumed that human volitions are of precisely the same order as physical phenomena, or the actions of animals; and that Divine control means, in the human case, exactly the same mechanical or other compulsion as is illustrated in all nature apart from man. Such an assumption is wholly without warrant, and is flatly contradicted by facts.[1]

The third sentence again assumes that which should be proved, i.e. that in all things, including human acts, God 'decrees the ends.' There is thus no 'consequently' whatever. For the whole force of the strong words—'must be inevitably foreordained'—turns upon the unwarranted assumption —'if He decrees the ends.' But Omnipotence *cannot* decree, and cannot be expected to decree, the ends which depend upon the actions of a free being. Any assertion to that effect would be but senseless verbiage. So that before the 'decrees' can be taken

---

[1] One may fairly ask why do not Determinedists frankly meet the plain objection to which Miss Benson, amongst others, calls such definite attention. 'The fundamental mistake lies in the attempt to extend exactly that conception of law which is drawn from the physical world, to the rational world. To do this is indeed to put the cart before the horse, for our only direct experience of causation, it must be remembered, is in our own volition; that is, in the heart of the "delusion" itself.'— *The Venture of Rational Faith*, p. 73.

for granted, the freedom of human acts must be disproved. Which is exactly what has not been done, and cannot be done, without giving the lie direct to experience.

The fourth sentence also assumes a ' scheme ' for which there is no warrant, hence the supposition of its being wrecked or imperilled (as if the two were the same !) need not be considered.

The fifth sentence takes as a premiss that which ought to be the conclusion; so that its inference is null and void. ' If it is part of God's scheme that a man should do a particular act,' is but a mailed fist in a velvet glove. That it *is* part of God's scheme so to compel men's actions that in reality they never act at all, is what is really connoted. Such an assertion assumes precisely what is under dispute. If, on the contrary, it is shown by appeal to the whole philosophy of experience, that a human volition is *not* so foreordained as to exclude any power of real choice, then the whole notion of foreordination goes by the board as a fiction of false Determinism.

The old confusion between foreknowledge and foreordination, of course appears once more. After acknowledging that ' it has been urged on behalf of free will that though God foresees, He does not foreordain man's conduct, that prescience is not the same as predestination, and consequently God's prescience renders no actions necessary '—which is not only perfectly sound but unshakable philosophy —refuge is sought, as so often before, in Jonathan Edwards. What is the suggested reply ? This—

' Prescience need not be the cause of the necessity of the events foreknown ; it may equally well be the effect. But in either case it proves the necessity ; for there must be a certainty in things themselves before they are certainly known or, which is the same thing, known to be certain.' [1]

It is difficult indeed to understand how any keen intelligence, in America or in this country, could ever satisfy itself with this merely verbal confusion; for it is nothing better. 'Prescience may equally well be the effect of the necessity of the events foreknown.' Why is 'necessity' foisted in here, when there is not the slightest warrant for it? Keeping to the plainer word foreknowledge—which, it must never be forgotten, is in its time-relation a mere accommodation to the limitations of human thought—what is the true relationship between the Divine foreknowledge of a human action and the action itself? To put it plainly—is the action derived from, or caused by, the foreknowledge? Or is the foreknowledge proleptically derived from and conditioned by the action? Most assuredly, and beyond all contradiction, is this last the true statement. Whence it follows that foreknowledge has no more to do with foreordination, than the flight of a swallow over the ocean has to do with its mighty currents. Thus Divine foreknowledge does not and cannot touch human action or volition; let alone predetermine it. Until, therefore, it is shown that a man is—what we have seen it is the fashion just now so often to assert without proof—a machine or an automaton (and this will never be so long as sane human experience endures), the predestination of a human will is simply unthinkable. The volition that could be predestined, is no more a volition than a mummy is a man. When, therefore, we are told, as in these words—which are quoted because they are typical of so much more of the kind—that—

---
[1] *Problems of Existence*, p. 103.

'The Libertarian, the religious Libertarian at any rate, cannot deny that there is a divinely ordered scheme of things; yet the existence of such a scheme is absolutely fatal to the freedom of his will'—[1]

it is necessary to meet such assertions with point-blank denial, the following reason for which ought to be both sufficient and final. Those who plead for the moral free agency of man, do not indeed deny that there is a 'divinely ordered scheme of things,' but they do emphatically deny that man is to be classed amongst 'things' at all. That is the utterly unwarranted assumption which vitiates the whole so-called 'deterministic argument.' There is no argument in it. It is pure assumption, as degrading in its issues as contrary to human experience. So far from there being on the part of true Determinists any need or desire ' to torture the facts of nature into conformity with their religious or philosophical theories,' they are entirely warranted in the retort that it is the false Determinist who tortures to death—i.e. into avowed delusion—the most irrefragable fact of nature known to us, viz. our own consciousness.[2]

As to the general question of the difficulty of reconciling the moral government of the world with free will, 'whose essence it is to be immune from compulsion,' there is no difficulty at all. We read that

---

[1] *Problems of Existence*, p. 161.
[2] Prof. Poynting's words already quoted on p. 107 above, are so weighty as to merit repetition here. ' It is better to face the situation boldly and claim for our mental experience as great certainty as that which the physicist claims for his experience in the outside world. If our mental experience convinces us that we have freedom of choice, we are obliged to believe that in mind there is territory which the physicist can never annex. Some of his laws may still hold good, but somewhere or other his scheme must cease to give a true account.'

'Libertarians may fairly be asked, if the will be governed, what becomes of its freedom? If the will be free, what becomes of the moral government?' But it surprises one not a little that cultured intelligence should find a moment's support for Determinedism in such an artificial dilemma. Either horn of it is perfectly harmless to handle. As for the latter, the straightforward answer is that only if the will be free, can there be any moral government at all. To talk about the moral government of compelled wills, is as absurd as to demand moral government for a row of steam-engines. The closing words of Dr. J. Ward's incisive Gifford Lectures ought to be writ large for their truth's sake. Premising only what will not be denied, that spiritual government and moral government are one, it is well said that—

'Here we may at least say that a principle which resolves the freedom of the many into their own private illusion, and so reduces divine government to an empty make-believe, in no sense deserves to be called spiritual. If Divine government is a reality, our souls must be ours, though we know not how. And yet God must be veritably supreme.'

As to what becomes of its freedom if the will be governed, any child in a well-governed household can answer. It is governed in its submission to and co-operation with a higher will. There is no other possible way of governing a moral being; and there is no truer exercise of genuine moral freedom. For those who specially desire a philosophical solution, the statement of Prof. Romanes holds good—

'The absolute volition and the relative volition are always in unison. It is not that the absolute volition unconditionally determines the relative volition, else the relative volition would not be free. But it is that the absolute volition invariably

---

[1] *Naturalism and Agnosticism*, Vol. II, p. 294.

assents to the relative volition, as to the activity of an integral part of itself. All relative volitions are constitutional parts of the absolute volition, which therefore cannot act causally on them, though it always acts substantially with them.'[1]

But a simpler attitude may after all be deeper and correspondingly truer, if one can be content to say, in the realm of religion—

> Oh blessed life! the heart at rest
> When all without tumultuous seems:
> That trusts a higher Will, and deems
> That higher Will, not mine, the best.

At all events the very soul and substance of moral government, is, and must for ever be, in the blended self-assertion and self-submission expressed by the never-too-often-quoted lines—

> Our wills are ours, we know not how;
> Our wills are ours, to make them Thine.

(4) It is not even true that the Bible, as the alleged basis of 'religious Determinism,' gives us an antinomy between Divine government and human free agency. For whether, when the originals are properly repeated in our own tongue, we can reconcile all its statements one with another or not, there runs through the whole Bible, from beginning to end, an unmistakable, never hesitating, always emphatic, assumption of human moral responsibility, and therefore, to that extent, moral freedom for every man. The degrees vary, but the reality is never for a

---

[1] *Mind and Motion and Monism*, pp. 168, 169. It is manifest that the assent of the absolute volition to the relative, as here expressed, does not involve assent to the evil of an evil volition, It is assent to the exercise of volition, but not necessarily to the direction of the volition. But the non-assent could not be prevention, without annihilating the freedom of the relative volition.

moment in doubt. The modern reader, indeed, is confidently assured that—

'As a rule the attempt to reconcile free will with the Divine government of the world is abandoned as hopeless; and those who affirm the co-existence of the two are obliged to admit that it is a mystery, or in plain language, that the Determinist argument is unanswerable.'[1]

If one were to use concerning such a statement, the 'plain language' which is called for, it would hardly be deemed philosophical. Let us be content to reply deliberately that there is here a double fallacy. The reconciliation of Divine government with moral free agency is *not* and never has been 'abandoned as hopeless.' If there be some phases of it which are lost to us in mystery, that is the very opposite of allowing that the allegations of false Determinism are unanswerable. Such an assertion is as unwarranted as it is audacious. Again; no reasonable man, and assuredly no philosopher, is surprised at mystery in such a region. As indeed mystery and reality ever go hand in hand, the true Determinist might well claim the region where the human will yields itself to the Divine, or the opposite, as his own. But the very most that can possibly be made of it on behalf of Determinedism, is expressed in the more modest and more scientific words of Mr. McCabe above quoted, that ' at a point in the obscure recesses of the brain, we lose the sequence of events.' As well we may. But neither the Bible nor science gives us any permission, let alone encouragement, for such a reason, to echo the ancient blasphemy—

> Oh Thou, who Man of baser Earth didst make,
> And who with Eden didst devise the Snake;
> For all the Sin wherewith the face of Man
> Is blackened, Man's Forgiveness give—and take![2]

---

[1] Pearson, *Some Problems*, p. 108.   [2] *Omar Khayyám*, LVIII.

'The Divine purpose,' well says Sir Oliver Lodge, 'is fulfilled in many ways.' Physical evolution in the past has been a slow process; spiritual evolution cannot be precipitated by Divine decree. But in all the bygone ages, back far beyond the period of Biblical records, 'it is to be assumed that help and guidance have been in constant activity all along, operating on, or rather in, the refractory materials so as slowly to develop in them the power of manifesting not only life and body but also consciousness, spiritual perception, and free will.'[1]

(5) The only approach to predestination which is found in the Bible, or is thinkable in the realm of real religion, is precisely that process which is taking place still in and around us all. It may be called 'election,' though 'selection' is a better term; but it stands for certain foundation elements of every human life, which it were sheer fatuity, or indeed dishonesty, to deny. We are elected, each of us, through our heredity and environment, to such differing degrees of capacity and opportunity as are quite beyond language to describe. But the more frankly these differences are acknowledged, the more unmistakably must it also be pointed out that two great principles are thereby involved. In the first place, these differences are certainly not matters of arbitrary Divine decree. All is law, yet all is free. Heredity and environment represent Divine laws, but the operation of those laws is decided by human volitions. The heredity which blesses or curses children before they are born, and the environment which blasts or brightens their earlier years, are the results of human wills working

---

[1] *The Substance of Faith allied with Science*, p. 75.

with, or contending against, the Divine will.[1] Where the Divine ends and the human begins, can never be precisely indicated. But it is enough, alike for practical and philosophical purposes, to say that the potentiality is God's, and the actuality is man's. It is in this actuality that the substance of his moral responsibility resides.

Again, nothing can possibly be more plain than that this very election to indescribable degrees of capacity and opportunity, is that which both implies and emphasizes moral responsibility, and therefore moral freedom. On the lines of false Determinism there are no degrees of responsibility, simply because responsibility anywhere is unthinkable. The human babe welcomed with joy and reared in the royal palace, is on a level of irresponsibility with the slum-child unwanted at birth and dragged up in squalor. Both are completely determined; neither can help anything; neither is responsible for anything. But the recognition of moral free agency opens the way to a juster balance. 'Unto whomsoever much is given, of him shall be much required.' On such lines, and on no other, can Divine government be even thought of, or religion merit a moment's consideration.

(6) In final summary, therefore, all these main elements of the case show that the true Determinism is the only basis of religion, when the latter is regarded as a potent contributor to the present condition of human society, no less than to individual character. Into the dim region of the future with which religion

---

[1] The principle is well expressed in the old word—'The Lord commanded us to do all these statutes, to fear the Lord our God, for our good always, that He might preserve us alive as at this day.'—Deut. vi. 24.

in its eschatological phases is concerned, we need not here enter. It is as manifest as it is sufficient that the principles of true Determinism which avail at present, can alone be extended into any hereafter which religion may contemplate. 'Whatever a man sows, that will he also reap,' is valid as a principle now, because a man, as a man, is a real sower and to that extent makes his own harvest. Out of his heredity and environment he, and he alone, determines his acts, whence arise his habits, and thence his character and conduct. Destiny is neither more nor less than the natural development of these. The religion which refuses to see in human death the mere expiry of a complex candle-flame, insists that the just degree of responsibility attaching to each man now, will be projected into his *post mortem* future, with all the exactness which a Divine government at once righteous and tender guarantees.

What is left, therefore, as the supreme lesson of the true religious Determinism, is the constant need of a blending of the sense of dependence with that of independence. Christian Theism represents each human soul as responsibly independent, because unmistakably dependent. In such an attitude there is neither anomaly nor antinomy. There is nothing in it either abnormal or mystical. It is but the extension, on a transcendent and universal scale, of that principle which proves itself valid and effectual on the humbler scale of every child's development under wise discipline. Through happy childhood into promising youth, on into the nobility of adult life, the process is ever double. The consciousness of loving guidance and authoritative control, works ever in and with the consciousness of necessity for personal decision. To ask which is the more necessary, would be as profitless and as unanswerable a question as to inquire which is more essential for bodily health, pure air or normal breathing. It would be still more so in regard to the blending of Divine sovereignty and human free agency in the course of humanity's development.

There are at present equal reasons for encouragement and for concern. 'A thousand years,' says a brave and thoughtful modern teacher, 'see the rise and fall of many generations, yet they are but a short period in the history of the race, and on the most flattering estimate of progress, the most we can claim for humanity, in science and in morals, is that it is emerging from a troublesome childhood into a somewhat petulant youth.'[1] But this at least is certain, that if Christian Theism contains any hope or inspiration for the hastening on of a better day, alike for human individuals and for society, its whole promise turns upon the development of the true Determinism which reveres God in the degree in which it honours man, and finds in the co-operation between human wills and the Divine, the only hope of any final victory of good over evil. Without such true Determinism, which treats every man as a man in order that he may work together with God, religion is but a mechanical delusion, as morally impotent in the present, and as devoid of promise for the future, as the prayer-wheel of a Buddhist or the love-song of a gramophone.

---

[1] *Bampton Lectures for* 1907, J. H. F. Peile, p. 130.

III

EPILOGUE

III.—EPILOGUE

In the preceding pages, the real and significant distinction between 'hard' and 'soft' Determinism has been fully acknowledged, each theory being considered upon its merits. But for all who are capable of following such a discussion, there is something of even greater importance than philosophical exactitude, viz. rational and moral life. In view of this, there can be no doubt that ultimately we have to face not Hegelian subtleties but plain logical and practical issues. The dilemma which confronts us is in very deed as unmistakable and inevitable as Mr. Mallock has represented. 'Man is either a free being with an intelligent Deity as his counterpart, or else he and his fellows are a mere procession of marionettes which strut, or jig, or laugh, or groan, or caper, according as their wires are pulled by forces admittedly less intelligent than themselves.'[1] If we may revert to our opening pages, man is either moral or non-moral. Half moral he cannot be. If he is in all his volitions and actions but the unalterable result of a character which was made for him before his birth, then not only is his inalienable consciousness of freedom an illusion, but all morality is an illusion with it. If the freedom is a delusion, so is the manhood, and the marionette alone remains. For such a being, as we have seen, character is as

---

[1] *Reconstruction of Belief*, p. 303.

impossible as morality. Hereupon Mr. Mallock deserves to be heard yet once more—

'Three quarters of our life is made up of the judgements which we form of one another, and of the judgements which we each of us suppose that others form of us. All these judgements are founded on the supposition of freedom. Every time we are grateful to a man because he has done us a kindness, we are asserting that he was kind when he might just as easily have been callous. Every time we honour any public character for heroism in war, or for disinterested sincerity in politics, we are asserting that he did for his country what he was not compelled to do.'[1]

No academical subtlety of thought or speech can ever shake the substantial certainty of such a statement. Whether we can succeed in obtaining the metaphysical formula for the freedom which it connotes or not, upon it, as a true principle, all human life deserving the name has proceeded since the dawn of history. Upon it all decent society is now working together, and will go on to work whilst sanity remains to humanity. If, therefore, Hume was right in his view that when an opinion leads to an absurdity it must be taken as false, the falsity of 'hard' Determinism is simply immeasurable. The extremes to which its advocates are driven, condemn themselves by their very desperation. Take but one, which for sheer audacity deserves to be the last, 'It is hardly too much to say that the moral improvement of the race has proceeded *pari passu* with a decline in men's belief in free will.'[2] It is indeed

---

[1] *Reconstruction of Belief*, p. 281.

[2] Dr. Callaway, in *The Agnostic Annual for* 1905, p. 26. Such a sentence is well matched by another to the effect that—'The only great religion which is based upon the reign of law is the most just and the most humane of all.' If this were the occasion, the triple falsity of such a side reference to Buddhism could

'hardly too much to say' that a falser statement could not be made. If we may assume, what appears generally to be conceded, that with all the faults of the present age it embodies moral improvement to a degree never known before, or—to repeat Mr. Kidd's well-chosen words—that we are in the midst of an 'ethical movement in which the very highest qualities and attributes of which human nature is capable find the completest expression they have ever reached in the history of the race,' is such moral progress due to the 'decline in men's belief in free will'? Is it truly to be attributed to the spread of the Determinism which asserts that no man can help anything he does? Most assuredly *it is not*. No negative is strong enough to give the lie to such an assumption as directly as it deserves. The truth to the contrary is threefold.

(i) The false or 'hard' Determinism, as represented above, is *not* spreading. Those who hear it, do not heed it. Those who preach it, do not practise it. It fills the air with reckless assertions and compels us to stand upon the defensive; but beyond that it effects no more than did Giant Despair in Bunyan's dream. (ii) What is spreading, is the fuller and wiser recognition of the strong influences upon human nature which spring from heredity and environment. These did indeed call for larger recognition, and it would be difficult to exaggerate their importance. But at their very utmost they do not constitute or justify Determinedism. (iii) What they do point to, with equal sternness

---

be vividly exposed. For the reign of law, justice, and humaneness, are, to say the least, every whit as real in Christianity as in Buddhism, and much more potent for highest human development.

and promise, is the exact opposite. They put unmeasured emphasis upon the true as against the false Determinism. For what they emphasize in all directions, and demand shall be intensified beyond measure, is the sense of personal responsibility. Whether heredity shall bless or curse the child, whether environment shall brighten or blacken a human life, depends ultimately upon a person. Traced truly to its root, the good or evil influence comes always ultimately from a human character. The very sting of the curse, is not only that it ought not to have been, but that it need not have been. The very heart-beat of the inspiration of the good, is that it might have been otherwise. It is to this double knowledge that the improvement in human character is thus far due, together with its promise to become still better. If anything is certain to sane and honest perception, it is that wherever the sense of irresponsibility obtains, there degradation follows. If its universal acceptance throughout humanity could be contemplated, then in a sense Tennyson never intended, we must say concerning man, that—

> The dragons of the prime,
> That tare each other in their slime,
> Were mellow music matched with him.

Happily there is no more fear of that, than there is that all the world of men will become one vast crowd of lunatics. Every modern movement of thought and of social life is tending to the contrary. It is increasingly seen that the more the influences of heredity and environment are recognized as potent, the more emphatically necessary it is practically, as well as entirely right philosophically, to hold some one, some man, some woman, somewhere, responsible for each and all of them. Whether viewed on the larger scale of the nations or the smaller scale of the individual, the issue and the prospect of the contrast between true and false Determinism are the same. It is the sacred importance of the individual human being, as a creature whose moral as well as intellectual potentialities are boundless, which is emerging into ever greater prominence. The most popular advocate in this country of the false Determinism which would reduce man to marionette, himself declares that as he grows older he becomes more and more impressed with 'the wonder and the complexity, the beauty, magnificence, and awfulness of human nature.'[1]

If a better social ideal is ever to prevail than the merciless competition and cruelly unjustifiable inequalities which at present blight and blast civilization, it can come and will come only upon the lines of the true Determinism which calls for the development of personality and moral responsibility to the very utmost. It is the still further development of this same estimate of human nature's capabilities and duties, which alone yields any hope of the time when the monstrous sums expended on the ghastly ironies of an 'armed peace,' shall be turned into the nobler channels of a real human brotherhood. All the much-asserted uncertainties of free beings may be fully taken into account, without in the least affecting the general result. Growth by appeal, which is the only method of moral evolution, may be slow in fact and beyond the power of human philosophy to predict. But it has come to pass; and it is actually proceeding. That is all the prediction that a creature capable of doing his duty needs,

---

[1] R. Blatchford in *The Clarion*, January, 1911.

to prompt him to be and to do his utmost. The ultimate reason for each genuine individual choice may be an insoluble mystery, defying alike the keenness of the psychologist and the subtlety of the metaphysician. But it does not follow, as Emerson truly said, that man is a nest of boxes with nothing in the innermost. Mystery is the pledge of reality. And after all, there is no more impenetrable mystery in the free causal agency of the human self, than inheres in the life of the simplest cell or the construction of the ultimate atom with its miniature universe of electrons. The former may well, therefore, be as real and as inevitable as the latter.

The reality of our consciousness is sufficient guarantee for the reality of our freedom. The reality of our freedom is the pledge of our responsibility. The deeper the sense of responsibility, the more applicable—if only they are taken in their true sense—will be the closing words of the noblest poem of the departed century—

> O living will that shalt endure,
> When all that seems shall suffer shock,
> Rise in the spiritual rock,
> Flow through our deeds, and make them pure.[1]

That 'living will' is the only final clue to the philosophical problem, as it is also the only practical hope for humanity's future. For as the nature of matter turns upon the ultimate electron, so does the fate of nations turn upon the character of the individual. And the character of the individual

---

[1] *In Memoriam*, cxxxi. See Mr. Robinson's note—'Tennyson explained this to mean that which we know as free will; the higher and enduring part of man. Free will was undoubtedly, he said, the main miracle, apparently an act of self-limitation by the Infinite, and yet a revelation by Himself of Himself.'— Cambridge University Press edition, p. 260.

depends upon the true Determinism which calls upon every man, as man, whatever his temperament or circumstances, to determine his own volitions, his own acts, his own character, his own conduct, his own destiny. It is at once his greatest privilege and most pressing duty, thereby to contribute his utmost to the present well-being of those about him, as well as to the future upward evolution of the whole human race.

AUTHORS QUOTED OR MENTIONED, &c.

REPRESENTING DETERMINEDISM.

BLATCHFORD, R.	*God and My Neighbour.*	Clarion Press.
	Not Guilty.	
BRADLEY, DR. F. H.	*Appearance and Reality.*	Sonnenschein.
CALLAWAY, DR. C.	*Does Determinism Destroy Responsibility?*	
	'Agnostic Annual,' 1905, Watts & Co.	
MORISON, COTTER	*The Service of Man.*	Watts & Co.
GÜNTHER, DR. CONRAD	*Darwinism and the Problems of Life.*	Owens & Co.
HAECKEL, PROF. ERNEST	*The Riddle of the Universe.*	Watts & Co.
HAMON, PROF. A.	*The Illusion of Free Will.*	University Press.
HUXLEY, PROF. T. H.	*Hume.*	Macmillan
MAUDSLEY, DR. H.	*Life, in Mind and Conduct.*	Macmillan.
MCCABE, JOSEPH	*The Evolution of Mind.*	A. & C. Black.
	Haeckel's Critics Answered.	Watts & Co.
	Free Will in Modern Psychology.	
	'R.P.A. Annual' for 1910, Watts & Co.	
MCTAGGART, DR. J. E.	*Some Dogmas of Religion*	Arnold.
MILL, JOHN STUART	*Logic.*	
PEARSON, NORMAN	*Some Problems of Existence.*	Arnold.
RUBÁIYÁT OF OMAR KHAYYÁM	*Translated by FitzGerald.*	Macmillan.
RUSSELL, HON. BERTRAND	*Philosophical Essays.*	Longmans.
	Determinism and Morals.	'Hibbert Journal.'
	October 1908, Williams & Norgate.	
SPENCER, HERBERT	*Psychology, Principles of*	
	Data of Ethics.	
'VIVIAN, PHILIP'	*The Churches and Modern Thought.*	Watts & Co.

INTERMEDIATE.

CAIRD, DR. E.	*The Evolution of Religion.*	Maclehose.
CAIRD, PRINCIPAL J.	*The Fundamental Ideas of Christianity.*	Maclehose.
GREEN, PROF. T. H.	*Prolegomena to Ethics.*	Clarendon Press.
HERBERT, DR. S.	*First Principles of heredity.*	A. & C. Black.
KIDD, BENJAMIN	*Social Evolution.*	Macmillan.
MACKENZIE, PROF. A. S.	*Manual of Ethics.*	University Tutorial Press.
DONCASTER L.	*Heredity and recent research.*	Camb. Univ. Press.
STOUT, DR. G. F.	*Manual of Psychology.*	University Tutorial Press.
SIDGWICK, DR. H.	*Methods of Ethics.*	
TAYLOR, A. E.	*Elements of Metaphysics.*	Methuen.

REPRESENTING DETERMINISM.

ANON	*Fiat Lux.*	Sonnenschein.
ARNOLD, R. B.	*Scientific Fact and Metaphysical Reality*	Macmillan.
ARTHUR, W.	*Physical and Moral Law.*	C. H. Kelly.
BALFOUR, A. J.	*Foundations of Belief.*	Longmans.
BENSON, MARGARET	*The Venture of Rational Faith.*	Macmillan.
BEVAN, J. O.	*The Genesis and Evolution of the Individual Soul.*	
		Williams & Norgate.
BOWNE, DR. BORDEN. P.	*Personalism.*	Constable.

BRADFORD, DR. AMORY	*Heredity and Christian Problems.*	Macmillan.
CALDERWOOD, H.	*Handbook of Moral Philosophy.*	Macmillan.
	Relations of Mind and Brain.	Macmillan.
CLARKE, DR. W. N.	*Outline of Christian Theology.*	T. & T. Clark.
D'ARCY, DR. C. F.	*Idealism and Theology.*	Hodder & Stoughton.
DEUSSEN, DR. PAUL	*Metaphysics.*	Macmillan.
FAIRBAIRN, DR. A. M.	*The Philosophy of the Christian Religion.*	
		Hodder & Stoughton.
GIBSON, BOYCE	*Personal Idealism.* Ed. Hy. Sturt.	Macmillan.
HARRIS, CHAS.	*Pro Fide.*	John Murray.
HENSON, HENSLEY	*Notes on Popular Rationalism.*	Isbister.
HOWISON, DR. G. H.	*The Limits of Evolution.*	Macmillan.
ILLINGWORTH, DR. J. R.	*Personality, Human and Divine.*	Macmillan.
	Divine Immanence.	Macmillan.
INGE, DR. W. R.	*Personal Idealism and Mysticism.*	Longmans.
JACKS, L. P.	*The Alchemy of Thought.*	Williams & Norgate.
JAMES, DR. WILLIAM	*The Varieties of Religious Experience.*	Longmans.
	The Will to Believe.	Longmans.
	Pragmatism.	Longmans.
LIGHTFOOT, DR. J.	*Studies in Philosophy.*	Blackwood & Sons.
LODGE, SIR OLIVER	*Man and the Universe.*	Methuen.
	The Substance of Faith Allied with Science.	Methuen.
	Reason and Belief.	Methuen.
LOTZE, HERMANN	*Outlines of the Philosophy of Religion.*	
		R. D. Dickinson.
MACDONALD, GREVILLE	*The Religious Sense in its Scientific Aspect.*	
		Hodder & Stoughton.
MALLOCK, W. H.	*Religion as a Credible Doctrine.*	Chapman & Hall.
	The Reconstruction of Belief.	Chapman & Hall.
MARSHALL, DR. NEWTON	*Theology and Truth.*	Jas. Clarke.
MELLONE, DR. S. H.	*Laws of Life.*	Sunday School Association.
MOMERIE, DR. A. W.	*Personality.*	Blackwood & Sons.
OTTO, DR. RUDOLF	*Naturalism and Religion.*	Williams & Norgate.
PIGOU, A. C.	*The Problem of Theism.*	Macmillan.
POYNTING, DR. J. H.	*Physical Law and Life.*	'Hibbert Journal' for
		July 1903, Williams & Norgate.
RICE, DR. W. N.	*Christian Faith in an Age of Science.*	
		Hodder & Stoughton.
ROMANES, DR. G. J.	*Mind and Motion and Monism.*	Longmans.
ROWLAND, ELEANOR H.	*The Right to Believe.*	Hodder & Stoughton.
SCHILLER, DR. F. C. S.	*Freedom and Responsibility.*	'Oxford & Cambridge
		Review,' Michaelmas, 1907.
SETH, DR. ANDREW	*Two Lectures on Theism.*	Wm. Blackwood & Sons.
TEMPLE, ARCHBISHOP	*Relations between Religion and Science.*	Macmillan.
TEMPLE, W.	*The nature of Personality.*	Macmillan.
THOMSON, DR. W. H.	*Brain and Personality.*	Hodder & Stoughton.
RASHDALL, DR. HASTINGS	*Philosophy and Religion.*	Duckworth.
TYLER, PROF. J. M.	*The Whence and Whither of Man.*	
		W. Blackwood & Sons.
UPTON, PROF. C. B.	*Dr. Martineau's Philosophy.*	Nisbet.
	Bases of Religious Belief.	Williams & Norgate.
WALKER, W. L.	*Christian Theism and Spiritual Monism.*	
		T. & T. Clark.
WARD, DR. JAS.	*Naturalism and Agnosticism.*	A. & C. Black.
WARDELL, R. J.	*First Lessons in Philosophy.*	C. H. Kelly.
WARSCHAUER, DR. J.	*Problems of Immanence.*	Jas. Clarke.
WATERHOUSE, E. S.	*Modern Theories of Religion*	C. H. Kelly.
WELLS, H. G.	*First and Last Things.*	Constable.
WENSLEY, DR. R. M.	*Kant and the Philosophical Revolution.*	T. & T. Clark.

INDEX

A

Absolute Idealism: in an impasse, 220
Action: series of steps in, 219
Acts: inseparable from the agent, 286
American crow-bar case, 325
Animal life: non-moral, 3, 40
Appeal: only method of moral evolution, 421
Aristotle and Free Will, 10
Arthur, Rev. W.:
  on Law and Cause, 228
  on Physical and Moral Law, 230
Attention and Will, 219
Automatism: 33
  conscious, absurd, 208

B

Bain, Prof., on 'A Fiction from Nonentity,' 192
Balfour, Mr. A. J., on responsibility, 296
Barnardo, Dr., on Environment, 288
Benson, Miss M.:
  on laws in the rational world, 404
  on laws of character, 370
  protest of, 266
Bentham: *Deontology* and the word 'ought,' 12, 289
Bergson, Prof.: Philosophy of, 24
Berlin, the wreck of the, 343
  and Predestination, 411
Bible, The: Doctrine of Divine Government, 403, 409
  no Support to Determinedism, 400
Birkenhead, men of the, 343
Blatchford, Mr. Robert: 4, 6, 24, 212, 349
Bowne, Dr. Borden P.:
  on Causation, 227
  on Explanation of Life, 235
  on Freedom, 158
  on Personality, 199
  on Science, 229
  on Volitional Causality, 240, 268
Bradford, Dr. A. H.:
  on Freedom, 262
  on the presumption of Freedom, 370
Bradley, Mr. F. H.:
  on Appearance and Reality, 5, 28
  on Free Will, 168
  on the Self, 178, 193
Brain:
  instrument of Self, 330
  and personality, 191
Brennus, at Rome, 51
Buddhism, 83, 84, 418
Bunyan, John, 260
Buridan's Ass: 329, 301

C

Calderwood, Prof.:
  on Consciousness of Freedom, 150
  on Mind and brain, 331
  on Phineas Gage, 325, 334
  on Will, 212, 223

INDEX

Callaway, Dr. C.: and Free Will, 22, 44, 66, 76, 83, 153, 225, 348, 418
Calvin, John, 32
Calvinism, 32
Carlyle's protest, 368
Carpenter, Dr. W. B., on responsibility, 289
Cassius, witness of, 341
Causality: mechanical and volitional, 231
Causation: universality of, 226
Cause: the sufficient, 225
Character:
   and true Determinism, 321
   animal character, 339
   and heredity, 171
   and motives, 171
   compelled unthinkable, 343
   distinct from Self, 312–314
   only possibility of, 303
Choice, and compulsion, 221
Christ, example of, 396
Clarion, The, 7, 15, 41, 61, 63, 139
Clifford, Prof. W. K.:
   on 'mind stuff,' 193
   on soul and matter, 18
   on will and matter, 235
Complete determination, 118, 121, 140
Conduct, expectation of, 273
Conscience, 35, 36
Consciousness, indefinable, 198
Contingency:
   in character, 139
   in words, 42
Conversion, Prof. W. James, on, 259
Cooley, Mr. W. F.:
   on Evolution, 358
   on repugnance to Determinedism, 358
Courtenay, Dr., on Sub-consciousness, 196, 197
Creationism, 246

D

D'Arcy, Dr. C. F.:
   on character, 239
   on consciousness of freedom, 151
   on freedom of will, 212

Darwin's pangenesis, 246
Delboeuf on Freedom, 17
Determinedism:
   and character, 67–171
   and disobedience, 72
   and ethics, 71
   and lying, 65
   and mental realm, 170
   and metaphysics, 165
   and morality, 63
   and moral philosophy, 57
   and personality, 190
   and psychology, 145
   and religion, 54
   and responsibility, 62
   and self-respect, 60
   and the Bible, 400
   as untrue as unworthy, 47
   a triple failure, 238
   Effects of, 127, 304, 352, 353
   Failure of:
      in a home, 48
      in business, 49
      in education, 48
      internationally, 50
      municipally, 50
      politically, 50
   False:
      in fact, 35
      in name, 32
      in principle, 54
   impracticable, 128
   irreconcilable with Determinism, 318
   makes religion impossible, 375, 391
   recklessness of, 75
   'See-saw philosophy,' 257
   self-contradictory, 259, 346–351
   significance of, 52
   worship impossible in, 392
Determinism:
   Conviction of, threefold, 366
   Explanation of experience, 263
   False: as distinct from true, 34
   Four points of, 203
   Hard and soft, 31
   In past history, 9
   Only basis of religion, 373–412

INDEX

Determinism:
  Only possibility of character, 303
  Only way of upward evolution, 345
  Practical considerations, 281
  Present-day recrudescence, 12
  Questions involved in, 8
  Relation to heredity and environment, 242
  Sufficient estimate of future, the, 270
  The only real, 223
  Valid foundation of morals, 281

Determinisms: two distinct, 27
Deterrent punishment, 7
Deussen's:
  Elements of Metaphysics, 5, 166
  Free Will, 174, 177, 179, 184
  the real guest, 169

Dilemma of Mr. J. S. Mill, false, 381
Divine Immanence, Dr. Illingworth's, 7

E

Edison, Mr. T., on Man, 61
Edwards, Jonathan:
  and Foreknowledge, 405
  and Freedom of Will, 10, 32
Eimer, on heredity, 246
Emerson, on Man, 422
Environment, 254, 256
Eucken, Prof. R., on character, 305, 309, 329, 371
Experience: not mere consciousness, 269

F

Facts and automatism, 46
Fairbairn, Dr. A. M.:
  on Freedom, 240
  on Man and heredity, 253
  on Motives, 239
Fatalism, 32
Ferrier, Prof.:
  Man: free and self-sustained, 319
  on cerebral disease, 332
Fisher, Dr. G. P., on Freedom, 110
Fiske, Mr. John, on Evolution and progress, 364

Freedom:
  and motive, 217
  and selection, 220
  two plain questions of, 211
Freedom of Self: acknowledged by Determinedists, 321

G

Gage, Phineas: case of, 325, 334
Gibson, Mr. W. R. B., on conservation of energy, 234–235
Gimblett, Mr. C. A.: letter of, 161
God and My Neighbour, 9, 13, 24, 48, 55, 56, 67, 244, 247, 256, 286, 348, 352, 373, 378
God: in need of man, 387
Goethe on the divine need, 388
Green, Prof. T. H.:
  on a free cause, 157
  on character and action, 316
  on desires and motives, 217
  on evidence of consciousness, 163, 314
  on free will, 317
Günther, Prof.:
  on Darwinism and ethics, 16, 71, 73
  Self-contradiction of, 43

H

Haeckel, Prof., 14, 15, 35, 71
  on Christian morals, 347
  on consciousness, 193
  on dog and man, 251
  on human nature, 335
  on mechanism, 168
  on thought, 188
Hamon, Prof.:
  and Irresponsibility, 16, 242
  on illusion of Free Will, 3, 62
Hegel on Freedom of Will, 212
Henley, Mr. W. E.: Poem on Freedom, 152
Herbert, Dr., on heredity, 255
Heredity:
  and environment, 253
  human, 245

Hibbert Journal, The, 23
History, and automatism, 45
Hobbes, Thos.: and ethical theory, 11
Holmes, Dr. W., on Elsie Venner, 260
Homicidal mania, 125
Human power, the need of, 28
Hume on Liberty and Necessity, 11
Huxley:
  and Determinism, 17 33, 146
  and Materialism, 188
  and unbroken continuity, 203
  on Hume, 11, 17, 155, 156
  on man as machine, 346
  on microcosm, 361, 364

I

Iago, on ourselves, 267
Illingworth, Dr. J. R., 7
  on freedom, 163, 224
  on consciousness of freedom, 150
  on illusion, 202
  on self-assertion, 309
Indeterminism:
  and future volitions, 137
  and morality, 133
Intention and moral quality, 287

J

Jacks, Rev. J. L.:
  Alchemy of thought, 5
  on reality, 163
  on the thinker, 194
James, Prof. Wm: 'Dilemma of Determinism,' 351; 6, 13, 14, 27, 31, 34, 42, 58, 61, 65, 75, 259, 262, 263, 266, 268, 291, 355, 357, 359, 363, 366, 367
Jerry McAulay, 260
Jesus:
  character of, 398
  teaching of, 120, 129
Jevons, Prof.: 385
Jowett, Dr. J. H., and character, 340
Judgements of obligation, 115

K

Kant:
  on causality, 232
  on God, Freedom, and Immortality, 39
  on kategorical imperative, 35, 145, 288
  and Leibnitz's Monads, 132
  and moral excellence, 120
  on purposeful activities, 337
Keller, Helen, 268
Keshub Chunder Sen., on greatness of Jesus, 399
Kidd, Mr. Benj., on the New Democracy, 28, 368, 419
Knowledge: formation of, 208

L

Laing, Mr. S.: consciousness of freedom, 152
Law, and dynamical causation, embodiment of volition, 228
Lecky, Mr. W. E. H.: on character of Jesus, 398
Leibnitz's 'pre-established harmony,' 189
Liberty not liberty of indifference, 215
Limitation of omnipotence, 382
Literature, human, and freedom, 44
'Living-will,' the final clue, 422
Lodge, Sir Oliver, 37 57, 94, 172, 218, 285, 308, 385, 411
Lotze, Hermann, on moral responsibility, 296

M

Mackenzie, Prof. J.:
  on animal instinct, 337
  on character, 342
  on character, and circumstances, 255
  on Freedom, 223
  on moral conduct, 288
  on the moral imperative, 291
  on the animal self, 338

INDEX

Mackenzie, Prof. J.:
  on the only hindrance to progress, 356
Mallock, Mr. W. H.: on Determinism, 19, 53, 58, 59, 70, 81, 243, 279, 287, 292, 294, 299, 300, 303, 309, 324, 325, 327, 329, 344, 417. 418.
Man :
  a determiner, 184
  as marionette, 340
  distinct from animal, 3, 40
  free as to volitions, 236
  more than heredity, 247, 250
  more than motives, 299
Marcus Aurelius, 260
Mark Twain: 'Man a machine,' 6, 25, 37, 53, 206, 350, 352, 386
Martineau, Dr., on self and character, 314
Maudsley, Dr. H.:
  on mind and conduct, 18, 334
  predetermined destiny, 243
McCabe, Mr. Joseph :
  13, 22, 28, 40, 78, 89, 133, 322, 336
  Consciousness of responsibility, 152
  human power, 368
  man v. heredity, 319
  Obscurity of personality, 240
  Self-determination, 307, 308
McDonald, Mr. J. Ramsay, on character, 74, 360
McTaggart Prof.:
  on acknowledgement of freedom, 148, 21, 113–143
  on causation, 226
  on determined volitions, 282
  on Determinism, 168, 349
  on freedom, 158
  on life of Jesus, 397
  misrepresentation of omnipotence, 378
  prediction, 271, 276, 278
  on raindrop and man, 160
  self-contradictory statement, 376
  Some Dogmas of Religion, 375

Mendelism, 246
Mill, Jas., 12
Mill, John Stuart, 12, 65, 146, 154, 196, 223, 264, 266, 275 277, 295, 320, 323, 346, 371, 381, 382, 389, 398.
Momerie, Dr. :
  on man as an exception, 284
  on metaphysics, 188
  on the Ego, 192, 195, 295
Moore, Mr. Aubrey L., on Calvinism, 402
Moral responsibility :
  denied 1, 3
  universal assumption of, 1, 285
Moral :
  moral consciousness of mankind, 39
  moral evil, 358
  moral philosophy—five elements of, 59
Morals, only foundation of, 302
Morgan, Prof. Lloyd, 97, 138
Morison, Mr. Cotter: on moral responsibility, 3, 19
Motives :
  and character, 110
  and freedom, 217

N

Naturalistic Determinism, 226
Naturalism :
  doubly condemned, 203, 227
  Shibboleth of, the, 340
Necessity, philosophical, 33
Nelson's signal at Trafalgar, 42, 73, 290
Nero and character, 136
  and heredity, 261
  and indeterminism, 134
Not Guilty, by Mr. R. Blatchford, 25, 43, 48, 55, 64, 69, 77, 74, 115, 123, 242, 244, 249, 253, 254, 257, 259, 327, 348, 352
Novelists and automatism, 46

O

Obligation and responsibility, 374
Oman, Mr. C. W., on importance of individual soul, 390
Omar Khayyám, 33, 56, 183, 207, 341, 372, 402, 410
Omnipotence:
  confusion in regard to, 378-385
  limit to, 404
Otto, Dr. Rudolf: 35, 37
  on consciousness, 200
  on consciousness of freedom, 151
  on external world, 205
  on guarantee of experience, 248
  on instrument and player, 328
  on man v. animal, 245, 338, 339
  on mental diseases, 332
  on mystery of psychical, 265
  on physical and mental causality, 230
  on self-activity, 207
  on the child and its parents, 251

P

Paul, 261
Peace, Charles, 260
Pearson, Mr. N., on Determinism, 20, 75, 97-107, 282, 283, 311, 321, 349, 383, 385, 387, 391, 392
Peile, Mr. J. H. F., Bampton Lectures, 401, 403, 410
  on Pain, 380
  on Progress, 414
Person, a creature of three dimensions, 248
Personality:
  and character, 135
  inexplicable, 237
  reality of, 192, 362
'Philip Vivian' on Free Will, 23
Picton, Mr. A., on Spontaneity, 215
Poets and automatism, 45
Poynting, Prof., on choice, 107, 113, 171, 172, 174, 276, 302, 407
Pragmatism, 61, 63, 65, 165, 359
Praise and blame, 87

Predestination, not in Bible, 407
Probability of human actions, 280
Progress, ethical, 365

R

Religion:
  four human essentials, 375
  three essential factors of, 373
  two distinct impulses of, 325
Remorse: real reason of, 298
Repentance:
  essential to religion, 395
  impossible for Determinedism, 395
Responsibility:
  and reciprocity, 77
  for volitions, 122
Ribot on heredity, 258
Rice, Dr. W., cause of volitions, 109, 236
Richet, Prof. Chas.: on Man, 61
Right Volition, 120
Romanes, Prof. G. J.:
  environment, 258
  freedom, 297
  idea of causation, 233
  on absolute and relative volition, 408
  our idea of causation, 233
  moral quality, 288
  moral responsibility, 223, 275, 291
  volitions and motives, 218, 265
Rorke's Drift: defence of, 343
Row, Mr. C. A., on predestination, 401
Russell, Hon. Bertrand:
  on causation, 226
  on Determinism, 20, 90-97, 148, 282, 348

S

Sadler, Rev. G. T., 7, 23, 56, 107-113
Sandow, Mr. Eugen, 82
Schäfer, Prof., on cerebral lesions, 331
Schiller, Dr. F. C. S., 52, 148, 154, 165

INDEX

Schmiedel, Prof., on Jesus in modern criticism, 396
Schopenhauer: men v. animals, 337
Science, function of, 229
Seeley, Prof., on character of Christ, 398
Self:
  creative activity of, 201, 204
  distinct from heredity, 252
  free, 210, 221, 316
  not character, 241
  objectivity of, 196
  reality of, 186, 199
  related to heredity and environment, 242
  the only mover of a, 311
  the sufficient cause, 225
  unity of, 195
Self-consciousness, unanalysable, 237
Self-limitation of the divine, 389
Seth, Dr. Andrew:
  consciousness of freedom, 149
  real action of man, 210
  man's personal agency, 267
Shakespeare's excellence, 119
'Shall' and 'will' in R. V., 400
Sidgwick, Prof. H.:
  on conscious choice, 314-345, 320, 347
  on Determinism, 154
Sin, as viewed in Bible, 402
Sodom, the men of, 279
'Soft Determinism:'
  absurdity of, 130
  and its pleas, 75-144
  no improvement on 'hard,' 144
Solipsism, 190
Solon and tyrants, 341
Speech, human, 39
Spencer, Mr. Herbert:
  and free-will, 19
  causation and volition, 232
Spinoza:
  on desires, 209
  and Free Will, 10
Spontaneity, 79, 80, 81
Stephen, Sir Leslie, on character, 307, 384

Stoics, and Free Will, 10
Storr, Mr. V. F:
  consciousness of freedom, 164
  self-determination, 245
  the creative self, 207
Stout, Dr.:
  on self-consciousness, 196
  on Truth and Freedom, 166
Strauss, Dr. D. F., on character of Jesus, 398

T

'Taboo,' witness of, 47
Taylor, Mr. A. E.:
  on character, 306
  on freedom, 165, 214, 216, 300
Tennant, Dr. F. R., on moral evil, 380
Tennyson, on human nature, 62, 200, 204, 354, 363, 364, 365, 372, 409, 420
Theism, Christian, assumed, 373, 396
Thompson, Dr. W. H.:
  Brain and Personality, 192, 264, 333
  mind subservient to will, 325
Thomson, Prof. J. A., 8, 162
Tiele, Prof.: *History of Religion*, 39
Traducianism, 246
Tylor, Prof., on primitive culture, 39
Tyndall, Prof.:
  and Determinism, 126, 147
  and free will, 18, 44, 67, 68, 243, 244

U

Uberweg: *History of Philosophy*, 10
Upton, Prof.:
  on freedom, 219
  on inconceivability, 301, 324
  on libertarian question, 222
  on man as moral being, 391
  on man's relations with God, 388
  on significance of moral evil, 394
  on voluntary attention, 237

V

Vindictive punishment, 142
Volitions and desire, 293
    and law, 228
    and motives, 171
Volitions not mere consequences, 277

W

Wallace, Dr.: views of, 189
Ward, Dr. Jas., 138, 175, 201, 367
    on conservation of energy, 234
    on divine government, 408
    on false axioms, 233
    on passivity and activity, 202
    on spontaneity, 209
Ward, Dr. W. G., on spontaneous impulse and resolve, 293
Warschauer, Dr.:
    on choice, 238
    on Christ's character, 129
Warschauer, Dr.:
    on determinedism—a doctrine of despair, 356
    on effects of determinedism, 106, 126
    on environment, 258
    on Man no machine, 146
    on Nietzsche, 368
    on Will, 213
Weismann, on theory of heredity, 246
Wells, Mr. H. G., on Freedom, 44, 54, 74, 144, 362
Will and complete determination, 117
    definition of, 212
    not a pair of scales, 6, 112
    reality of, 211
Willoughby, on moral responsibility, 362
World: external and internal, the, 204

Important Sixpenny Editions.

Large Crown 8vo, Paper Covers, 6d. net each.

THE PEOPLE'S RELIGIOUS DIFFICULTIES. By Frank Ballard, D.D., M.A., B.Sc., &c. In Five Parts, each Part complete in itself. Also in One Vol., Cloth, 3s. 6d. net.

    I. POPULAR 'DETERMINISM.'
    II. GOD, PRAYER, and the MYSTERY OF PAIN.
    III. THE BIBLE IN MODERN LIGHT.
    IV. CHRIST and CHRISTIANITY.
    V. SOCIAL QUESTIONS and SOCIALISM.

CHRISTIANITY AND WOMAN. A Reply to some recent Sceptical Assertions. By J. E. Gun, Lecturer for the Christian Evidence Society. With an Introduction by Frank Ballard, D.D., M.A., B.Sc.

THE NOTHING THAT DID. A Discussion of Christian Evidences. By J. E. Ramsden.

NEW THEOLOGY. Its Meaning and Value—An Eirenicon. By Frank Ballard, D.D., M.A., B.Sc. Tenth Thousand. Also in Cloth, 1s. net.

GUILTY! A Tribute to the Bottom Man, and a Plain Reply to 'Not Guilty, a Defence of the Bottom Dog.' By Frank Ballard, D.D., M.A., B.Sc. Sixteenth Thousand. Also in Cloth, 1s. net.

IS THERE A GOD? And other Lectures on Modern Scepticism. By Vallance Cook. Third Thousand. Also in Cloth, 1s. net.

CHRISTIAN HEALING. The Words and Facts of the New Testament on the subject, and some arguments and conclusions to be drawn from them. By T. Farmer Hall.

CHARLES H. KELLY, 25-35 CITY ROAD, AND 26 PATERNOSTER ROW, LONDON, E.C.
AND OF ALL BOOKSELLERS.

OTHER WORKS BY THE SAME AUTHOR.

THEOMONISM TRUE: God and the Universe in Modern Light. Second Thousand. Demy 8vo, cloth, gilt. 6s. net.

'A very able book, sensitively in touch with recent scientific and philosophical developments—a book as fair in temper as it is strong in resource. Every important phase of the Theistic argument is touched on, and we have the satisfaction of knowing that the battle is being fought with the newest weapons.'—*Literary World*.

HAECKEL'S MONISM FALSE. An Examination of 'The Riddle of the Universe,' 'The Wonders of Life,' 'The Confession of Faith of a Man of Science,' by Professor Haeckel. Together with 'Haeckel's Critics Answered,' by Joseph McCabe. Demy 8vo, cloth, gilt. 5s. net.

'There is no Christian, to whatever church he may belong, who will not be benefited by a perusal of Dr. Ballard's book.'—*Catholic News*.
'The exposition is the most crushing exposure.'—*Expository Times*.

CHRISTIAN ESSENTIALS: A Re=statement for the People of To=day. Demy 8vo, cloth. 5s. net.

'The volume admirably sums up such teaching as will be found in the evidential writings of Westcott, Sanday, Milligan, Briggs, Bruce and Fairbairn. Students who do not possess the productions of these authors will find ample compensation in this valuable work.'—*Homiletic Review*.

DOES IT MATTER WHAT A MAN BELIEVES? and other Themes for Thought. Third Thousand. Large crown 8vo, cloth, gilt. 2s. 6d. net.

'The title relates only to the first chapter, but the other sections deal with equally important topics. The whole treatise is a weighty blow at scepticism. A vein of fine philosophy runs through the whole work.'—*Homiletic Review*.

THE TRUE GOD: A Modern Summary of the Relations of Theism to Naturalism, Monism, Pluralism and Pantheism. Second Thousand. Crown 8vo, cloth, gilt. 2s. 6d. net.

'The book cannot fail to be helpful. The author exposes with absolute clearness the unwarrantable nature of the assumptions which underlie naturalistic and materialistic theories. We heartily recommend this volume.'—*Guardian*.

EDDYISM, MISCALLED 'CHRISTIAN SCIENCE': A Delusion and a Snare. Fourth Thousand. Paper cover, 1s. net. Limp cloth, 1s. 6d. net. Cloth boards, 2s. net.

'Closely reasoned, relentless, unanswerable. It is certainly severe, but not a whit too severe; its logic is irrefutable; and to any one who reads with an open mind there can only be one result—conviction.'—*Foreign Field*.

CHARLES H. KELLY, 25-35 CITY ROAD, AND 26 PATERNOSTER ROW, LONDON, E.C.
AND OF ALL BOOKSELLERS.

Reprint Publishing

FOR PEOPLE WHO GO FOR ORIGINALS.

This book is a facsimile reprint of the original edition. The term refers to the facsimile with an original in size and design exactly matching simulation as photographic or scanned reproduction.

Facsimile editions offer us the chance to join in the library of historical, cultural and scientific history of mankind, and to rediscover.

The books of the facsimile edition may have marks, notations and other marginalia and pages with errors contained in the original volume. These traces of the past refers to the historical journey that has covered the book.

ISBN 978-3-95940-080-0

Facsimile reprint of the original edition
Copyright © 2015 Reprint Publishing
All rights reserved.

www.reprintpublishing.com

www.ingramcontent.com/pod-product-compliance
Lightning Source LLC
Chambersburg PA
CBHW081933170426
43202CB00018B/2922